McGraw-Hill's Torts
for Paralegals

The McGraw-Hill Paralegal List

WHERE EDUCATIONAL SUPPORT GOES BEYOND EXPECTATIONS.

Introduction to Law & Paralegal Studies
Connie Farrell Scuderi
ISBN: 0073524638
© 2008

Introduction to Law for Paralegals
Deborah Benton
ISBN: 007351179X
© 2008

Basic Legal Research, Second Edition
Edward Nolfi
ISBN: 0073520519
© 2008

Basic Legal Writing, Second Edition
Pamela Tepper
ISBN: 0073403032
© 2008

Contract Law for Paralegals
Linda Spagnola
ISBN: 0073511765
© 2008

Civil Law and Litigation for Paralegals
Neal Bevans
ISBN: 0073524611
© 2008

Wills, Trusts, and Estates for Paralegals
George Kent
ISBN: 0073403067
© 2008

The Law Office Reference Manual
Jo Ann Lee
ISBN: 0073511838
© 2008

The Paralegal Reference Manual
Charles Nemeth
ISBN: 0073403075
© 2008

The Professional Paralegal
Allan Tow
ISBN: 0073403091
© 2009

Ethics for Paralegals
Linda Spagnola and Vivian Batts
ISBN: 0073376981
© 2009

Family Law for Paralegals
George Kent
ISBN: 0073376973
© 2009

McGraw-Hill's Torts for Paralegals
ISBN: 0073376930
© 2009

McGraw-Hill's Real Estate Law
for Paralegals
ISBN: 0073376957
© 2009

Legal Research and Writing for Paralegals
Pamela Tepper and Neal Bevans
ISBN: 007352462X
© 2009

McGraw-Hill's Criminal Law
for Paralegals
ISBN: 0073376965
© 2009

McGraw-Hill's Law Office Management
for Paralegals
ISBN: 0073376949
© 2009

Legal Terminology Explained
Edward Nolfi
ISBN: 0073511846
© 2009

For more information or to receive desk copies, please contact your McGraw-Hill Sales Representative.

McGraw-Hill's Torts for Paralegals

Lisa Schaffer

Contributing Author

Andrew Wietecki

Contributing Editor

McGraw-Hill
Higher Education

Boston   Burr Ridge, IL   Dubuque, IA   New York   San Francisco   St. Louis
Bangkok   Bogotá   Caracas   Kuala Lumpur   Lisbon   London   Madrid   Mexico City
Milan   Montreal   New Delhi   Santiago   Seoul   Singapore   Sydney   Taipei   Toronto

McGraw-Hill
Higher Education

MCGRAW-HILL'S TORTS FOR PARALEGALS
Published by McGraw-Hill, a business unit of The McGraw-Hill Companies, Inc., 1221 Avenue of the
Americas, New York, NY, 10020. Copyright © 2009 by The McGraw-Hill Companies, Inc. All rights reserved.
No part of this publication may be reproduced or distributed in any form or by any means, or stored in a
database or retrieval system, without the prior written consent of The McGraw-Hill Companies, Inc.,
including, but not limited to, in any network or other electronic storage or transmission, or broadcast for
distance learning.

Some ancillaries, including electronic and print components, may not be available to customers outside the
United States.

This book is printed on acid-free paper.

1 2 3 4 5 6 7 8 9 0 QPD/QPD 0 9 8

ISBN   978-0-07-337693-6
MHID   0-07-337693-0

Vice president/Editor in chief: *Elizabeth Haefele*
Vice president/Director of marketing: *John E. Biernat*
Associate sponsoring editor: *Natalie J. Ruffatto*
Developmental editor II: *Tammy Higham*
Marketing manager: *Keari Bedford*
Lead media producer: *Damian Moshak*
Media producer: *Marc Mattson*
Director, Editing/Design/Production: *Jess Ann Kosic*
Lead project manager: *Susan Trentacosti*
Senior production supervisor: *Janean A. Utley*
Designer: *Marianna Kinigakis*
Media project manager: *Mark A. S. Dierker*
Outside development house: *Beth Baugh*
Cover and Interior design: *Pam Verros, pv design*
Typeface: *10.5/13 Times New Roman*
Compositor: *Aptara, Inc.*
Printer: *Quebecor World Dubuque Inc.*
Cover credit: *© Johanna Goodyear/iStockphoto*
Text credits: *Material reprinted from* Prosser and Keeton on the Law of Torts, *§58 and §100 (5th ed. 1984) with
permission of ThomsonWest.*

Restatement, 2d, Torts, © 1965 by the ALI. Reprinted with permission. All rights reserved.

Model Penal Code, © 1985 by the ALI. Reprinted with permission. All rights reserved.

Library of Congress Cataloging-in-Publication Data
Schaffer, Lisa.
   McGraw-Hill's torts for paralegals / Lisa Schaffer, contributing author;
Andrew Wietecki, contributing editor.
      p. cm.—(The McGraw-Hill paralegal list)
   Includes index.
   ISBN-13: 978-0-07-337693-6 (alk. paper)
   ISBN-10: 0-07-337693-0 (alk. paper)
   1. Torts—United States. 2. Legal assistants—United States—Handbooks,
manuals, etc. I. Wietecki, Andrew. II. Title. III. Title: Torts for paralegals.
KF1250.Z9S33 2009
346.7303—dc22

                                                                            2007046672

The Internet addresses listed in the text were accurate at the time of publication. The inclusion of a Web site
does not indicate an endorsement by the authors or McGraw-Hill, and McGraw-Hill does not guarantee the
accuracy of the information presented at these sites.

About the Authors

Curriculum Technology

Curriculum Technology works with McGraw-Hill on several projects related to the paralegal series. Curriculum Technology serves education organizations and publishing companies by providing a source of intellectual property development, media, technology, as well as consultation, and research.

Lisa Schaffer, JD, MBA

Contributing Author/Editor

- Bachelor of Arts in History from University of California, Los Angeles
- Juris Doctorate in law from Chapman University School of Law
- Masters in Business Administration from Chapman University
- Advanced Management Certificate from University of California, Riverside
- Executive Management Certificate from University of California, Riverside

Lisa worked in the legal industry for more than 20 years in a variety of positions for law firms that specialized in the areas of criminal law, real estate law, corporate law, and personal injury. She served as in-house counsel for regulatory compliance in the legal affairs department of National Water & Power, Inc., doing business in 43 states. Lisa taught a variety of courses in paralegal studies for InterCoast Colleges over a period of five years. She was offered and accepted the position of Director of Education. She was later promoted to School Director of the Riverside campus before accepting the position of Chief Administrative Officer for all campuses. Lisa served as an assistant vice president in the accreditation and licensing department for Corinthian Colleges, Inc.

Andrew Wietecki, JD, MPA

Contributing Editor

- Bachelor of Arts in English from St. Thomas Aquinas College
- Masters in Public Administration from Hamline University, Graduate School
- *Juris Doctor* in law from Hamline University, School of Law

Andrew was born and raised in New York City. He has been in the education business for 13 years, having practiced real property law before that. He has taught at the high school level in New York City as well as instructing college-level paralegal students. He has been Academic Dean, Legal Program Chair, and a college instructor for the past 11 years. Currently, Andrew works in the education field with Curriculum Technology producing a wide variety of learning tools while also tutoring children in English skills.

Amy Eisenhower JD, BS

Contributing Writer

- Bachelor of Science in English from Wayne State College
- Doctorate in *Jurisprudence* from the University of South Dakota

Amy was born in Nebraska and has spent much of her life there. She currently resides in Grand Island, Nebraska. Amy is a member of both the South Dakota and the Nebraska State Bars. Amy taught five years of high school English before attending law school. She is currently employed as assistant general counsel for Credit Management, Inc. Amy has been with Curriculum Technology for approximately a year and a half as a senior consultant.

Rastin Ashtiani

Contributing Writer

- Bachelor of Arts in Psychology from University of California at Irvine
- Doctorate in *Jurisprudence* from Chapman University

Rastin was born in Los Angeles, California, has spent much of his life living in the Los Angeles area, and currently resides in Orange County, California. Rastin has worked with the Orange County District Attorney's office and the law offices of Dyke Huish. He has been with Curriculum Technology for approximately a year as a consultant for both paralegal and legal projects.

Preface

Tort law is an exciting legal subject to study and become familiar with, particularly in our world today. Tort law has been on the forefront of legal news for the past 25 to 30 years with the number of lawsuits filed skyrocketing each year, along with possible enormous monetary judgments at stake. The issue of lawsuits and the massive damage awards, and whether or not there should be caps placed on those awards, has even been debated recently in the U.S. Congress.

This text helps to prepare students for the practical world of tort law. It contains a variety of subject areas introducing the student to a useful array of topics necessary to be successful in the real-world practice of tort law while not overwhelming the student with dry, textual, dull material.

McGraw-Hill's Torts for Paralegals examines the basics of tort law, ranging from topics on intentional torts against person and property, followed by defenses to those torts, continuing with negligence and its elements, and finishing off with chapters on product and strict liability. Additional chapters also address subjects such as vicarious liability, nuisances, immunities, and other torts like malpractice and an assortment of business-related torts. However, the most exciting aspect of this textbook will be the myriad of learning resources to aid students in their torts journey.

McGraw-Hill's Torts for Paralegals contains 14 chapters and an appendix. By providing a hands-on approach to learning, each chapter has a recent, applicable case opinion, along with many ancillaries—including charts, tables, figures, and exercises—placed throughout each chapter to aid in the student's development.

TEXT DESIGN

Pedagogy

This text has numerous features that capitalize on the various learning styles that students use to gain knowledge. Based on the notion that students who use their newly acquired knowledge often retain it much better that those who do not, this text requires students to apply the knowledge they have acquired. Chapters are designed in a manner that assures students will have the opportunity to learn the appropriate legal concepts, the necessary vocabulary, develop their legal reasoning skills, and demonstrate their knowledge of the material. Each chapter contains the following features:

- **Spot the Issue**—Student is presented with a fact pattern and asked to "spot" the issue(s) present.
- **A Day in the Life of a Real Paralegal**—Practical application designed to help students build a specific skill set.
- **Legal Research Maxim**—General statement of a principle in law.
- **Case Fact Pattern**—Simple fact pattern with story and outcome.
- **Research This**—Hands-on assignment designed to develop students' research skills.
- **Eye on Ethics**—Students are presented with ethical issue(s) related to the subject in the chapter.

- **You Be the Judge**—Students are presented with a fact pattern and issue and asked to be the "judge" and decide on the issue set forth.
- **Surf's Up**—Hands-on research presents students with numerous websites where they can *surf* and gather material.
- **Case in Point**—A significant case designed to expand on the topics discussed in chapter.
- **Portfolio Assignment**—Students are given an assignment by which to begin, creates, and add to a portfolio.
- **Vocabulary Builders**—Crossword puzzle for the students to complete using vocabulary words found in the chapter.

The text is written in clearly presented language that engages the student, keeps the reader's interest and presents information in a variety of styles.

OTHER LEARNING AND TEACHING RESOURCES

Supplements

The **Online Learning Center (OLC)** is a Web site that follows the text chapter by chapter. OLC content is ancillary and supplementary germane to the textbook—as students read the book, they can go online to review material or link to relevant Web sites. Students and instructors can access the Web sites for each of the McGraw-Hill paralegal texts from the main page of the Paralegal Super Site. Each OLC has a similar organization. An Information Center features an overview of the text, background on the author, and the Preface and Table of Contents from the book. Instructors can access the instructor's manual, and PowerPoint presentations, and Test Bank. Students see the Key Terms list from the text as flashcards, as well as additional quizzes and exercises.

Acknowledgments

Special thanks need to be given to the reviewers who provided valuable feedback during the steps to completion of the final draft.

Belinda J. Clifton
International Institute of the Americas

Regina Dowling
Branford Hall

Tameiko Allen Grant
Florida Metropolitan University

Carol Halley
National American University

Walter Junewick
Everest College

M.H. Libby
PEG Schools (The Salter School)

Terri Lindfors
Minnesota School of Business

Annalinda Ragazzo
Bryant & Stratton

Kathleen Reed
University of Toledo

Heather Tucker
McCann School of Business and Technology

Babette Wald
California State University, Dominguez Hills

A Guided Tour

McGraw-Hill's Torts for Paralegals explores the wide variety of civil wrongs that can harm an individual and the remedies available to that injured party. Utilizing many practical learning tools, the text takes a step-by-step approach in understanding private harms and proving their prima facie elements. The text is written in a very concise and sequential manner, beginning with intentional torts, continuing through the steps of negligence, and finishing with the different liabilities and agency law. The many practical assignments allow students to enjoy the study of torts and apply it to their work as practicing paralegals. The pedagogy of the book applies three main goals:

- Learning outcomes (critical thinking, vocabulary building, skill development, issues analysis, writing practice).

- Relevance of topics without sacrificing theory (ethical challenges, current law practices, technology application).

- Practical application (real-world exercises, practical advice, portfolio creation).

Chapter Objectives

CHAPTER OBJECTIVES

Upon completion of this chapter, you will be able to:

- Understand and define a tort.
- Identify what constitutes reasonable conduct.
- Explain the difference between a tort and a crime or a contract.
- Identify the elements of a tort.
- Discuss the major categories of torts.

Introduce the concepts students should understand after reading each chapter as well as provide brief summaries describing the material to be covered.

Case Fact Pattern

Describes simple fact patterns and asks students to apply concepts learned from the chapter to understand the legal issues at hand.

CASE FACT PATTERN

Harry owns a seven-acre property in a remote area outside of Omaha. An avid admirer of lions and tigers, Harry has built a small sanctuary for his six lions and tigers on his property. Harry is very conscious of the potential damage and harm these animals could possibly inflict if they were to get out of the sanctuary. Therefore, Harry has built an enclosure on his property to keep the animals from running loose. Harry has taken every possible measure to ensure the animals do not get out. Harry has invested in the best cages and fences he could buy. An animal gets out of Harry's sanctuary. It kills two people. Harry will be held strictly liable.

A Day in the Life of a Real Paralegal

Presents scenarios depicting what a usual day is like for practicing paralegals and provides practical application designed to help students build a skill set to prepare for a career as a paralegal.

 A DAY IN THE LIFE OF A REAL PARALEGAL

Most jurisdictions do not allow "mistake" as a defense against trespass to land, as duly noted. However many people, and sometimes jurisdictions, mistakenly believe that a "proper notice" must be given to potential trespassers alerting them of private property. Many times you will see NO TRESPASS signs on property to alert bystanders, with many having the local, jurisdictional code against trespass listed as well. On numerous occasions, trespassers believe they are within the bounds of law because they failed to see—or there failed to be—a NO TRESPASS sign. The reality is, in most cases, that mistake will not work as a defense. It's important to know your local ordinances regarding trespass to land.

Spot the Issue

Is a hands-on exercise that presents students with a fact pattern and asks them to apply concepts learned in the chapter to "spot" the issues present.

SPOT THE ISSUE

Patrick loves baseball. He and his friends know all the members of their local minor league baseball team, and they love to go to games. Patrick likes to sit as close to the action as possible. When Patrick's team makes the finals, he buys tickets to go to the game. Patrick wants to view the game from a clear vantage point, so he purchases tickets that are in the front row right beside third base.

Patrick and his friends go to the game. They are having a great time. The count is 3-2 for Patrick's favorite player, and the game is tied at 2-2 in the top of the eighth inning. Patrick is standing up yelling at the batter. The batter swings a line drive foul ball right up the third field line, and it hits Patrick in the head. Patrick sustains a severe concussion and is taken to the hospital.

Patrick sues the ball park for negligence.

What issue may be present on behalf of the defendant, the baseball park?

Legal Research Maxim

LEGAL RESEARCH MAXIM

Many times culture, environment, and daily routine play a part in how law and society can indirectly be affected by these subtle, yet powerful, underlying forces. Would it be reasonable, as an example, to file a lawsuit against a person for the tort of battery in New York City for bumping into you on a crowded subway? No, it wouldn't be, as the subway is part of a daily routine that many millions follow each day and bumps and knocks here and there are part of the norm.

Highlights some of the major principles in law covered in each chapter.

Surf's Up

SURF'S UP

When the *Exxon Valdez* dumped millions of barrels of oil into the ocean off the coast of Alaska, the oil spill created a public nuisance because it damaged wildlife and destroyed protected habitat. In addition, fishermen in the area were subjected to a special damage as it destroyed their ability to fish in the area. Exxon was fined for the incident. To learn more about this public nuisance, research the following sites:

- www.uga.edu
- www.evostc.stateak.us
- www.wikipedia.org
- www.epa.gov/oilspill/exxon
- www.fakr.noaa.gov

Presents students with numerous and varied websites to "surf" and gather additional information on the important legal concepts and issues discussed in each chapter.

Research This

LEGAL RESEARCH MAXIM

Remember, the basis for this defense is that the plaintiff must not take unreasonable risks of injuring himself. The plaintiff will be contributorily negligent only if the risk that he created to his own safety was unreasonable and was the same risk that led to his injury.

Gives students the opportunity to investigate issues more thoroughly through hands-on assignments designed to develop critical research skills.

You Be the Judge

Places students in the judge's seat. Students are presented with facts from a fictitious case and they use concepts learned from the chapter to make a legal determination.

Eye on Ethics

Recognizes the importance of bringing ethics to the forefront of paralegal education. It raises ethical issues facing paralegals and attorneys in today's legal environment.

Chapter Summary

Provides a comprehensive review of the key concepts presented in the chapter.

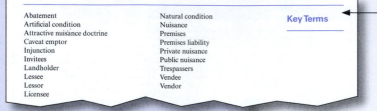

Abatement	Natural condition	**Key Terms**
Artificial condition	Nuisance	
Attractive nuisance doctrine	Premises	
Caveat emptor	Premises liability	
Injunction	Private nuisance	
Invitees	Public nuisance	
Landholder	Trespassers	
Lessee	Vendee	
Lessor	Vendor	
Licensee		

Key Terms

Used throughout the chapters are defined in the margin and provided as a list at the end of each chapter. A common set of definitions is used consistently across the McGraw-Hill paralegal titles.

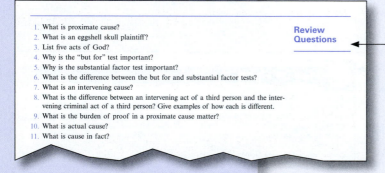

1. What is proximate cause?
2. What is an eggshell skull plaintiff?
3. List five acts of God?
4. Why is the "but for" test important?
5. Why is the substantial factor test important?
6. What is the difference between the but for and substantial factor tests?
7. What is an intervening cause?
8. What is the difference between an intervening act of a third person and the intervening criminal act of a third person? Give examples of how each is different.
9. What is the burden of proof in a proximate cause matter?
10. What is actual cause?
11. What is cause in fact?

Review Questions

Review Questions and Exercises

Emphasize critical thinking and problem-solving skills as they relate to tort law. The Review Questions focus on more specific legal concepts learned in each chapter. The Exercises introduce hypothetical situations and ask students to determine the correct answers using knowledge gained from studying topics in each chapter.

 PORTFOLIO ASSIGNMENT

Make a list of possible attractive nuisances that may be found on someone's property. Then, observe your own property, home, or apartment complex and list any possible attractive nuisances that you think are present on the property. If none, ask your neighbor if you could walk the area of his or her property to see if you think any attractive nuisances are present there. Compare your first possible list of attractive nuisances with the list for your property or your neighbor's property.

Portfolio Assignments

Ask students to use the skills mastered in each chapter to reflect on major legal issues and create documents that become part of the paralegal's portfolio of legal research. The Portfolio Assignments are useful as both reference tools and as samples of work product.

Vocabulary Builders

Provides a crossword puzzle in each chapter that uses the key terms and definitions from that chapter to help students become more proficient with the legal terminology.

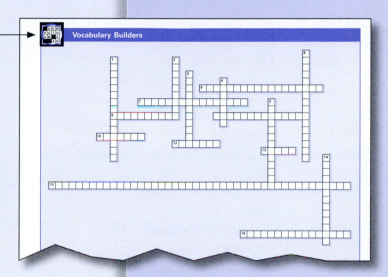

Case in Point

At the end of each chapter exposes students to real-world examples and issues through a case chosen to expand on key topics discussed in the chapter.

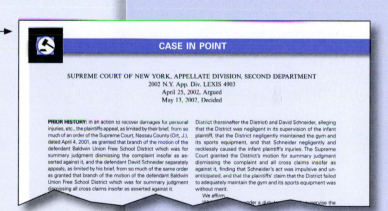

Brief Contents

Chapter 1   Tort Law: An Introduction   1

Chapter 2   Intentional Torts Against the Person   17

Chapter 3   Intentional Torts Against Property   39

Chapter 4   Defenses to Intentional Torts   53

Chapter 5   Negligence: Duty and Breach of Duty   70

Chapter 6   Negligence: Proximate Cause   87

Chapter 7   Negligence: Defenses   100

Chapter 8   Damages   114

Chapter 9   Vicarious Liability   130

Chapter 10   Premises Liability and the Doctrine of Nuisance   149

Chapter 11   Strict Liability   167

Chapter 12   Product Liability   181

Chapter 13   Other Torts   197

Chapter 14   Immunity from Tort Liability   214

APPENDIX

United States Constitution and Bill of Rights   232

GLOSSARY   248

INDEX   254

Table of Contents

Chapter 1
Tort Law: An Introduction   1

What Is a Tort?   1
   Reasonable Care   2
Torts: Not Criminal and Not Contractual   3
   Crimes   3
   Contracts   4
Elements of All the Torts   5
Categories of Torts   6
   Intentional Torts   6
   Negligence   7
   Strict Liability   7
   Other Torts   7
Major Types of Personal Injury
Tort Litigation   7
Summary   8

Chapter 2
Intentional Torts Against the Person   17

Intent   17
Transferred Intent   19
Types of Intentional Torts Against the
Person   19
   Battery   19
   Assault   21
   False Imprisonment   22
   False Arrest   24
   Intentional Infliction of Emotional Distress   24
   Malicious Prosecution   26
   Wrongful or Unjustified Civil Proceedings   27
   Defamation   27
   Invasion of Privacy   29
Summary   32

Chapter 3
Intentional Torts Against Property   39

Harm to Property   39
Trespass to Land   39
Trespass to Chattels   41
Trespass in Cyberspace   42
Conversion   43
Summary   45

Chapter 4
Defenses to Intentional Torts   53

Concept of a Defense   53
Types of Defenses   54
   Consent   54
   Self-Defense   55
   Defense of Others   57
   Defense of Property   58
   Reentry onto Land   58
   Recapture of Chattels   59
   Necessity   59
   Justification   60
   Discipline   60
Summary   61

Chapter 5
Negligence: Duty and Breach of Duty   70

Negligence   70
The Elements of Negligence   71
The Reasonable Person   73
Duty   74
   Breach of Duty   75
   Res Ipsa Loquitur   78
Other Considerations   79
   Custom and Usage   79
   Violation of a Law   79
   Negligence Per Se   80
   Presumption of Negligence   80
Summary   81

Chapter 6
Negligence: Proximate Cause   87

Causation in Fact   87
The "But For" Test   88
Substantial Factor   89
Causation   90
   Common Sense   90
   Market Share   90
   Foreseeability   91
Intervening Causes   92
Proximate Cause Overview   93
Summary   94

Chapter 7
Negligence: Defenses 100

Contributory Negligence 100
  Cause in Fact 101
Last Clear Chance 102
  Helpless Plaintiff, Defendant Discovers 102
  Helpless Plaintiff, Inattentive Defendant 102
  Inattentive Plaintiff, Aware Defendant 103
  Inattentive Plaintiff, Inattentive Defendant 103
  Imputed Contributory Negligence 103
Comparative Negligence 103
  Pure Comparative Negligence 104
  Modified Comparative Negligence 104
Assumption of the Risk 105
  Express Assumption 105
  Implied Assumption 106
Summary 107

Chapter 8
Damages 114

Compensatory Damages 114
Other Types of Damages 116
  Hedonic Damages 116
  Nominal Damages 116
  Liquidated Damages 117
  Property Damages 117
  Loss of Consortium 117
Punitive Damages 117
Mitigation 118
Joint Tortfeasors 119
  Release 120
  Contribution 120
  Indemnity 120
Summary 121

Chapter 9
Vicarious Liability 130

Vicarious Liability 130
Employer-Employee Relationship 131
  Scope of Employment 132
  Frolic and Detour 132
Employer's Liability Based on Own Negligence 135
  Negligent Selection 135
  Negligent Instruction 135
  Negligent Supervision 135
Independent Contractor 136
Intentional Torts 139
Joint Enterprise 140
Automobile Consent Statutes 140
Family Purpose Doctrine 140
Summary 142

Chapter 10
Premises Liability and the Doctrine of Nuisance 149

Duties of a Landowner 149
  Outside the Land 149
  Artificial Condition 150
  Entry upon Land 150
Trespassers 151
  Discovered Trespasser 151
  Constant Trespasser 151
  Child Trespassers 152
Licensees 152
Invitees 153
Lessors and Lessees 154
Vendors and Vendees 154
Nuisance 155
  Private Nuisance 155
  Public Nuisance 157
Defenses to Nuisance 158
Summary 159

Chapter 11
Strict Liability 167

Strict Liability 167
Animals 168
  Wild Animals 168
  Domesticated Animals 168
  Liability to Third Parties 170
  Livestock 171
Abnormally Dangerous Activities 172
Defenses to Strict Liability 174
Summary 176

Chapter 12
Product Liability 181

Product Liability 181
Negligence 182
  Manufacturer 182
  Retailer 183
  Defenses 183
Warranty and Strict Liability 184
  Express Warranty 185
  Implied Warranty 185
  Defenses to Warranty Actions 187
Design Defects 189
Duty to Warn 190
Summary 190

Chapter 13
Other Torts 197

Medical Malpractice 197
Legal Malpractice 199

Survival Tort   201
  Personal Tort   201
  Personal Property Tort   202
  Real Property Tort   202
Wrongful Death Tort   202
Wrongful Birth Tort   203
Business Tort   203
  Disparagement   204
  Injurious Falsehood   205
  Interference with Contractual Relationships   205
  Interference with Prospective Advantage   206
  Interference with Employment   206
Summary   207

Chapter 14
Immunity from Tort Liability   214

Public Policy   214
Family Immunity   215
  Interspousal Immunity   215
  Spousal Privilege   216
  Parent and Child   218

Charitable Immunity   219
Sovereign Immunity   221
  Federal Government   221
  State Government   223
  Local Government   223
Public Officers   224
Diplomatic Immunity   224
Summary   225

APPENDIX

United States Constitution and Bill
of Rights   232

GLOSSARY   248

INDEX   254

McGraw-Hill's Torts
for Paralegals

Chapter 1

Tort Law: An Introduction

CHAPTER OBJECTIVES

Upon completion of this chapter, you will be able to:

- Understand and define a tort.
- Identify what constitutes reasonable conduct.
- Explain the difference between a tort and a crime or a contract.
- Identify the elements of a tort.
- Discuss the major categories of torts.

Tort law can be overwhelming. Numerous situations and injuries can be categorized as torts, and the court system is constantly changing its view of what constitutes a tort. Who is responsible for damages caused to a piece of property by a trespasser? Who is responsible for the dog bite suffered by a little girl? Who is responsible for the damages that a celebrity suffers for untrue remarks made about his or her character? All of these situations, as well as many others, fall into various areas of tort law. This chapter gives an introduction to and an overview of the major aspects of tort law and provides a foundation on which to build discussions on specific areas of tort law in later chapters.

tort
A civil wrongful act, committed against a person or property, either intentional or negligent.

civil
Relating to private rights and remedies sought in an action brought to enforce, redress, or protect private rights.

WHAT IS A TORT?

One of the most frequently asked questions when beginning the study of tort law is: What is a tort? It is not a dessert or a breakfast Danish. Nor is it a sour taste. So what is a tort? A **tort** is defined as a private or **civil** wrong or injury for which the

CASE FACT PATTERN

A man was using a public telephone booth to make a telephone call. While he was in the booth, an alleged drunk driver sped down the street, lost control of his vehicle, and crashed into the man in the telephone booth, severing his leg. The door to the telephone booth had jammed and the man could not open it in time to retreat once he noticed the speeding car careening out of control. The accident left the injured man unable to walk or work. The injured man sued the telephone company for placing the booth near a known hazardous intersection and because the door to the booth had jammed, trapping the man inside the booth.

- Who should the man sue and why? Is the telephone company the right party to sue or the drunk driver? Why?
- Are there public policy issues present?
- If so, might the public policy issues have an impact on the trial? Why or why not?

1

remedy
The means by which a right is enforced or the violation of a right is prevented, redressed, or compensated.

damages
Money paid to compensate for loss or injury.

court will provide a **remedy** in the form of an action for **damages**. If a tort occurs, the law permits the injured party to seek to recover damages equal to the value of the injury. Damages are awarded in an effort to make the injured party whole again.

Money, the usual form of damages awarded in a tort case, can assist to rectify many things, but it cannot always make the injured party whole again; nevertheless, it is the best remedy that the law affords for the situation. The underlying theory in tort law is that socially unreasonable conduct should be penalized. Public policy becomes a prime focus in tort law. What is just and fair and promotes equality is the underlying theme that permeates this area of the law.

Reasonable Care

reasonable care
Conduct that an ordinary person would exhibit under the same or similar circumstances.

The concept of reasonable care underlies tort law. The court tries to compensate a victim for harm suffered from another person who did not take **reasonable care**. The reasonableness of a person's conduct is objective. Therefore, to understand what constitutes unreasonable conduct, one must first examine what constitutes reasonable care. Reasonable care generally means any type of conduct that might be exhibited by an ordinary person under the same or similar circumstances. Another way of looking at what is *reasonable* is to determine "what a reasonable person would do under the circumstances."

The concept of reasonable care does not mean that a person must act *perfectly*; it means an individual must act *appropriately*, as any other ordinary person might in the same or similar circumstances. A person violates the premise of reasonable care if he or she acts intentionally toward another person. The concept of reasonable conduct is used to determine whether or not a person's conduct complied with how others might behave or act under similar circumstances.

For example, suppose a corporate executive is running late for a business deal. The business deal could be worth a substantial amount of money to his corporation should he consummate the deal. He decides to speed through a residential area where a school is located in order to save time on his drive to the office. He is traveling 70 mph in a 30 mph zone. The executive is drinking coffee and placing a CD into the CD player of the car. A short distance up the street, a little boy is crossing the road on his way to school. The corporate executive notices the little boy at the last minute, but cannot stop his vehicle in time. His vehicle strikes the little boy and kills him. Is the corporate executive's conduct reasonable? Would an ordinary person in the same or similar circumstances have acted in the same manner? The answer is no. Speeding laws are enacted to protect the public. Traveling at excessively high rates of speed in a residential area is not conduct that would be exhibited by an ordinary or average person under those circumstances. It would be assumed that an ordinary person would obey speed limits and call the office to say he would be late. Therefore, the executive's conduct violates social utility or public policy, and he will be held responsible for the death of the little boy.

 A DAY IN THE LIFE OF A REAL PARALEGAL

Tort law is a very important area of law in the legal industry and, as such, many paralegals are employed at firms and companies that work in this area. A paralegal may work for a personal injury law firm helping injured people obtain compensation for their injuries and damages. On the other hand, an insurance company may employ paralegals to work in defending the people who are insured by the insurance company from false claims of damages and injuries made by individuals for money. A paralegal working in this field can expect to become very familiar with court rules and regulations as well as state statutes. Deadlines are commonplace and the atmosphere can be fast paced at times. Many paralegals employed in this area of the law like the fact that they can help people who are in need.

In the preceding example, the unreasonable conduct of the executive can be called the **tortious conduct** in a case involving tort law. The executive is called the **tortfeasor**, and the lawsuit for the death of the boy would be a **cause of action** against the executive. If the executive is found **liable** for the death of the little boy, the court will award damages in favor of the little boy's family and against the executive.

TORTS: NOT CRIMINAL AND NOT CONTRACTUAL

When a person sues another under tort law, the purpose is not to punish the person who committed the act, but rather to compensate the victim for his or her loss, injury, or damages. When a tort case is initiated, the rules of civil procedure dictate how the case will proceed. The burden of proof is a **preponderance of the evidence**. A tort is different from a crime and different from a contract. Those differences are discussed next.

Crimes

A tort is not a **crime**. A crime is considered an offense against society as a whole. When people are punished for committing crimes, they are punished for committing wrongs against society. For example, a person is being tried in state court for committing a murder. The prosecutor works for the state. The state represents the people or the public at large, not an individual. The interests of society are served when the offending person is punished for committing the crime. When a criminal case is being prosecuted, the rules of criminal procedure dictate how the case is to proceed. The **burden of proof** in a criminal case is **beyond a reasonable doubt**. In a tort action, the burden of proof is the responsibility of the plaintiff. That is, it is the responsibility of the plaintiff or plaintiff's attorney to prove the defendant is liable for the plaintiff's damages or injury. (See Figure 1.1.)

A single action can be both a crime against society and a tort against a person. For example, take the infamous O.J. Simpson case. O.J. Simpson, a former professional football player, was accused of killing his ex-wife, Nicole, and a male friend in front of her home. Simpson was tried in a criminal court in the state of California for the murder of both people. The case was entitled *People of the State of California v. Orenthal J. Simpson.* The prosecutors prosecuted O.J. Simpson on behalf of the public because a crime of **murder** is viewed as a crime against society. Simpson was found not guilty of the murders. However, in a later civil action brought by the families of the victims, he was sued for the **wrongful deaths** of both people. In the civil case, O.J. Simpson was found liable for the wrongful deaths of his ex-wife and her friend, and a monetary award of millions of dollars was awarded to the families in an effort to compensate them for their loss. As already indicated, although no amount of money can make up for the lives of those two people, it is the best way that the courts have to compensate the victims for their loss. O.J. Simpson was tried

	Torts	Crimes
Purpose	Compensation	Punishment
Theory of Offense	Offense to individual	Offense to society
Initiating Party	The victim	The state
Verb/Noun	Sue/suit	Try/trial
Category of Responsibility	Liability	Guilt
Standard of Proof	Preponderance of evidence	Beyond a reasonable doubt
Procedural Rules	Civil rules	Criminal rules
Domain of Law	Civil	Criminal

FIGURE 1.1   **Torts Versus Crimes**

---

tortious conduct
The intentional or unintentional behavior or conduct that results in harm to another person.

tortfeasor
Actor committing the wrong, whether intentional, negligent, or strict liability.

cause of action
A personal, financial, or other injury for which the law gives a person the right to receive compensation.

liable
A determination of financial responsibility of the tortfeasor for tortious conduct that has resulted in some form of injury to an individual's property or person.

preponderance of the evidence
The weight or level of persuasion of evidence needed to find the defendant liable as alleged by the plaintiff in a civil matter.

crime
An act that violates the penal law of the local, state, or federal government.

burden of proof
Standard for assessing the weight of the evidence.

beyond a reasonable doubt
The requirement for the level of proof in a criminal matter in order to convict or find the defendant guilty. It is a substantially higher and more-difficult-to-prove criminal matter standard.

murder
The killing of a human being with intent.

wrongful death
A death attributable to the willful or negligent act of another.

SPOT THE ISSUE

A woman is walking down the sidewalk in front of City Hall. The concrete of the sidewalk is chipped, and in many areas the roots of the trees that line Main Street have raised the sidewalk. The woman trips over one of the raised areas of concrete, falls, and breaks her arm. What is the tort? Who can the woman sue?

both for a crime (murder) and a tort (wrongful death) from the commission of one act. In the murder trial, Simpson was held to the standard of beyond a reasonable doubt. Defense attorneys argued that since the infamous glove found at the scene of the crime did not fit Simpson when he tried to put it on that reasonable doubt existed as to whether or not Simpson committed the murders. Simpson was found not guilty of the murders. In the civil case, the standard of a preponderance of the evidence was used to find Simpson liable for the murders.

A tort does have some similarities to crimes. For example, both are considered to be actions against societal utility or public policy. The intention of the perpetrator is at the heart of an action for both crimes and torts. In a crime, the question is whether the intent was malicious. In a tort, the intent is looked at slightly differently to determine if it is blameworthy.

Contracts

contract
A legally binding agreement between two or more parties.

mutual agreement
A meeting of the minds on a specific subject, and a manifestation of intent of the parties to do or refrain from doing some specific act or acts.

An action in contracts, like a tort, is a civil action; however, a tort action is not based on a **contract**. A tort differs from a contract in that the action of contracting involves a voluntary action wherein each party agrees to be bound to certain duties and obligations. There is a **mutual agreement** between the parties. In tort law, obligations and duties are imposed by law and are not agreed to by the parties. Those involved do not voluntarily assume the duties and obligations. In contract law, the duties and obligations are specific to the contracting individuals. In tort law, the obligations and duties are to society. They are those duties and obligations that are imposed by society as to what conduct is considered fair and ethical. For example, David agrees to pay Ernie $2,000 for painting his house. The two sign a contract that defines the terms of their agreement. If Ernie paints David's house and then David refuses to pay him, then David has violated the contract with Ernie. Ernie can sue David for breach of contract. In contrast, suppose that David knocked the ladder by walking under it while Ernie was painting, causing Ernie to fall and break his arm. Ernie could sue David for causing his injury. In contracts, money damages are paid for violating the agreement. In tort law, money damages are paid for the injury. (See Figure 1.2.)

FIGURE 1.2
Torts Versus Contracts

	Torts	Contracts
Duties Assigned	Imposed by law	By parties' consent
Injuries Arise From	Injuries are not the result of a breach of an agreement	Injuries are the result of a breach of an agreement
Obligations Made To	Specific individuals Society in general	Specific individuals
Compensation	Monetary	Monetary Court-imposed specific performance
Procedural Rules	Civil rules	Civil rules
Domain of Law	Civil	Civil

ELEMENTS OF ALL TORTS

Tort law has evolved over time through Anglo-Saxon societies. The concept of paying monetary compensation for damages sustained was a product of Anglo-Saxon society and was based primarily on a person's rank in the society. People learned over time which decisions when rendered consistently were most advantageous to the society as a whole. Eventually, those decisions became local rules, and these local rules developed into what is now called **common law**.

Tort law comes into existence either by the court making a ruling in a case, which makes it common law, or by the legislature enacting a law, which makes it **statutory law**. Common law is judge-made law in the absence of any other controlling type of law. However, if a legislative statute exists, the court must follow the statute because statutory law takes priority over common law. When a court, such as a supreme court or an appellate court, makes a ruling or a decision in a case, that ruling is to be bound and adhered to and establishes **precedent**. Adhering to and abiding by decisions and rulings that have gone before is known as the doctrine of stare decisis. The doctrine of *stare decisis* does not mean that court rulings should never be overturned. In fact, over time, many are due to changes in circumstances or statutory law. However, *stare decisis* provides for the principle that a court should not overturn its own precedents unless there is a strong reason to do so and should be guided by principles from lateral and lower courts.

Every tort is a cause of action, which means that the injured party has a legally acceptable reason for bringing a lawsuit. To bring a lawsuit, a party must allege facts that support every element of the cause of action in torts. The components of a cause of action in torts are called **elements**. When a party has alleged facts that satisfy every element of the tort cause of action, then that party has presented a **prima facie** case.

The person who brings the lawsuit and who sustained the injury is called the **plaintiff**. If a case involves more than one person who sustained injuries or damages, they may bring suit together as **co-plaintiffs**. The wrongdoer is the tortfeasor and is called the **defendant**. If more than one defendant is involved in an action, a lawsuit can be brought against both of them as **co-defendants**. The law of torts provides remedies under the law for those plaintiffs who can prove that the basic elements of a cause of action for torts exists. If the plaintiff fails to prove the elements that make a prima facie case for the tort, the plaintiff has failed to prove that there is a cause of action in tort; as such, he is not entitled to avail himself to the court on a lawsuit for that tort. During the course of the lawsuit, while the plaintiff alleges facts to state a prima facie case against the defendant, the defendant is able to provide evidence or defenses that dispute the plaintiff's allegations.

A cause of action for torts has four basic elements. These elements are as follows:

- A *legal right* resides with the plaintiff.
- A *duty* resides in the defendant.
- There is a *violation of the duty* by the defendant.
- The plaintiff *sustained damages* as a result of the defendant's violation of his or her duty.

When analyzing a tort issue, three major questions should be considered for each possible tort that may be involved. These questions are:

1. Are the basic elements for the tort satisfied? Is the prima facie case established? If any of the basic elements are missing, then the plaintiff will probably not have a tort cause of action against the plaintiff.

common law
Judge-made law, the ruling in a judicial opinion.

statutory law
Derived from the Constitution in statutes enacted by the legislative branch of state or federal government; primary source of law consisting of the body of legislative law.

precedent
The holding of past court decisions that are followed in future judicial cases where similar facts and legal issues are present.

stare decisis
(Latin) "Stand by the decision." Decisions from a court with substantially the same set of facts should be followed by that court and all lower courts under it; the judicial process of adhering to prior case decisions; the doctrine of precedent whereby once a court has decided a specific issue one way in the past, it and other courts in the same jurisdiction are obligated to follow that earlier decision in deciding cases with similar issues in the future.

elements
A constituent part of a claim that must be proved for the claim to succeed.

prima facie
(Latin) "At first sight." A case with the required proof of elements in a tort cause of action; the elements of the plaintiff's (or prosecutor's) cause of action; what the plaintiff must prove; accepted on its face, but not indisputable.

plaintiff
The party initiating legal action.

co-plaintiff
More than one plaintiff who is involved in the same lawsuit.

defendant
The party against whom a lawsuit is brought.

co-defendant
More than one defendant who is being sued in the same lawsuit.

2. Are there any reasons or justifications or defenses that the defendant can offer that would negate any presumed liability by the defendant? For example, did the defendant act in self-defense, or did the plaintiff's actions help contribute to the alleged tort?

3. If the prima facie case has been established and the defendant can offer no defenses to his conduct, then what type of damages may the plaintiff recover from the defendant?

CATEGORIES OF TORTS

There are three main categories of torts:

- Intentional torts
- Negligence
- Strict liability torts

(See Figure 1.3.)

Intentional Torts

intentional tort
An intentional civil wrong that injures another person or property.

intent
Having the knowledge and desire that a specific consequence will result from an action.

omission
The failure to act when there exists a legal duty to do so.

An **intentional tort** is just that—intentional. It is a tort that is committed on purpose by the defendant. The **intent** of the defendant drives this cause of action. The defendant intended for her actions to happen and to cause the result to the plaintiff. The defendant must either desire to bring the result or knew with substantial certainty that the result would follow from what she did or failed to do. A failure to act by the defendant is known as an **omission**. Intentional torts are differentiated from other torts because they involve the state of mind of the defendant at the time that the person performed the action or failed to act.

The causes of action that fall under the category of intentional torts are:

- Assault and battery
- False imprisonment
- False arrest
- Infliction of emotional distress
- Conversion
- Trespass to land and/or chattels
- Invasion of privacy
- Defamation
- Malicious prosecution
- Abuse of process

Intentional torts will be discussed in more detail in later chapters in this book.

FIGURE 1.3
Categories of Torts

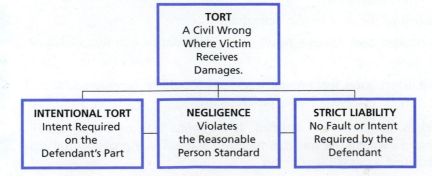

TORT A Civil Wrong Where Victim Receives Damages.		
INTENTIONAL TORT Intent Required on the Defendant's Part	**NEGLIGENCE** Violates the Reasonable Person Standard	**STRICT LIABILITY** No Fault or Intent Required by the Defendant

YOU BE THE JUDGE

Joey and Sarah are dating each other. Joey is obsessed with Sarah and becomes very jealous whenever she speaks with anyone of the opposite sex. Sarah has a good friend, Tom. Tom and Sarah have been friends since their childhood. Joey is jealous of Sarah's relationship with Tom. One day, Joey sees Tom speaking to Sarah. Joey becomes angry that Tom would speak to his girlfriend. Joey walks up to Tom and punches him in the face, breaking Tom's nose. Is Joey liable for a tort? Does Tom have any recourse?

Negligence

Some torts are caused by the **negligence** of the defendant. The defendant's intent to cause the injury to the plaintiff is not involved. This is distinguishable from the intentional torts that center on the intent of the defendant. Negligence covers harm due to actions or inactions that were unreasonable under the circumstances. It is the blameworthy conduct of the defendant that was the direct cause of the plaintiff's injuries. In an action for negligence, in order for there to be a cause of action against the defendant, there must have been harm to the plaintiff. For example, suppose that Keith spills some water on a hardwood floor and fails to clean it up. A short time later, Dan enters the room, slips on the water, and falls to the ground breaking his arm. As a result of Keith's failure to wipe up the water on the floor, Dan was injured. Keith's actions were considered negligent and were the cause of Dan's injury.

negligence
The failure to use reasonable care to avoid harm to another person or to do that which a reasonable person might do in similar circumstances.

Strict Liability

The general meaning of **strict liability** is liability without fault. If the defendant engages in a certain kind of conduct that causes harm to the plaintiff, then liability will result, irrespective of intent, negligence, or innocence. Certain types of conduct are inherently dangerous; therefore, any harm that results from these types of activities will result in liability being assessed to the defendant. Activities that fall into this category include blasting to clear land for development or transporting hazardous waste.

strict liability
The defendant is liable without the plaintiff having to prove fault.

Other Torts

There are other torts that do not fit neatly into the three categories of intentional tort, negligence, and strict liability. These torts are premises liability, nuisance, vicarious liability, and product liability. These torts will be discussed in more detail in later chapters.

LEGAL RESEARCH MAXIM

Various texts exist that explain the law created by statutes or judicial opinions. One source that is particularly helpful in understanding tort law is the *Restatement of Torts*. This text is not a source of law but will provide detailed explanations and sources of law for the various areas and concepts that are found in torts.

MAJOR TYPES OF PERSONAL INJURY TORT LITIGATION

Tort litigation in state and federal courts in this country is estimated to be between $30 billion and $40 billion per year. The litigation falls into three types:

- Routine personal injury—Automobile accidents, slips and falls, and so on.
- High-stakes personal injury—Products liability, medical malpractice, business torts, and so on.
- Mass latent injury—Products liability but on a broader scale because the injury is not discovered right away.

tort litigation
Legal action that involves an injury that falls under the definition of a tort.

DCA decisions

SURF'S UP

Court decisions in tort law are being rendered all the time at the local, state, and federal levels. To learn about recent federal decisions in tort law, try visiting the website for the Cornell Law School Legal Information Institute. Go to www.law.cornell.edu and click on "Recent Tort Law Decisions" for the United States Supreme Court. Read the recent cases that are listed and how they were decided using tort law.

YOU BE THE JUDGE

Bryan likes to play jokes on people. One day, Bryan and his mom, Marci, go to meet their friends, David and David's mom, Brenda, at a restaurant. Just as Brenda is about to take a seat in the restaurant, Bryan decides to play a joke on her. Bryan pulls Brenda's chair out from under her just as she is about to sit down. Brenda falls on the hard floor and injures her back. Has Bryan committed a tort? If so, which category of torts does his action fall into? Last, do you think that Marci is liable for Brenda's injuries?

EYE ON ETHICS

Remember that each state has its own laws. It is always important to stay abreast of all current local, state, and federal laws when dealing with any type of legal theory.

Although there are numerous other types of tort litigation, the types in the preceding list constitute a large majority of the common types found in most law firms.

black letter
An informal term indicating the basic principles of law generally accepted by the courts and/or embodied in the statutes of a particular jurisdiction.

RESEARCH THIS

Although numerous resources are available for information on tort law, the principal resource for **black letter** rules of tort law comes from the *Restatement (Second) of Torts* that was drafted by the American Law Institute. The *Restatement* is an excellent source of information and should be referred to frequently when studying this area of the law.

Summary

A tort is defined as a private or civil wrong or injury for which the court will provide a remedy in the form of an action for damages. If a violation of a tort occurs, the law permits the injured party to seek to recover damages equal to the value of the injury. Damages are awarded in an effort to make the injured party whole again.

Money is the usual form of damages awarded in a tort case. While money can assist to rectify many things, it cannot always make the injured party whole again, but it is the best remedy that the law affords for the situation. The underlying theory in tort law is that socially unreasonable conduct should be penalized. Public policy becomes a prime focus in tort law. What is just and fair and promotes equality is the underlying theme of this area of the law.

Reasonable care generally means any type of conduct that might be exhibited by an ordinary person under the same or similar circumstances. Individuals can violate the premise of reasonable care if they act intentionally toward another person. The definition of a reasonable person can be interpreted as "what a reasonable person would do under the circumstances."

A tort is different from a crime. A crime is considered an offense against society as a whole. When people are punished for committing a crime, they are punished for committing a wrong against society. For example, a person being tried in state court for committing a murder.

A tort is different from a contract. An action in contracts, like a tort, is a civil action, but a tort action is not based on a contract. The action of contracting involves a voluntary action wherein each party agrees to be bound to certain duties and obligations. There is a mutual agreement between the parties. In tort law, obligations and duties are imposed by law and are not agreed to by the parties. Those involved do not voluntarily assume the duties and obligations. In contract law, the duties and obligations are specific to the contracting individuals. In tort law, the obligations and duties are to society. They are those duties and obligations that are imposed by society as to what conduct is considered fair and ethical.

Tort law comes into existence either by the court making a ruling in a case, which makes it common law, or by the legislature enacting a law, which makes it statutory law. If a statute exists, the court must follow the statute because statutory law takes priority over common law.

Every tort is a cause of action, which means that the injured party has a legally acceptable reason for bringing a lawsuit. To bring a lawsuit, a party must allege facts that support every element of the cause of action in torts. The components of a cause of action in torts are called elements. When a party has alleged facts that satisfy every element of the tort cause of action, then that party has presented a prima facie case.

A cause of action for torts has four basic elements. These elements are as follows: a legal right resides with the plaintiff; a duty resides in the defendant; there is a violation of the duty by the defendant; and the plaintiff sustained damages as a result of the defendant's violation of his or her duty.

An intentional tort is just that—intentional. It is a tort that is committed on purpose by the defendant. The defendant intended for his actions to happen and to cause the result to the plaintiff. The defendant must either desire to bring the result or know with substantial certainty that the result will follow from what she did, or failed to do. A failure to act by the defendant is known as an omission. Intentional torts are differentiated from other torts because they involve the state of mind of defendants at the time that they performed the action or failed to act.

Torts that are caused by the negligence of the defendant involve the lack of intent to cause the injury to the plaintiff. This is distinguishable from the intentional torts that center on the defendant's intent. Negligence covers harm due to actions or inactions that were unreasonable under the circumstances. It is the blameworthy conduct of the defendant that was the direct cause of the plaintiff's injuries. In an action for negligence, in order for there to be a cause of action against the defendant there must have been harm to the plaintiff.

The general meaning of strict liability is liability without fault. If the defendant engages in a certain kind of conduct that causes harm to the plaintiff, then liability will result, irrespective of intent, negligence, or innocence. It is thought that certain types of conduct are inherently dangerous; therefore, any harm that results from these types of activities will result in liability being assessed to the defendant.

Key Terms

Beyond a reasonable doubt	Civil
Black letter	Co-defendant
Burden of proof	Common law
Cause of action	Contract

Co-plaintiff   Precedent
Crime   Preponderance of the evidence
Damages   Prima facie
Defendant   Reasonable care
Elements   Remedy
Intent   *Stare decisis*
Intentional tort   Statutory law
Liable   Strict liability
Murder   Tort
Mutual agreement   Tortfeasor
Negligence   Tort litigation
Omission   Tortious conduct
Plaintiff   Wrongful death

Review Questions

1. What is a tort?
2. What is tortious conduct?
3. What is a tortfeasor?
4. How is reasonable care measured?
5. What distinguishes intentional torts from negligence?
6. What are the elements of a tort?
7. What is the similarity between torts and crimes?
8. What is the similarity between torts and contracts?
9. What is a plaintiff?
10. What is the difference between preponderance of the evidence and beyond a reasonable doubt?
11. What is common law?
12. What is statutory law?
13. What is a prima facie case?
14. Can a tort be both a crime and a civil wrong? Explain.
15. What does "liable" mean?

Exercises

1. Look in your local telephone directory. Identify 25 attorney's offices that practice in the area of torts. List the firm name and identify the different types of torts that they practice.
2. Bill and Jenny are wrestling. Bill pushes Jenny and she falls into Sara. Sara is injured. Write an essay describing whether or not a tort was committed by Bill, Jenny, Sara, or all of them and, if so, into which category the tort falls.
3. Has a tort ever been committed against you, a family member, or one of your friends? Write an essay about the tort, making sure you cover the following items:
   a. the facts surrounding the tort;
   b. into what category the tort falls;
   c. who the plaintiff and defendant were;
   d. what the cause of action was; and
   e. what the injury was that was sustained.
4. Interview a neighborhood/community attorney working in personal injury. What are the different types of payment attorneys may receive as compensation?
5. The terms *assault* and *battery* are heard frequently not only in criminal settings but tort settings as well. Are there different elements to each? What is different?

6. Can a person be successful in a lawsuit claiming *assault* if the victim never saw the perpetrator? Research and list your discoveries about that issue.

7. Explain in laypeople's' terms what the difference is between the two very different standards for criminal law and torts, "beyond a reasonable doubt" versus "by a preponderance of the evidence," respectively.

8. Why does society make room for, *allow,* people to seek reimbursement for injuries sustained when society may hold the perpetrator responsible by arresting and incarcerating the guilty party?

PORTFOLIO ASSIGNMENT

Write a memorandum about an episode in your life in which you believe a tort was committed. Explain the facts of the scenario and tell why you believe that the action of the defendant rises to the level of a tort.

Vocabulary Builders

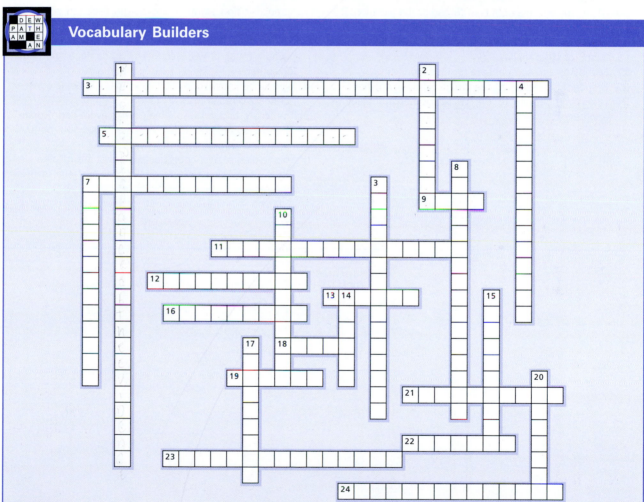

Instructions

Use the key terms from this chapter to fill in the answers to the crossword puzzle.

NOTE: When the answer is more than one word, leave a blank space between the words.

ACROSS

3. The weight or level of persuasion of evidence needed to find the defendant liable as alleged by the plaintiff in a civil matter.

5. An intentional civil wrong that injures another person or property.

DOWN

1. The requirement for the level of proof in a criminal matter in order to convict or find the defendant guilty. It is a substantially higher and more-difficult-to-prove criminal matter standard.

2. The party against whom a lawsuit is brought.

Vocabulary Builders

7. Derived from the Constitution in statutes enacted by the legislative branch of state or federal government; primary source of law consisting of the body of legislative law.
9. A civil wrongful act, committed against a person or property, either intentional or negligent.
11. Intentional or unintentional behavior or conduct that results in harm to another person.
12. Judge-made law, the ruling in a judicial opinion.
13. Determination of financial responsibility of the tortfeasor for tortious conduct that has resulted in some form of injury to an individual's property or person.
16. The party initiating legal action.
18. Act that violates the penal law of the local, state, or federal government.
19. Means by which a right is enforced or the violation of a right is prevented, redressed, or compensated.
21. Actor committing the wrong, whether intentional, negligent, or strict liability.
22. Money paid to compensate for loss or injury.
23. Standard for assessing the weight of the evidence.
24. Death attributable to the willful or negligent act of another.

4. A personal, financial, or other injury for which the law gives a person the right to receive compensation.
6. The defendant is liable without the plaintiff having to prove fault.
7. (Latin) "Stand by the decision." Decisions from a court with substantially the same set of facts should be followed by that court and all lower courts under it; the judicial process of adhering to prior case decisions; the doctrine of precedent whereby once a court has decided a specific issue one way in the past, it and other courts in the same jurisdiction are obligated to follow that earlier decision in deciding cases with similar issues in the future.
8. Conduct that an ordinary person would do under the same or similar circumstances.
10. (Latin) "At first sight." A case with required proof of elements in a tort cause of action; the elements of the plaintiff's (or prosecutor's) cause of action; what the plaintiff must prove; accepted on its face, but not indisputable.
14. Having the knowledge and desire that a specific consequence will result from an action.
15. The failure to use reasonable care to avoid harm to another person or to do that which a reasonable person might do in similar circumstances.
17. The holding of past court decisions that are followed in future judicial cases where similar facts and legal issues are present.
20. A legally binding agreement between two or more parties.

CASE IN POINT

Getchell v. Lodge
65 P.3d 50
February 28, 2003
Alaska

I. INTRODUCTION

When Barbara Lodge saw a moose in her lane of traffic, she braked and skidded on ice into the oncoming lane of traffic, causing a collision with Joyce Getchell's car. Getchell sued Lodge, and the case proceeded to a jury trial. The jury found that Lodge was not negligent. Getchell appeals the superior court's denial of her motions for judgment notwithstanding the verdict (JNOV) and new trial. She also appeals the trial court's admission of the investigating state trooper's testimony. Because we conclude that the trial court did not err in denying Getchell's motions for JNOV or new trial, or in admitting the trooper's testimony, we affirm.

II. FACTS AND PROCEEDINGS

On the morning of January 16, 1998, Joyce Getchell and Barbara Lodge drove to work on the Kenai Spur Highway. Getchell headed south on the highway towards Kenai. Lodge headed north towards Nikiski. A thin layer of ice covered the unsanded road; the morning was dark. There was a dispute at trial about what happened next. However, because we draw all factual inferences in favor of the non-moving party when reviewing motions for JNOV and new trial, what follows is Lodge's account.

Because of the darkness, the icy road conditions, and the possibility of moose crossing the highway, Lodge was driving at about forty-five miles per hour, even though the speed limit was fifty-five. A moose emerged out of the darkness from Lodge's right and tried to cross the road as Lodge neared Mile 20 of the highway. Lodge hit her brakes as hard as she could. She testified that her car skidded immediately and began to rotate in a counterclockwise direction. Lodge lost control of her car as it continued to rotate and slide. Ultimately, the car crossed the center line of the road. The car finished rotating and came to a stop in the southbound lane. As Getchell headed south towards Mile 20, driving between forty-five and fifty-five miles per hour, she saw a car in her lane. Getchell hit the passenger side of Lodge's car. The impact injured Getchell's ankle, requiring surgery. State Trooper Harold Leichliter investigated the accident and completed an accident report based upon his observations of the scene and witness interviews.

Getchell brought a personal injury negligence action against Lodge. Before trial, Getchell objected to the introduction of portions of Trooper Leichliter's videotaped deposition. Getchell argued that the objectionable portions of the deposition should be excluded as impermissible opinion testimony under Alaska Rules of Evidence 701 and 702. Additionally, she argued that Trooper Leichliter's testimony was irrelevant and more prejudicial than probative, and therefore excludable under Alaska Rules of Evidence 402 and 403. The superior court admitted Trooper Leichliter's testimony over Getchell's objections.

Superior Court Judge Harold M. Brown conducted a three-day jury trial in July 2001. Getchell moved for a directed verdict, which the trial court denied. The jury found Lodge not negligent. After hearing the verdict, Getchell orally moved for a judgment in her favor notwithstanding the verdict or, alternatively, a new trial. The court entered judgment in favor of Lodge and against Getchell in September 2001, for $17,042.50 in attorney's fees and $5,473.18 in costs, a total of $22,515.68. Shortly thereafter, Getchell filed a motion for judgment notwithstanding the verdict and a motion for new trial. Judge Brown heard arguments on Getchell's motions in November 2001. Judge Brown denied Getchell's motions.

Getchell appeals Judge Brown's denial of her motions for JNOV and new trial. She also appeals the trial court's admission of Trooper Leichliter's testimony.

[Text omitted]

III. DISCUSSION

A. The Trial Court Did Not Err in Denying Getchell's Motions for Judgment Notwithstanding the Verdict and New Trial.

Getchell argues that the trial court erred in denying her motions for JNOV and new trial, contending that reasonable jurors could have only concluded that Lodge acted negligently. Getchell structures her argument around the tort consequences of Lodge's alleged violation of two Alaska traffic regulations. Getchell contends that because Lodge crossed the center lane of traffic into Getchell's lane she violated 13 AAC 02.085 and 13 AAC 02.050. Because Lodge violated these traffic regulations, Getchell argues, the burden of proof shifted to Lodge to show by a preponderance of the evidence that her conduct was excused. To prove excuse in the instant case, Getchell asserts that Lodge had to demonstrate that she exercised reasonable care in two ways: "first, that she refrained from steering into oncoming traffic, and second, that she exercised reasonable care in handling her sliding vehicle." Getchell contends that Lodge steered into oncoming traffic, took no steps to control her skidding car, and that therefore "reasonable persons could only have concluded that Lodge failed to meet her burden of proving excuse by a preponderance of the evidence."

Getchell is correct that Lodge can only claim excuse if she handled her moose-avoidance maneuver and the resulting skid in a non-negligent manner. However, contrary to Getchell's argument, there is evidence in the record that Lodge did not purposefully steer into the oncoming lane and that the skid was not caused by her negligence. We will affirm a trial court's denial of a motion for judgment notwithstanding the verdict "unless the evidence, viewed in the light most favorable to the non-moving party, is such that reasonable persons could not differ in their judgment as to the facts." A factual dispute exists here. Similarly, we affirm a trial court's denial of a motion for a new trial unless the court abused its discretion. We will find an abuse of discretion when no evidence supported the verdict or when the evidence was "so slight and unconvincing as to make the verdict plainly unreasonable and unjust." Ample evidence supports the verdict in this case.

Both Getchell and Lodge agree that it would have been negligent to steer into the oncoming lane of traffic on purpose under the circumstances of this case. However, Lodge testified that she did not steer into the other lane.

Q But you deny that you attempted to turn, correct?
A Yes.
Q Okay. And when asked in your deposition if you swerved to the right or to the left, you said: I did not turn and I did not swerve to the right or left, true?
A That's what I said, yes.
Q And you maintain that today?
A Yes, mmm-hmm.

James Stirling, Lodge's accident reconstruction expert, testified similarly:

Q Mr. Lewis testified that tire marks in the trooper photos indicate that Ms. Lodge's vehicle was sideslipping and rotating as it crossed the center line in the roadway. Do you agree with that position?
A Yes I do.
Q What's the significance of that information?
A The rotation started in her lane.
Q Are you aware of any evidence in this case that Ms. Lodge intended to steer into or swerve into the oncoming lane of traffic?
A No, I'm not.

In addition to the evidence that Lodge did not steer into the oncoming lane of traffic, Lodge testified that she slammed on her brakes to avoid a moose in her lane. According to Lodge, her brakes locked and she skidded into Getchell's lane. Reasonable jurors could have concluded that the presence of the moose in the road excused Lodge's skid into the oncoming lane of traffic. Skidding to avoid a moose is the type of excuse contemplated by 288A of the *Restatement (Second) of Torts*, adopted by this court in *Ferrell v. Baxter*. Comment h of this section aptly describes this situation:

> Emergency. As in other cases of negligence (see 296), the violation of an enactment or regulation will ordinarily be excused when the actor is confronted with an emergency which is not caused by his own misconduct.

It is plausible that the jury concluded that the moose created an emergency situation for Lodge and that they therefore excused the unfortunate consequences of her attempt to avoid the moose.

The jury also heard other evidence from which it could have reasonably concluded that Lodge was not negligent. Lodge points out that she had very little time to react after she saw the moose in the road. Lodge's accident reconstruction expert, James Stirling, expressed his opinion that Lodge had approximately "three-point-some seconds before" she would have collided with the

moose. According to Stirling, Lodge's perception of the danger, before she took any evasive action, would have consumed one-and-a-quarter to one-and-a-half seconds. Thus, Lodge argues, she had one-and-a-half seconds at most to slow the car down and correct the slide. Stirling testified that "[g]iven the surface and how slick it was, and given the speed of 45 miles an hour, [Lodge's attempts to correct her car's rotation] would have had to have been almost instantaneous to stop. . . . I would think she would have to perform higher than the average driver to do it." Based upon this testimony, reasonable jurors could have concluded that "Lodge was unable after reasonable care to comply with [13 AAC 02.085 and 13 AAC 02.050]." The trial court did not abuse its discretion in denying Getchell's motions for JNOV or new trial.

B. The Trial Court Did Not Err in Admitting Trooper Leichliter's Testimony.

1. Trooper Leichliter testified as a hybrid witness.

Trooper Leichliter responded to the accident in this case and wrote an accident report. Before trial, Getchell objected to Trooper Leichliter's proposed testimony about causation and fault. She argued in a motion in limine that Trooper Leichliter should not be able to offer expert opinions because Lodge listed him as a fact witness rather than an expert witness in her witness list. Getchell asserted that because Trooper Leichliter was a fact witness, his testimony should be excluded as improper lay opinion evidence under Alaska Rule of Evidence 701 because, contrary to Rule 701's requirements, he did not see the accident. Alternatively, Getchell argued that if the court considered Trooper Leichliter an expert, his testimony should be barred because it did not satisfy Rule 702's helpfulness requirement. Although Lodge listed Trooper Leichliter as a fact witness, rather than an expert, the trial court apparently considered his testimony to be expert testimony. Judge Brown permitted Trooper Leichliter to testify regarding causation based upon his investigation of the accident.

In his testimony, Trooper Leichliter focused on the accident report that he prepared when he arrived at the accident scene. He testified that the moose was the only contributing factor and that no human factors contributed to the accident. Trooper Leichliter gave the opinion that drivers generally react to the sight of a moose in the road in front of them by braking, which could lead to skidding and loss of control in icy road conditions. He testified that he found no evidence indicating any improper conduct by Lodge. Lodge's defense attorney used this testimony in his closing statement as opinion evidence that Lodge was not negligent in responding as she did to the sighting of the moose. Trooper Leichliter's testimony incorporated both his observations as a percipient witness investigating the scene and his conclusions about causation based on over twenty-two years as a state trooper investigating accidents. Thus, we find that the label "expert" or "fact" witness lacks significance in this situation because Trooper Leichliter provided hybrid testimony.

We discussed the concept of hybrid witnesses in *Miller v. Phillips*. In *Miller*, parents of an injured newborn sued their midwife for negligence. The jury found for the midwife. On appeal, the parents argued that the trial court erred in allowing the midwife's supervising physician to testify as an expert because the midwife called him as a fact witness. The trial court allowed the doctor to testify as a hybrid witness; he could not testify "in general terms about the appropriate standard of care," but he could testify to "his expert observations [and] his own opinions as to what he observed," as well as his "expert opinions based on his review of hospital records." We held that the physician could express expert opinions formed as a supervisory participant, reasoning that "[w]hen physicians are called to testify about matters pertaining to the treatment of their patients, the distinction between an expert witness and a fact witness inevitably becomes blurred." Like the treating physician in *Miller,* Trooper Leichliter, the investigating officer, was "intimately involved in the underlying facts giving rise to the litigation and . . . would reasonably be expected to form an opinion through that involvement." Thus, despite Lodge's choice to list Trooper Leichliter as a fact witness, it was not error to permit him to base his opinions on his expertise. Moreover, Getchell was fully aware of the content of Trooper Leichliter's proposed testimony. She was able to depose Trooper Leichliter and thus suffered no prejudice from Lodge's decision to list him as a fact witness.

2. The trial court did not err in admitting Trooper Leichliter's testimony under Rule 702.

Getchell also argues that the trial court abused its discretion by admitting Trooper Leichliter's testimony as an expert witness because his testimony did not comply with Alaska Rule of Evidence 702. She contends primarily that Trooper Leichliter's testimony did not help the jury because the jury was at least as capable as Trooper Leichliter of determining whether Lodge acted reasonably.

Alaska Rule of Evidence 702(a) allows a witness to give opinion testimony if the witness is qualified "by knowledge, skill, experience, training or education," and if "scientific, technical, or other specialized knowledge will assist the trier of fact to understand the evidence or to determine a fact in issue." To be admissible, then, expert opinion testimony must be helpful to the jury. This helpfulness standard requires experts to "stop short of stating their own conclusions" on points that the jury is at least equally capable of determining. In *Spenard Action Committee,* we relied on this rationale in holding that the superior court had erred in permitting police officers to express their opinion that a massage parlor was operating as a house of prostitution. On the other hand, in cases such as *Adkins v. Lester* and *State v. Phillips,* we have approved of the admission of police officers' opinions as to the cause of particular traffic accidents that they have investigated.

Trooper Leichliter's testimony satisfies Rule 702's requirements. First, his knowledge and experience qualified him as an expert. He served as a state trooper in Kenai for twenty years, and, as Lodge points out, Trooper Leichliter "routinely determined whether there were any human factors contributing to [accidents involving moose], such as speeding, or whether the accident was simply the result of a moose interfering with motor vehicle traffic." Second, Trooper Leichliter's testimony was at least of arguable assistance to the jury. His implied opinion that Lodge had not been negligent was not different in kind than the police testimony permitted in *Adkins v. Lester* and *State v. Phillips.* Finally, it is analogous to the type of testimony given by the accident reconstruction experts who testified at the trial without objection. The trial court did not abuse its discretion in admitting Trooper Leichliter's testimony under Rule 702.

3. The trial court did not err in declining to exclude Trooper Leichliter's testimony under Alaska Rule of Evidence 403.

Getchell finally argues that the trial court should have barred Leichliter's testimony under Alaska Rule of Evidence 403 because it was more prejudicial than probative.

Alaska Rule of Evidence 403 provides that the trial court may exclude relevant evidence "if its probative value is outweighed by the danger of unfair prejudice, confusion of the issues, or misleading the jury, or by considerations of undue delay, waste of time, or needless presentation of cumulative evidence." The commentary to the rule explains that "[s]ituations in this area call for balancing the probative value of and need for the evidence against the harm likely to result from its admission. . . . [T]here is a slight presumption in favor of admitting relevant evidence. . . . [T]o overcome this minimal presumption, the prejudicial effect must be demonstrably greater than the probative value of the evidence."

It is true that Trooper Leichliter's testimony was prejudicial to Getchell in the sense that it bolstered Lodge's argument that her conduct was excused because she skidded to avoid a moose. However, "undue prejudice connotes not merely evidence that is harmful to the other party, but evidence that will result in a decision being reached by the trier of facts on an improper basis." We recognize that there is a danger that a police investigator's conclusion will be given undue weight by a jury. In any particular case this may be a real danger. The officer may be focusing on whether the evidence will support a quasi-criminal traffic citation that must be proven beyond a reasonable doubt, rather than whether there is civil negligence that need only be proven by a preponderance of the evidence. Nonetheless, this possibility may be ignored by a jury, and because of the neutrality and prestige of an investigating officer, the officer's testimony may be given decisive weight. There is case law in other jurisdictions holding that a police officer's decision whether to issue a traffic citation is inadmissible on the question of negligence. These authorities are based in part on the rationale that such testimony amounts to an opinion on an ultimate issue that is for the trier of fact to decide, an exclusionary rationale that our rules reject, and in part on the undue weight concerns. The answer we have accepted in response to these legitimate concerns is not a rule of blanket exclusion. Instead, vigorous advocacy including cross-examination is expected to serve as a safeguard against undue weight being given to police testimony. A second safeguard is the discretionary power of the trial court under Rule 403 to exclude testimony when, on balance, its probative force is outweighed by the danger of unfair prejudice. In the present case the record does not suffice to persuade us that the trial court abused its discretion in striking the balance mandated by Evidence Rule 403 in favor of the admission of Trooper Leichliter's implied opinion testimony.

IV. CONCLUSION

Because we find that there was evidence from which reasonable jurors could have differed in their judgment of the facts as to whether Lodge acted negligently, we AFFIRM the trial court's denial of Getchell's motions for JNOV and new trial. Because the trial court did not abuse its discretion in admitting Trooper Leichliter's testimony, we AFFIRM the decision to admit the testimony.

Matthews, Eastaugh, Bryner, and Carpeneti, Justices.
FABE, Chief Justice.
[Footnotes omitted]

Source: LexisNexis, *Getchell v. Lodge* 65 P.3d 50 Alaska, 2003. Reprinted with permission from LexisNexis.

Chapter 2

Intentional Torts Against the Person

CHAPTER OBJECTIVES

Upon completion of this chapter, you will be able to:

- Discuss intent.
- Identify the concept of transferred intent.
- Explain the reasonable person test.
- Understand the elements of each intentional tort against the person.

As you will remember from Chapter 1, for an action to be considered an intentional tort, four elements are required: (1) a legal right resides with the plaintiff; (2) a duty resides in the defendant; (3) there is a violation of the duty by the defendant; and (4) the plaintiff sustains damages as a result of the defendant's violation of his or her duty. An intentional tort is the intentional act of an individual against another person that violates the victim's right to be free from harm.

The same intentional tort may be the basis for either a criminal action or a civil action or both. A criminal action is a wrong committed against society and is usually punishable by some type of jail time or the threat of jail time, such as probation. A civil action is considered a wrong against the victim and usually results in monetary damages being awarded to the victim to compensate him for the damages that resulted from the harm. When learning about intentional torts, it bears remembering that a tort is neither a crime nor a contract but has similarities to both, as discussed in Chapter 1.

INTENT

The state of mind of the defendant who committed the tort is the central concept of intentional torts. The defendant must have **intent** to commit the act, and the intent must be sufficient in nature to bring about a physical or mental effect upon the plaintiff. Intent is different from a desire to harm; intent involves planning and acting. There need not be any desire or intent to harm the plaintiff in order to satisfy the element of intent for an intentional tort.

There are two types of intent: specific and general. In **specific intent**, the defendant intends that his actions will cause the consequence. In other words, the defendant's goal is to cause the consequences that resulted from his action. General intent means that the defendant did not necessarily intend for her actions to cause harm, but she

intent
Having the knowledge and desire that a specific consequence will result from an action.

specific intent
The mental desire and will to act in a particular way.

17

substantial certainty
The defendant knows that the plaintiff's damage is probably going to occur as a result of the defendant's actions.

knew with **substantial certainty** that some type of consequences would result from her actions. The defendant must have intended or been reasonably certain that the desired result would occur from her actions. However, if there is doubt that a consequence would occur, but it is merely *likely* to occur, then an intentional tort has not resulted. The fact that something is likely to occur as a result of the defendant's actions does not rise to the level of intent necessary to fulfill the element of intent for a cause of action for an intentional tort.

The *Restatement (Second) of Torts,* section 8A, states as follows: "The word 'intent' is used throughout the Restatement of this Subject to denote that the actor desires to cause consequences of his act or that he believes that the consequences are substantially certain to result from it." The act is not the focus of intent; rather, it is the consequences that stem from that act that are the focus. For example, suppose as a practical joke Morton pulled a chair out from under Sam as Sam was about to take a seat. Morton caused the act, intended to do it, and was substantially certain that Sam would fall as a result of Morton's actions. Morton may not have intended harm to come to Sam, but Morton knew with substantial certainty that Sam would fall.

Typically, three elements must be present in order to have an intentional tort. Those elements are:

- The defendant's state of mind or intent.
- An intentional act by the defendant.
- Consequences or substantially certain consequences caused by the defendant.

When these three elements are met, then a cause of action can be brought for an intentional tort. If one of the three is missing, the intent, conduct, or consequences involved, then the situation does not rise to the level necessary for an intentional tort.

A DAY IN THE LIFE OF A REAL PARALEGAL

Distinguishing between different types of intents is a paramount skill to learn and have knowledge of, as it can mean the difference in whether an intentional tort occurred or can have an effect on the ultimate judgment and award that may or may not be awarded to the plaintiff.

SPOT THE ISSUE

Boisterous Barney attended a party held at Meek Mary Sue's on Saturday night. There was drinking and partying and many people going in and out all night long. Most were drunk or at least had one or two drinks too many, including both Meek Mary and Boisterous Barney. Nearing early morning hours, Meek Mary began to ask people to leave; without warning Boisterous Barney blurted out, "Hey, Mary, you prude, don't break the party up yet. We are just beginning to have some fun. Besides, you need all the friends you can get because you are so ugly." Hearing that, Meek Mary ran out of the house crying hysterically. Has a tort been committed? If so, what are the potential issues and defenses, if any?

Just because the situation cannot be classified as an intentional tort does not mean that the plaintiff is not entitled to relief. As will be discussed in later chapters, the level of intent, conduct, and consequences may very well fit the elements of another tort.

TRANSFERRED INTENT

Suppose that Dan gets angry with Pete. Dan decides that he is going to punch Pete in the face because he is so angry. Dan swings his fist at Pete but misses Pete and hits Martha. Martha's nose is broken by Dan's swing. Is Dan liable for an intentional tort against Martha, since he did not intend to hit Martha? This is classic case of transferred intent. There are many instances in tort law where the **transferred intent doctrine** may apply. The list includes:

- Assault
- Battery
- False imprisonment
- Trespass to land
- Trespass to chattels

The doctrine states that if a defendant intends to commit a tort against one person but accidentally commits it against another person, then the defendant will be held liable for an intentional tort for the consequences of his actions against the second person. Using the preceding example, Dan meant to hit Pete, but instead hit Martha. Dan's intent will be transferred to Martha under the doctrine of transferred intent. Dan will be liable for the intentional tort committed against Martha even though it was not Dan's intent to hit Martha. The transferred intent doctrine provides that Dan will be held liable just as if he had intended to hit Martha.

The doctrine of transferred intent will apply when the defendant intends to commit a tortious action against one person but instead:

- Commits a different tortious act against the intended plaintiff;
- Commits the intended tortious act, but against a different person; or
- Commits a different tortious act against a different person.

To establish a prima facie case for an intentional tort using the transferred intent doctrine, one of the three preceding scenarios must have occurred. In an intentional tort, whether the transferred intent doctrine comes into play or not, the tortfeasor will be liable for almost every consequence that results from his conduct. If the defendant's conduct results in the commission of a tort against another person, then he is liable for that tort.

transferred intent doctrine
The doctrine that holds a person liable for the unintended result to another person not contemplated by the defendant's actions.

LEGAL RESEARCH MAXIM

Tort law is driven by the facts of a case. What facts prove that the defendant possessed the requisite intent to demonstrate that an intentional tort was committed? What facts demonstrate that the defendant caused the plaintiff's injuries? Paralegals who work in the legal arena will spend time investigating the facts of each case to determine what happened or the chronology of the events. Paralegals who are skilled in basic investigative techniques such as interviewing clients, interviewing witnesses, and reviewing documentation are valuable assets to their employer. It is important for a paralegal to develop these basic skills. As you read the intentional torts described next, think about each example and what type of investigative skills would be required to flush out the facts of each case.

TYPES OF INTENTIONAL TORTS AGAINST THE PERSON

Battery

Personal **integrity** is entitled to protection under the law. The tort of battery is concerned with maintaining the plaintiff's body. Individuals should be able to be free from any intentional, not permitted, unwanted, or uninvited physical contact with

integrity
A standard of values having soundness or moral principle and character.

FIGURE 2.1

Elements of the Tort of Battery

> **Battery**
> * An act
> * Harmful or offensive contact
> * Intent
> * Cause

battery

An intentional and unwanted harmful or offensive contact with the person of another; the actual intentional touching of someone with intent to cause harm, no matter how slight the harm.

their body or anything associated with their body. A **battery** is a harmful or offensive contact with a person that occurs as a result of the defendant's intent to cause the harmful or offensive contact or the defendant's intent to cause apprehension in the person of an imminent contact.

A battery consists of the following elements:

* An *act* by the defendant;

* That creates a *harmful or offensive contact* to the plaintiff;

* An *intent* on the part of the defendant to cause the harm or contact to the plaintiff; and

* The defendant must be the *cause* of the harmful or offensive contact.

To establish a prima facie case against the defendant, all of the preceding elements must be proved. (See Figure 2.1.)

To begin to establish a tort of battery, there must first be an act by the defendant that leads to contact with the plaintiff's person. An act is a voluntary movement of the body. A person decides to physically move his or her body so as to cause it to do something. It is a conscious decision to act. Not all harmful or offensive contacts are the result of acts. In order to determine whether or not the contact was harmful or offensive, the court will look to the **reasonable person test**. Would a reasonable person of ordinary sensitivity consider the contact harmful or offensive? If the answer is yes, then the act may well be a battery. If the answer is no, then it is likely that a battery has not occurred.

reasonable person test

Asking whether or not an ordinary or average person would find the action offensive or harmful.

Battery is an intentional tort. Therefore, if the harmful or offensive contact is caused by negligent or reckless contact, the element of intent is not sufficient for a tort of battery. The defendant must have intended to cause the harm. The notable Professor W. Page Keeton in *Prosser and Keeton on Torts* section 9, at 41 (5th ed., 1984), described the necessary level of intent as follows: "The act must cause, and must be intended to cause, an unpermitted contact. Mere negligence, or even recklessness, which creates only a risk that the contact will result, may afford a distinct cause of action in itself, but under modern usage of the term it is not enough for battery."

If a situation exists in which touching occurred that is normally customary or traditional, such as shaking hands or greeting people by kissing them on both cheeks, then most jurisdictions will not find that contact offensive or harmful even if the plaintiff considers it to be so. Contact is harmful if it brings about physical damage, impairment, pain, or illness. Contact is offensive if it offends the personal dignity of an ordinary person who is not unduly sensitive. If the contact is not harmful, the plaintiff can still recover under the objective standard of the reasonable person test. Again, the test is whether a reasonable person, a person who is not unduly sensitive, would be offended by the contact. However, if the defendant knows that a plaintiff is unduly sensitive and exploits those sensitivities, then he will be found liable for the consequences of the harmful and offensive contact.

For example, Sheila was the victim of a rape a year ago. The rape was well publicized in the local newspapers. Sheila goes to school with Ron. Everyone at school knows that Sheila is very apprehensive about being touched by anyone, especially by men, since the rape. Ron thinks it will be amusing to go up to Sheila and put his arm around her waist. The next day at school, in front of his friends, Ron goes up to Sheila and suddenly puts an arm around her waist, pulling her close to him. Sheila becomes hysterical and faints to the floor. Ron will be liable for a battery upon Sheila because Ron knew that Sheila had sensitivity to the touching of her person by men and he exploited that sensitivity for his own amusement.

The motive of the defendant is irrelevant. If the defendant does not intend a harmful or offensive contact, it may be battery, even if the defendant was trying to help the plaintiff in making the contact. For example, John was walking down the street and saw a woman walking in front of him crossing the street. John also noticed that a truck was traveling very fast, and the driver did not see the woman who was crossing the street. John ran to the woman and pushed her out of the way just as the speeding truck passed by. The truck would have struck the woman. The woman fell to the ground and was injured. Did John commit a battery on the woman? The answer is yes. Even though John was trying to help the woman, she could sue him for battery should she choose to do so.

The tort of battery is designed to protect the personal integrity of one's body against intentional invasions, which can occur even if one does not know it at the time. In the example just described, the woman was not aware that John was going to push her, yet a battery has occurred because there was an invasion of her personal integrity even though it was for her benefit.

The term **person** means one's body, anything attached to one's body, or anything so closely associated with one's body as to be identified with it. If someone grabs a woman's purse, the purse is considered part of her body. If a boy kicks an old man's cane out from under him, the cane is considered an extension of his body. If you knock a glass out of someone's hand, the glass is considered part of the person's body. Anything connected to the person is considered to be part of the plaintiff's body. It is also not necessary for the defendant to make contact with another person with the defendant's own body. For example, the defendant can beat the plaintiff with a baseball bat and no part of the defendant's body ever touches the plaintiff. The defendant would still be liable to the plaintiff for battery even though the defendant's body never touched the plaintiff.

As long as the plaintiff can establish that an intentional harmful or offensive contact occurred, the plaintiff can recover damages. If no physical injury was involved, the plaintiff may be awarded **nominal damages**. If the defendant's contact was deemed to be outrageous in nature, the plaintiff may be awarded **punitive damages**.

Assault

Assault is a tort that is very similar to battery, and that is why many tort actions are brought against defendants for both assault and battery. Assault involves the threat of a harmful and offensive touching, not the contact. Assault does not need actual contact, just the fear or apprehension of the contact. The plaintiff just needs to think that she will be touched by the defendant. The injury sustained by the plaintiff in this type of tort involves mental harm or anguish.

Recall the earlier example of Sheila, whose fear of physical touch stemmed from a rape. Assume that Ron approaches Sheila and acts as though he is going to place his arm around her, but never touches her. Sheila's fear that Ron may touch her is enough to establish the tort of assault. Sheila should be free from the apprehension of being touched; that is the essence of the tort of assault.

The elements of the tort of assault are:

- An *act* by the defendant;

- That creates a *reasonable apprehension* of immediate harmful or offensive contact;

- To the *plaintiff's person*; with

person
The body and clothing of an individual as well as anything attached or an extension of the body such as a purse.

nominal damages
A small amount of money given to the nonbreaching party as a token award to acknowledge the fact of the breach.

punitive damages
An amount of money awarded to a nonbreaching party that is not based on the actual losses incurred by that party, but as a punishment to the breaching party for the commission of an intentional wrong.

assault
Intentional voluntary movement that creates fear or apprehension of an immediate unwanted touching; the threat or attempt to cause a touching, whether successful or not, provided the victim is aware of the danger.

FIGURE 2.2
Elements of the Tort
of Assault

> **Assault**
> - An act
> - Reasonable apprehension of an immediate harmful or offensive contact
> - Plaintiff's person
> - Intent
> - Cause

- *Intent* by the defendant to cause that contact; and
- The defendant was the *cause* of that reasonable apprehension in the plaintiff.

(See Figure 2.2.)

The act of the defendant must create a reasonable apprehension of harm. Again, the court will turn to the reasonable person test to determine if a person of ordinary sensitivities would be fearful or apprehensive that an immediate harmful or offensive contact may occur. The act does not have to necessarily cause fear. The act by the defendant can cause an expectation that contact will occur. As was the case with Sheila, she would reasonably expect that Ron may very well put his arm around her waist. Sheila does not have to fear Ron to have a reasonable expectation that he will put his arm around her waist. In addition, the apprehension must be about an immediate contact, not a contact that may happen out in the future or that happened in the past. In addition, it is not necessary for the defendant to intend to cause harm. Ron did not intend to cause Sheila any harm, yet he can still be liable for an assault.

In an assault action, the plaintiff must have knowledge or awareness that the defendant is going to act to have contact with the plaintiff. This is different from battery where the plaintiff can have a contact from the defendant and not have awareness that the contact is about to occur. If someone points a gun at someone but never pulls the trigger or touches the other person, then the person pointing the gun can be guilty of assault. However, if the defendant points the gun at the plaintiff's back and the plaintiff is unaware of the action, then if the defendant removes the gun, no assault has occurred because the plaintiff was unaware of the defendant's action.

Transferred intent can be applied in the tort of assault. If the defendant intends to assault one person, but in fact assaults the plaintiff, whom the defendant did not intend to assault, the defendant will still be liable for the assault.

Words alone do not constitute an assault. There must be some type of action above and beyond the utterance of words by the defendant in order to rise to the level required for an assault. Also, the plaintiff does not need to prove that she or he was damaged. Establishing the prima facie case for assault against a defendant is enough for an award of damages.

RESEARCH THIS

Using the *Restatement (Second) of Torts*, look up how the *Restatement* defines assault. What does the *Restatement* tell us about the awareness required of the plaintiff in an assault? If you do not have access to the *Restatement*, research your state's statute and see how assault is defined in your state.

False Imprisonment

false imprisonment
Any deprivation of a person's freedom of movement without that person's consent and against his or her will, whether done by actual violence or threats.

False imprisonment is a violation of the right to be free from intentional restraints on one's freedom of movement. The elements of this tort are:

- An *act* that completely *confines* the plaintiff *within fixed boundaries* set by the defendant;
- *Intent* to confine the plaintiff or a third party;

FIGURE 2.3
Elements of the Tort
of False Imprisonment

False Imprisonment

- An act
- Confines within fixed boundaries
- Intent
- Cause
- Consciousness of confinement, or physical harm to plaintiff

- *Causation* of the confinement; and
- The plaintiff was either *conscious* of the confinement or was *physically harmed* by it.

(See Figure 2.3.)

As with assault and battery, the plaintiff does not need to show that actual damages occurred in order to prove a prima facie case. The confinement is considered to be damage enough. Once the elements have been proven, the **trier of fact** will be allowed to consider damages for humiliation, physical discomfort, illness, injury to the plaintiff's reputation, or loss of earnings or other personal property due to the confinement. If the defendant acted out of hatred or malice, punitive damages are also possible.

trier of fact
Jury.

False imprisonment consists of an illegal confinement of the plaintiff by the defendant. The first element of false imprisonment is an act that completely confines the plaintiff within fixed boundaries as set by the defendant. The tort occurs when there is simply a confinement of the plaintiff's freedom of movement. The confinement can be caused by tangible, physical restraints or barriers that are imposed on the plaintiff, or it can be confinement that is placed on the plaintiff through duress by threatening the plaintiff. The confinement is effectively imposed in these situations when actual physical force is used on a plaintiff's body. A person's freedom of movement is certainly restricted if the defendant threatens immediate force or violence against the plaintiff, against a member of the plaintiff's immediate family, or against the plaintiff's valuable property. The threat is that some harm will befall the plaintiff, the plaintiff's family, or the valuable property of the plaintiff if the plaintiff tries to escape or move out of an area of confinement as determined by the defendant. If the plaintiff submits to the threat and remains in the area the defendant designated, a confinement has occurred. It does not matter how long or short the duration of confinement. There is no time limit that automatically states that the confinement constitutes a false imprisonment.

The confinements just listed will establish the first element of a prima facie case for false imprisonment. It does not matter if there appears to be a way in which the plaintiff can escape as long as the plaintiff is unaware that a way to escape exists.

The use of words alone to confine the plaintiff does not constitute confinement under the tort of false imprisonment. In addition, threats of future harm are not sufficient. The threat must be of imminent harm. The plaintiff must be aware of the confinement in order to have a tort of false imprisonment.

If the defendant claims that he has the legal authority to confine or arrest the plaintiff, then the confinement of the plaintiff occurs when the defendant takes the plaintiff into custody. For example, a shopkeeper detaining a shoplifter for hours before calling the police falls into this category. The shopkeeper, by catching the shoplifter, appears to have legal authority to detain the shoplifter. However, the shopkeeper does not have legal authority to confine the shoplifter for hours before calling the police. Shopkeepers may only detain shoplifters for a reasonable period of investigation, but they do not have legal authority to confine them for an unreasonable amount of time. If the defendant does not have a privilege that gives her authority to arrest the plaintiff, then confinement has occurred. No physical force or touching need be used as long as the plaintiff has reason to believe that force will be used if the plaintiff either moves outside an area designated by the defendant or fails to follow the defendant's directions. There is no set amount of time that the confinement must last.

Defendants must have the intent to confine or know with substantial certainty that the confinement will result from their actions. For damages in a false imprisonment case, the plaintiff need not show anything other than the fact that the confinement occurred. As with assault and battery, the transferred intent doctrine applies to false imprisonment cases. To establish causation, the plaintiff must be able to show that either:

- But for the act of the defendant, the plaintiff would not have been confined; or
- The defendant was a substantial factor in producing the plaintiff's confinement.

False Arrest

When a law enforcement officer has a warrant to arrest someone, the arrest is privileged as long as the warrant is fair on its face. *Fair on its face* means that the warrant does not appear to be obviously defective; for example, a warrant that does not have the name of the party to be arrested, does not state the crime charged, or appears to be missing important information usually necessary to obtain a warrant from a judge. A law enforcement officer is only required to recognize blatant irregularities in the warrant, not specific problems with its issuance. Once a judge issues an arrest warrant, the judge has already found that probable cause exists so that the officer may arrest on the basis of the warrant as long as the warrant is regular on its face.

If the law enforcement officer arrests the wrong person under the warrant, the privilege is lost. There is no transference of the privilege. However, the privilege is not lost if the law enforcement officer's mistake was reasonable under the circumstances, such as if there existed circumstantial evidence to make her believe that she had the right person. A law enforcement officer may also make an arrest without a warrant. The principles of the privilege to arrest without a warrant differ depending on why the arrest is being made, such as in connection with a bank robbery or an assault and battery. Basically, the officer needs to be able to make the assertion that probable cause existed that the arrest without a warrant was justified. An arrest is false when it is not privileged.

Private citizens as well as law enforcement officers have a privilege to arrest. A private citizen may make a citizen's arrest under particular circumstances. The requirements for the privilege of a citizen's arrest differ between jurisdictions, and legal assistants should be familiar with the laws in their jurisdiction.

Intentional Infliction of Emotional Distress

intentional infliction of emotional distress
Intentional act involving extreme and outrageous conduct resulting in severe mental anguish.

Emotional distress relates to the plaintiff's state of mind. Mental anguish in the form of fear, anxiety, grief, humiliation, embarrassment, and other types of mental distress make up the basis for emotional distress. The tort of **intentional infliction of emotional distress** involves a violation of a person's right to be free from emotional distress or psychological harm that is intentionally (or recklessly) caused by someone else.

The elements for the tort of intentional infliction of emotional distress are:

- An *act* of extreme or outrageous conduct.
- *Intent* to cause severe emotional distress.
- Plaintiff suffers *extreme emotional distress*.
- Defendant is the *cause* of this distress.

(See Figure 2.4.)

The plaintiff can recover for the mental distress suffered as well as for any physical harm or illness that may have resulted from the defendant's conduct. If the defendant acted out of hatred or malice, punitive damages may be recovered.

Intentional Infliction of Emotional Distress

- An act
- Extreme or outrageous conduct
- Intent
- Cause
- Extreme emotional distress

The defendant's conduct must be so extreme or outrageous that an ordinary person would regard it as appalling and totally intolerable The act required for intentional infliction of emotional distress must shock the conscience and sensibilities of society. For example, telling a woman that her husband has just been killed when he has not may rise to the level of intentional infliction of emotional distress if the defendant intended to cause her mental anguish. If the defendant is aware that the plaintiff is vulnerable because of his age, mental illness, or physical illness, it is usually easier to establish that the defendant's conduct was extreme or outrageous under the circumstances.

The plaintiff cannot recover for intentional infliction of emotional harm from mere insults, obscenities, or indignities as they do not rise to the level of severe emotional distress in the ordinary person. These actions are insufficiently extreme or outrageous to be actionable.

In most states, the defendant must intend to cause severe emotional distress. This means that the defendant must either desire to have such a consequence occur as a result of his actions or know with substantial certainty that the consequence will result from his actions.

Sometimes reckless conduct is enough to establish intent. If the defendant knows that his or her conduct creates a very great risk that the plaintiff will suffer severe emotional distress, then this reckless conduct may be enough to satisfy the element of intent. For example, John knows that Mary once had an abortion and has never told her parents. John threatens to tell Mary's parents. John decides not to tell Mary's parents, but, with the intent of causing her severe emotional distress, John tells his mother, who is Mary's mother's best friend. John's behavior is reckless, since he knows with substantial certainty that his mother will probably tell Mary's mother about the abortion.

If the defendant is merely negligent in causing the severe emotional distress, there is no intentional infliction of emotional distress. On January 2, 2006, in Sago, West Virginia, thirteen coal miners were trapped in a mine after an apparent gas explosion. After conflicting reports, the mining company representatives first told the families of the trapped miners that the miners had been found alive. The families, of course, were elated and celebratory, but the information proved to be erroneous. Some two hours later, the company informed the families that only one miner had been brought out alive. The case is still being investigated. However, some people feel that the mining company's actions rose to the level of recklessness.

The plaintiff must, in fact, experience severe emotional distress in order to have a cause of action for intentional infliction of emotional distress. It is not enough that the defendant committed the extreme or outrageous conduct, but the plaintiff must have experienced the severe emotional distress as well. Minor inconvenience or annoyance is not enough to establish severe emotional distress. There must be severe fright, horror, grief, humiliation, embarrassment, anger, worry, or nausea. The severity of these feelings is measured by their intensity and duration as well as other factors such as the sensitivity, age, and size of the plaintiff.

If the plaintiff experiences physical illness or harm, damages are likely to increase and the plaintiff's case will be easier to prove as it is thought that the plaintiff would not have experienced physical harm unless the emotional distress was severe. The plaintiff will not be able to recover unless an ordinary person, who is not unduly sensitive, would have suffered severe emotional distress from what the defendant did under similar circumstances.

The plaintiff can use either of the following tests to establish that the defendant was the cause of the severe emotional distress:

- But for the defendant's act, the plaintiff would not have suffered severe emotional distress; or

- The defendant was a substantial factor in producing the plaintiff's severe emotional distress.

The second test is used when there is more than one causal factor producing the plaintiff's severe emotional distress. Intentional infliction of emotional distress is difficult to prove and the likelihood of the plaintiff's success on this type of claim is usually not successful.

Malicious Prosecution

malicious prosecution
Initiating a criminal prosecution or civil suit against another party with malice and without probable cause.

Malicious prosecution is a violation of a person's right to be protected from unreasonable or unjustifiable criminal litigation brought against the plaintiff. Unreasonable and unjustifiable criminal proceedings can harm a plaintiff both in reputation and by confinement. The elements of this tort are:

- The *initiation or continuance of a criminal proceeding* against the plaintiff;
- Without *probable cause;*
- With *malice;* and
- The *criminal proceedings* terminate in favor of the plaintiff.

probable cause
The totality of circumstances leads one to believe certain facts or circumstances exist; applies to arrests, searches, and seizures.

(See Figure 2.5.)

The first element of a tortious action for malicious prosecution is that the tortfeasor initiates or procures the initiation of criminal proceedings against the plaintiff. The tortfeasor will later become the defendant in the malicious prosecution action brought by the plaintiff.

The legal proceeding must be initiated without probable cause. Probable cause is a suspicion based on the manifestation of circumstances that are strong enough to allow a reasonable person to believe that a criminal charge against a person is true. If there is probable cause, then the tort of malicious prosecution cannot be established, and it does not matter if the tortfeasor has ill will or malice toward the plaintiff.

malice
Person's doing of any act in reckless disregard of another person.

Malice means doing something for an improper motive. Malice does not mean that the tortfeasor has shown any ill will or hatred toward the plaintiff. The proper motive for initiating criminal proceedings is to bring an alleged criminal to justice. If the tortfeasor has another purpose for initiating such an action, such as harassment through litigation, then person is acting with malice.

To bring a cause of action for malicious prosecution, the criminal proceedings must have been completed, and the plaintiff must have won the case. Most states require that the plaintiff must have prevailed in the criminal action by an acquittal or dismissal on the merits of the case and not on a technicality. If the plaintiff does not prevail, it is more likely than not that the initial prosecution against the accused was made with probable cause rather than with malice.

FIGURE 2.5
Elements of the Tort of Malicious Prosecution

Malicious Prosecution
- Initiation or continuing a criminal proceeding
- Without probable cause
- Malice
- Terminates in favor of the plaintiff

Wrongful or Unjustified Civil Proceedings

Generally, the same elements apply for the causes of action of wrongful civil proceedings as are required for malicious prosecution. The defendant must maliciously initiate civil proceedings without probable cause, and the proceedings must end in the plaintiff's favor. Probable cause here means a reasonable belief that good grounds exist to begin a civil proceeding against the plaintiff.

The elements of the tort of **abuse of process** are the following:

- Use of *civil or criminal proceedings,*
- For an *improper or ulterior motive.*

This tort involves the initiation of either a civil or criminal case. Probable cause may exist. The proceeding does not have to terminate in favor of the person who initiated the abuse-of-process action. The civil or criminal case must have been initiated for an improper purpose or with an ulterior motive.

In other words, the tort of abuse of process involves the misuse or misapplication of the legal process to accomplish a result for which the legal process did not intend; that is, extortion. For example, suppose a mortgage company has misapplied a mortgagee's payments and demands additional payment in fees to correct the error. The mortgagee refuses, so the mortgage company files foreclosure proceedings to force the mortgagee to pay the additional fees to keep his property out of foreclosure. If the mortgagee refuses, he may lose his property even though the fees are improper. The filing of a foreclosure proceeding for improper purposes is abuse of process.

abuse of process
Using the threat of resorting to the legal system to extract agreement to terms against the other party's will.

Defamation

Defamation involves individuals' right to be free from harm to their reputation and good name. Defamation is any false and intentional oral or written communication that causes injury or harm to the plaintiff's reputation or good name. Defamation covers two torts: slander and libel.

The elements of the tort of defamation are:

- A *defamatory statement* by the defendant;
- *Of and concerning the plaintiff;*
- *Publication;*
- *Damages;* and
- *Causation.*

defamation
An act of communication involving a false and unprivileged statement about another person, causing harm.

(See Figure 2.6.)

A defamatory statement is a statement of fact that would tend to harm the plaintiff's reputation in the eyes of at least a substantial and respectable minority of people by lowering the plaintiff in the esteem of those people or by deterring them from associating with the plaintiff. More specifically, it is a statement of fact that tends to

LEGAL RESEARCH MAXIM

There are two types of defamation claims: defamation per se and defamation per quod. Defamation per se occurs when a statement is defamatory on its face; defamation per quod occurs when a statement is defamatory through interpretation or innuendo.

Defamation

- Defamatory statement
- Of and concerning
- Publication
- Damages
- Causation

FIGURE 2.6
Elements of the Tort of Defamation

disgrace individuals by holding them up to hatred or ridicule, or by causing others to avoid them. For example, Mohammad owns a local grocery store that has a meat counter. Steve begins making statements in the store that Mohammad is not selling beef but dog. Since a statement such as this would cause disdain in the United States, as Americans do not eat dog, people stop shopping at Mohammad's store. The statement is defamatory because it is untrue and concerns Mohammad. Steve publishes the false statement by telling people the falsity. The false statement has caused Mohammad damages, since people have stopped shopping at his store as a result of Steve's comments.

In general, a defamatory *opinion* made by one person about another is not actionable. It is when an untrue and harmful statement is made as fact that it is actionable. A major distinction between a fact and an opinion is that it is possible to prove the truth or falsity of a fact, whereas an opinion cannot be proved to be true or false but is based on subjectivity.

At common law, the plaintiff was not required to prove that the defamatory statement was false. It was assumed to be false. Truth was an affirmative defense, which meant that the defendant had to allege and prove the truth of the statement. However, the U.S. Supreme Court has changed the common law as it relates to the media as a defendant.

If the plaintiff is a public official or a public figure, he must establish constitutional malice, which is proof by clear and convincing evidence that the defendant knew the statement was false or was reckless in regard to its truth or falsity. Public officials are public employees who have significant government authority. Public figures are people who have assumed special prominence in the affairs of society because of power or influence or because of voluntary involvement in interest to the general public. It is not enough to prove the media published a false defamatory statement about public officials or figures with carelessness or negligence. The media must know that it is false or be reckless as to its truth or falsity when they publish it.

If the plaintiff is not a public official or figure, she is considered to be a private person. If the media defames a private person, a state court can either require the plaintiff to establish the same degree of fault as public officials or figures or impose a less demanding standard, such as proving that the media defendant was negligent in determining the truth or falsity of the defamatory statement before publishing it.

The defamatory statement must be of and concerning the plaintiff. This requires proof by the plaintiff that someone who sees or hears the statement will reasonably understand that the statement referred to the plaintiff.

There must be a publication of the defamatory statement by the defendant to a third party. A publication is when the statement is communicated to a third person by reading it, hearing it, or seeing it.

libel
Written defamatory statement.

presumed damages
Damages that are presumed under the law to result naturally and necessarily from an act and do not require proof.

Libel is the writing or printing of the defamatory statement about the plaintiff in a medium that will be seen or read by a third person. In most libel cases, the jury is allowed to presume that the plaintiff suffered humiliation and harm to her reputation or good name. This presumption is called **presumed damages**. The plaintiff does have to prove that she suffered special damages, which are actual economic losses such as medical expenses and/or lost wages as a result of the publishing of the defamatory statement. Special damages must be shown when there is a written statement that requires additional facts in order for someone to understand its defamatory meaning or to understand its reference to the plaintiff. If Steve had written up signs saying that Mohammad sells dog meat and posted them out for everyone to see, then he would have committed an act of libel.

Slander is a defamatory statement made orally to a third person about the plaintiff. Slander per se does not require proof of special damages. **Slander per se** is an oral statement that is defamatory in one of the following four ways:

- It accuses the plaintiff of a crime.
- It accuses the plaintiff of having a communicable disease.
- It accuses the plaintiff of sexual misconduct.
- It adversely affects the plaintiff's trade, profession, or office.

> In order for a statement to constitute defamation per se, it must "consist of words which import an indictable criminal offense involving moral turpitude or infamous punishment, impute . . . some loathsome or contagious disease which excludes one from society or tend . . . to injure one in his trade or occupation." (Norman v. Whiteside v. Thomas Williams et al., 2007 Ohio App. LEXIS 1017.)

In the example used previously, the statement made by Steve concerning Mohammad's meat demonstrates slander. Steve's statement was a defamatory statement that was made orally to other people that adversely affected Mohammad's trade, which is operating a store that sells meat.

A slanderous statement that does not fall into one of the preceding four categories is known as **slander per quod** because it requires additional facts in order to be associated to the plaintiff. This type of slander requires proof of special damages.

Judges, lawyers, parties, and witnesses have an absolute privilege to make defamatory statements in judicial proceedings without legal ramifications. The same is true of legislators and high executive officers who make such statements while performing their duties. This issue—governmental immunity—will be covered in a later chapter. It offers protection to governmental officials whose ability to perform their duties would be affected by undue fear of making defamatory statements.

Individuals have a qualified privilege to publish defamatory statements in order to protect their own legitimate interests. This privilege can be lost by abusing the privilege in some manner, as to be decided by the trier of fact.

Invasion of Privacy

Invasion of privacy consists of four torts: intrusion, appropriation, public disclosure of private facts, and false light. Each has its own elements. The torts are designed to protect an individual's interest in being left alone, and that is violated because of an unreasonable form of attention or publicity on the plaintiff.

Intrusion

Intrusion is the violation of one's solitude in a manner that would be considered highly offensive to the ordinary person. The elements of intrusion are:

- An *act* of intrusion.
- Into someone's private affairs or concerns.
- *Highly offensive* to a reasonable person.

slander
Oral defamatory statements.

slander per se
Slander that is actionable without the plaintiff providing proof of damages.

slander per quod
Slander that requires proof of damages.

intrusion
Trespassing on or encroachment on the possessions of another.

🔍 **SURF'S UP**

Research the following: Over the past 10 years, have the number of lawsuits in California, with the claim of invasion of privacy, gone up or down? If on the rise, by how much and what was the percentage of results awarding damages to the plaintiff?

Intrusion consists of prying, peering, or probing of some kind that is directed at information that is considered to be someone's private affairs. The intrusion must be highly offensive to the reasonable person. For example, Martha believes that her boss is having an affair with one of his employees. Unbeknownst to him she has his cell phone wiretapped so that she can record his telephone conversations without him knowing. Sure enough, Martha obtains taped conversations between her boss and his employee that evidence an affair. Martha turns the tapes over to the company and her boss loses his job. The boss sues Martha for intrusion because his privacy of his telephone conversations had been invaded and the information that Martha sought was confidential in nature. Martha's conduct was unreasonably intrusive.

Appropriation

appropriation
Stealing and using someone's identity or image.

The essence of the tort of **appropriation** is stealing and using someone's image. The elements of appropriation are:

- The *use* of the *plaintiff's name, likeness, or personality.*
- For the *benefit* of the defendant.

The first element is present if the plaintiff is specifically identifiable through the use of his or her name, likeness, or personality. The defendant must obtain an advantage from the use of the plaintiff's name, likeness, or personality. The use of people's names, likenesses, or personalities by the media is protected under the First Amendment of the United States Constitution.

In 1992, a VCR manufacturer ran an advertisement that depicted a robot dressed like celebrity Vanna White next to a game board that resembled the *Wheel of Fortune* game show set. Vanna White sued the manufacturer alleging that the manufacturer misappropriated her identity without her consent. The court found for Vanna stating that the manufacturer exploited her identity and celebrity value for its own gain. See *White v. Samsung Electronics America, Inc.,* 971 F.2d 1395 (9th Cir. 1992).

Public Disclosure

Publicity is different from publication. Publication is the communication of the defamatory statement to at least one person other than the plaintiff. Publicity means communication to the public at large. There is no disclosure of a private fact when publicity is given to something that is already considered a matter of public record. If a private fact is disclosed, it is not a defense that the fact is true. Falsity is not one of the elements of this tort. The disclosure must be highly offensive to the reasonable person.

public disclosure
Stated in the news or printed in a newspaper.

The elements of the tort of **public disclosure** of private facts are:

- *Publicity;*
- Concerning the *private life* of the plaintiff; and
- *Highly offensive* to a reasonable person.

For example, suppose a young girl was raped at the hands of a known sex offender. It is against the law in the particular state where the rape occurred to release the name of a rape victim, especially if the individual is a minor. Because the victim was a minor, her actual name did not appear on any documents that are available to the public. A newspaper discovers the identity of the victim and publishes her name in the newspaper. The publication of the young girl's name in the paper stating the facts concerning her private life and making them public would be an example of public disclosure.

CASE FACT PATTERN

John is a well-known international rock star. ABC Movie company decides to make a movie loosely based on John's life without his permission. Although the character portrayed in the movie does not have John's name, his appearance as well as the story depicted in the movie lead reasonable people to belief that the movie is about John. In the movie, the filmmakers suggest that the character that resembles John is a homosexual. John is highly offended and believes that the public might believe that he is a homosexual should they see the movie. What can John do?

If the defendant is part of the media, the constitutional freedoms of the press and the First Amendment right to free speech may bar the plaintiff from recovering damages for this tort. If publicity is given to a matter of legitimate public interest and hence is newsworthy, then the plaintiff will not be able to recover damages. A great deal of information about public figures falls into this category. A public figure is a celebrity, someone in whom the public has a legitimate interest because of their achievements, reputation, or occupation, such as Michael Jordan, Michael Jackson, or Tom Cruise.

False Light

False light is similar to defamation in that the statement made about the plaintiff must be false. Unlike defamation, false light can be established without the statement causing harm to the plaintiff's reputation or good name. False light occurs whenever an impression or conclusion is given about a person that is not accurate. The impression or conclusion must be considered highly offensive by a reasonable person. If the defendant is part of the media, constitutional law requires that the plaintiff prove that the defendant either knew the statement placed the plaintiff in a false light or acted in reckless disregard of whether or not the statement caused the plaintiff to be perceived in a false light.

The elements for false light are:

- *Publicity;*
- Placing the plaintiff in a *false light;* and
- *Highly offensive* to a reasonable person.

false light
An untrue and misleading portrayal of a person.

YOU BE THE JUDGE

Maurice White is a successful quarterback for an NFL team. Maurice grew up in the Lower East Side of Manhattan in the projects. He has had a sensational life. He was abandoned by his mother when he was very young, and he never knew his father. His grandmother raised him. When he was fourteen years old, Maurice was almost killed in a robbery in which he was stabbed and shot. Maurice received good grades and was a high school football star. He then went to Notre Dame where he became an all-star quarterback, taking the team to the national championships. Maurice was drafted for a professional football team in the first round of the NFL draft. His rookie season he led his team to the Super Bowl. Maurice's life is one that movies are made about. Joe Judd is a Hollywood producer. He decided to make a movie based largely on the life of Maurice. The movie is fictional, but the comparisons are such that the ordinary person knows that the main character is referring to Maurice White. In the movie, the main character is physically assaulted and raped by a high school football coach. Maurice saw the movie and was highly offended. The incident with the high school coach never happened and is totally fictional. Does Maurice have a tort claim? If so, what type of tort claim can Maurice bring? What are the facts that support Maurice's tort claim and why do they support his claim?

Summary

The state of mind of the defendant who caused the act is the central concept of intentional torts. The intent needs to be sufficient in nature as to bring about a physical or mental effect upon the plaintiff that is caused as a result of the defendant's actions. Intent is different from a desire to harm. There need not be any desire to harm the plaintiff in order to satisfy the element of intent for an intentional tort.

There are two types of intent: specific and general. In specific intent, the defendant intends that his actions will cause the consequence. In other words, the defendant's goal is to cause the consequences that resulted from his action. In general intent, the defendant knows with substantial certainty that the consequences will result from his actions. The defendant must have intended or been reasonably certain that the desired result would occur from his actions. However, if there is doubt that a consequence would occur, but it is merely likely to occur, then an intentional tort has not resulted. The fact that something is likely to occur as a result of the defendant's actions does not rise to the level of intent necessary to fulfill the element of intent for a cause of action for an intentional tort.

If a defendant intends to commit a tort against one person, but accidentally commits it against another person, then the defendant will be held liable for an intentional tort for the consequences of her actions against the second person.

The tort of battery is either a harmful or offensive contact with a person that occurs as a result of the defendant's intent to cause the harmful or offensive contact or the defendant has the intent to cause apprehension in the person of an imminent contact.

Assault involves the fear of a harmful and offensive touching, not the contact. Assault does not need actual contact, just the fear or apprehension of the contact. The injury sustained by the plaintiff in this type of tort entails mental harm or anguish.

False imprisonment consists of an illegal confinement of the plaintiff by the defendant. The tort occurs when there is simply a confinement of the plaintiff's freedom of movement by tangible, physical restraints or barriers or by duress by threatening the plaintiff. The confinement is imposed in these situations when actual physical force is used on a plaintiff's body or if the defendant threatens immediate force or violence against the plaintiff, against a member of the plaintiff's immediate family, or against the plaintiff's valuable property.

When a law enforcement officer has a warrant to arrest someone, the arrest is privileged as long as the warrant is fair on its face; that is, it does not appear to be obviously defective. A law enforcement officer is only required to recognize blatant irregularities in the warrant, not specific problems with its issuance.

Emotional distress involves mental anguish in the form of fear, anxiety, grief, humiliation, embarrassment, and other types of mental distress. The tort of intentional infliction of emotional distress concerns the right to be free from emotional distress or psychological harm that is intentionally (or recklessly) caused by someone else.

The plaintiff must experience severe emotional distress in order to have a cause of action for intentional infliction of emotional distress. There must be severe fright, horror, grief, humiliation, embarrassment, anger, worry, or nausea. The severity of these feelings is measured by their intensity and duration as well as other factors such as the sensitivity, age, and size of the plaintiff.

The tort of malicious prosecution concerns the right to be protected from unreasonable or unjustifiable criminal litigation brought against the plaintiff. Unreasonable and unjustifiable criminal proceedings can harm plaintiffs both in reputation and by confinement. The proper motive for initiating criminal proceedings is to bring an alleged criminal to justice. If the tortfeasor has another purpose for initiating such an action, then she is acting with malice.

Generally, the same elements apply for the causes of action of wrongful civil proceedings as are required for malicious prosecution. The defendant must maliciously initiate civil proceedings without probable cause, and the proceedings must end in the plaintiff's favor. Probable cause here means a reasonable belief that good grounds exist to begin a civil proceeding against the plaintiff.

Abuse of process involves the initiation of either a civil or criminal case. Probable cause may exist. The proceeding does not have to terminate in favor of the person who initiated the abuse-of-process action. The civil or criminal case must have been initiated for an improper—or with an ulterior—motive.

Defamation involves individuals' right to be free from harm to their reputation and good name. Defamation is any false and intentional oral or written communication that causes injury or harm to plaintiffs' reputation or good name. Defamation covers two torts, slander and libel.

In general, the defamatory opinion made by one person about another is not actionable. A major distinction between a fact and an opinion is that it is possible to prove the truth or falsity of a fact, whereas an opinion cannot be proved to be true or false but is based on subjectivity.

If the plaintiff is a public official or a public figure, he or she must establish constitutional malice, which is proof by clear and convincing evidence that the defendant knew the statement was false or was reckless in regard to its truth or falsity. Public officials are public employees who have significant government authority. Public figures are people who have assumed special prominence in the affairs of society because of power or influence or because of voluntary involvement in interest to the general public. It is not enough to prove the media published a false defamatory statement about public officials or figures with carelessness or negligence. The media must know that it is false or be reckless as to its truth or falsity when they publish it.

Libel is the writing or printing of the defamatory statement about the plaintiff in a medium that will be seen or read by a third person. In most libel cases, the jury is allowed to presume that the plaintiff suffered humiliation and harm to his or her reputation or good name. This presumption is called presumed damages. Plaintiffs do have to prove that they suffered special damages, which are actual economic losses such as medical expenses and/or lost wages as a result of the publishing of the defamatory statement. Special damages must be shown when there is a written statement that requires additional facts in order for someone to understand its defamatory meaning or to understand its reference to the plaintiff.

Slander is a defamatory statement made orally to a third person about the plaintiff. Slander per se does not require proof of special damages.

Invasion of privacy consists of four torts: intrusion, appropriation, public disclosure of private facts, and false light. Each has its own elements.

Intrusion is the violation of one's solitude that would be considered highly offensive to the ordinary person.

Appropriation is essentially stealing and using someone's image.

Publicity is different from publication. Publication is the communication of the defamatory statement to at least one person other than the plaintiff. Publicity means communication to the public at large. There is no disclosure of a private fact when publicity is given to something that is already considered a matter of public record. If there has been a disclosure of a private fact that the fact is true is not a defense. Falsity is not one of the elements of this tort. The disclosure must be highly offensive to the reasonable person.

False light is similar to defamation in that the statement made about the plaintiff must be false. Unlike defamation, false light can be established without the statement causing harm to the plaintiff's reputation or good name. False light occurs whenever an impression or conclusion is given about a person that is not accurate. The impression or conclusion must be considered highly offensive by the reasonable person. If the defendant is part of the media, constitutional law requires that the plaintiff prove that the defendant either knew the statement placed the plaintiff in a false light or acted in reckless disregard of whether or not the statement caused the plaintiff to be perceived in a false light.

Key Terms

Abuse of process	Nominal damages
Appropriation	Person
Assault	Presumed damages
Battery	Probable cause
Defamation	Public disclosure
False imprisonment	Punitive damages
False light	Reasonable person test
Integrity	Slander
Intent	Slander per quod
Intentional infliction of emotional	Slander per se
distress	Specific intent
Intrusion	Substantial certainty
Libel	Transferred intent doctrine
Malice	Trier of fact
Malicious prosecution	

Review Questions

1. What is the difference between assault and battery?
2. What is intent?
3. What is the reasonable person test?
4. What happens if a person has an unusual sensitivity to touch and a person threatens to pinch him or her?
5. What is the key element in a defamation case?
6. What is the difference between libel and slander?
7. What is abuse of process?
8. What is the transferred intent doctrine?
9. What are nominal damages?
10. What does prima facie mean?
11. What element is necessary for an arrest to be lawful?
12. What is substantial certainty?
13. What is the trier of fact?
14. How is a public figure treated differently than a private figure in a defamation case?
15. What is outrageous conduct?
16. List some examples of outrageous conduct.

Exercises

1. Using the Internet, locate a recent case (within the past two years) from your state in which the plaintiff recovered damages for intentional infliction of emotional distress. Brief the case focusing on the facts surrounding the emotional distress as well as the ruling by the court. You might want to try www.findlaw.com.
2. Go to the website for you local state bar and find an article on malicious wrongful prosecution. If your state bar does not have an article, use a global search engine

such www.findlaw.com to locate an appropriate legal article. Read the article and then write a memorandum on what actions can be brought against the instigator and the attorney. What are the elements of the tort as listed in the article?

3. A doctor is eating dinner in a restaurant. The man sitting at the table next to him begins to choke. After several unsuccessful attempts to dislodge the obstacle from the man's throat, the doctor performs a tracheotomy. Is the doctor liable for assault? Is he liable for battery? Explain your answer.

4. Susie is about to sit down in her chair when unruly Eddie pulls the chair from under her, having her fall down and injuring her back. Has a tort been committed and which one, if any?

5. Do you have to be cognizant, awake, conscience to have a battery committed upon you? Explain your answer.

6. In this day and age, should the tort of infliction of emotional distress be renamed to infliction of severe emotional distress? Why? Why not? Argue both sides in your answer.

7. Why are the torts of assault and battery usually linked together? Does one have to be committed for the other to be present/occur? Explain your answer fully with examples.

8. Might the tort of false imprisonment be dependent upon a person's perception as to its elements and facts? Explain your answer.

 PORTFOLIO ASSIGNMENT

Over the past few years, much has been made in the press and in Congress about limiting jury awards for personal injury cases to a total amount of damages not exceeding $250,000.00. Interview three people; your doctor, a lawyer, and an insurance agent. Ask them what they think about such a proposal. Are their viewpoints different and if so, how? Be complete in your explanation and research.

Vocabulary Builders

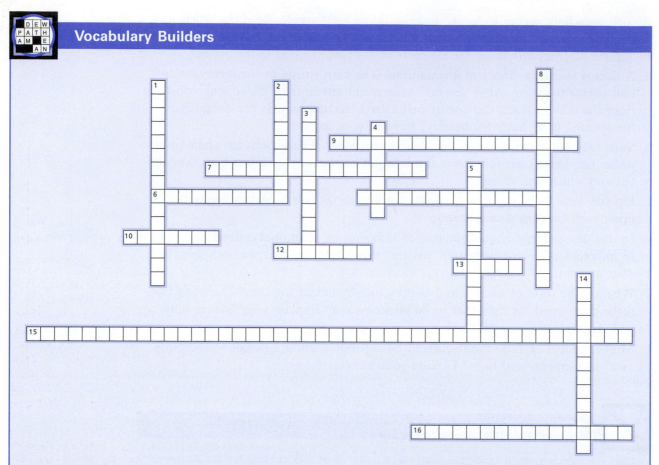

Instructions

Use the key terms from this chapter to fill in the answers to the crossword puzzle.

NOTE: When the answer is more than one word, leave a blank space between words.

ACROSS

6. Any deprivation of a person's freedom of movement without that person's consent and against his or her will, whether done by actual violence or threats.
7. An amount of money awarded to a nonbreaching party that is not based on the actual losses incurred by that party, but as a punishment to the breaching party for the commission of an intentional wrong.
9. An act of communication involving a false and unprivileged statement about another person, causing harm.
10. Slander that is actionable without the plaintiff providing proof of damages.
11. Written defamatory statements.
12. An intentional and unwanted harmful or offensive contact with the person of another; the actual intentional touching of someone with intent to cause harm, no matter how slight the harm.
13. Oral defamatory statements.
15. Intentional act involving extreme and outrageous conduct resulting in severe mental anguish.
16. Using the threat of resorting to the legal system to extract agreement to terms against the other party's will.

DOWN

1. Slander that requires proof of damages.
2. A small amount of money given to the nonbreaching party as a token award to acknowledge the fact of the breach.
3. Trespassing on or encroachment on the possessions of another.
4. An untrue and misleading portrayal of a person.
5. Intentional voluntary movement that creates fear or apprehension of an immediate unwanted touching; the threat or attempt to cause a touching, whether successful or not, provided the victim is aware of the danger.
8. Stealing and using someone's identity or image.
14. Jury.

Norman v. Whiteside v. Thomas Williams et al.
CASE NO. CA2006-06-021
COURT OF APPEALS OF OHIO, TWELFTH APPELLATE DISTRICT, MADISON COUNTY
2007 Ohio 1100
March 12, 2007, Decided
PRIOR HISTORY: CIVIL APPEAL FROM MADISON COUNTY COURT OF COMMON PLEAS.
Case No. 2006 CV-02-063.

CASE SUMMARY

PROCEDURAL POSTURE: Appellant prisoner sought review of the judgment of the Madison County Court of Common Pleas (Ohio), which dismissed the prisoner's defamation action against appellee fellow prisoners for failure to state a claim for which relief could be granted.

OVERVIEW: In his complaint, appellant alleged that appellees published false statements made by one appellee that appellant was involved in racist activity designed to disrupt Black History Month activities. The court held that the trial court properly dismissed appellant's defamation action. Appellant did not state a claim for defamation per se as he did not allege that the statements imported an indictable criminal offense involving moral turpitude or that the statements imputed a loathsome or contagious disease that excluded one from society. Moreover, appellant could not show that the statements injured him in his occupation as a musician. Appellant also did not state a claim for defamation per quod as he did not adequately plead special damages, in compliance with Civ. R. 9(G). Further, since appellant's complaint did not state a claim for which relief could be granted, the trial court did not err in denying appellant's motion for default judgment as to one appellee who never filed an answer to the complaint. Finally, contrary to the inmate's contention, the record did not indicate that the trial court considered matters outside the pleadings in deciding to dismiss the complaint.

OUTCOME: The court affirmed the judgment of the trial court.

JUDGES: POWELL, J., YOUNG, P.J., and WALSH, J., concur.

OPINION BY: POWELL

POWELL, J.

This is an accelerated appeal by plaintiff-appellant, Norman Whiteside, of the decision of the Madison County Court of Common Pleas dismissing appellant's defamation action for failure to state a claim for which relief can be granted.

In his complaint, appellant, a prisoner at Madison Correctional Institution, alleged that defendant-appellee, Thomas Williams, a fellow prisoner, "maliciously told third parties that * * * [appellant] was involved in racist activity designed to disrupt and/or to prevent Black History Month activities." Appellant alleged that Williams' statements were false, and that defendants-appellees, William Nelson and Michael Sheets, also fellow prisoners, further published Williams' statements, knowing they were false.

Appellant raises four assignments of error. In his third assignment of error, which we will address first, appellant argues that the common pleas court erroneously applied Ohio law regarding defamation and Civ.R. 12(B)(6). According to appellant, his complaint stated a claim for defamation.

There are two types of defamation claims: defamation per se and defamation per quod. Defamation per se occurs when a statement is defamatory on its face; defamation per quod occurs when a statement is defamatory through interpretation or innuendo. *Whiteside v. United Paramount Network,* Madison App. No. CA2003-02-008, 2004 Ohio 800, P14. When a complaint alleges defamation per se, damages are presumed; when a complaint alleges defamation per quod, the complaint must allege special damages. *Williams v. Gannett Satellite Information Network, Inc.,* 162 Ohio App.3d 596, 2005 Ohio 4141, P7, 834 N.E.2d 397.

In order for a statement to constitute defamation per se, it must "consist of words which import an indictable criminal offense involving moral turpitude or infamous punishment, impute[] some loathsome or contagious disease which excludes one from society or tend[] to injure one in his trade or occupation." *Heidel v. Amburgy,* Warren App. No. CA2002-09-092, 2003 Ohio 3073, P30, citing *McCartney v. Oblates of St. Francis de Sales* (1992), 80 Ohio App.3d 345, 353, 609 N.E.2d 216.

We find no error in the common pleas court's determination that appellant's complaint did not state a claim for defamation per se. The complaint did not allege that the statements imported an indictable criminal offense involving moral turpitude or infamous punishment, or that the statements imputed a loathsome or contagious disease that excludes one from society. The complaint did allege that the statements "affected * * * [appellant] in his profession as a musician who relies on music for therapy and as a future livelihood." However, the alleged defamatory statements, as described in the complaint, related to appellant's character and not to his competence or ability as a musician. As such, the statements were not actionable. See, generally, 35 Ohio Jurisprudence 3d (2002) 461, Defamation and Privacy, section 35. Further, appellant was a prisoner and not employed as a professional musician at the time of the alleged statements, rendering suspect the argument that the statements tended to injure appellant in his trade or occupation.

Because the alleged statements did not constitute defamation per se and could only have constituted defamation per quod, appellant was required to allege special damages. Appellant did allege, in conclusory fashion, that he suffered special damages as a result of the defendants' conduct. However, there is no indication in the complaint that appellant could have possibly suffered special damages, which have been described as an actual, temporal loss of something having economic or pecuniary value. See, generally, 2 Smolla, Law of Defamation (2 Ed.2003), 7-3, Section 7:2. Further, appellant did not comply with Civ.R. 9(G), which states that "when items of special damage are claimed, they shall be specifically stated." See *Wheeler v. Yocum* (Mar. 25, 1986), Franklin App. No. 85AP-828, 1986 Ohio App. LEXIS 6075 (applying Civ.R. 9(G) in defamation context).

Accordingly, because appellant did not adequately plead special damages, we find no error by the common pleas court in determining that appellant did not state a claim for defamation per quod. Because appellant did not state a claim for defamation per se or per quod, we overrule appellant's third assignment of error.

In appellant's first assignment of error, he argues that the common pleas court erred by dismissing his defamation action as to all pro se defendants based on the motion to dismiss of only one of the defendants, Williams.

We overrule appellant's first assignment of error. As appellant asserts, Williams, who is not an attorney, did not have the authority to bring a motion to dismiss on behalf of his pro se co-defendants. Nevertheless, the common pleas court did have the authority to sua sponte dismiss appellant's complaint as to all the defendants for failure to state a claim if appellant obviously could not prevail based on the facts alleged in the complaint. See *State ex rel. Bruggeman v. Ingraham*, 87 Ohio St.3d 230, 231, 1999 Ohio 27, 718 N.E.2d 1285. Because appellant obviously could not prevail based on the facts alleged in the complaint, we find no error by the common pleas court in dismissing the action.

In his second assignment of error, appellant argues that the common pleas court erred in denying his motion for default judgment as to defendant Sheets when Sheets never filed an answer.

We overrule appellant's second assignment of error. When a complaint fails to state a claim for which relief can be granted, it is not error for a trial court to deny a motion for default judgment. *Graham v. Byerly*, Hancock App. No. 5-04-09, 2004 Ohio 4530, P18; *Morgan v. Chamberlin* (Oct. 13, 2000), Clark App. No. 00CA0017, 2000 Ohio App. LEXIS 4744. Because appellant's complaint did not state a claim for which relief could be granted, the common pleas court did not err in denying appellant's motion for default judgment as to Sheets.

In his fourth assignment of error, appellant argues that the common pleas court erred in considering matters outside the pleadings. Appellant also argues that the court erred by not permitting appellant to respond to Williams' motion to dismiss.

We overrule appellant's fourth assignment of error. The record does not indicate, as appellant contends, that the common pleas court considered matters outside the pleadings in deciding to dismiss the complaint. In support of his argument that the court erred by not permitting a response to Williams' motion, appellant cites no authority. As previously noted, the court had the authority to sua sponte dismiss the complaint because appellant obviously could not prevail based on the facts alleged. *State ex rel. Bruggeman*, 87 Ohio St.3d at 231. In those circumstances, we do not find that the court was required to give appellant notice or to wait for a response from appellant before dismissing the complaint. See *State ex rel. Fogle v. Steiner*, 74 Ohio St.3d 158, 161, 1995 Ohio 278, 656 N.E.2d 1288. (Sua sponte dismissal without notice is appropriate where the complaint is frivolous or the claimant obviously cannot prevail on the facts alleged in the complaint.)

Having overruled appellant's four assignments of error, we affirm the judgment of the common pleas court.

YOUNG, P.J. and WALSH, J., concur.

Source: LexisNexis, 2007 Ohio App. LEXIS 1017. Reprinted with the permission of LexisNexis.

Chapter 3

Intentional Torts Against Property

CHAPTER OBJECTIVES

Upon completion of this chapter, you will be able to:

- Identify and discuss torts against personal property.
- Explain the revival of trespass to chattels as it relates to cyberspace.
- Understand conversion.

The torts that most people hear about are torts against the person. However, torts can also occur against property, both personal property and real property. This chapter focuses on those torts that have to do with a person's property.

HARM TO PROPERTY

As with assault and battery, when people think of violations concerning a person's property, they think of the crimes of theft or burglary. Torts' causes of action against property rights are similar to their crimes' counterparts. As is the case with the torts of assault and battery, torts against property rights are civil wrongs against property and not crimes. Torts against property can be perpetrated against **personal property** or **real property**. The tort involves individuals' exclusive right to freely use the property that they own. Interference with the right to freely enjoy both their personal and real property is the basis for tort actions concerning property rights.

TRESPASS TO LAND

Prior to the nineteenth century, English common law was very strict when it came to **trespass to land**. The plaintiff only had to show that the defendant entered the land; there was no concern as to whether or not the entry was intentional or negligent. Today's law in America does not look at the tort of trespass to land in the same way. Under American jurisdictions, trespass to land occurs when the defendant enters the plaintiff's land without **consent**. The tort of trespass to land protects the interest in the exclusive possession of land in its present physical condition.

The elements for the tort of trespass to land are:

- An *act;*
- *Intrusion* on land;

personal property
Movable or intangible thing not attached to real property.

real property
Land and all property permanently attached to it, such as buildings.

trespass to land
Intentional and unlawful entry onto or interference with the land of another person without consent.

consent
All parties to a novation (substitution of a new contract) must knowingly assent to the substitution of either the obligations or parties to the agreement.

39

FIGURE 3.1
Elements of the Tort
of Tresspass to Land

> **Trespass to Land**
> - An act
> - Another
> - Intent
> - Intrusion
> - Cause

- In possession of *another;*
- *Intent* to intrude; and
- *Causation* of the intrusion.

(See Figure 3.1.)

A trespass to land can also occur if the defendant causes an object or another person to enter the plaintiff's land. In addition, a trespass can occur when the defendant remains on the plaintiff's land without the right to be there. If the plaintiff causes an object to enter the land, he may still be liable for trespass even though the defendant never personally entered the property. For example, suppose the defendant decides to throw eggs at the plaintiff's house. He drives by one night and pelts the plaintiff's house with eggs. The defendant has trespassed on the plaintiff's land by throwing the eggs.

Land does not consist solely of the ground. It also includes that portion of the airspace above the ground, over which the plaintiff can claim a reasonable or beneficial use. As such, the plaintiff cannot keep airplanes from flying over her house. The plaintiff has the use of the airspace immediately above the ground. For example, a plaintiff can assert the tort of trespass to land if another neighbor's tree extends over the fence and leans on the roof of the plaintiff's house. The plaintiff has the right to the quiet enjoyment of the airspace above her roof such that she should not have to deal with the neighbor's tree trespassing into that space.

In addition to airspace, the plaintiff also is entitled to the use of the subterranean space below the plaintiff's property. Again, the land below the plaintiff's property is considered as land under this tort so long as the plaintiff can claim a reasonable or beneficial use of that space. Only the person who owns the land or is in possession of the land, such as a tenant, can sue for trespass. A tenant can only recover damages for any interest that he has up to the end of the lease term.

As people become more environmentally conscious, another example of a trespass to land that has been getting attention as of late is in the area of toxic torts. With residential housing tracts springing up near manufacturing plants, this tort has become more prevalent in the modern era. A toxic tort is the toxic interference by the defendant with the plaintiff's ownership and enjoyment of his or her property. For example, a chemical plant adjacent to a residential neighborhood manufactures a pesticide known as Toxaphene. The water in the neighborhood began to have a bad taste and smell. Tests run by the homeowners discover that Toxaphene has leached into the groundwater under the residential neighborhood. The leaching of the chemicals into the groundwater below the homes is a trespass to land that takes the form of a toxic tort.

With an intentional trespass to land, the defendant does not need to have the intent to harm in order to be liable for a trespass to land. The only requisite intent is that of intentionally entering the plaintiff's land. A defendant can have the requisite intent even if he makes a mistake entering the plaintiff's land. For example, if the defendant enters into the plaintiff's property thinking it was his property, the defendant has still committed an intentional trespass because he intentionally entered the plaintiff's property even if it was by mistake. Even if the defendant's mistake is reasonable, reasonableness is not a defense for this tort.

Plaintiffs do not have to demonstrate actual destruction or harm to the land. The actual entry onto the land is damage enough. The plaintiff only needs to prove actual entry onto the land in order to prove damages. If nothing other than just an entry onto the land has occurred, the plaintiff can recover nominal damages, but only if the trespass was intentional.

"This court has also recognized that ownership of an easement is a valid defense to trespass."

An easement is a defense as it is the use of property of another, such as the utility company coming on to your property to read meters. (*VILARR RANSOM, as Trustee of the VILARR B. RANSOM REVOCABLE TRUST v. TOPAZ MARKETING, L.P., and DENNIS LOWER & FARR WEST INVESTMENTS v. TOPAZ MARKETING, L.P., and MR. AND MRS. DENNIS LOWER,* 152 P.3d 2; 2006 Ida. LEXIS 160.)

Once a trespass has been established, the defendant will be responsible for all of the consequences of that trespass. For example, suppose John decides that he is going to cross through Suzy's backyard to reach the street on the other side of Suzy's house. John could easily have gone around the housing track to reach the street, but he intentionally decides to jump Suzy's fence to get to the street on the other side. It is dusk when John jumps the fence and begins to cross the street. Suzy is coming around the corner of her house, sees John out of the corner of her eye, and thinks John is an intruder. She turns to run away, slips and falls, and injures her back. John will be responsible for Suzy's personal injuries because they were a consequence of his trespass.

Likewise, if the defendant is blasting with explosives near the plaintiff's property so that vibrations or concussions are felt on the plaintiff's property, the plaintiff may have a cause of action for trespass. If the defendant is conducting some type of activity such that it causes particulates or gases to cross onto the plaintiff's land, then the plaintiff may have a cause of action for trespass against the defendant.

A trespass can be continuing. A **continuing trespass** is usually caused when the defendant causes an object to enter the plaintiff's land. As long as the object remains on the plaintiff's property, the harm to the plaintiff continues.

continuing trespass
Remaining in force or being carried on without letup.

TRESPASS TO CHATTELS

Individuals are entitled to be free from interference or intermeddling of their enjoyment of their personal property. Personal property is akin to all movable property or any property that is not real property. A **chattel** is another name for personal property. If the interference with the chattel by the defendant is intentional, then the plaintiff can bring a cause of action for trespass to chattels.

chattel
Tangible personal property or goods.

FIGURE 3.2
Elements of the Tort of Tresspass to Chattel

Trespass to Chattel
- Intent to interfere or intermeddle
- An act
- Cause
- Damages

The elements of the tort of trespass to chattels are:

- *Intent to perform the interference or intermeddling* with plaintiff's right to possession of the personal property;
- The *act* by the defendant;
- *Causation;* and
- *Damages.*

(See Figure 3.2.)

The tort of trespass to chattels involves protecting plaintiffs from interference or intermeddling with the right of possession of their personal property. Therefore, any interference, intermeddling, or unauthorized use of the chattel is a violation of the right of plaintiffs' possession to the property and is sufficient to establish the elements necessary for this tort. It is not necessary for the defendant to intend to cause the plaintiff's personal property harm. Only the intent to interfere with the plaintiff's possession of his personal property is enough. Any person who is in possession of personal property can bring a cause of action for trespass to chattels; however, the interference must have been caused by some act by the defendant.

The interference must be intentional. It must involve a serious infringement of the rights of plaintiff to her property or actual harm to the property, and it must involve a physical act by the defendant. Intermeddling involves any action by the defendant that causes harm to the property, causes the owner to have loss of use of the chattel, or lessens the value of the property.

Most courts hold that in order to bring a cause of action for trespass to chattels, some damage must have occurred to the property. This is different from trespass to land where the mere entry can entitle the plaintiff to nominal damages. In trespass to chattels, there must be damage to the personal property in order to bring the cause of action.

TRESPASS IN CYBERSPACE

Trespass to chattels used to be an old and rarely used tort law that was only spoken about in law schools and paralegal classes. However, recently, trespass has received renewed attention as it applies to **cyberspace**. In 1996, a California appellate court found in *Thrifty-Tel, Inc. v. Bezenek,* 54 Cal. Rptr. 2d 468 (Ct. App. 1996) that computer-generated signals used to access a telephone system were sufficiently tangible to constitute an object sufficient to establish a trespass. In this case, two minor children used a computer to hack into a telephone system. The court determined that electronic signals constituted a tangible object, and since the children caused the signals to enter the computer systems, a trespass of chattel had occurred. The court borrowed the concepts from trespass to land wherein particulate materials and gases are sufficiently tangible to be objects that can cause a trespass to land.

The revival of trespass to chattel as it pertains to cyberspace was first tested in *CompuServe, Inc. v. Cyber Promotions, Inc.,* 962 F. Supp. 1015 (S.D. Ohio 1997). In this case, CompuServe, Inc., which is an Internet service provider, sued Cyber Promotions, Inc. for sending spam to its account holders. The court found that the electronic touches from sending spam constituted a trespass to chattel. The court also granted CompuServe the remedy of an **injunction** without CompuServe having to demonstrate

cyberspace
Computer network consisting of a worldwide network of computer networks that use the TCP/IP network protocols to facilitate data transmission and exchange.

injunction
A court order that requires a party to refrain from acting in a certain way to prevent harm to the requesting party.

CASE FACT PATTERN

Bob works for Computerworks, Inc. Computerworks is a huge Internet company and has thousands of employees. Bob is unhappy that he did not receive a significant raise even though the company made a huge profit last year. Bob uses his access to the e-mails of thousands of Computerworks employees criticizing Computerworks' policies and procedures and advocating that the employees of Computerworks join a union. Computerworks sues Bob, claiming that he has committed a trespass to chattel as a result of his e-mails to Computerworks' employees. Has a trespass to chattel occurred? See *Intel v. Hamidi*, 30 Cal. 4th 1342.

SURF'S UP

Trespass to chattels has been used in other cyber cases beside those just listed. Using the Internet, research the case of *Intel Corp. v. Hamidi* and determine what the court held in this case. What part of cyberspace constituted an object? What was the ruling by the court?

EYE ON ETHICS

Laws are constantly changing. Cyberspace is constantly evolving, and laws are being interpreted in new ways to cover situations as they evolve. The evolution of the tort of trespass to chattels is a perfect example. It is important for legal assistants and attorneys to stay abreast of these changes. Remember, when citing case law, you must use the most current laws when presenting a case.

conversion
An overt act to deprive the owner of possession of personal property with no intention of returning the property, thereby causing injury or harm.

actual damages had occurred. The court determined that the spam broke the communications between CompuServe and its account holders and constituted a harm due to the damage to CompuServe's reputation, its employee time, and the goodwill of its customers.

With this new interpretation of trespass to chattels as well as with advances in technology, it is no doubt that this rarely used law will see a change in adoption and interpretation as time goes by.

CONVERSION

Conversion is similar to trespass to chattels as it involves an intentional interference by the defendant to plaintiff's property. However, this tort goes one step further. Trespass to chattels involves an intentional interference, but the plaintiff retains possession of his or her property. In the tort of conversion, the interference is of such a substantial nature that the plaintiff is deprived of his property and the defendant converts the property to his own use. The plaintiff is denied her ownership rights to the property. The distinction is in the seriousness of the interference. If the interference is minor, trespass to chattels applies. If the interference is serious, then conversion applies.

LEGAL RESEARCH MAXIM

The *Restatement (Second) of Torts* is an important secondary source that a paralegal can consult in order to gain a better understanding of tort concepts and theories. The *Restatement (Second) of Torts* defines conversion in section 222A as follows:

1. Conversion is an intentional exercise of dominion or control over a chattel which so seriously interferes with the right of another to control it that the actor may justly be required to pay the other the full value of the chattel.

2. In determining the seriousness of the interference and the justice of requiring the actor to pay the full value, the following factors are important:
   (a) the extent and duration of the actor's exercise of dominion or control;
   (b) the actor's intent to assert a right in fact inconsistent with the other's right of control;
   (c) the actor's good faith;
   (d) the extent and duration of the resulting interference with the other's right of control;
   (e) the harm done to the chattel;
   (f) the inconvenience and expense caused to the other.

Source: American Law Institute.

Conversion protects the plaintiff's right to be free from serious intentional interferences with personal property caused by the defendant. Conversion is the intentional and substantial interference with the plaintiff's use or possession of her personal property. Damages are not necessary to have occurred in order for the tort of conversion to be established.

The elements for this tort are:

- *Personal property;*
- The *plaintiff is in possession* of the chattel or is entitled to immediate possession;
- *Intent* to exercise **dominion** or control over the chattel;
- *Serious interference* with the plaintiff's possession; and
- *Causation.*

dominion
The perfect control in right of ownership.

(See Figure 3.3.)

Any tangible personal property can be converted. Also, some intangible objects have been considered personal property by the court and as such can be converted. Some of these intangible items are promissory notes, stocks, and insurance policies, to name a few.

The plaintiff may be allowed to recover the full fair-market value of the chattel at the time and place of the conversion. If malice or hatred existed, punitive damages may also be possible against the defendant.

The court looks at several factors to determine the extent of the interference with the chattel. Those factors include:

- The extent and duration of the defendant's exercise of control or dominion over the chattel; the more substantial and lengthy the interference, the more likely it will be found to constitute a conversion.
- Whether the defendant intended to assert a right in the chattel that was inconsistent with the plaintiff's right of control.
- Whether the defendant acted in good faith or bad faith when interfering with the chattel.
- Whether the interference caused any damage or harm to the chattel.
- Whether the plaintiff suffered any inconvenience or expense as a result of the interference.

It is not a defense that the defendant acted in good faith or made a reasonable mistake, although this is one of the overall factors that the court will take into consideration.

If the defendant removes the plaintiff's property from one place to another, he may be liable for conversion if the removal constitutes a sufficiently serious interference to the plaintiff's right to possession or control of the property. If the defendant refuses to return the property to the owner, then a conversion may exist. The defendant will have exercised dominion and control over the plaintiff's property. For example, suppose Ron borrows Bob's skis so that he can go skiing in Utah. Bob allows Ron to borrow the skis. Ron thinks that skis are great. Ron comes back from his ski trip and puts Bob's skis in the garage. The skis remain there for three months. After three months, Bob asks Ron for the skis back. Ron wants to keep the skis. He tells Bob that the skis were stolen. Ron has committed conversion because he substantially

FIGURE 3.3
Elements of the Tort of Conversion

Conversion
- Personal property
- Plaintiff has possession
- Intent to exercise dominion or control
- Serious interference
- Cause

YOU BE THE JUDGE

Sheri's watch was not working. She decided that she was going to leave it with Oti, the jeweler, for repairs. Sheri was going to be out of town for the next couple of weeks on vacation, so she asked Oti to send the watch to her house once the repairs were completed. Oti did the repairs and then shipped the watch to Sheri via Federal Parcel Service. Federal Parcel Service delivered the watch, but to the wrong house. The watch was delivered to a house down the street and not to Sheri. Sheri called Oti when she returned because she had not received the watch. Oti contacted Federal Parcel Service, who conducted an investigation. Federal Parcel Service discovered that its courier had delivered the watch to the wrong house. The courier retrieved the watch and returned it to Sheri. Did a trespass to chattel occur? Did a conversion occur?

SPOT THE ISSUE

When dealing with lawsuits involving intentional torts, one of the most important items that a paralegal has to keep track of is the statute of limitations. Statute of limitations is the time limit within which plaintiffs can bring a lawsuit against the defendant seeking remedies for their damages and injuries. If a lawsuit is not filed within the time period prescribed by the statute of limitations, the plaintiff may be barred forever from seeking legal remedies against the defendant who caused her injuries and damages. It is extremely important to gather factual information from the client so that you know exactly what the time limit is for the statute of limitations in your state with regard to the tort issues in your client's matter. Make sure that the supervising attorney is well aware of the date and record it appropriately in whatever calendar system that your firm utilizes.

If a paralegal and/or attorney missed the filing of a complaint within the allowed prescribed statute of limitations time frame, on what issue could the plaintiff file an action against the attorney, paralegal, and firm?

interfered with Bob's right to possession of his skis so as to dispossess Bob of his property rights.

Using the preceding example, if Ron had been skiing, crashed, and broken Bob's skis, then Ron would be liable for conversion. If the defendant destroys or alters the goods of the plaintiff, then he is liable for conversion as the defendant has substantially interfered with the plaintiff's ownership rights by altering or destroying the plaintiff's property.

Some acts by the defendant that constitute a serious interference with the plaintiff's property interest are:

- Wrongful acquisition of the property, such as theft or embezzlement;
- Wrongful transfer, such as selling, misdelivering, or pledging of plaintiff's property;
- Wrongful detention, such as refusing to return the plaintiff's property;
- Substantially changing the plaintiff's property;
- Severely damaging or destroying the plaintiff's property; and
- Misusing the property.

Summary

As with assault and battery, when people think of violations concerning a person's property, they think of the crimes of theft or burglary. Torts' causes of action against property rights are similar to their crimes' counterparts. As is the case with the torts of assault and battery, torts against property rights are civil wrongs against property and not crimes. Torts against property can be perpetrated against personal property or real property. The tort involves an individual's exclusive right to freely use the property that the person owns. Interference with individuals' right to freely enjoy both their personal and real property is the basis for tort actions concerning property rights.

Under American jurisdictions, trespass to land occurs when the defendant enters the plaintiff's land without consent. The interest protected by the tort of trespass to land is the interest in the exclusive possession of land in its present physical condition.

The elements for the tort of trespass to land include the following: an act, intrusion on land, in possession of another, intent to intrude, and causation of the intrusion.

A trespass to land can also occur if the defendant causes an object or another person to enter the plaintiff's land. Also, a trespass can occur when the defendant remains on the plaintiff's land without the right to be there. If the plaintiff causes an object to enter the land, he or she may still be liable for trespass even though the defendant never personally entered the property.

Land does not consist solely of the ground. It also includes that portion of the airspace above the ground, over which the plaintiff can claim a reasonable or beneficial use. In addition to airspace, the plaintiff also is entitled to the use of the subterranean space below the plaintiff's property. Again, the land below the plaintiff's property is considered as land under this tort as long as the plaintiff can claim a reasonable or beneficial use to that space.

Only the person who owns the land or is in possession of the land, such as a tenant, can sue for trespass. Tenants can only recover damages for any interest that they have up to the end of the lease term.

Individuals are entitled to be free from interference or intermeddling of their enjoyment of their personal property. Personal property is all movable property or any property that is not real property. Chattel is another name for personal property. If the interference with the chattel by the defendant is intentional, then the plaintiff can bring a cause of action for trespass to chattels.

The elements of the tort of trespass to chattels are intent to perform the interference or intermeddling with plaintiff's right to possession of the personal property, the act by the defendant, causation, and damages.

Conversion is similar to trespass to chattels as it involves a defendant's intentional interference to plaintiff's property. However, this tort goes one step further. Trespass to chattels involves an intentional interference, but the plaintiff retains possession of his property. In the tort of conversion, the interference is of such a substantial nature that the plaintiff is deprived of his property and the defendant converts the property to his own use. The plaintiff is denied her ownership rights to the property. The distinction is in the seriousness of the interference. If the interference is minor, trespass to chattels applies. If the interference is serious, then conversion applies.

Key Terms

Chattel	Dominion
Consent	Injunction
Continuing trespass	Personal property
Conversion	Real property
Cyberspace	Trespass to land

Review Questions

1. What is the main difference between trespass to chattel and conversion?
2. What is personal property?
3. What is real property?
4. Does the defendant have to intend to harm the property in order to have a trespass to chattel?
5. What is dominion?
6. What is consent?
7. If someone steals property, is that a trespass to chattel?

8. What is a trespass to land?
9. What is an injunction?
10. What is a chattel?

---

1. Sara owns a business where she sprays crops for pests. She does this from an airplane that she owns. She usually flies within 15 feet of the ground and sprays insecticides on the crops. She was hired to spray a customer's orchards. The owners of the orchards told Sara that the land where the orchard was located was parcel 727 on the county assessor's map. However, the orchard was really parcel 772 on the county assessor's map. Because of the mistake, Sara accidentally sprayed the wrong property. She sprayed Bill's avocado orchard instead. The insecticide caused all of Bill's avocados to die so that he lost his entire crop of avocados for the year. If Bill asserts a claim for damages resulting from the trespass of Sara to his land, the court should find for:
   a. Bill, because crop dusting is a dangerous activity.
   b. Bill, because Sara intentionally flew through the airspace above his land.
   c. Sara, because she reasonably believed that the farm which she was spraying belonged to her client.
   d. Sara, because her client gave her the wrong information.
2. Peter goes to Dan, who is a car dealer, to discuss trading in his old car for a new one. Dan asks Peter for his old car keys so that he can inspect the possibility of using Peter's old car for a trade-in toward the purchase of a new car. Peter gives Dan the keys. After Peter declines to do a trade-in of his old car, Dan refuses to give Peter his keys back and laughs at him. Peter is compelled to call the police, after which his keys are returned. Is Dan liable for conversion? Explain.
3. Pam climbs on the back of Jake, a dog owned by David. Pam pulls the dog's ears, and the dog snaps at Pam's nose. Pam's parents sue for damages from the dog bite. David contends that under local law, Pam may not recover if Pam was a trespasser, and that Pam was in fact committing a trespass to chattels at the time she was bitten. Did a trespass to chattels occur? Explain.
4. Research your state or county and determine what the time frame would be for a landowner in your jurisdiction to wait after warning an intruder that he or she was trespassing before taking further action.
5. Although chattel is referred to as personal property, what did the word represent *generally speaking* back in agricultural days? Were human beings ever considered chattel? Who and when?
6. Provide three examples of tangible property and intangible property.
7. Provide three examples of trespass to chattel and three examples of conversion, with analysis on each action, as to why they fit as trespass to chattel or conversion.

PORTFOLIO ASSIGNMENT

Using your local law library or resources on the Internet, locate a sample complaint for personal injuries. Prepare a complaint for a Tom Jones who has suffered a trespass to land when Manufacturing Corp. allowed smoke to waft over his land, which caused a film to build up on his house and vehicles. Prepare the complaint as if you were completing a draft for your supervising attorney to review. Complaints are the initiation of an intentional tort lawsuit and are a very important document that many paralegals who work in this area are asked to prepare.

Vocabulary Builders

Instructions

Use the key terms from this chapter to fill in the answers to the crossword puzzle.

NOTE: When the answer is more than one word, leave a blank space between the words.

ACROSS

2. A court order that requires a party to refrain from acting in a certain way to prevent harm to the requesting party.
7. Computer network consisting of a worldwide network of computer networks that use the TCP/IP network protocols to facilitate data transmission and exchange.
8. Tangible personal property or goods.
9. The perfect control in right of ownership.

DOWN

1. Remaining in force or being carried on without letup.
3. Movable or intangible thing not attached to real property.
4. Land and all property permanently attached to it, such as buildings.
5. Intentional and unlawful entry onto or interference with the land of another person without consent.
6. All parties to a novation must knowingly assent to the substitution of either the obligations or parties to the agreement.
7. An unauthorized assumption and exercise of the right of ownership over goods or personal chattels belonging to another.

VILARR RANSOM, as Trustee of the VILARR B. RANSOM REVOCABLE TRUST, Plaintiff-Respondent,
v. TOPAZ MARKETING, L.P., and DENNIS LOWER, Defendants-Appellants. FARR WEST
INVESTMENTS, Plaintiff-Respondent, v. TOPAZ MARKETING, L.P., and
MR. AND MRS. DENNIS LOWER, Defendants-Appellants.

SUPREME COURT OF IDAHO

152 P.3d 2; 2006 Ida. LEXIS 160

December 22, 2006, Filed

SUBSEQUENT HISTORY: Rehearing denied by *Ransom v. Topaz Mktg., L.P.,* 2007 Ida.
LEXIS 50 (Idaho, Feb. 26, 2007)

PRIOR HISTORY: Appeal from the District Court of the Sixth Judicial District of the State of Idaho,
Franklin County. Hon. Don L. Harding, District Judge.

DISPOSITION: Decision of the district court awarding damages for trespass, nominal damages for a
continuing tort and attorney fees is: Reversed in part, vacated in part and remanded.

CASE SUMMARY

PROCEDURAL POSTURE: Appellant easement holders challenged a decision from the District Court of the Sixth Judicial District of the State of Idaho, which entered judgment in favor of respondent owner in a trespass and breach of duty action.

OVERVIEW: After purchasing the easement in question, the holders began to change it and cut a new road. The owner filed a **trespass** action, and this appeal was commenced after judgment was entered in the owner's favor. On review, the supreme court determined that the ownership of an easement was a valid defense to a **trespass** action. The district court failed to distinguish whether the actions were permissible or were excessive. Also, it failed to distinguish between permanent and temporary damages. Next, the award of nominal damages was reversed because the sum of $25 per day was not trifling in nature. Since they amounted to over $35,000, this was really in the nature of punitive damages. The district court erred by decreeing the proper use of the easement since nothing in the owner's complaint asked for the district court to set the parameters of the easement. Attorney's fees were improperly awarded under Idaho Code Ann. § 6-202 because the owner was unable to collect treble damages. The issue of a fence was not properly before the district court. Finally, given the mixed result of the case, neither party was awarded attorney's fees on appeal under Idaho Code Ann. § 12-121.

OUTCOME: The district court's award of nominal damages and attorney's fees, together with the order limiting the terms of the easement and the order to build a fence were reversed. The case was remanded for further proceedings regarding the award of damages. Specifically, the district court was ordered to find if the actions were excessive and to distinguish between temporary to and permanent damages.

JUDGES: TROUT, Justice. Chief Justice SCHROEDER and Justices EISMANN, BURDICK and JONES.

OPINION BY: TROUT

OPINION

TROUT, Justice

Topaz Marketing, L.P. and its owner/officer/agent, Dennis Lower (collectively Lower), appeal from a district court's decision finding it guilty of **trespass** and in breach of a duty as the non-exclusive owner of an easement.

I. FACTUAL AND PROCEDURAL BACKGROUND

Two lawsuits against Topaz Marketing and Dennis Lower were combined for purposes of the district court trial: *Vilarr Ransom, as Trustee of the Vilarr B. Ransom Revocable Trust (Ransom) v. Topaz and Dennis Lower* (Ransom suit) and *Farr West v. Topaz and Dennis Lower.* The *Ransom* suit was resolved through mediation; consequently, the only remaining case on appeal is *Farr West v. Topaz and Lower.*

Lower originally bought 120 acres of property lying east of property owned by Ransom and Farr West, and then later bought an additional 80 acres in 2000. Lower's **land** is accessed by a road easement crossing Farr West's property. Farr West's predecessors in interest, Ransom, granted the right-of-way easement to several grantees in 1977, including Mahlon Rupp. The easement consisted of a "dug way" or seasonal dirt road utilized for non-commercial use for nearly 24 years. In 2000, Rupp conveyed his interest in the easement to Lower, which subsequently attempted to purchase additional **land** from Farr West. When Farr West rejected the offer, Lower had the property surveyed and concluded that the right-of-way easement did not match the legal description in the document from Rupp. In 2001, over Farr West's objections, Lower began to change the easement and cut a new road, which everyone agrees, does conform to the legal description contained in the 1977 easement agreement.[1]

While it's not clear from the parties' briefing on appeal or the record, it appears that problems arose when, in creating the road, Lower pushed dirt onto other property owned by Farr West and made cuts onto Farr West's property, which had nothing to do with the creation or maintenance of the road itself. Additionally, during construction, Lower blocked off areas where water had traditionally crossed Farr West's property, altering the natural flow of the water runoff causing sink holes and sloughs. At some point, Lower also took out a fence bordering the property between Ransom and Farr West. These parties then filed lawsuits against Lower for **trespass** and damages. Specifically, in Farr West's complaint, it requested that title to the property be quieted in Farr West and that damages for **trespass** be awarded; there was no allegation about Lower's right to an easement. After making several trips to view the premises and listening to several days of testimony, the district court concluded there was a **trespass**, including continuing **trespass**, onto Farr West's property and that Farr West was entitled to a $42,685 judgment for the cost to repair the damage done in constructing the easement and the attendant **trespass**. The district judge also awarded nominal damages in the amount of $25 per day based upon what the judge called a "continuing tort," which amounted to $35,350. Additionally, the judge awarded attorney's fees to Farr West pursuant to Idaho Code section 6-202. Finally, the court ordered that a fence be erected on the boundary line between the Ransom and Farr West property and defined the proper use of the easement. Lower now appeals from that decision.

II. STANDARD OF REVIEW

A district court's findings of fact will not be set aside on appeal unless they are clearly erroneous. *Camp v. East Fort Ditch Company, Ltd.*, 137 Idaho 850, 55 P.3d 304 (2002); *Bramwell v. South Rigby Canal Co.*, 136 Idaho 648, 39 P.3d 588 (2001); Idaho Rules of Civil Procedure 52(a). When deciding whether findings of fact are clearly erroneous, this Court does not substitute its view of the facts for that of the trial court. *Bramwell, supra.* It is the province of the trial court to weigh conflicting evidence and to judge the credibility of witnesses. *Rowley v. Fuhrman*, 133 Idaho 105, 982 P.2d 940 (1999). On appeal, this Court examines the record to see if challenged findings of fact are supported by substantial and competent evidence. *Id.* Evidence is regarded as substantial if a reasonable trier of fact would accept it and rely upon it in determining whether a disputed point of fact has been proven. *Bramwell, supra.*

The awarding of attorney's fees and costs is within the discretion of the trial court and subject to review for an abuse of discretion. *See Burns v. Baldwin*, 138 Idaho 480, 486, 65 P.3d 502, 508 (2003); *Bowles v. Pro Indiviso, Inc.*, 132 Idaho 371, 374, 973 P.2d 142, 145 (1999); *O'Boskey v. First Fed. Sav. & Loan Ass'n of Boise*, 112 Idaho 1002, 1008, 739 P.2d 301, 307 (1987). However, whether a statute awarding attorney's fees applies to a given set of facts is a question of law. *Kidd Island BayWater Users Coop. Ass'n, Inc. v. Miller*, 136 Idaho 571, 573, 38 P.3d 609, 611 (2002). The standard of review for questions of law is one of free review. *Electrical Wholesale Supply Co., Inc. v. Nielson*, 136 Idaho 814, 825, 41 P.3d 242, 253 (2001).

III. DISCUSSION

A. Measure of damages for trespass

At oral argument the parties agreed that Lower had the right to enter the property and create a graveled road over Farr West's property, conforming to the legal description of the right-of-way easement. The problems between the parties result from damage allegedly done in excess of that reasonably necessary in building the road. An affirmative easement, according to the Restatement of Property § 451, at 2912 (1944), "entitles the owner thereof to use the **land** subject to the easement by doing acts which, were it not for the easement, he would not be privileged to do." The comments to § 451 explain that the easement allows the owner to intrude upon **land** in many ways which, "were it not for the easement, would make him a trespasser upon the **land.**" This court has also recognized that ownership of an easement is a valid defense to **trespass.** *See Deer Creek, Inc. v. Hibbard*, 94 Idaho 533, 493 P.2d 392 (1972).

It is not clear from the district judge's decision on what he was basing the award of damages; he simply made reference to **trespass** in various locations and then awarded a significant amount for repair costs. While the district court acknowledged Lower's right to maintain and improve the right-of-way easement, it also stated that "[Lower] also had a duty not to do so at the Plaintiff's expense by damaging or creating an additional burden on the Plaintiff's property." It is not clear that the court differentiated between damages attributable to the lawful creation of an easement and excessive or wrongful damage to the property. There was no dispute over the validity of the 1977 deed or Lower's right to change the easement to conform to the legal description therein. Thus, Lower had the right to encroach or **trespass** onto Farr West's **land,** since an easement is, in essence, permission to encroach or **trespass** onto another's property. *See Deer Creek, Inc. v. Hibbard, 94 Idaho 533, 493 P.2d 392 (1972)*; Restatement of Property § 451, at 2912 (1944). In its findings on **trespass,** the district court stated:

> Contrary to the Defendant's arguments he did **trespass** onto the Plaintiff's property and the effects of that conduct canal so be classified as a continuing **trespass.** The facts show that the Defendant intentionally and without the Plaintiff's consent, entered onto the Plaintiff's property with heavy construction equipment, that the Defendant placed and removed soil from the Plaintiff's property, and that the Defendant altered and made several critical changes to the Plaintiff's property.

It is not a **trespass** for Lower to go on the Farr West property to construct a road over the easement, nor does it require Farr West's consent. When a road easement is developed, the **land** may be modified: trees may be cleared, gravel may be laid, and fences may be built. The question becomes, what damage was the natural effect of creating the easement and what damage was excessive, unnecessary and compensable under the law. Here, the district court did not address this distinction when awarding damages.

The district court also failed to identify and distinguish between permanent and temporary damages. **land** is permanently injured, but not totally destroyed, the owner is entitled to the difference between the fair market value before and after the injury. *Nampa & Meridian Irrigation Dist. v. Mussell*, 139 Idaho 28, 33, 72 P.3d 868, 873 (2003). However, if the **land** is only temporarily injured, the owner is entitled to recover the amount necessary to put the **land** in the condition it was immediately preceding the injury. *Id.* In regard to temporary injury to property, "if the cost of restoration exceeds the value of the premises in their original condition, or in the diminution in market value, the latter are the limits of recovery." *Id.* citing *Alesko v. Union Pac.R. Co.*, 62 Idaho 235, 109 P.2d 874 (1941). However, as the Court in *Mussell* indicated, because the goal of compensatory damages is reimbursement of the actual loss suffered, the rule precluding recovery in excess of the diminution in value is not of "invariable application." *Nampa & Meridian Irrigation Dist.*, 139 Idaho at 33-34; 72 P.3d at 873-74. It's apparent that in this case, there are damages that are temporary and others that appear to be continuous in nature, or "permanent." For example, the district court refers to harm caused from water erosion that has "rendered the property unsuitable for its natural use," implying permanent damage, yet the court never labels it as such. Additionally, the court failed to determine the fair market value of the **land.** While there is some indication in the record that the property damaged was about ten acres in size and was valued at approximately $3,800 per acre (making the court's damage award in excess of the property's total value), the judge made no determination about how much property was actually damaged or what the value of the property was, making it impossible to tell whether an award for temporary damages wrongly exceeded the diminution in value of the property. Therefore, the case must be remanded back to the district court for further findings of fact. On remand, the district court should distinguish between damages caused by Lower's permissible **trespass** to build the road, for which Farr West is not entitled to compensation, and damages caused by impermissible **trespass,** for which Farr West is owed the cost to repair the property. Further, the court should identify and distinguish between temporary and permanent damages. If the district court awards temporary damages to Farr West and believes that an award of damages in excess of value is appropriate, it should articulate a justification for such an award. *Nampa & Meridian Irrigation Dist.*, 139 Idaho at 33-34; 72 P.3d at 873-74. As to permanent damages, if any are found, the district court must determine the fair market value before and after the injury in order to properly compensate Farr West.

B. Award of nominal damages

Nominal damages generally refers to a "trifling sum" awarded to "demonstrate, symbolically, that the plaintiff's person or property has been violated." *Myers v. Workmen's Auto Insurance Company*, 140 Idaho 495, 508, 95 P.3d 977, 990 (2004) citing C. McCORMICK, THE LAW OF DAMAGES, § 20 (1935). The district court awarded the sum of $25 a day beginning from August 1, 2001, the day the **trespass** began, until the date of the court's decision, for an award totaling $35,350. That amount is not, by any reasonable analysis, a nominal amount. Further, nominal damages are only appropriate when there are no actual damages or actual damages are so small as to be incalculable and, therefore, the court will enter a nominal award simply to indicate a recognition that some damage was done, although not a significant amount.

In its findings, the district court stated:

> Evidence presented at the hearings and a walk of the property affected by the Defendant revealed that in addition to the water damage, the Defendant also damaged several trees on the Plaintiff's property. Furthermore, the road constructed by the Defendant does in fact encroach in several places on to the Plaintiff's property. The damage to the trees and the continuing **trespass** are acts that merit some relief.

These are in fact the damages discussed in Section A above for which compensation should be awarded under the **trespass**

theory. Instead, the district court deemed these to be damages for "continuing **trespass**" for which there had been no actual damage amount proven and, therefore, the court created its own remedy of nominal damages. The district court did not state how the $25 per day award bears any relationship to what it believed to be additional uncompensated damages, nor is it clear why those damages were not properly included in the actual damage award. Suffice it to say, these are not mere "nominal damages."

Further, based upon the district court's comments that the award was also "based on the fact that this **trespass** was particularly egregious," it appears that the trial court may have been attempting to award punitive damages, even though they were not requested by the Plaintiff. Based on the foregoing, the district court's award of nominal damages is reversed.

C. Limits on the easement.

In its decision, the district court found that the easement was intended for private use and should be limited "to the private use of the owner of the easement and not for any public or commercial use." In its complaint, however, Farr West requested only damages for **trespass** and a decree quieting title in Farr West, free and clear from any claim by Lower. Nothing in Farr West's complaint relates to the easement or prays for relief that the district court should decree that an easement exists or setting its parameters. As a part of the cause of action for **trespass**, the district court could appropriately consider whether there was an easement and could consider whether the work done by Lower exceeded the scope of work necessary to maintaining that easement. Going beyond that, however, and decreeing its proper use was not before the court and the district court erred in making any findings or conclusions about the nature of the easement.

D. Attorney's fees pursuant to Idaho Code section 6-202.

In its complaint, Farr West demanded that it be awarded damages, including treble damages, costs and attorney's fees pursuant to I.C. § 6-202. That provision governs actions for **trespass** and reads in pertinent part:

> Any person who, without permission of the owner, . . . enters upon the real property of another person which property is posted with "No Trespassing" signs . . . or otherwise injures any tree or timber on the **land** of another person . . . is liable to the owner of such **land** . . . for treble the amount of damages which may be assessed therefor or fifty dollars ($50.00), plus a reasonable attorney's fee which shall be taxed as costs. . . .

I.C. § 6-202. As explained by the district court, Farr West was unable to collect treble damages for **trespass** under the statute because Farr West failed to post "No Trespassing" signs on its property and failed to prove any damages for lost timber. Nevertheless, the district court awarded attorney's fees based upon the statute. There is no independent claim for attorney's fees if the plain language of the statute does not so indicate. *Barbee v. Barbee*, 146 P.3d 657, 2006 WL 2795613 (Idaho 2006). In *Barbee*, this Court held that the plain language of I.C. § 30-1446, did not support a suit solely for attorney's fees filed after an arbitration award assigning damages was fully paid. In support of its decision, this Court referred to the language of the statute, which stated that a claimant is entitled to sue for consideration paid, "*together with* interest, costs and fees." The plain language of I.C. § 6-202 also indicates that attorney's fees may be awarded *in addition to* any amounts awarded for damages ("plus a reasonable attorney's fee"). Because the district court determined that Lower did not violate the statute, the court's award of attorney's fees was in error and is reversed.

E. Order regarding new fence

In the *Ransom* suit, settled through mediation, Lower and Ransom agreed that a section of fence, which had been previously removed and relocated by Lower, would be rebuilt at its historical location. While it's not clear from the record, it appears that had not been accomplished as of the time of the trial in this case. That fence line was not an issue raised by Farr West. Moreover, the district judge acknowledged that it was not an issue before him, telling the parties that he would not settle the dispute over the fence line. Nevertheless, in the district court's memorandum opinion in this case, the court ordered Lower to erect a fence on the proper boundary line between the Ransom and Farr West property. Because that was not an issue before the court in this case, the district court erred in directing Lower to erect a new fence.

F. Attorney's fees on appeal

Both parties have requested attorney fees on appeal based on I.C. § 12-121. Attorney's fees may be awarded to the prevailing party pursuant to this section if this Court finds that the case was brought, pursued or defended frivolously, unreasonably or without foundation. *Hutchinson v. State of Idaho*, 134 Idaho 18, 22, 995 P.2d 363, 367 (2000); I.R.C.P. 54 (e)(1). Because this case is reversed in part, vacated in part and remanded, there is no basis for finding that the appeal was frivolous or unreasonable and, therefore, attorney's fees are not awarded to either party.

IV. CONCLUSION

The district court improperly measured actual damages for Lower's **trespass,** as it failed to distinguish between damages attributable to Lower's permissible **trespass** to create or maintain an access road and damages attributable to excessive intrusion exceeding the scope of the easement. There has also been no distinction between costs to repair temporary damage and an award of damages for permanent damage to the property. The district court's award of nominal damages and attorney's fees, together with the order limiting the terms of the easement and ordering Lower to build a fence are reversed. This case is remanded for further proceedings consistent with this opinion. Given the mixed result, no costs or fees are awarded to the parties on appeal.

[Footnotes omitted]

Chief Justice SCHROEDER and Justices EISMANN, BURDICK and JONES **CONCUR.**

Source: 152 P.3d 2; 2006 Ida. LEXIS 160. Reprinted with the permission of LexisNexis.

Chapter 4

Defenses to Intentional Torts

CHAPTER OBJECTIVES

Upon completion of this chapter, you will be able to:

- Understand the concept of a defense to a tort.
- Identify the traditional defenses available in a cause of action for an intentional tort.
- Explain each defense to an intentional tort.
- Discuss the defenses that are applicable to each intentional tort.

In intentional torts, it is up to plaintiffs to prove their prima facie case against defendants. Once the plaintiff has proven the case, the defendant gets the opportunity to defend her- or himself from the plaintiff's allegations. This chapter focuses on the various types of defenses that are available to a defendant who is involved in a cause of action for an intentional tort.

CONCEPT OF A DEFENSE

A **defense** may be raised by the defendant against a plaintiff's claim that an intentional tort has been committed against the plaintiff. A defense is a legal justification or excuse. The concept of a defense is such that even if the defendant committed a tort or a violation, she may not be held liable for her actions because she may have a legal justification for the action.

A defense is not an element to a tort. A defense is brought up after the intentional tort has already been completed. That means the defendant has committed the intentional tort against the plaintiff and the plaintiff has met his burden of proof by demonstrating that all of the elements of the intentional tort have been satisfied. At that time, the defendant can bring up a defense in order to avoid liability for his actions.

Defenses are largely grouped into two categories: (1) the defense that the plaintiff consented to the action or invasion into her interest; and (2) defenses that are imposed as a matter of law. Defenses that are imposed as matter of law are called **privileges**. A defendant may be entitled to use a privilege if her actions further a social interest that is entitled to protection.

defense
Legally sufficient reason to excuse the complained-of behavior.

privilege
Reasonable expectation of privacy and confidentiality for communications in furtherance of the relationship such as attorney–client, doctor–patient, husband–wife, psychotherapist–patient, and priest–penitent.

TYPES OF DEFENSES

Consent

consent
All parties to a novation must knowingly assent to the substitution of either the obligations or parties to the agreement.

If a person legally consents to a particular action by the defendant, then that action is not a tort. **Consent** means that the plaintiff was in possession of her full mental capacity and was completely knowledgeable of all of the facts. With full mental capacity and complete knowledge, the plaintiff granted the defendant permission to commit the act. The theory behind the defense of consent is that once consent is given, the first element of an intentional tort—the act—is negated. Consent negates the wrongful act by the defendant.

Consent may be distinguished in one of three ways.

- The first is *express* consent. In this situation, the person explicitly gives his or her consent to the action.
- The second category is *implied* consent. In circumstances where an individual has not expressly given consent, consent may be implied through conduct, including inaction or silence.
- The third category is *exceeding* consent. Exceeding consent occurs where the actions or conduct go beyond what the person has consented to. This concept often arises in situations where an individual consents to a specific medical procedure, but a different one is performed.

To establish consent, the following must be present:

- Willingness to accept the defendant's action; and
- Full understanding by the plaintiff of the consequences of the action.

If either of the preceding is lacking, then a defense of consent cannot be asserted by the defendant.

Consent cannot be asserted if any of the following conditions is present:

capacity
The ability to understand the nature and significance of a contract; to understand or comprehend specific acts or reasoning.

- The plaintiff lacked the **capacity** to consent;
- Consent was coerced from the plaintiff;
- The plaintiff did not understand the nature and extent of the defendant's actions to which he was consenting; and
- The conduct by the defendant was so egregious that no reasonable person would consent.

There are circumstances in which the plaintiff lacks the mental capacity to give consent. For example, in the eyes of the law, a child lacks the mental capacity to give consent. Also, when someone is unconscious, they lack mental capacity to give consent. If the defendant knew, or should have known, that the plaintiff lacked mental capacity to give consent, then the consent will not be effective as a defense by the defendant.

However, in certain circumstances, consent by the plaintiff will be implied as a matter of law. If all of the following factors are met, then consent will be implied as a matter of law:

- Incapacitated—the plaintiff is unable to give consent for some reason (e.g., mentally incapacitated, in a coma);
- Emergency—in order to save the plaintiff's life or protect her health, immediate action is necessary;
- Lack of consent is not indicated—no indication exists that the plaintiff would not give consent under the circumstances; and
- Reasonable person—a **reasonable person** would give consent in the same or similar circumstances.

For example, Jenny is hit by a car and taken to the hospital, where she is unconscious. Bruce is the resident doctor at the hospital. It reasonably appears to Bruce that Jenny has bleeding on the brain and will die if emergency surgery is not performed immediately. Bruce performs the surgery on Jenny before she regains consciousness and without obtaining the consent of a relative. Jenny will be deemed to have consented to the surgery because of its emergent and vital nature.

LEGAL RESEARCH MAXIM

Many times culture, environment, and daily routine play a part in how law and society can indirectly be affected by these subtle, yet powerful, underlying forces. Would it be reasonable, as an example, to file a lawsuit against a person for the tort of battery in New York City for bumping into you on a crowded subway? No, it wouldn't be, as the subway is part of a daily routine that many millions follow each day and bumps and knocks here and there are part of the norm.

reasonable person
A hypothetical person used as a legal standard, especially to determine whether someone acted with negligence; specifically, a person who exercises the degree of attention, knowledge, intelligence, and judgment that society requires of its members for the protection of their own and of others' interests.

RESEARCH THIS

Consent is a major part of medical practice. Doctors obtain patients' written consent all the time. Research the following scenario and determine whether Kathy consented to the medical treatment she received.

Kathy visits an ear specialist, Dr. Smith. Dr. Smith tells Kathy that her right ear is very infected and needs an operation. Kathy consents to the operation. After Dr. Smith administers the anesthetic, Dr. Smith determines that the right ear is not as infected as he had first thought, but Kathy's left ear is. Dr. Smith therefore operates on Kathy's left ear without obtaining Kathy's consent for this operation. Kathy sues Dr. Smith for battery. Dr. Smith brings up the defense of consent.

Consent can be asserted as a defense in the following torts:

- Assault
- Battery
- Conversion
- Deceit
- Defamation
- Emotional distress
- False imprisonment
- Injurious falsehood
- Misuse of legal proceedings
- Privacy
- Trespass to chattels
- Trespass to land

Self-Defense

The privilege of **self-defense** has been handed down for centuries. The law has recognized the need to excuse defendants' actions if they are based on the necessity to take

self-defense
A defendant's legal excuse that the use of force was justified.

SPOT THE ISSUE

Johnny had been leery of fighting with Tim. Tim was a professional black belt in karate and Tim looked—and was—physically powerful. One night after leaving the bar, Johnny and his girlfriend were accosted by Tim and two of his friends, as Johnny and his girlfriend were walking to their car. Johnny screamed at him to leave them alone, and with that, Tim backed up into his trained karate stance ready to attack Johnny. With that fear and threat, Johnny pulled out a gun and fired two shots at Tim, killing him. Is anyone here liable for a tort? Explain your answer fully. Is there any defense under law for Johnny? Explain your answer fully.

reasonable steps to prevent harm to themselves, to someone else, or to property. The defense of self-defense is applied similarly in both criminal law and tort law.

To determine whether a defendant can assert the privilege of self-defense, two questions need to be answered: (1) was the defendant privileged to use some kind of force to defend himself? and (2) was it necessary to use the degree of force that was exerted? A person is entitled to use reasonable force to prevent any threatened or harmful offensive bodily contact and any threatened confinement or imprisonment. The defendant has the burden to prove that reasonable force was necessary in defending himself, someone else, or his property. Self-defense may be used when there is a threat of harm but also when the defendant reasonably believes that a threat exists. Also, the defendant may not use force to avoid a harm that is not immediate or imminent unless there may be no opportunity in the future to prevent the harm.

For example, Victor is walking down the street when he comes upon Darren walking on the opposite side of the street. Darren shouts out to Victor that he hates him and is going to kill him in one year. Victor then takes out a gun and shoots down Darren. Victor would not be able to use self-defense as justification because the threat of harm from Darren was not imminent.

Reasonable force means that the force used must match the threat, meaning that one cannot use more force than is reasonably necessary to defend herself. In other words, the defendant may only use the force reasonably required to protect herself against the harm. The *Restatement (Second) of Torts,* section 63, determines the type of force that may be exerted should the threat to the defendant not involve the threat of death or bodily harm:

1. *An actor is privileged to use reasonable force, not intended or likely to cause death or serious bodily harm, to defend himself against unprivileged harmful or offensive contact or other bodily harm which he reasonably believes that another is about to inflict intentionally upon him.*

2. *Self-defense is privileged under the conditions stated in Subsection (1), although the actor correctly or reasonably believes that he can avoid the necessity of so defending himself,*
   a. *by retreating or otherwise giving up a right or privilege, or*
   b. *by complying with a command with which the actor is under no duty to comply or which the other is not privileged to enforce by the means threatened.*

Defendants may not use deadly force unless the danger to them is a threat of death or serious bodily harm. The *Restatement (Second) of Torts,* section 65 states:

1. *Subject to the statement in Subsection (3), an actor is privileged to defend himself against another by force intended or likely to cause death or serious bodily harm, when he reasonably believes that*
   a. *he other is about to inflict upon him an intentional contact or other bodily harm, and that*
   b. *he is thereby put in peril of death or serious bodily harm or ravishment, which can safely be prevented only by the immediate use of such force.*

2. *The privilege stated in Subsection (1) exists although the actor correctly or reasonably believes that he can safely avoid the necessity of so defending himself by*
   a. *retreating if he is attacked within his dwelling place, which is not also the dwelling place of the other, or*
   b. *permitting the other to intrude upon or dispossess him of his dwelling place, or*
   c. *abandoning an attempt to effect a lawful arrest.*

3. *The privilege stated in Section (1) does not exist if the actor correctly or reasonably believes that he can with complete safety avoid the necessity of so defending himself by*
   a. *retreating if attacked in any place other than his dwelling place, or in a place which is also the dwelling of the other, or*
   b. *relinquishing the exercise of any right or privilege other than his privilege to prevent intrusion upon or dispossession of his dwelling place or to effect a lawful arrest.*

Self-defense can be asserted as a defense for the following intentional torts:

- Assault
- Battery
- Conversion
- False imprisonment
- Infliction of emotional distress
- Injurious falsehood
- Trespass to chattels
- Trespass to land

Defense of Others

Like self-defense, the law recognizes that there are instances when a person may have to use force to defend others from a threat of harm. This defense is known as the **defense of others**. If another person or other persons are exposed to a threat of death or serious bodily harm, a defendant can assert the defense of others as a defense in that situation. The courts allow the use of reasonable force to defend others. However, as with the self-defense, the defendant must use only the force that is reasonably necessary for the situation and can use deadly force only if others are threatened with death or serious bodily injury. If the person being attacked would not be able to assert a privilege of self-defense, then the defendant will not be entitled to assert the privilege either.

defense of others
A justification available when one harms or threatens another in defense of a person other than oneself.

For example, Fred is walking downtown late at night on his way home from work. As he reaches a dark alley, he notices that a man in the alley is attacking a woman. Fred runs down the alley and jumps on the man, and a fight ensues. Fred knocks the man unconscious. In a lawsuit brought against Fred for battery by the attacker, Fred can assert the defense of defense of others because he was defending the woman being attacked.

YOU BE THE JUDGE

Jared was walking toward his car after work on a late night at the shopping mall on a very cold night. As he left the building he heard what he thought were screams coming from a woman in a parked automobile. He walked over to where the car was parked and had trouble seeing anything, as the windows were steamed up and foggy. The screams continued. Not knowing what to expect, Jared picked up a piece of wood lying on the ground and began to move closer to the car. As he made his way closer, he yelled out to see if anyone could hear him or if the occupant screaming in the car could hear him. As the screams continued, Jared, fearing the worst, began beating the wood on the car and demanding the door be opened. Just as Jared began to take a big swing to try and smash the window in, the door flew open, and Jared, not able to stop himself, slammed the wood onto the head of the male who was exiting the car, killing him with one blow. It all ended up as a very bad mistake. The man Jared killed was with his girlfriend in the car that night celebrating their anniversary. Can a claim of action be brought against Jared and does he have any defenses to his actions, if sued?

The privilege of defense of others can be asserted for the same intentional torts that have been listed previously for self-defense.

Defense of Property

A person who owns property, be it personal or real, is entitled to protect that property and to the peaceful enjoyment of its use. As such, the law provides for individuals to be able to defend their property from unauthorized invasions. This privilege is known as the **defense of property**. Like self-defense and defense of others, the defendant may use only as much force as appears to be reasonably necessary to protect the property. A property owner is required to make a verbal demand to the intruder before the use of force can be exerted except in circumstances in which it appears that the violence or harm is immediate and a demand would be useless to stop the intruder.

defense of property
A justification for the use of force in protecting one's property through such force as must be reasonable under all circumstances.

A property owner does not have a right to use deadly force to defend property even if this is the only way to prevent the intrusion. A property owner may use deadly force only if, coupled with the intrusion, there is a threat of serious bodily harm or death. The law does not generally recognize that the defense of a person's property alone is sufficient enough to use deadly force where a life could be lost. However, the property owner may be able to use deadly force to prevent certain felonies, such as burglary, which is the breaking and entering of the property owner's home or **dwelling place**. However, the property owner can use deadly force against a burglar only if the property owner reasonably believes that this would be the only way to keep the burglar out of the dwelling. This privilege is limited to the cases that involve dwelling places.

dwelling place
The home or other structure in which a person lives.

Some property owners use various devices to protect their property. These devices can range from the use of barbed wire to guard dogs to mechanically rigged devices such as spring guns. The general rule concerning such devices is that a property owner is privileged to use such devices if using the device would equal the same amount of force that the property owner would assert if he or she were defending the property without such a device.

The defense of property can be asserted as a defense for the following intentional torts:

- Assault
- Battery
- Conversion
- False imprisonment
- Infliction of emotional distress
- Trespass to chattels
- Trespass to land

Reentry onto Land

The Model Penal Code is an effort by all 50 states, and has been adopted by many, to make uniform the various state definitions of crimes. Crimes were previously defined by old common law, culminating in various definitions of the same criminal act. The Model Penal Code attempts to make definitions of crimes more concise and standardized.

The Model Penal Code, section 3.06(1)(b), permits the use of non-deadly force to re-enter land if:

1. *the defendant believes that he or the person for whom he is acting was unlawfully dispossessed of the property; and either*

2. *the force is used immediately after dispossession; or*

3. *even if it is not immediate, the defendant believes that the other person has no claim of right to possession of the property. Here, however, re-entry of land (as distinguished from recapture of personal property)* is *not permitted unless the defendant also believes that it would constitute an "exceptional hardship" to delay re-entry until he can obtain a court order.*

Recapture of Chattels

As was seen previously in defense of property, there are instances in which property owners may use force to defend their property. This legal premise is also applied to chattels. This defense is known as a **recapture of chattels**. Property owners, under certain circumstances, may have the right to use force to defend or regain possession of their chattels that have been taken from them.

Certain conditions must be met before a property owner can assert force to recapture a chattel. First, there must have been a tortious dispossession of the property owner from her property by force or fraud or without some type of claim of ownership being asserted by the invader. Second, the property owner must be entitled to immediate possession of the property. Next, the recapture of the chattel must be made promptly upon the property owner discovering the dispossession. If the owner waits a substantial length of time, she cannot use force to regain possession of the chattel. Last, a peaceful demand for a return of the property must have been made first by the property owner.

The owner of a chattel may sometimes use reasonable force to enter the invader's land to recover the missing chattels. The entry onto the land must be made in a reasonable manner and within a reasonable time limit. A delay could negate any privilege asserted by the property owner. Reasonable force may be used to enter the property, but only such force as might have been used reasonably against the landowner personally. However, if the chattels are located on another's property due to the fault of the property owner, that property owner is not entitled to re-enter the land but must bring a court action for the return of the chattels. If the chattels are located on someone else's land due to the fault of the property owner, force or re-entry cannot be used to recover them.

> **recapture of chattels**
> The act of recovering personal property by a property owner.

Necessity

The defense of **necessity** does not involve an excuse for the defendant to cause harm to the plaintiff in order to prevent a threatened injury from some force of nature. The defendant may harm the property interests of another person where it is necessary to prevent great harm to himself or other people. If the action is used to protect a substantial number of people, then the privilege is said to be that of public necessity. If the defense is asserted because the defendant alone was facing the harm, then the

> **necessity**
> Individuals are excused from criminal and sometimes tortious liability if they act under a duress of circumstances to protect life or limb or health in a reasonable manner and with no other acceptable choices.

EYE ON ETHICS

Each state provides its own legal processes for recovering property. The reason that such legal processes are established is to provide a method for property owners to recapture their property without resorting to the use of force. Preserving the public interest of keeping the peace is more important than preventing inconvenience to a property owner.

CASE FACT PATTERN

During Hurricane Katrina, many people faced tremendously harmful, perilous, and even deadly situations as a result of the hurricane and subsequent flooding of the city of New Orleans when the levies broke. To protect themselves and others, individuals broke into houses and buildings to seek shelter from the potentially deadly consequences of remaining where they were. Under ordinary conditions, the breaking and entering of houses, buildings, and property would be not only criminal but also tortious interference with the owner's property rights. However, under such extreme conditions, in which many people were facing death or serious injury, it was a necessity for them to seek safe shelter. Therefore, should any property owners bring an action against individuals who sought refuge on their property during the hurricane, the defendants could assert a defense of necessity.

privilege is known as a private necessity. If the privilege is asserted as a public necessity, the defendant will not be responsible to pay for any damages sustained by the plaintiff. However, if the defendant is protecting himself as a private necessity, then he will be responsible to pay for any damages resulting from the intrusion.

The fundamental nature of this defense is the avoidance of the greater harm to oneself or others by choosing a lesser injury or harm. The elements required to assert a defense of necessity are:

- The defendant must commit an intentional tort against the property or person of another.
- A threat of a more serious injury to the defendant or others must exist.
- The threat of serious injury must be coming from some other source that is not the plaintiff.
- Avoiding the threat would result in a greater harm than the injury caused by the defendant's actions.

The defense of necessity can be asserted for the following intentional torts:

- Assault
- Battery
- Trespass to chattels
- Trespass to land

Justification

It is often said that when all other tort defenses fail, a defendant may use the defense of justification. Justification essentially states that the tortfeasor was somehow warranted in his action. This defense will often arise when the court believes that it would be unfair to hold the person liable for his actions. *See Sindle v. New York Transit Authority* 33 N.Y.2d 293.

Discipline

discipline
Instruction, comprehending the communication of knowledge and training to observe and act in accordance with rules and order.

At times, a person's job requires that she maintain a degree of **discipline** in order to maintain order. Jobs that require the maintenance of discipline are teachers and military officers. Also, parents and guardians may be able to assert this defense when having to discipline a child. A person asserting discipline must exert only reasonable force necessary for the situation. The *Restatement (Second) of Torts*, section 147, provides the following guidance toward reasonable discipline:

1. *A parent is privileged to apply such reasonable force or to impose such reasonable confinement upon his child as he reasonably believes to be necessary for its proper control, training, or education.*

> 2. *One other than a parent who has been given by law or has voluntarily assumed in whole or in part the function of controlling, training, or educating a child, is privileged to apply such reasonable force necessary for its proper control, training, or education, except in so far as the parent has restricted the privilege of one to whom he has entrusted the child.*

The privilege does not extend to any person whose conduct is considered unreasonable under the circumstances, and circumstances will vary greatly depending on the age of the child, the child's size, or the child's behavioral tendencies, such as mental impairment or other special circumstances. Local and state laws regulate this area. Many defendants have asserted the defense of discipline when in fact their conduct has violated state child abuse laws. Each situation is different, and each state highly regulates these areas.

Loco Parentis

With discipline, the idea of **loco parentis,** Latin for "in place of the parent," should also be mentioned. This concept essentially states that the person placed in the position of the parent has all the discipline defenses and rights that the parent could potentially raise. These rights include the use of reasonable force and corporal punishment for discipline and control.

When dealing with intentional torts, always keep in mind that the defendant will more than likely assert a defense. These defenses can absolve defendants from liability to plaintiffs for their actions.

loco parentis
Of, relating to, or acting as a temporary guardian or caretaker of a child, taking on all or some of the responsibilities of a parent.

Summary

The defendant may raise a defense against a plaintiff's claim that an intentional tort has been committed against the plaintiff. A defense is a legal justification or excuse. The concept of a defense is such that even if the defendant committed a tort or a violation, he may not be held liable for his actions because he may have a legal justification to the action.

A defense is not an element to a tort. A defense is brought up after the entire intentional tort has already been completed. That means the defendant has committed the intentional tort against the plaintiff and that the plaintiff has met her burden of proof by demonstrating that all of the elements of the intentional tort have been satisfied. At that time, the defendant can bring up a defense in order to avoid liability for her actions.

Defenses are largely grouped into two categories: (1) the defense that the plaintiff consented to the action or invasion into his interest; and (2) defenses that are imposed as a matter of law. Defenses that are imposed as matter of law are called privileges. A defendant may be entitled to use a privilege if his actions further a social interest that is entitled to protection.

If a person legally consents to a particular action by the defendant, then that action is not a tort. Consent means that the plaintiff was in possession of her full mental capacity and was completely knowledgeable of all of the facts. Consent negates the wrongful act by the defendant.

With the privilege of self-defense, the law has recognized the need to excuse a defendant's actions if they were based on the necessity to take reasonable steps to prevent harm to himself, to someone else, or to property. Just as in criminal law, tort law provides for the defense of self-defense. The defense is applied similarly in both criminal law and tort law.

Reasonable force means that the force used must match the threat, meaning that people cannot use more force than is reasonably necessary to defend themselves.

As is true with self-defense, the law recognizes that there are instances when a person may have to use force to defend others from a threat of harm. This defense is known as the defense of others. If another person or persons is exposed to a threat of death or serious bodily harm, a defendant can assert the defense of others in that situation. The courts allow the use of reasonable force to defend others. However, as with the self-defense, the defendant must only use that force that is reasonably necessary for the situation and can only use deadly force if others are threatened with death or serious bodily injury.

A person who owns property, be it personal or real, is entitled to protect that property and to the peaceful enjoyment of its use. As such, the law provides for individuals to be able to defend their property from unauthorized invasions. This privilege is known as the defense of property. Like self-defense and defense of others, the defendant may only use as much force as appears to be reasonably necessary to protect the property. A property owner is required to make a verbal demand to the intruder before the use of force can be exerted, except in circumstances where it appears that the violence or harm is immediate and a demand would be useless to stop the intruder.

As was seen previously in defense of property, there are instances in which property owners may use force to defend their property. This legal premise is also applied to chattels. This defense is known as a recapture of chattels. Property owners, under certain circumstances, may have the right to use force to defend or regain possession of their chattels that have been taken from them.

The defense of necessity does not involve an excuse for the defendant to cause harm to the plaintiff in order to prevent a threatened injury from some force of nature. Defendants may harm the property interests of another person where it is necessary to prevent great harm to themselves or other people. If the action is used to protect a substantial number of people, then the privilege is said to be that of public necessity. If the defense is asserted because the defendant alone was facing the harm, then the privilege is known as a private necessity. If the privilege is asserted as a public necessity, the defendant will not be responsible to pay for any damages sustained by the plaintiff. However, if defendants are protecting themselves as a private necessity, then they must pay for any damages resulting from the intrusion.

At times, individuals' jobs require that they maintain a degree of discipline in order to maintain order. Jobs that require the maintenance of discipline are teachers and military officers. Also, parents and guardians may be able to assert this defense when having to discipline a child. A person asserting discipline must only exert reasonable force necessary for the situation.

Key Terms

Capacity	Loco parentis
Consent	Necessity
Defense	Privilege
Defense of others	Reasonable person
Defense of property	Recapture of chattels
Discipline	Self-defense
Dwelling place	

Review Questions

1. When is consent ineffective?
2. What is reasonable force?
3. What is the difference between private necessity and public necessity?
4. What is a defense?
5. What is a privilege?
6. When can self-defense be used?
7. When can defense of others be used?

8. When can discipline be used?

9. What types of positions do people hold that may be entitled to the use of the defense of discipline?

10. Is a defense an element of a tort? If so, why? If not, why not?

---

1. At an elementary school in Anytown, California, a five-year-old girl throws a tantrum in her classroom. The teacher calls the principal, who brings the girl to the office. The little girl's tantrum escalates, and she begins to hit the principal. The principal proceeds to tie up the little girl and calls both her mother and the police. The little girl is released once the police have arrived. Research California law and determine whether the principal can assert a defense of discipline if an action for assault and battery is brought on behalf of the little girl by her mother.

2. Peter is sailing his sailboat on a lake. While he is sailing, a severe thunderstorm comes up and begins to violently toss the boat around the lake. Peter heads for shore where he sees a nearby dock at a house. Peter ties the boat to the dock and breaks into the house until the storm passes. The boat damages the dock, and Peter broke a window in the house. If the landowners bring a lawsuit against Peter for trespass to land and damages, what will be the results? Explain.

3. Leslie and Cindy are competing at a horse show. The two often see each other at horse shows as they compete regularly in the same local area. Cindy has forgotten her riding pants and asks Leslie if she can borrow her pants so that she can compete as scheduled. Leslie consents and gives Cindy the pants. Unbeknownst to Cindy, Leslie had placed her diamond ring in the pocket of the pants for safekeeping while she rode her horse in the horse show. Cindy borrows the pants and finishes the competition. After the competition, Leslie leaves the show grounds, forgetting that she has lent the pants to Cindy. Cindy cannot find Leslie in order to return the pants, so Cindy heads home thinking that she will return the pants at the next horse show. If Leslie brings an action for trespass to chattels for both the pants and the diamond ring, what will be the results? Explain.

4. Is a reasonable person standard truly based on an objective standard? Is there such a standard in reality? Is the standard based on a male or female viewpoint and/or bias? Please explain your answer in terms of law. Research where and how the standard developed.

5. We may defend ourselves and others against attack on our persons. Do we have to, though, by law? Is there anything in the law that states whether or not you must come to the aid of another? Does it depend on who you are?

6. Can booby traps be used by homeowners to defend their property, house and land? Can the homeowner resort to a pre-emptive defense, of sorts, before anything has happened?

 PORTFOLIO ASSIGNMENT

Contact the State of Louisiana, the New Orleans mayor's office, and/or the parish authorities in New Orleans to see if they have any numbers or any percentages of people who took refuge by entering another's home during Katrina and claimed necessity as a reason for doing such. Check the police authorities as well to see if they have statistics on the issue.

Vocabulary Builders

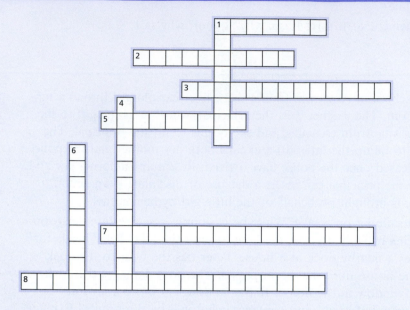

Instructions

Use the key terms from this chapter to fill in the answers to the crossword puzzle.

NOTE: When the answer is more than one word, leave a blank space between the words.

ACROSS

1. All parties to a novation must knowingly assent to the substitution of either the obligations or parties to the agreement.
2. Instruction, comprehending the communication of knowledge and training to observe and act in accordance with rules and order.
3. Of, relating to, or acting as a temporary guardian of caretaker of a child, taking on all or some of the responsibilities of a parent.
5. Individuals are excused from criminal and sometimes tortious liability if they act under a duress of circumstances to protect life or limb or health in a reasonable manner and with no other acceptable choices.
7. A hypothetical person used as a legal standard, especially to determine whether someone acted with negligence; specifically, a person who exercises the degree of attention, knowledge, intelligence, and judgment that society requires of its members for the protection of their own and of others' interests.
8. A justification for the use of force in protecting one's property through such force as must be reasonable under all circumstances.

DOWN

1. The ability to understand the nature and significance of a contract; to understand or comprehend specific acts or reasoning.
4. A defendant's legal excuse that the use of force was justified.
6. Reasonable expectation of privacy and confidentiality for communications in furtherance of the relationship such as attorney–client, doctor–patient, husband–wife, psychotherapist–patient, and priest–penitent.

VERNONIA SCHOOL DIST. 47J v. ACTON, ___ U.S. ___ (1995)

No. 94-590.

Argued March 28, 1995

Decided June 26, 1995

[Text omitted]

JUSTICE SCALIA delivered the opinion of the Court.

The Student Athlete Drug Policy adopted by School District 47J in the town of Vernonia, Oregon, authorizes random urinalysis drug testing of students who participate in the District's school athletics programs. We granted certiorari to decide whether this violates the Fourth and Fourteenth Amendments to the United States Constitution.

I

A

Petitioner Vernonia School District 47J (District) operates one high school and three grade schools in the logging community of Vernonia, Oregon. As elsewhere in small-town America, school sports play a prominent role in the town's life, and student athletes are admired in their schools and in the community.

Drugs had not been a major problem in Vernonia schools. In the mid-to-late 1980's, however, teachers and administrators observed a sharp increase in drug use. Students began to speak out about their attraction to the drug culture, and to boast that there was nothing the school could do about it. Along with more drugs came more disciplinary problems. Between 1988 and 1989 the number of disciplinary referrals in Vernonia schools rose to more than twice the number reported in the early 1980's, and several students were suspended. Students became increasingly rude during class; outbursts of profane language became common.

Not only were student athletes included among the drug users but, as the District Court found, athletes were the leaders of the drug culture. 796 F. Supp. 1354, 1357 (D. Ore. 1992). This caused the District's administrators particular concern, since drug use increases the risk of sports-related injury. Expert testimony at the trial confirmed the deleterious effects of drugs on motivation, memory, judgment, reaction, coordination, and performance. The high school football and wrestling coach witnessed a severe sternum injury suffered by a wrestler, and various omissions of safety procedures and misexecutions by football players, all attributable in his belief to the effects of drug use.

Initially, the District responded to the drug problem by offering special classes, speakers, and presentations designed to deter drug use. It even brought in a specially trained dog to detect drugs, but the drug problem persisted. According to the District Court:

"[T]he administration was at its wits end and . . . a large segment of the student body, particularly those involved in interscholastic athletics, was in a state of rebellion. Disciplinary problems had reached 'epidemic proportions.' The coincidence of an almost three-fold increase in classroom disruptions and disciplinary reports along with the staff's direct observations of students using drugs or glamorizing drug and alcohol use led the administration to the inescapable conclusion that the rebellion was being fueled by alcohol and drug abuse as well as the student's misperceptions about the drug culture."

At that point, District officials began considering a drug-testing program. They held a parent "input night" to discuss the proposed Student Athlete Drug Policy (Policy), and the parents in attendance gave their unanimous approval. The school board approved the Policy for implementation in the fall of 1989. Its expressed purpose is to prevent student athletes from using drugs, to protect their health and safety, and to provide drug users with assistance programs.

B

The Policy applies to all students participating in interscholastic athletics. Students wishing to play sports must sign a form consenting to the testing and must obtain the written consent of their parents. Athletes are tested at the beginning of the season for their sport. In addition, once each week of the season the names of the athletes are placed in a "pool" from which a student, with the supervision of two adults, blindly draws the names of 10% of the athletes for random testing. Those selected are notified and tested that same day, if possible.

The student to be tested completes a specimen control form which bears an assigned number. Prescription medications that the student is taking must be identified by providing a copy of the prescription or a doctor's authorization. The student then enters an empty locker room accompanied by an adult monitor of the same gender. Each boy selected produces a sample at a urinal, remaining fully clothed with his back to the monitor, who stands approximately 12 to 15 feet behind the student. Monitors may (though do not always) watch the student while he produces the sample, and they listen for normal sounds of urination. Girls produce samples in an enclosed bathroom stall, so that they can be heard but not observed. After the sample is produced, it is given to the monitor, who checks it for temperature and tampering and then transfers it to a vial.

The samples are sent to an independent laboratory, which routinely tests them for amphetamines, cocaine, and marijuana. Other drugs, such as LSD, may be screened at the request of the District, but the identity of a particular student does not determine which drugs will be tested. The laboratory's procedures are 99.94% accurate. The District follows strict procedures regarding the chain of custody and access to test results. The laboratory does not know the identity of the students whose samples it tests. It is authorized to mail written test reports only to the superintendent and to provide test results to District personnel by telephone only after the requesting official recites a code confirming his authority. Only the superintendent, principals, vice-principals, and athletic directors have access to test results, and the results are not kept for more than one year.

If a sample tests positive, a second test is administered as soon as possible to confirm the result. If the second test is negative, no further action is taken. If the second test is positive, the athlete's parents are notified, and the school principal convenes a meeting with the student and his parents, at which the student is given the option of (1) participating for six weeks in an assistance program that includes weekly urinalysis, or (2) suffering suspension from athletics for the remainder of the current season and the next athletic season. The student is then retested prior to the start of the next athletic season for which he or she is eligible. The Policy states that a second offense results in automatic imposition of option (2); a third offense in suspension for the remainder of the current season and the next two athletic seasons.

C

In the fall of 1991, respondent James Acton, then a seventh-grader, signed up to play football at one of the District's grade schools. He was denied participation, however, because he and his parents refused to sign the testing consent forms. The Actons filed suit, seeking declaratory and injunctive relief from enforcement of the Policy on the grounds that it violated the Fourth and Fourteenth Amendments to the United States Constitution and Article I, 9, of the Oregon Constitution. After a bench trial, the District Court entered an order denying the claims on the merits and dismissing the action. 796 F. Supp., at 1355. The United States Court of Appeals for the Ninth Circuit reversed, holding that the Policy violated both the Fourth and Fourteenth Amendments and Article I, 9, of the Oregon Constitution. 23 F.3d 1514 (1994). We granted certiorari. 513 U.S. ___ (1994).

II

The Fourth Amendment to the United States Constitution provides that the Federal Government shall not violate "[t]he right of the people to be secure in their persons, houses, papers, and effects, against unreasonable searches and seizures, ..." We have held that the Fourteenth Amendment extends this constitutional guarantee to searches and seizures by state officers, *Elkins v. United States*, 364 U.S. 206, 213 (1960), including public school officials, *New Jersey v. T.L.O.*, 469 U.S. 325, 336–337 (1985). In *Skinner v. Railway Labor Executives' Assn.*, 489 U.S. 602, 617 (1989), we held that state-compelled collection and testing of urine, such as that required by the Student Athlete Drug Policy, constitutes a "search" subject to the demands of the Fourth Amendment. *See also Treasury Employees v. Von Raab*, 489 U.S. 656, 665 (1989).

As the text of the Fourth Amendment indicates, the ultimate measure of the constitutionality of a governmental search is "reasonableness." At least in a case such as this, where

there was no clear practice, either approving or disapproving the type of search at issue, at the time the constitutional provision was enacted, whether a particular search meets the reasonableness standard "'is judged by balancing its intrusion on the individual's Fourth Amendment interests against its promotion of legitimate governmental interests.'" *Skinner, supra,* at 619 (quoting *Delaware v. Prouse,* 440 U.S. 648, 654 (1979)). Where a search is undertaken by law enforcement officials to discover evidence of criminal wrongdoing, this Court has said that reasonableness generally requires the obtaining of a judicial warrant, *Skinner, supra,* at 619. Warrants cannot be issued, of course, without the showing of probable cause required by the Warrant Clause. But a warrant is not required to establish the reasonableness of all government searches; and when a warrant is not required (and the Warrant Clause therefore not applicable), probable cause is not invariably required either. A search unsupported by probable cause can be constitutional, we have said, "when special needs, beyond the normal need for law enforcement, make the warrant and probable-cause requirement impracticable." *Griffin v. Wisconsin,* 483 U.S. 868, 873 (1987) (internal quotation marks omitted).

We have found such "special needs" to exist in the public-school context. There, the warrant requirement "would unduly interfere with the maintenance of the swift and informal disciplinary procedures [that are] needed," and "strict adherence to the requirement that searches be based upon probable cause" would undercut "the substantial need of teachers and administrators for freedom to maintain order in the schools." *T.L.O., supra,* at 340, 341. The school search we approved in *T.L.O.,* while not based on probable cause, was based on individualized suspicion of wrongdoing. As we explicitly acknowledged, however, "'the Fourth Amendment imposes no irreducible requirement of such suspicion,'" *id.,* at 342, n. 8 (quoting *United States v. Martinez-Fuerte,* 428 U.S. 543, 560–561 (1976)). We have upheld suspicionless searches and seizures to conduct drug testing of railroad personnel involved in train accidents, *see Skinner, supra;* to conduct random drug testing of federal customs officers who carry arms or are involved in drug interdiction, *see Von Raab, supra;* and to maintain automobile checkpoints looking for illegal immigrants and contraband, *Martinez-Fuerte, supra,* and drunk drivers, *Michigan Dept. of State Police v. Sitz,* 496 U.S. 444 (1990).

III

The first factor to be considered is the nature of the privacy interest upon which the search here at issue intrudes. The Fourth Amendment does not protect all subjective expectations of privacy, but only those that society recognizes as "legitimate." *T.L.O.,* 469 U.S., at 338. What expectations are legitimate varies, of course, with context, *id.,* at 337, depending, for example, upon whether the individual asserting the privacy interest is at home, at work, in a car, or in a public park. In addition, the legitimacy of certain privacy expectations vis-a-vis the State may depend upon the individual's legal relationship with the State. For example, in *Griffin, supra,* we held that, although a "probationer's home, like anyone else's, is protected by the Fourth Amendmen[t]," the supervisory relationship between probationer and State justifies "a degree of impingement upon [a probationer's] privacy that would not be constitutional if applied to the public at large." 483 U.S., at 873 , 875. Central, in our view, to the present case is the fact that the subjects of the Policy are (1) children, who (2) have been committed to the temporary custody of the State as schoolmaster.

Traditionally at common law, and still today, unemancipated minors lack some of the most fundamental rights of self-determination—including even the right of liberty in its narrow sense, i.e., the right to come and go at will. They are subject, even as to their physical freedom, to the control of their parents or guardians. *See* 59 Am. Jur. 2d 10 (1987). When parents place minor children in private schools for their education, the teachers and administrators of those schools stand in loco parentis over the children entrusted to them. In fact, the tutor or schoolmaster is the very prototype of that status. As Blackstone describes it, a parent "may . . . delegate part of his parental authority, during his life, to the tutor or schoolmaster of his child; who is then in loco parentis, and has such a portion of the power of the parent committed to his charge, viz. that of restraint and correction, as may be necessary to answer the purposes for which he is employed." 1 W. Blackstone, *Commentaries on the Laws of England* 441 (1769).

In *T.L.O.* we rejected the notion that public schools, like private schools, exercise only parental power over their students, which of course is not subject to constitutional constraints. *T.L.O.,* 469 U.S., at 336 . Such a view of things, we said, "is not entirely 'consonant with compulsory education laws,'" *ibid.* (quoting *Ingraham v. Wright,* 430 U.S. 651, 662 (1977)), and is inconsistent with our prior decisions treating school officials as state actors for purposes of the Due Process and Free Speech Clauses, *T.L.O., supra,* at 336. But while denying that the State's power over schoolchildren is formally no more [than the delegated power of their parents), *T.L.O.* did not deny, but indeed emphasized, that the nature of that power is custodial and tutelary, permitting a degree of supervision and control that could not be exercised over free adults. "[A] proper educational environment requires close supervision of schoolchildren, as well as the enforcement of rules against conduct that would be perfectly permissible if undertaken by an adult." 469 U.S., at 339. While we do not, of course, suggest that public schools as a general matter have such a degree of control over children as to give rise to a constitutional "duty to protect," *see DeShaney v. Winnebago County Dept. of Social Servs.,* 489 U.S. 189, 200 (1989), we have acknowledged that for many purposes "school authorities ac[t] in loco parentis," *Bethel School Dist. No. 403 v. Fraser,* 478 U.S. 675, 684 (1986), with the power and indeed the duty to "inculcate the habits and manners of civility," *id.,* at 681 (internal quotation marks omitted). Thus, while children assuredly do not "shed their constitutional rights . . . at the schoolhouse gate," *Tinker v. Des Moines Independent Community School Dist.,* 393 U.S. 503, 506 (1969), the nature of those rights is what is appropriate for children in school. *See, e.g., Goss v. Lopez,* 419 U.S. 565, 581–582 (1975) (due process for a student challenging disciplinary suspension requires only that the teacher "informally discuss the alleged misconduct with the student minutes after it has occurred"); *Fraser, supra,* at 683 ("[I]t is a highly appropriate function of public school education to prohibit the use of vulgar and offensive terms in public discourse"); *Hazlewood School Dist. v. Kuhlmeier,* 484 U.S. 260, 273 (1988) (public school authorities may censor school-sponsored publications, so long as the censorship is "reasonably related to legitimate pedagogical

concerns"); *Ingraham, supra,* at 682 ("[I]mposing additional administrative safeguards [upon corporal punishment] . . . would . . . entail a significant intrusion into an area of primary educational responsibility").

Fourth Amendment rights, no less than First and Fourteenth Amendment rights, are different in public schools than elsewhere; the "reasonableness" inquiry cannot disregard the schools' custodial and tutelary responsibility for children. For their own good and that of their classmates, public school children are routinely required to submit to various physical examinations, and to be vaccinated against various diseases. According to the American Academy of Pediatrics, most public schools "provide vision and hearing screening and dental and dermatological checks. . . . Others also mandate scoliosis screening at appropriate grade levels." Committee on School Health, American Academy of Pediatrics, *School Health: A Guide for Health Professionals* 2 (1987). In the 1991–1992 school year, all 50 States required public-school students to be vaccinated against diphtheria, measles, rubella, and polio. U.S. Dept. of Health & Human Services, Public Health Service, Centers for Disease Control, *State Immunization Requirements 1991–1992,* p. 1. Particularly with regard to medical examinations and procedures, therefore, "students within the school environment have a lesser expectation of privacy than members of the population generally." *T.L.O.,* 469 U.S., at 348 (Powell, J., concurring).

Legitimate privacy expectations are even less with regard to student athletes. School sports are not for the bashful. They require "suiting up" before each practice or event, and showering and changing afterwards. Public school locker rooms, the usual sites for these activities, are not notable for the privacy they afford. The locker rooms in Vernonia are typical: no individual dressing rooms are provided; shower heads are lined up along a wall, unseparated by any sort of partition or curtain; not even all the toilet stalls have doors. As the United States Court of Appeals for the Seventh Circuit has noted, there is "an element of 'communal undress' inherent in athletic participation," *Schaill by Kross v. Tippecanoe County School Corp.,* 864 F.2d 1309, 1318 (1988).

There is an additional respect in which school athletes have a reduced expectation of privacy. By choosing to "go out for the team," they voluntarily subject themselves to a degree of regulation even higher than that imposed on students generally. In Vernonia's public schools, they must submit to a preseason physical exam (James testified that his included the giving of a urine sample, App. 17), they must acquire adequate insurance coverage or sign an insurance waiver, maintain a minimum grade point average, and comply with any "rules of conduct, dress, training hours and related matters as may be established for each sport by the head coach and athletic director with the principal's approval." Somewhat like adults who choose to participate in a "closely regulated industry," students who voluntarily participate in school athletics have reason to expect intrusions upon normal rights and privileges, including privacy. *See Skinner,* 489 U.S., at 627; *United States v. Biswell,* 406 U.S. 311, 316 (1972).

IV

Having considered the scope of the legitimate expectation of privacy at issue here, we turn next to the character of the intrusion that is complained of. We recognized in *Skinner* that collecting the samples for urinalysis intrudes upon "an excretory function traditionally shielded by great privacy." *Skinner*, 489 U.S., at 626. We noted, however, that the degree of intrusion depends upon the manner in which production of the urine sample is monitored. *Ibid.* Under the District's Policy, male students produce samples at a urinal along a wall. They remain fully clothed and are only observed from behind, if at all. Female students produce samples in an enclosed stall, with a female monitor standing outside listening only for sounds of tampering. These conditions are nearly identical to those typically encountered in public restrooms, which men, women, and especially school children use daily. Under such conditions, the privacy interests compromised by the process of obtaining the urine sample are in our view negligible. The other privacy-invasive aspect of urinalysis is, of course, the information it discloses concerning the state of the subject's body, and the materials he has ingested. In this regard it is significant that the tests at issue here look only for drugs, and not for whether the student is, for example, epileptic, pregnant, or diabetic. *See Skinner, supra,* at 617. Moreover, the drugs for which the samples are screened are standard, and do not vary according to the identity of the student. And finally, the results of the tests are disclosed only to a limited class of school personnel who have a need to know; and they are not turned over to law enforcement authorities or used for any internal disciplinary function. 796 F. Supp., at 1364; *see also* 23 F.3d, at 1521. Respondents argue, however, that the District's Policy is in fact more intrusive than this suggests, because it requires the students, if they are to avoid sanctions for a falsely positive test, to identify in advance prescription medications they are taking. We agree that this raises some cause for concern. In *Von Raab,* we flagged as one of the salutary features of the Customs Service drug-testing program the fact that employees were not required to disclose medical information unless they tested positive, and, even then, the information was supplied to a licensed physician rather than to the Government employer. *See Von Raab,* 489 U.S., at 672–673, n. 2. On the other hand, we have never indicated that requiring advance disclosure of medications is per se unreasonable. Indeed, in *Skinner* we held that it was not "a significant invasion of privacy." *Skinner,* 489 U.S., at 626 , n. 7. It can be argued that, in *Skinner,* the disclosure went only to the medical personnel taking the sample, and the Government personnel analyzing it, *see id.,* at 609, *but see id.,* at 610 (railroad personnel responsible for forwarding the sample, and presumably accompanying information, to the Government's testing lab); and that disclosure to teachers and coaches—to persons who personally know the student—is a greater invasion of privacy. Assuming for the sake of argument that both those propositions are true, we do not believe they establish a difference that respondents are entitled to rely on here.

The General Authorization Form that respondents refused to sign, which refusal was the basis for James's exclusion from the sports program, said only (in relevant part): "I . . . authorize the Vernonia School District to conduct a test on a urine specimen which I provide to test for drugs and/or alcohol use. I also authorize the release of information concerning the results of such a test to the Vernonia School District and to the parents and/or guardians of the student." App. 10-11. While the practice of the District seems to have been to have a school official take medication information from the student at the time of the test, see App. 29, 42, that practice is not set forth in, or required by, the Policy, which says simply: "Student athletes who . . . are or have been taking prescription medication must provide verification (either by a copy of the prescription or by doctor's authorization) prior to being tested." App. 8. It may well be that, if and when James was selected for random testing at a time that he was taking medication, the School District would have permitted him to provide the requested information in a confidential manner—for example, in a sealed envelope delivered to the testing lab. Nothing in the Policy contradicts that, and when respondents choose, in effect, to challenge the Policy on its face, we will not assume the worst. Accordingly, we reach the same conclusion as in *Skinner:* that the invasion of privacy was not significant.

V

Finally, we turn to consider the nature and immediacy of the governmental concern at issue here, and the efficacy of this means for meeting it. In both *Skinner* and *Von Raab,* we characterized the government interest motivating the search as "compelling." *Skinner, supra,* at 628 (interest in preventing railway accidents); *Von Raab, supra,* at 670 (interest in insuring fitness of customs officials to interdict drugs and handle firearms). Relying on these cases, the District Court held that because the District's program also called for drug testing in the absence of individualized suspicion, the District "must demonstrate a 'compelling need' for the program." 796 F. Supp., at 1363. The Court of Appeals appears to have agreed with this view. *See* 23 F.3d, at 1526. It is a mistake, however, to think that the phrase "compelling state interest," in the Fourth Amendment context, describes a fixed, minimum quantum of governmental concern, so that one can dispose of a case by answering in isolation the question: Is there a compelling state interest here? Rather, the phrase describes an interest which appears important enough to justify the particular search at hand, in light of other factors which show the search to be relatively intrusive upon a genuine expectation of privacy. Whether that relatively high degree of government concern is necessary in this case or not, we think it is met.

That the nature of the concern is important—indeed, perhaps compelling can hardly be doubted. Deterring drug use by our Nation's schoolchildren is at least as important as enhancing efficient enforcement of the Nation's laws against the importation of drugs, which was the governmental concern in *Von Raab, supra,* at 668, or deterring drug use by engineers and trainmen, which was the governmental concern in *Skinner, supra,* at 628. School years are the time when the physical, psychological, and addictive effects of drugs are most severe. "Maturing nervous systems are more critically impaired by intoxicants than mature ones are; childhood losses in learning are lifelong and profound"; "children grow chemically dependent more quickly than adults, and their record of recovery is depressingly poor." Hawley, The Bumpy Road to Drug-Free Schools, 72 *Phi Delta Kappan* 310, 314 (1990). *See also* Estroff, Schwartz, & Hoffmann, Adolescent Cocaine Abuse: Addictive Potential, Behavioral and Psychiatric Effects, 28 *Clinical Pediatrics* 550 (Dec. 1989); Kandel, Davies, Karus, & Yamaguchi, The Consequences in Young Adulthood of Adolescent Drug Involvement, 43 *Arch. Gen. Psychiatry* 746 (Aug. 1986). And of course the effects of a drug-infested school are visited not just upon the users, but upon the entire student body and faculty, as the educational process is disrupted. In the present case, moreover, the necessity for the State to act is magnified by the fact that this evil is being visited not just upon individuals at large, but upon children for whom it has undertaken a special responsibility of care and direction. Finally, it must not be lost sight of that this program is directed more narrowly to drug use by school athletes, where the risk of immediate physical harm to the drug user or those with whom he is playing his sport is particularly high. Apart from psychological effects, which include impairment of judgment, slow reaction time, and a lessening of the perception of pain, the particular drugs screened by the District's Policy have been demonstrated to pose substantial physical risks to athletes. Amphetamines produce an "artificially induced heart rate increase, [p]eripheral vasoconstriction, [b]lood pressure increase, and [m]asking of the normal fatigue response," making them a "very dangerous drug when used during exercise of any type." Hawkins, Drugs and Other Ingesta: Effects on Athletic Performance, in H. Appenzeller, *Managing Sports and Risk Management Strategies* 90, 90–91 (1993). Marijuana causes "[i]rregular blood pressure responses during changes in body position," "[r]eduction in the oxygen-carrying capacity of the blood," and "[i]nhibition of the normal sweating responses resulting in increased body temperature." *Id.*, at 94. Cocaine produces "[v]asoconstriction[,] [e]levated blood pressure," and "[p]ossible coronary artery spasms and myocardial infarction." *Ibid.*

As for the immediacy of the District's concerns: We are not inclined to question—indeed, we could not possibly find clearly erroneous—the District Court's conclusion that "a large segment of the student body, particularly those involved in interscholastic athletics, was in a state of rebellion," that "[d]isciplinary actions had reached 'epidemic proportions,'" and that "the rebellion was being fueled by alcohol and drug abuse as well as by the student's misperceptions about the drug culture." 796 F. Supp., at 1357. That is an immediate crisis of greater proportions than existed in *Skinner*, where we upheld the Government's drug testing program based on findings of drug use by railroad employees nationwide, without proof that a problem existed on the particular railroads whose employees were subject to the test. *See Skinner*, 489 U.S., at 607. And of much greater proportions than existed in *Von Raab*, where there was no documented history of drug use by any customs officials. *See Von Raab*, 489 U.S., at 673; *id.*, at 683 (SCALIA, J., dissenting).

As to the efficacy of this means for addressing the problem: It seems to us self-evident that a drug problem largely fueled by the "role model" effect of athletes' drug use, and of particular danger to athletes, is effectively addressed by making sure that athletes do not use drugs. Respondents argue that a "less intrusive means to the same end" was available, namely, "drug testing on suspicion of drug use." Brief for Respondents 45–46. We have repeatedly refused to declare that only the "least intrusive" search practicable can be reasonable under the Fourth Amendment. *Skinner, supra*, at 629, n. 9 (collecting cases). Respondents' alternative entails substantial difficulties—if it is indeed practicable at all. It may be impracticable, for one thing, simply because the parents who are willing to accept random drug testing for athletes are not willing to accept accusatory drug testing for all students, which transforms the process into a badge of shame. Respondents' proposal brings the risk that teachers will impose testing arbitrarily upon troublesome but not drug-likely students. It generates the expense of defending

lawsuits that charge such arbitrary imposition, or that simply demand greater process before accusatory drug testing is imposed. And not least of all, it adds to the ever-expanding diversionary duties of schoolteachers the new function of spotting and bringing to account drug abuse, a task for which they are ill prepared, and which is not readily compatible with their vocation. *Cf. Skinner, supra*, at 628 (quoting 50 Fed. Reg. 31526 (1985)) (a drug impaired individual "will seldom display any outward 'signs detectable by the lay person or, in many cases, even the physician.'"); *Goss*, 419 U.S., at 594 (Powell, J., dissenting) ("There is an ongoing relationship, one in which the teacher must occupy many roles - educator, adviser, friend, and, at times, parent-substitute. It is rarely adversary in nature . . . ") (footnote omitted). In many respects, we think, testing based on "suspicion" of drug use would not be better, but worse.

VI

Taking into account all the factors we have considered above—the decreased expectation of privacy, the relative unobtrusiveness of the search, and the severity of the need met by the search—we conclude Vernonia's Policy is reasonable and hence constitutional.

We caution against the assumption that suspicionless drug testing will readily pass constitutional muster in other contexts. The most significant element in this case is the first we discussed: that the Policy was undertaken in furtherance of the government's responsibilities, under a public school system, as guardian and tutor of children entrusted to its care. Just as when the government conducts a search in its capacity as employer (a warrantless search of an absent employee's desk to obtain an urgently needed file, for example), the relevant question is whether that intrusion upon privacy is one that a reasonable employer might engage in, *see O'Connor v. Ortega*, 480 U.S. 709 (1987); so also when the government acts as guardian and tutor the relevant question is whether the search is one that a reasonable guardian and tutor might undertake. Given the findings of need made by the District Court, we conclude that in the present case it is.

We may note that the primary guardians of Vernonia's schoolchildren appear to agree. The record shows no objection to this districtwide program by any parents other than the couple before us here—even though, as we have described, a public meeting was held to obtain parents' views. We find insufficient basis to contradict the judgment of Vernonia's parents, its school board, and the District Court, as to what was reasonably in the interest of these children under the circumstances.

* * *

The Ninth Circuit held that Vernonia's Policy not only violated the Fourth Amendment, but also, by reason of that violation, contravened Article I, Section 9 of the Oregon Constitution. Our conclusion that the former holding was in error means that the latter holding rested on a flawed premise. We therefore vacate the judgment, and remand the case to the Court of Appeals for further proceedings consistent with this opinion.

It is so ordered.

[Footnotes omitted]

Source: Reprinted with Permission from Westlaw.

Chapter 5

Negligence: Duty and Breach of Duty

CHAPTER OBJECTIVES

Upon completion of this chapter, you will be able to:

- Define the tort of negligence.
- Identify the elements of negligence.
- Explain foreseeability.
- Understand the reasonable person test.
- Discuss the concept of the duty of care.
- Explain breach of duty.
- Understand *res ipsa loquitur.*

Perhaps the most common civil actions in the area of tort law are based on negligence. Negligence differs from intentional tort actions in that the tortfeasor in a cause of action for negligence did not intend or desire for the harmful event to occur. In an action for negligence, unlike an intentional tort, the mental state of the defendant is not a consideration. The basis of a tort of negligence centers on the conduct of the defendant and the unreasonable risk that the defendant's conduct placed upon others.

NEGLIGENCE

In the English language, the word *negligence* is synonymous with *carelessness*. In the legal sense, it is similar. Negligence is the failure of individuals to appreciate the risks caused by their conduct. Negligence is sometimes known as the "catchall" tort in that it covers a wide variety of unreasonable actions and inactions by a defendant that cause injury to a plaintiff or plaintiffs.

In negligence, an injury or harm is caused by unreasonable conduct. To determine whether negligence exists in a given situation, two questions need to be considered:

- Was the defendant's conduct unreasonable?
- Did the defendant cause the plaintiff's injury?

The law of negligence was formulated to establish a standard by which to protect others from the unreasonable risk of harm from careless acts of individuals. The

Restatement (Second) of Torts, section 282, provides the following definition: "Negligence is conduct which falls below the standard established by law for the protection of others against unreasonable risk of harm."

THE ELEMENTS OF NEGLIGENCE

To bring a cause of action for negligence, the plaintiff must demonstrate that the following four elements exist:

- *Duty* by the defendant;
- The defendant *breached the duty* of reasonable care;
- The defendant's actions were the ***proximate cause*** of the harm to plaintiff; and
- The plaintiff sustained *damages*.

Foreseeability is an essential element of tort law. It plays a role in three of the four elements of negligence. Foreseeability in the legal sense means the extent to which something can be known in advance; that is, the extent to which something is predictable. A person must examine the circumstances surrounding an event before it happens to determine whether or not the event was foreseeable.

To determine foreseeability, the event needs to be examined in such a way as to determine whether the event was foreseeable in any shape, fashion, or form and to what extent it was foreseeable. When something is so foreseeable as to become a certainty, the law says that the person intended the event or result to occur. For example, if a person leaves a piece of lumber lying in the street, she should be able to foresee that the lumber would be a danger to motorists.

Intent has two meanings in the law:

- The wish to have something happen; and
- The knowledge, with substantial certainty, that the result will happen from what someone did or failed to do.

Foreseeability is normally measured using an **objective standard**. The question is to what extent the event or result should have been foreseeable to the defendant. The question is not whether the defendant *knew* that harm or injury would result, but whether the defendant *should have known* harm or injury would likely result from his actions.

To reach an intelligent conclusion regarding foreseeability in a given situation, one must interview the parties involved and witnesses to the event and thoroughly investigate the facts. One will typically begin the analysis of the situation by identifying the subject matter of the foreseeability question (e.g., personal injury, product liability, etc.). After identifying the subject matter, eight factors need to be considered in determining foreseeability:

- Area
- Activity
- People
- Preparation
- Human nature
- History
- Sensory data
- Common sense

Each factor is considered separately in the following paragraphs, even though, in reality, some factors will overlap.

proximate cause
The defendant's actions are the nearest cause of the plaintiff's injuries.

foreseeability
The capacity for a party to reasonably anticipate a future event.

objective standard
A legal standard that is based on conduct and perceptions external to a particular person.

Area involves the physical situation and location in which the event occurred. Was the incident foreseeable given the conditions of the area? For example, was it raining with a slick road when the defendant went speeding down a residential street? In addition, one must consider how, if at all, would the area affect the foreseeability of what happened? For instance, the foreseeability of harm is more pronounced for a defendant speeding down a residential street near a school when school is letting out than for the defendant speeding in the middle of a desert. Where the incident occurred can lead to a determination of whether the damage or injury sustained by the plaintiff was foreseeable. Certainly, if the defendant was speeding on a wet residential street, in a school zone, while school was letting out, a reasonable person would expect that someone may be injured or harmed as a result of the defendant's conduct.

Area and *activity* are significantly related. What specific activities were going on at the time of the accident or event? The nature of the activity needs to be examined. In the preceding example, the defendant was driving a vehicle, and the defendant was speeding. What types of injuries may occur as a result of these activities? Is it foreseeable that an automobile accident could occur as a result of the defendant speeding in his automobile?

Another issue is what types of *people* were involved in the activities that led to the event or result. How would those people be characterized? What normal expectations are associated with such types of people? What precautions are usually taken or what precautions were not taken? In the automobile example, if the defendant was a teenager, what types of expectations would a reasonable person associate with a teenage driver? Would it be expected that a teenager might not use reasonable care, that he would speed, that he might even street race in a residential area? The answers to these types of questions may determine whether or not an event was foreseeable.

The amount of *preparation* that is involved in an activity may also assist in determining if injury or damage from an activity was foreseeable. Was long-term preparation necessary for the activity? Was any short-term preparation required? For example, the long-term preparation for a mining operation is very different from the short-term activity of repairing a sinkhole. The longer time that one has to prepare, the more likely it is that she will foresee possible damages or injuries that could result.

What kind of *behavior* is usually expected of someone engaged in the kind of activity that is being examined? Human nature is predictable to some extent. Assumptions about people, when they can be made, may be relevant to whether a harm that resulted from an activity was foreseeable.

Historical data can be informative and relevant when examining foreseeability. The more frequently something has occurred in the past, the more foreseeable it is that it will occur again. Have incidents of a similar nature occurred in the past? For example, in determining whether or not it is foreseeable that accidents will occur at a particular intersection, traffic and safety engineers will look at historical data to see how frequently accidents have occurred at the same intersection in the past.

Sensory data are also important. What did the eyes, ears, nose, fingers, feet, and so on tell the parties just before the incident? Did any of this sensory data provide signs of what might happen? Visibility is often relevant to foreseeability. Did she see the car coming? Could she hear the train? The answers to these questions are oftentimes relevant to determining foreseeability.

Common sense also plays a role on determining foreseeability. Based on common sense, to what extent was something foreseeable or not? If a person speeds down a wet residential street near a school, common sense tells us that it is foreseeable that there could be an accident, a child could be struck, the car could skid, or a host of other foreseeable possibilities could occur.

THE REASONABLE PERSON

Lawmakers have attempted to institute an objective standard for measuring whether or not a defendant's conduct was careless, reckless, or unreasonable. The test is known as the reasonable person standard. The *Restatement (Second) of Torts,* section 283, defines the reasonable person standard as follows: "Unless the actor is a child, the standard of conduct to which he must conform to avoid being negligent is that of a reasonable man under like circumstances." We have discussed the reasonable person standard in previous chapters. To review, the reasonable person standard measures the defendant's conduct by determining whether a reasonable and prudent person would act the same way as the defendant in the same or similar circumstances.

The standard also looks at characteristics of the defendant to determine whether a reasonable person *in the same circumstances* as the defendant would act in the same manner. For example, if the defendant is disabled, the court would determine whether a person with the same disability as the defendant would have acted in the same way. But if a defendant is stupid, hot-tempered, or careless, then those attributes will not be considered in determining the reasonable person standard. Such attributes are not considered reasonable. Having said that, some courts have determined that if the defendant is not capable of understanding or avoiding the danger of his actions because he is insane, then the defendant may not be held negligent for his actions because he was incapable of understanding them. A person who is intoxicated or under the influence at the time of an accident will still be held to a reasonable person standard, and her intoxication or other mental impairment due to a controlled substance will not be taken into account as a mitigating factor.

Minors (under the age of 18) are an exception to the reasonable person standard. A minor's conduct will be analyzed against the conduct of what a reasonable person or minor of like age, intelligence, and experience would do under the same or similar circumstances. However, if the minor is engaged in a potentially dangerous activity that is normally performed only by adults, then the minor will be held to the reasonable person standard as if he or she were an adult doing the same activity.

The reasonable person standard requires that a defendant possess a certain minimum level of **knowledge** or understanding that enables a person to survive through life. For example, a defendant should know that if an object is dropped it will fall, that fire burns, and that people cannot breathe in water. The *Restatement (Second) of Torts,* section 289, discusses this topic as follows:

knowledge
Understanding gained by actual experience.

> The actor is required to recognize that his conduct involves a risk of causing an invasion of another's interest if a reasonable man would do so while exercising
> a. such attention, perception of the circumstances, memory, knowledge of other pertinent matters, intelligence, and judgment as a reasonable man would have; and
> b. such superior attention, perception, memory, knowledge, intelligence, and judgment as the actor himself has.

LEGAL RESEARCH MAXIM

The professional standard of care holds that various professionals such as doctors, lawyers, and accountants are held to a standard of care of a reasonable professional in similar circumstances. This standard measures the professional's conduct by determining whether a reasonable and prudent professional would act the same way as the defendant in the same or similar circumstances. For example, if a doctor is accused of acting negligently in her work, her actions will be compared with those of a "reasonable doctor under the same circumstances."

However, if individuals possess superior knowledge or understanding, such as a doctors, lawyers, or accountants, then they will be held to a higher standard than those individuals who are not trained in such professions and who do not possess that type of expertise. Their behavior and actions will be compared with persons possessing the same or similar knowledge and with what those individuals would do in the same or similar circumstances.

DUTY

A duty is an obligation or a requirement to conform to a standard of conduct prescribed by law. But what duty does the defendant have toward a plaintiff? That is where the reasonable person test comes into play. A defendant owes a **duty of care** to the plaintiff; that is, the defendant needs to behave toward the plaintiff with the degree of care that a reasonable person would use in the same or similar circumstances.

duty of care
Such a degree of care, precaution, or diligence as may fairly and properly be expected or required, having regard to the nature of the action, or of the subject matter, and the circumstances surrounding the transaction.

To determine if a duty is required, some very specific questions must be asked. These questions are:

- Who owes this duty?
- To whom is the duty owed?
- When does the duty arise?
- What is the standard of conduct to which there must be conformity?

The general rule on duty is that whenever one's acts and omissions create a foreseeable risk of injury or damage to someone else's person or property, a duty of reasonable care requires that a person take precautions to prevent that injury or damage. The more foreseeable is the injury to the plaintiff, the greater is the need for the defendant to take precautions. Under the general rule, the duty is for the defendant to use reasonable care.

The defendant owes a duty of reasonable care to any foreseeable plaintiff. A foreseeable plaintiff is someone to whom it can be determined that the defendant clearly owes a duty of reasonable care. The determination that a duty is owed to a particular plaintiff or plaintiffs establishes the first element of negligence, which is duty. An unforeseeable plaintiff is someone to whom it cannot definitely be determined that the defendant clearly owes a duty of reasonable care. If it is determined that there is not a duty of care owed, then the first element of negligence cannot be established; therefore, the entire negligence cause of action will fail.

To better understand the concept of the foreseeable plaintiff and the unforeseeable plaintiff, consider this scenario. Lee is driving too fast on College Avenue and rear-ends a car. The car that he hits lurches forward and runs into a pedestrian. The driver of the car is the foreseeable plaintiff. It could be assumed that a person driving too fast would hit another car. The pedestrian is the unforeseeable plaintiff.

To determine whether or not a duty is owed to a particular plaintiff, two major tests have been developed: the Cardozo test, or zone-of-danger test; and the Andrews test, or world-at-large test.

The *Cardozo test,* or *zone-of-danger test,* states that a duty is owed to a specific plaintiff within a zone of danger if the zone of danger and persons injured in it were foreseeable. For example, a defendant is conducting target practice in a vacant lot. The defendant has simply set up cans and is shooting them. The plaintiff is hiking in the woods just behind the vacant lot. While hiking, the plaintiff is struck by one of the defendant's stray bullets. The plaintiff was in the zone of danger created by the defendant. In this case, the zone of danger is any place within the range of the defendant's bullets.

The *Andrews test,* or *world-at-large test,* states that a duty is owed to anyone in the world at large (any plaintiff) if: (1) the plaintiff suffers an injury as a result of the conduct of the defendant, and (2) the conduct of the defendant was unreasonable toward anyone, whether or not the plaintiff was in the zone of danger. This plaintiff does not have to have been in the zone of danger as long as someone (in the world at large) was in this zone because of the defendant's action or inaction. Using the preceding example, anyone, not just the plaintiff, needed to be within the zone of danger the defendant created. The defendant owed a duty of care to anyone who might be hit by a stray bullet, not just the plaintiff.

These two tests focus only on the element of duty. All of the other elements of negligence must also be established in order to bring the cause of action. The Andrews test is much broader than the Cardozo test. More plaintiffs can establish duty under the Andrews test because they do not have to be in the foreseeable zone of danger in order to be owed a duty by the defendant. People only have to be injured as a result of the defendant's unreasonable conduct that created the zone of danger and placed someone, anyone, in the zone of danger.

Misfeasance is conduct or an action that is improper or unreasonable. A failure to act is called **nonfeasance.** With limited exceptions, negligence liability cannot be based on a mere omission or failure to act. However, if a special relationship exists between the plaintiff and defendant, then nonfeasance by the defendant could lead to being considered negligent. Many negligence cases fall into the misfeasance category. An example of misfeasance is the embezzlement of funds by a trustee handling a trust account.

Some examples of special relationships are the following:

- Common carrier/passenger
- Innkeeper/guest
- Employer/employee
- Landowner or possessor/invitee
- Parent/child
- Ship captain/sailor

In a nonfeasance case, in addition to the presence of a special relationship, the defendant's duty turns on whether the injury was foreseeable and whether the defendant had the opportunity to do something about it. The duty is not to prevent the injury. The duty that arises from the special relationship is simply to use reasonable care to avoid the injury to the plaintiff.

No duty exists requiring people to assist someone simply because it is possible for them to give assistance without harming themselves. There is no legal duty to be a Good Samaritan. In fact, if someone voluntarily decides to be a Good Samaritan and renders assistance to an injured person, even though there was no duty to do so, the Good Samaritan can be sued for negligence if he or she fails to use reasonable care in rendering this free assistance.

Breach of Duty

A breach of duty occurs when the defendant engages in unreasonable conduct. Reasonableness becomes the standard when determining negligence in a given situation. To determine if the defendant's actions were reasonable, one must examine all of the

misfeasance
The improper performance of some act that a person may lawfully do.

nonfeasance
The omission of an act that a person ought to do.

CASE FACT PATTERN

Suppose that Jim is in a restaurant, and he notices Steve clutching his chest. It appears that Steve is having a heart attack. Steve falls to the floor, his heart stops, and he stops breathing. Jim decides to see if he can resuscitate Steve. Jim begins CPR, applying concussions to Steve's chest. In the process of performing CPR, Jim applies too much pressure to Steve's chest; as a result, and unbeknownst to Jim or Steve at the time, Jim breaks Steve's sternum. Jim is able to revive Steve before the ambulance comes to the restaurant. It is apparent that Steve would have died had Jim not stepped in. However, at the hospital it is revealed that Jim's efforts caused a break in Steve's sternum. Steve sues Jim for negligence for failing to render reasonable care to him and causing him injuries. If it is determined that Jim did not use reasonable care when performing CPR on Steve, then Jim will be liable to Steve for his broken sternum.

factors leading up to and during the incident. No one factor by itself is conclusive as to reasonableness.

To determine if a defendant's conduct is reasonable, five elements need to be identified:

- State the injury that the plaintiff claims to have suffered.
- Identify the specific acts or omissions of the defendant that the plaintiff alleges caused the injury.
- Examine the circumstances before and during the incident and ask what a reasonable person, if he or she were in the defendant's position, would have done under the same or similar circumstances at that time.
- Compare the specific acts and omissions of the defendant with what a reasonable person would have done.
- Reach a conclusion.

If a reasonable person would have done the same thing in the same or similar circumstances, then there is no breach of duty. If a reasonable person would not have done the same thing in the same or similar circumstances, then the conduct was unreasonable and there was a breach of duty.

To avoid injuring others, the reasonable person tries to avoid the dangers or risks that could cause injury or harm to others. If the danger of a serious accident outweighs the burden or inconvenience of taking precautions to avoid the accident, the reasonable person would take those precautions to try to minimize injury or damage to others. The defendant's failure to take precautions would mean that the defendant was unreasonable and had committed a breach of duty. If the danger of a serious accident is so slight that the danger of injury or damage would not outweigh the relatively high burden or inconvenience of taking the precautions that would be needed to avoid the injuries or damages, then the reasonable person would not take these precautions. No breach of duty would have occurred by the defendant.

hypothesis
An assumption made especially in order to test its logical or empirical consequences.

For every group of facts, it is possible to state a **hypothesis** about the amount of danger that is present and the amount of caution or care that is needed to compensate for or eliminate the danger. The greater is the possible danger that exists, the greater is the need for the defendant to take precautions.

The standard of reasonableness does not require an individual to take every conceivable precaution necessary to prevent injury or damage. A reasonable person takes only reasonable precautions to avoid injuries or damages. Reasonableness does not require excessive caution. For example, a contractor could reasonably be expected to erect a chain-link fence around a construction site to protect the public. It would be unreasonable, however, to expect a 10-foot fence with barbed wire.

To determine the defendant's culpability, one must carefully weigh the elements for breach of duty:

- The foreseeability of an accident occurring.
- The foreseeability of the kind of injury of damage that would result from the accident if it occurs.
- The burden or inconvenience that would be involved in taking the precautions necessary to avoid the accident.
- The importance or social utility of what the defendant was trying to do before the accident.

When examining the foreseeability, the defendant needs to be concerned with the danger of an accident occurring as well as the danger of a particular kind of injury or damage happening. Once it can be determined what a reasonable person would have foreseen in the same or similar circumstances, then it can be determined what the defendant should have foreseen as well.

When examining the burden or inconvenience caused by taking the precautions, one does not look at who should accept this burden or inconvenience to take precautions, but rather at what exactly are the burdens or inconveniences. Burdens or inconveniences fall into several categories:

- Cost
- Time
- Effectiveness
- Aesthetics

How much will the precautions cost? How much time will it take to implement them? How effective will they be? Will they cause an unsightly mess? For example, before land that was once a part of a military base can be used for a housing development, the top layers of soil must be completely removed.

The more important or socially useful the activity engaged in by the defendant, the more likely it is that a reasonable person would take risks to accomplish the activity. If defendant does not evaluate all factors of a situation in the same manner in which a reasonable person would, then the defendant commits a breach of duty.

 ## A DAY IN THE LIFE OF A REAL PARALEGAL

Joan's parents came into the law office with Joan, a 15-year-old female, claiming she [*and her parents*] were being sued, as they had a complaint served upon them by the estate of a woman named Margie. Margie was killed in a car accident by the driver of the vehicle in which Joan was a passenger. Joan, who was sitting in that car's backseat, was with two other friends and a third friend, the driver of the vehicle. Although Margie's death was the fault of the driver of the car in which Joan was a passenger, the complaint stated that Joan was partly to blame for the death. It went on to say that had Joan not asked her friend for a ride home that day, Margie would still be alive. It seems as though the accident occurred right near Joan's house. The driver of the vehicle that hit Margie would not have normally gone home following that route. But because she did, Margie ended up dead.

This particular fact pattern does not place a duty upon Joan, as she was just a passenger. Nothing was breached by Joan. It also goes against public policy. If the estate of Margie was to succeed here, no one would ever do any favors for anyone else. Society and the law want citizens to help one another and offer favors. The foreseeability approach is also very weak. Accidents can always happen, at any time, regardless of the route one takes to get anywhere.

SPOT THE ISSUE

Simon and his friends, Alvin and Theodore, were looking for trouble. School was out for the summer and they had only another year left before graduation from high school. One afternoon, they were up to no good and were causing problems on the roof of a downtown building, 100 feet in height, throwing things off the roof at people as they walked by on the sidewalk below. Since more people walked by on the north side of the building, the boys planted themselves on that side. As they continued to hurl material at people below, a terrible scream sounded from the south side of the building. Startled, Alvin, Simon, and Theodore got up and ran to the south side of the roof, looked down, and saw that a barrel had crushed a woman below as she walked her baby in a carriage. The baby survived. It was discovered that the barrel came from the roof and fell to the ground. Will Simon and his friends be sued and held liable for the death of the mother? What issues may pop up as you think about the situation at hand?

Res Ipsa Loquitur

res ipsa loquitur
Doctrine in which it is assumed that a person's injuries were caused by the negligent act of another person as the harmful act ordinarily would not occur but for negligence.

inference
Arriving at a conclusion based on evidence.

Res ipsa loquitur is a Latin term that that means "the event speaks for itself." It is a doctrine used by a plaintiff who is having trouble proving that the defendant breached a duty or that defendant's conduct was unreasonable. This doctrine enables a plaintiff to point to the facts of an incident and create an **inference** that the defendant was negligent without specifically pointing to the defendant's behavior. A classic example of a *res ipsa loquitur* case is someone struck by an object that falls out of a second-floor window owned by, and under the exclusive control of, the defendant.

American courts have determined that the plaintiff must demonstrate four basic elements in order to attach liability to the defendant in a *res ipsa loquitur* situation. These elements are:

- No direct evidence is available to point to the defendant's behavior in the situation.
- The event must be of a kind that ordinarily does not occur in the absence of someone's negligence. It must be more likely than not that the accident was the result of the defendant's negligence.
- The event must be caused by an entity or instrumentality that was within the exclusive control of the defendant.
- The plaintiff must not be a responsible cause of the accident.

Most courts maintain that no direct evidence of how the defendant behaved in connection with the event can be available. *Res ipsa loquitur* can only be used to infer that the defendant's conduct was negligent.

A mere possibility of unreasonableness is not enough to establish the first element of a *res ipsa loquitur* case. The plaintiff does not have to prove that the only explanation for the accident was the defendant's unreasonableness. The plaintiff does not have to prove that no other cause is possible. The test for the first element is whether unreasonableness by the defendant is more likely than not the explanation for why the incident occurred. Therefore, a defendant does not defeat a *res ipsa loquitur* case by demonstrating that it is possible that the accident was not due to unreasonableness. In other words, it doesn't matter if the defendant can prove that he was being reasonable; a *res ipsa loquitur* tort wouldn't have happened if it hadn't been for the defendant.

The second element of *res ipsa loquitur* requires that the plaintiff demonstrate that it is more likely than not that the accident was caused by the defendant's unreasonableness. If the unreasonableness of the defendant is a mere possibility, or if there is a 50/50 chance that the accident was due to the unreasonableness of someone other than the defendant, then the second element of *res ipsa loquitur* has not been established.

Exclusive control of the situation by the defendant is only one of the ways to prove the unreasonableness causing the accident was that of defendant. However, it is not necessary for the defendant to be in exclusive control of what caused the accident in order to prove *res ipsa loquitur*. The second element of *res ipsa loquitur* can still apply if the plaintiff submits enough evidence to conclude that the incident was probably not due to anyone other than the defendant.

In a case with multiple defendants, if the plaintiff cannot show it is more likely than not that any single, individual defendant's unreasonableness caused the injury, then the court will allow the application of *res ipsa loquitur* against all of the defendants, forcing the defendants to have to decide among themselves who was responsible. This is the theory of joint and several liability that will be discussed in a later chapter.

The final element of *res ipsa loquitur* is that the plaintiff must establish that the plaintiff herself was not the cause of the accident. The plaintiff must show that she did not contribute to the accident or that unreasonable conduct on the part of the plaintiff was the cause the incident.

For example, Sue is walking down the street. She is not conducting herself in any unreasonable manner. She is just simply walking down the sidewalk in front of a two-story building. Brad is a piano mover. Brad is moving a piano into the second-floor apartment of a building. During the move, the piano slips and falls to the ground, injuring Sue. The first element of *res ipsa loquitur* is established: no apparent behavior on Brad's part can be examined to determine a breach of due care. The second and third elements are established as well; Brad had exclusive control of the piano, and pianos do not just simply fall out of second-story windows. As for the fourth element, Sue was doing nothing out of the ordinary. She was simply walking down the street in front of the building. Her conduct did not contribute to the accident. This situation would be considered a *res ipsa loquitur* event.

OTHER CONSIDERATIONS

Custom and Usage

In determining if the defendant breached a duty, one must consider what others in the defendant's field or industry are doing and whether or not the defendant's conduct is simply following what is standard for that industry. An inquiry must be performed as to why a business or profession has acted or failed to act in a certain manner to make a determination of negligence. If it is determined that defendants' actions are not standard for their particular industry or field, then defendants are more likely to be held to be negligent in their actions. Take again the example of the contractor building a chain-link fence around a construction site. Building a five- or six-foot-tall chain-link fence would be normal operating procedure for people in this field.

Violation of a Law

Sometimes it can be proved that defendant's conduct violated a statute, ordinance, or regulation. The following steps must be taken to determine if this violation was negligent:

- Determine what it is that the defendant did or failed to do that allegedly caused the accident.
- Determine what statutes, ordinances, or regulations might regulate the defendant's conduct.
- Determine if the defendant's conduct violated the statute, ordinance, or regulation.
- Determine whether the violation of the statute, ordinance, or regulation was the cause of the incident.

- Determine whether the plaintiff was within the class of persons the statute, ordinance, or regulation was designed to protect.
- Determine whether the statute, ordinance, or regulation was intended to avoid the kind of harm suffered by the plaintiff.

If the defendant proves that a statute was not violated, the plaintiff may still demonstrate that the defendant's conduct was unreasonable. To determine if the violation of the law caused the accident, one must determine whether the incident would not have occurred if the defendant's actions had been different. Was the defendant a substantial factor in the accident occurring? If there would have been no violation of the law, would the accident still have happened? If the accident probably would have still occurred, then the violation of the law did not cause the accident. If more than one possible cause for the incident exists, then the test is whether the violation of the law was a substantial factor in causing the accident.

If a violation of the law is a substantial factor in the accident, one must examine whether the plaintiff is the type of person whom the law was intended to protect. If the law was not intended to cover the kind of harm that resulted to the plaintiff, then the plaintiff cannot use the violation of the statute, ordinance, or regulation as the basis of a breach-of-duty argument against the defendant. However, the plaintiff might still prove that the defendant's conduct was unreasonable and caused the incident. For example, a law intended to protect someone in an automobile may not apply to someone on a bicycle, or a bystander on the sidewalk.

negligence per se
Results from statutes establishing that certain actions or omissions are impermissible under any and all circumstances; the failure to use reasonable care to avoid harm to another person or to do that which a reasonable person might do in similar circumstances.

Negligence Per Se

In determining **negligence per se**, a jury must find that there was unreasonableness in the defendant's conduct. The jury will not be permitted to consider any arguments by the defendant that he or she was, in fact, reasonable in spite of a violation of the statute, ordinance, or regulation. In other words, it doesn't matter how reasonable people feel they are being; if they violate a statute, they violate a statute.

presumption
A rule of law, statutory or judicial, by which finding of a basic fact gives rise to existence of presumed fact, until the presumption is rebutted.

Presumption of Negligence

A **presumption** of negligence is **rebuttable**. That is, the defendant has the right to offer a defense. A jury must find that the conduct by the defendant was unreasonable unless the defendant has introduced convincing evidence that he acted reasonably in spite of the injury.

rebut
To defeat, refute, or take away the effect of something.

The fact that a defendant can show that she was in compliance with a statute, ordinance, or regulation does not necessarily mean that the defendant was not negligent. In other words, just because she didn't break the law doesn't mean she isn't negligent. However, if the defendant can prove that her conduct was reasonable, it will help her case. The statute, ordinance, or regulation sets a minimum standard of conduct. However, the reasonableness of the defendant's conduct under the circumstances might require more due care than what the statute, ordinance, or regulation has established.

gross negligence
The intentional failure to perform a manifest duty in reckless disregard of the consequences as affecting the life or property of another.

Gross negligence is the failure to use even a small amount of care to avoid foreseeable harm. For example, driving an automobile into a crowd of people demonstrates gross negligence. When individuals act with knowledge that injury or harm will probably

SURF'S UP

For more information on negligence, visit the website for the National Personal Injury Attorneys as well as that for the Reference for Business. The links for these two websites are www.nationalpersonalinjuryattorneys.com, and www.referenceforbusiness.com.

EYE ON ETHICS

The law of negligence has not been established on a federal level. Most negligence laws are established at the state level. While some are based on common law, some are based on statutes. However, negligence can be found on a local or community level and can be enacted by an ordinance or regulation as well. Findings of negligence can vary from city to city, community to community, and state to state. It is important to recognize the jurisdiction that will govern the incident that you are examining and to determine what the rules, regulations, and laws of negligence are in that region.

result from their action or failure to act, it constitutes willful, wanton, and reckless conduct. In this instance, the harm is foreseeable. Street racing would be an example of willful, wanton, or reckless conduct.

RESEARCH THIS

One of the most famous cases that demonstrate some of the basic elements of negligence is the case of *Palsgraf v. Long Island R. Co.*, 248 N.Y. 339, 162 N.E. 99 (1928). Locate this case and brief it. What does the court say about foreseeability? What was the ruling? What was the issue and/or issues? Who won and why?

Summary

Negligence actions differ from intentional tort actions in that the tortfeasor in a cause of action for negligence did not intend or desire for the harmful event to occur. In an action for negligence, unlike an intentional tort, the defendant's mental state is not a consideration. The basis of a tort of negligence centers on the defendant's conduct and the unreasonable risk that the defendant's conduct placed upon others.

To bring a cause of action for negligence, the plaintiff must demonstrate the following four elements exist: (1) duty by the defendant; (2) the defendant breached the duty of reasonable care; (3) the defendant's actions were the proximate cause of the harm to plaintiff; and (4) the plaintiff sustained damages.

Foreseeability is an essential element of tort law. It plays a role in three of the four elements of negligence. Foreseeability in the legal sense means the extent to which something can be known in advance. It is the extent to which something is predictable. A person must examine the circumstances surrounding an event before it happens in order to determine whether or not the event was foreseeable.

Foreseeability is normally measured using an objective standard. The question is to what extent the event or result should have been foreseeable to the defendant. The question is not whether the defendant knew, but whether the defendant should have known harm or injury would likely result from his or her actions.

The reasonable person standard requires that a defendant possess a certain minimum level of knowledge or understanding that enables a person to survive through life. For example, a defendant should know that if an object is dropped it will fall, that fire burns, and that people cannot breathe in water.

However, if individuals possess superior knowledge or understanding, (for example, doctors, lawyers, or accountants), then they are held to a higher standard than those individuals who are not trained in such professions and who do not possess that type of expertise. People's behavior and actions will be compared with those of persons possessing the same or similar knowledge and what those individuals would do in the same or similar circumstances.

A duty is an obligation or a requirement to conform to a standard of conduct prescribed by law. A defendant owes a duty of care to the plaintiff. A duty of care means that the defendant needs to behave toward the plaintiff with the degree of care that a reasonable person would use in the same or similar circumstances.

The general rule on duty is that whenever one's acts and omissions create a foreseeable risk of injury or damage to someone else's person or property, a duty of reasonable care requires one to take precautions to prevent that injury or damage. The more foreseeable the injury to the plaintiff, the greater the need that arises for the defendant to take precautions.

The Cardozo test, or zone-of-danger test, states that a duty is owed a specific plaintiff in the zone of danger, if the zone of danger and persons injured in it were foreseeable.

The Andrews test, or world-at-large test, states that a duty is owed to anyone in the world at large (any plaintiff) if: (1) the plaintiff suffers an injury as a result of the conduct of the defendant, and (2) the conduct of the defendant was unreasonable toward anyone, whether or not the plaintiff was in the zone of danger. This plaintiff does not have to have been in the zone of danger as long as someone (in the world at large) was in this zone because of the action or inaction of the defendant.

Misfeasance is conduct that is improper or unreasonable. With limited exceptions, negligence liability cannot be based on a mere omission or failure to act. This failure to act is called nonfeasance. If a special relationship exists between the plaintiff and defendant, then nonfeasance by the defendant could lead to being considered negligent. Many negligence cases fall into the misfeasance category.

A breach of duty occurs when the defendant engages in unreasonable conduct. To determine if the defendant's actions were reasonable, one must examine all of the factors leading up to an incident and during the incident. No one factor by itself is conclusive as to reasonableness.

To avoid injuring others, the reasonable person tries to avoid the dangers or risks of injury that could be caused to others. If the danger of a serious accident outweighs the burden or inconvenience of taking precautions to avoid the accident, the reasonable person would take those precautions in order to try to minimize injury or damage to others. The defendant's failure to take precautions would mean that the defendant was unreasonable and had committed a breach of duty. If the danger of a serious accident is so slight that the danger of injury or damage would not outweigh the relatively high burden or inconvenience of taking the precautions that would be needed to avoid the injuries or damages, then the reasonable person would not take these precautions. No breach of duty would have occurred by the defendant.

For every group of facts, it is possible to state a hypothesis about the amount of danger that is present and the amount of caution or care that is needed to compensate for or eliminate the danger. The greater the possible danger that exists, the greater the need for the defendant to take precautions.

Res ipsa loquitur is a Latin term that means "the event speaks for itself." It is a doctrine used by a plaintiff who is having trouble proving that the defendant breached a duty or that the defendant's conduct was unreasonable. This doctrine enables a plaintiff to point to the facts of an incident and to create an inference that the defendant was negligent without specifically pointing to the defendant's behavior.

A mere possibility of unreasonableness is not enough to establish the first element of a *res ipsa loquitur* case. The plaintiff does not have to prove that the only explanation for the accident was the defendant's unreasonableness. The plaintiff does not have to prove that no other cause is possible. The test for the first element is whether unreasonableness by defendant is more likely than not the explanation for why the incident occurred. Therefore, a defendant does not defeat a *res ipsa loquitur* case by demonstrating that it is possible that the accident was not due to unreasonableness.

Custom and usage may be applied to determine if the defendant breached a duty. What others in the defendant's field or industry are doing and whether or not a defendant's conduct is simply following what is standard for that industry is a consideration. An inquiry must be conducted as to why a business or profession has acted or failed to act in a certain manner in order to make a determination of negligence.

If the defendant proves that a statute was not violated, the plaintiff may still demonstrate that the defendant's conduct was unreasonable. To determine if the violation of the law caused the accident, it needs to be asked whether the incident would not have occurred "but for" the defendant's actions, or whether the defendant was a "substantial factor" in the accident occurring. If there would have been no violation of the law, would the accident still have happened? If the accident probably would have still occurred, then the violation of the law did not cause the accident. If more than one possible cause for the incident exists, then the test is whether the violation of the law was a substantial factor in causing the accident. (The "but for" and substantial factor tests are discussed more in the next chapter.)

In determining negligence per se, a jury must find that there was unreasonableness in the defendant's conduct. The jury will not be permitted to consider any arguments by the defendant that he or she was in fact reasonable in spite of a violation of the statute, ordinance, or regulation.

Key Terms

Duty of care
Foreseeability
Gross negligence
Hypothesis
Inference
Knowledge
Misfeasance
Negligence per se
Nonfeasance
Objective standard
Presumption
Proximate cause
Rebut
Res ipsa loquitur

Review Questions

1. What is negligence?
2. List the elements of negligence?
3. What is a duty of reasonable care?
4. Describe what the reasonable person standard is?
5. What happens to the reasonable person standard if a person possesses superior skill or knowledge?
6. Define misfeasance and why is important to a claim for negligence?
7. Define nonfeasance and why it is important to a claim for negligence?
8. What constitutes a breach of duty of reasonable care?
9. Define negligence per se?
10. What is res ipsa loquitur and what makes it different from the reasonable care standard?
11. What is gross negligence?
12. If a defendant violates a law, is he or she liable for negligence?
13. What is foreseeability and why is it important to a cause of action for negligence?
14. What is a presumption of negligence?
15. What is the difference between gross negligence and willful, wanton, and reckless conduct?

Exercises

1. Bill is blind. While walking down the street, he stops to light a cigarette. Bill is not aware that he has stopped in a gasoline station in order to light his cigarette. All around the station are posted signs that say **HIGHLY FLAMMABLE—NO SMOKING**. Bill cannot see or read the signs. Bill starts a fire, and the vapors in the gasoline station explode, causing serious damage and injuries to many people. Is Bill negligent?

2. Looking at the following scenarios, state which theory of negligence you feel applies and why. There could be more than one theory for each one.
   a. An electrical wire is exposed on the side of a building and a child is injured because of it.
   b. An insect is found in a can of peas, and a consumer becomes ill because of ingestion of the insect.
   c. A can of soda explodes and injures the consumer.
   d. Two cars are involved in an accident and a pedestrian who was crossing the street was injured.

3. In Anytown, USA, there is a statute that requires all vacant lots to be fenced at all times. Erica owns a vacant lot within the city limits that is not fenced. Some children decide to cross Erica's vacant lot, fall into a hole, and are injured. The hole was covered with shrubbery and was not easily seen. The parents of the children sue Erica. Using the information discussed in this chapter, what causes of actions might the parents bring against Erica and why?

4. Billy, a 15-year-old boy, is playing on a construction site when he falls into a ditch dug by Construction Co. Billy claims that Construction Co. was negligent in leaving the ditch exposed without any warning of its existence. How should the court rule?

5. Baker owns a bakery, which he operates out of a two-story building. Victor is walking under the second-story window of the bakery when a barrel of flour falls on his head and injures him. Under what theory(s) of negligence may Victor seek to assert a claim of negligence against Baker?

6. Joe operates a cab in a big city. Joe stops in the middle of a busy street to pick up a passenger. As a result of Joe stopping in the middle of the street, he is involved in an accident with Wendy. What factors should the court look to when seeking to determine whether Joe was guilty of negligence?

7. Harry owns and operates a horse rental facility. Harry fails to check the saddle of a horse before sending it out for its first rental. Lauren is injured when the saddle falls off the horse. What does Lauren need to prove in order to sustain a negligence claim against Harry?

8. Due to various physical, painful symptoms in her leg, Jenny visits a doctor. The doctor fails to properly diagnose Jenny's condition. Due to this, her symptoms grow more painful, causing Jenny to ultimately contract gangrene. As a result, Jenny suffers the amputation of her leg. What standard of care will the doctor be held to if Jenny sues for negligence?

PORTFOLIO ASSIGNMENT

Interview your doctor, a neighborhood police officer, and a/your clergy person. Ask them if they owe a "reasonable" duty to another to act or whether they owe a special duty to act in a given circumstance. See if they know and whether they are correct or not. Research all three positions and their appropriate duties before the interviews.

Vocabulary Builders

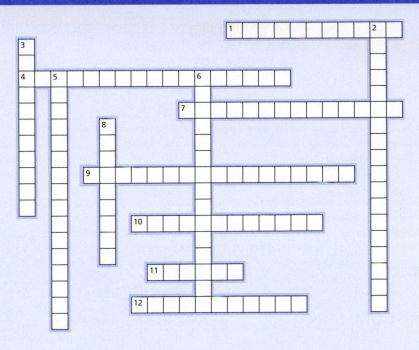

Instructions

Use the key terms from this chapter to fill in the answers to the crossword puzzle.

NOTE: When the answer is more than one word, leave a blank space between words.

ACROSS

1. A rule of law, statutory or judicial, by which finding of a basic fact gives rise to existence of presumed fact, until the presumption is rebutted.
4. Results from statutes establishing that certain actions or omissions are impermissible under any and all circumstances; the failure to use reasonable care to avoid harm to another person or to do that which a reasonable person might do in similar circumstances.
7. The capacity for a party to reasonably anticipate a future event.
9. Doctrine in which it is assumed that a person's injuries were caused by the negligent act of another person as the harmful act ordinarily would not occur but for negligence.
10. Such a degree of care, precaution, or diligence as may fairly and properly be expected or required, having regard to the nature of the action, or of the subject matter, and the circumstances surrounding the transaction.
11. To defeat, refute, or take away the effect of something.
12. The improper performance of some act that a person may lawfully do.

DOWN

2. A legal standard that is based on conduct and perceptions external to a particular person.
3. The omission of an act that a person ought to do.
5. The intentional failure to perform a manifest duty in reckless disregard of the consequences as affecting the life or property of another.
6. The defendant's actions are the nearest cause of the plaintiff's injuries.
8. Arriving at a conclusion based on evidence.

SUPREME COURT OF NEW YORK, APPELLATE DIVISION, SECOND DEPARTMENT
2002 N.Y. App. Div. LEXIS 4903
April 25, 2002, Argued
May 13, 2002, Decided

PRIOR HISTORY: In an action to recover damages for personal injuries, etc., the plaintiffs appeal, as limited by their brief, from so much of an order of the Supreme Court, Nassau County (Ort, J.), dated April 4, 2001, as granted that branch of the motion of the defendant Baldwin Union Free School District which was for summary judgment dismissing the complaint insofar as asserted against it, and the defendant David Schneider separately appeals, as limited by his brief, from so much of the same order as granted that branch of the motion of the defendant Baldwin Union Free School District which was for summary judgment dismissing all cross claims insofar as asserted against it.

CASE SUMMARY

PROCEDURAL POSTURE: Appellant injured student sued respondents, school district and tortfeasor student, in the Supreme Court, Nassau County (New York), for injuries caused by the tortfeasor. The trial court granted the school district's summary judgment motion, and the injured student and tortfeasor student appealed.

OVERVIEW: The injured student said the school district was negligent in its supervision of him and negligently maintained its gym and sports equipment and the tortfeasor negligently caused his injuries. The appellate court held the school district established its prima facie entitlement to summary judgment, as none of the evidence submitted by the injured student raised an issue of fact as to whether the district had actual or constructive notice of prior similar conduct on the part of the tortfeasor. An injury caused by the impulsive, unanticipated act of a fellow student would not ordinarily give rise to a finding of negligence.

OUTCOME: The trial court's judgment was affirmed.

JUDGES: ANITA R. FLORIO, J.P., CORNELIUS J. O'BRIEN, LEO F. McGINITY, HOWARD MILLER, JJ. FLORIO, J.P., O'BRIEN, McGINITY and H. MILLER, JJ., concur.

OPINION

On February 14, 1997, the infant plaintiff, a seventh grade student at Baldwin Middle School, was injured when he allegedly was pushed by a fellow classmate, the defendant David Schneider. After the incident, the plaintiffs commenced this action against the defendants Baldwin Union Free School District (hereinafter the District) and David Schneider, alleging that the District was negligent in its supervision of the infant plaintiff, that the District negligently maintained the gym and its sports equipment, and that Schneider negligently and recklessly caused the infant plaintiff's injuries. The Supreme Court granted the District's motion for summary judgment dismissing the complaint and all cross claims insofar as against it, finding that Schneider's act was impulsive and unanticipated, and that the plaintiffs' claim that the District failed to adequately maintain the gym and its sports equipment was without merit.

We affirm.

While schools are under a *duty* to adequately supervise the students in their care, they are *not* insurers of the students' safety since they cannot reasonably be expected to continuously supervise and control all of their movements and activities (see *Mirand v City of New York*, 84 NY2d 44, 49). To establish a cause of action to recover damages for breach of the duty to provide adequate supervision, a plaintiff must demonstrate that school authorities "had sufficiently specific knowledge or notice of the dangerous conduct which caused injury; that is, that the third-party acts could reasonably have been anticipated" (*Mirand v City of New York*, 84 NY2d at 49). "Actual or constructive notice to the school of prior similar conduct is generally required," and "an injury caused by the impulsive, unanticipated act of a fellow student ordinarily will not give rise to a finding of negligence" (*Mirand v City of New York*, 84 NY2d at 49). A plaintiff must also establish that the alleged breach of the duty to provide adequate supervision was a proximate cause of the injuries sustained (see *Mirand v City of New York*, 84 NY2d at 50). We agree with the Supreme Court that the District established its prima facie entitlement to summary judgment and that none of the evidence submitted by the plaintiffs raised an issue of fact as to whether the District had actual or constructive notice of prior similar conduct on the part of Schneider (see *O'Neal v Archdioceses of N.Y.*, 286 AD2d 757; *Convey v City of Rye School Dist.*, 271 AD2d 154; *Kennedy v Seaford Union Free School Dist. No. 6*, 250 AD2d 574; *Moores v City of Newburgh School Dist.*, 237 AD2d 265).

Accordingly, the District was entitled to summary judgment dismissing the complaint and all cross claims insofar as asserted against it.

Florio, J.P., O'Brien, McGinity and H. Miller, JJ., concur.

Source: 2002 N.Y. App. Div. LEXIS 4903. Reprinted with the permission of LexisNexis.

Chapter 6

Negligence: Proximate Cause

CHAPTER OBJECTIVES

Upon completion of this chapter, you will be able to:

• Define proximate cause.

• Understand causation in fact.

• Explain the "but for" test.

• Discuss the substantial factor test.

• Understand causation.

• Identify intervening causes.

The first element in negligence is to establish that the defendant owed a duty of due care to the plaintiff. The second element that must be established is whether the defendant breached the duty of due care. The third element necessary to be established by a plaintiff in a negligence cause of action is proximate cause. Was the defendant the cause of the incident and the injury to plaintiff? The fourth and final element that must be established is whether plaintiff sustained an injury or harm. This chapter explores how the defendant's actions are analyzed to determine if **proximate cause** exists in a negligence action.

proximate cause
The defendant's actions are the nearest cause of the plaintiff 's injuries.

CAUSATION IN FACT

Whether or not a defendant caused the plaintiff's injuries and damages is a question of fact. The legal question is whether or not the defendant's conduct was the **cause in fact** of the damages and injuries sustained by the plaintiff.

When trying to determine proximate cause, the following question—the causation question (cause in fact)—needs to be asked: Was the defendant the cause of the plaintiff's injury?

Actual harm to a plaintiff may not be present in a case; the harm may be to the public at large. For example, in 2006, California growers of spinach were forced to recall thousands of bags of prepackaged spinach from store shelves due to E. coli contamination. The actual harm or injuries could not be traced back to these specific growers, but the fact that they produced a product that might have caused the harm could be enough to establish legal cause.

cause in fact
The particular cause that produces an event and without which the event would not have occurred.

YOU BE THE JUDGE

Mary was drinking, *as usual,* down at the park, when one day she slipped and fell, cutting her left leg, very deeply, right below the knee. Unable to walk, she screamed out in pain for help to the next person walking down the sidewalk. This person happened to be a milk delivery person. Since the town has only 140 people in it and only one milk delivery person, she knew his name was Charlie. He stopped, decided not to help—because he didn't care to get screamed at by this obvious drunk—and walked on.

No one else passed Mary until two days later when a police officer walked by and smelled something terrible and found Mary still alive but passed out from gangrene, which had set into the leg. That afternoon, Mary had her left leg amputated below the knee to save her life from a deadly infection. Does Mary have a tort claim against Charlie for not helping her, which resulted in her losing her left leg to amputation? If so, what claim and what elements, if any, are satisfied?

A DAY IN THE LIFE OF A REAL PARALEGAL

In law, some would argue that there is no such thing as an accident; that nothing happens by chance, except maybe *acts of God;* and that someone must be behind the cause of the injury sustained. In many ways, the tort of negligence becomes the cause of action individuals would take to make themselves whole again by holding the defendant liable for an "*accident.*" The "*proximate cause*" element of negligence can be the most difficult element for the plaintiff to prove.

SPOT THE ISSUE

Tommy, a 2-year-old child, sneaks his way into a neighbor's yard, opens the unlocked gate to the pool (pool was fenced in), and falls into the pool *with no one around* and drowns. Has any tort occurred here? If so, which one? Are all elements of the tort satisfied?

Two methods are used to determine if the defendant's actions were the cause in fact of the plaintiff's injuries and damages. Those two methods are the "but for" test and the substantial factor test.

THE "BUT FOR" TEST

"but for" test
If the complained-of act had not occurred, no injury would have resulted.

The **"but for" test** is one of the tests that the courts use to determine whether or not the defendant was the cause in fact of the plaintiff's injury or damages. The but for test is used when there is only one defendant who is suspected of being the cause of the injury. The but for test asks the following question: Is it more likely than not that "but for" the defendant's unreasonable conduct, the injury or damages would not have been suffered by the plaintiff?

The trier of fact uses the but for test to determine that the defendant's conduct was the cause in fact not only of the incident but also of the plaintiff's injury. One of the great authors on torts, W. Page Keeton in *Prosser and Keeton on the Law of Torts* (5th ed. 1984), section 41 at 266, defines the but for test as follows:

> *From such cases many courts have derived a rule, commonly known as the "but-for" or "sine qua non" rule, which may be stated as follows: The defendant's conduct is a cause of the event if the event would not have occurred but for the conduct; conversely, the defendant's conduct is not a cause of the event, if the event would have occurred without it.*

burden of proof
Standard for assessing the weight of the evidence.

When a plaintiff is attempting to attach liability to the defendant using the but for test, the plaintiff has the **burden of proof** to demonstrate that the defendant caused the plaintiff's harm. However, the plaintiff does not have to prove with absolute certainty that the defendant was the cause of the harm. The plaintiff only has to prove that it is probable that the defendant's actions caused the harm sustained by the plaintiff.

The but for test is extremely broad, since there could be thousands of reasons why a plaintiff was harmed. In addition, some states have elected not to use this test to establish proximate cause because they find that it is difficult for juries to understand and apply the test because it is so broad.

The but for test looks at whether the plaintiff has been injured because of what the defendant did or failed to do. If the plaintiff would have been injured regardless of what the defendant did or failed to do, then the defendant did not cause the injury to the plaintiff. Every time liability is found using the but for test, then liability will also be established using the substantial factor test.

RESEARCH THIS

As already stated, some states have elected to no longer use the but for test to determine proximate cause. California is such a state. Locate and read the case of *Mitchell v. Gonzales,* 817 P.2d 872 (Cal. 1991). Brief the case and answer the following questions: What did the court say about the but for test, and what happened as a result of its conclusions?

SUBSTANTIAL FACTOR

The **substantial factor** test is more widely used than the but for test. The test is simple: if the defendant's conduct was a substantial factor in bringing about the injuries or damages to the plaintiff, then proximate cause can be established. The substantial factor test is used when there is more than one possible causal individual or entity. The question that needs to be asked in the substantial test is this: Is it more likely than not that the defendant's unreasonable acts or omissions were a substantial factor in producing the injury suffered by the plaintiff?

The substantial factor test is particularly useful when two or more events have occurred and each one by itself could have been enough to damage or harm the plaintiff. For each of the events, the substantial factor is used to determine whether or not it could have caused the harm. If so, then that event is determined to be a cause in fact of the harm. If it is determined that one of the events could not have brought harm to the plaintiff by itself, then that event or that defendant will not be found to be a substantial factor, and liability to the defendant will not attach. The *Restatement (Second) of Torts,* section 431, provides the following definition for the substantial factor rule and legal cause:

> The actor's negligent conduct is a legal cause of harm to another if
> a. his conduct is a substantial factor in bringing about the harm, and
> b. there is no rule of law relieving the actor from liability because of the manner in which his negligence has resulted in the harm.

Usually, the trier of fact will determine that the defendant's actions were a proximate cause of the harm if a reasonable person would conclude that they were. The trier of fact may also determine that the plaintiff's injuries would have occurred anyway despite the defendant's conduct, and, therefore, the defendant was not a substantial factor in causing the harm sustained by the plaintiff.

The substantial factor test requires simply that the defendant be a substantial factor in causing the harm sustained by the plaintiff. It is not necessary that the defendant be the sole or only cause of the harm in order to be the cause in fact of the

substantial factor
A material and active contributing activity or event that led to the plaintiff's injuries or damages.

harm that the plaintiff sustained. It is also not necessary for the plaintiff to demonstrate that the defendant was the dominant factor in producing the injury. The fact that the defendant's conduct was a substantial factor will be enough to demonstrate cause in fact.

CAUSATION

Common Sense

Perhaps one of the most resourceful methods for establishing a connection between cause and effect in analyzing a situation is through common sense. Common sense is based on a person's everyday experience. Common sense uses aspects of time, location, and history to draw conclusions. When assessing time, location, and history as they pertain to cause and effect, the following analysis can be helpful:

- Time—Did the injury to the plaintiff occur after the defendant's acts or omissions? The shorter the time period that occurs between the plaintiff's injury and the conduct of the defendant, the more likely than not that the defendant's conduct caused the injury. The more time that passes between the defendant's conduct and the injury to the plaintiff, then the more it is probable that the defendant's conduct did not cause the injury to the plaintiff.

- Location—Did the injury occur in the same area as the conduct of the defendant? The closer the physical proximity to each other, the more convincing it is that the defendant's conduct was the cause of the plaintiff's injury. The greater the distance between the conduct and the injury, the more likely it is that the defendant's conduct did not cause the injury to the plaintiff.

- History—Historically, has the same or similar conduct by the defendant or other people under similar situations produced the kind of injury sustained by the plaintiff? The more often this kind of injury has historically resulted from such conduct, then the more likely it is that the defendant's conduct caused the injury or harm to the plaintiff. If this kind of injury has never—or rarely—occurred due to such conduct, it is more likely that the defendant's conduct did not cause the injury.

The preceding analysis turns on the burden of proof that the plaintiff has offered. Remember, the burden of proof in civil cases is a preponderance of the evidence. The preponderance of the evidence standard is the minimum required that the plaintiff must establish to prove cause in fact. The plaintiff must produce evidence that is convincing enough for the trier of fact to conclude that it is more likely than not that the defendant was a substantial factor in producing the injury to the plaintiff.

Market Share

In circumstances in which numerous manufacturers may have caused the injuries to the plaintiff, and it is difficult to determine that any one manufacturer could have caused the injury to the plaintiff, then all of the manufacturers involved may be forced to pay a portion of the plaintiff's award that is proportional to each manufacturer's market share in the industry. This type of market share determination is typically found in cases that involve products. Good examples of these types of cases have involved breast implants, pesticides, and tobacco cases. Typically the courts will look for the products of the defendant manufacturers that are identical or very similar. In addition, a large number of manufacturers must be sued by the plaintiff or plaintiffs so that it can be said that they constitute a significant or substantial share of the market in the industry.

CASE FACT PATTERN

Molly decided to have breast implants. She saved for the surgery and finally had it done. Molly was very happy with the results. Two years after the surgery, Molly became ill. Initially, doctors could not figure out what was wrong with Molly. However, as time passed, her breasts became sore and swollen, one began to deflate, and Molly became more ill. Finally, it was discovered that Molly's silicone breast implants had begun to leak into her body, and that was the cause of her illness and injuries. Over 20 manufacturers produce the type of breast implants that were used in Molly. Molly had the implants removed, and the doctor was unable to determine which implant had caused Molly's injury. Molly sued all 20 manufacturers. The jury awarded Molly $1.2 million dollars. Since no one could determine which company had actually manufactured the breast implants used in Molly, all 20 companies were required to pay a portion of the $1.2 million dollar award to Molly based on their market share in the breast implant industry.

Foreseeability

The determination that needs to be made as to when liability will attach to a defendant is that the injury to the plaintiff must be the foreseeable consequence of the original risk created by the defendant's unreasonable acts or omissions. If the injuries are the foreseeable consequences of the original risk created by defendant, then the defendant will be determined to be the proximate cause of all of the plaintiff's injuries, and liability will attach. The plaintiff must take reasonable steps to **mitigate** any additional injury or harm that is the consequence of the original injury caused by the defendant.

> **mitigate**
> To make less severe or intense.

If it is foreseeable that a defendant's unreasonable conduct will result in any force on a plaintiff's body, and if this force to the plaintiff does occur, then the defendant will be liable for the foreseeable as well as the unforeseeable injuries that the plaintiff sustained. If it was foreseeable that the defendant's conduct will cause injuries to the plaintiff, then the defendant will be liable for unforeseeable injuries that follow from any foreseeable force that occurred to the plaintiff. If the defendant's conduct was unreasonable or intentional, the defendant will be held liable for the plaintiff's injuries. It will not matter if the plaintiff has a particular vulnerability to injury and, therefore, might be injured to a greater extent than a person who does not possess the same vulnerabilities as the plaintiff. A plaintiff who has particular vulnerabilities is known as an **eggshell skull** plaintiff. The defendant will still be held liable for the foreseeable and unforeseeable injuries sustained by the plaintiff that resulted from the defendant's actions.

> **eggshell skull**
> A person who is particularly vulnerable or susceptible to damage or injury as a result of a pre-existing condition or weakness that afflicts a particular person.

Note that eggshell skull plaintiffs do not necessarily have weak skulls; their weakness or vulnerability could involve any part of their anatomy.

A plaintiff with an eggshell skull usually has a pre-existing condition, disease, or injury that has been aggravated by the conduct and force sustained as a result of the defendant's actions. The defendant will be responsible for the aggravation of the plaintiff's condition that resulted from the defendant's actions or conduct. For example, if you already have a back problem and someone rear-ends your vehicle and aggravates your back problem, then the person who rear-ended you will be liable for your aggravated back injury.

The manner in which an injury occurs does not have to be foreseeable in order for the defendant to be deemed to be the proximate cause of the injury. A major factor is that the harm that resulted was within the risk originally created by the defendant's conduct. A defendant can be the cause of a foreseeable injury that occurs in an unforeseeable manner. Liability does not attach in this case when the harm that resulted to the plaintiff was in fact highly extraordinary or unusual.

If the plaintiff can establish that the defendant had a duty to the plaintiff, then the defendant will be held liable. However, if the injury is not foreseeable, then liability will not attach to the defendant. The *Restatement (Second) of Torts*, section 435, defines the foreseeability of harm as follows:

1. *If the actor's conduct is a substantial factor in bringing about harm to another, the fact that the actor neither foresaw nor should have foreseen the extent of the harm or the manner in which it occurred does not prevent him from being liable.*

2. *The actor's conduct may be held not to be a legal cause of harm to another where after the event and looking back from the harm to the actor's negligent conduct, it appears to the court highly extraordinary that it should have brought about the harm.*

INTERVENING CAUSES

intervening cause
An independent cause that intervenes between the original wrongful act or omission and the injury, turns aside the natural sequence of events, and produces a result that would not otherwise have followed and that could not have been reasonably anticipated.

There are circumstances in which the defendant will be absolved of liability for a plaintiff's injuries in a particular situation. This principle is known as **intervening causes**. An intervening cause is a force or an act by a third person that produces the injury or harm to the plaintiff after the defendant's unreasonable action, or failure to act (omission) has occurred.

An intervening cause will relieve the defendant from liability for the plaintiff's injury even if the defendant's conduct was a substantial factor that caused the plaintiff to sustain injury or damage. Most of the time, the courts will also look to determine if the intervening cause was foreseeable before applying the principle. The *Restatement (Second) of Torts*, section 44, explains the principle in this way:

The number and variety of causes which may intervene, after the negligence of the defendant is an accomplished fact, are obviously without any limit whatever. In the effort to hold the defendant's liability within some reasonable bounds, the courts have been compelled, out of sheer necessity and in default of anything better, to fall back upon the scope of the original foreseeable risk which the defendant has created. The question is always one of whether the defendant is to be relieved of responsibility, and the defendant's liability superseded, by the subsequent event. In general, this has been determined by asking whether the intervention of the later cause is a significant part of the risk involved in the defendant's conduct, or is so reasonably connected with it that the responsibility should not be terminated. It is therefore said that the defendant is to be held liable if, but only if, the intervening cause is foreseeable.

LEGAL RESEARCH MAXIM

Superseding causes and intervening forces are two very different definitions, yet may mistakenly seem the same. Research the history of both superseding causes and intervening forces and why the law separates the two ideas into different causations.

If the intervening force involves an act of nature that is truly unforeseeable, then it will oftentimes be determined to be a **superseding** cause. **Acts of God** such as hurricanes, earthquakes, and tsunamis are all examples of intervening forces of nature.

The negligent act of a third person may also absolve the defendant from liability and be considered an intervening force. An example is as follows:

supersede
To set aside, render unnecessary, suspend, or stay.

act of God
An act occasioned exclusively by forces of nature without the interference of any human agency.

intervening force
An act that actively operates in producing harm to another after an actor's negligent act or omission.

Julie is crossing the street in a crosswalk. A car hits Julie and throws her to the ground with only minor injuries. While Julie is lying on the ground, another car, whose driver does not see Julie in the street, runs over her, causing her grave injury. The second automobile running over Julie was a negligent act of a third person that could be considered an *intervening force*. It is the driver of the second car who is liable for Julie's injuries. Another example of an intervening force is called an *intervening negligent human force*. Suppose that Julie, after being run over, is taken to the hospital where she is operated on for internal bleeding. The doctors leave sponges in her abdomen, causing Julie to suffer from a severe infection. The actions or omissions of the doctors are considered to be intervening negligent human forces.

Another type of intervening force is one in which a third person's criminal conduct may be considered an intervening force. This is known as an *intervening intentional or criminal human force*. Julie, who has been hit by a car and taken to the hospital, bumps into her fiancé's former girlfriend. The former girlfriend, who is very upset by

EYE ON ETHICS

The acts of third persons are not always considered intervening causes. For example, many states have what is known as a Dram Shop Act. These acts hold that tavern or bar owners will be held liable for the negligent acts of their intoxicated patrons to whom bar owners served more liquor. The rational is that it is foreseeable that an intoxicated patron will cause damages or injuries to others. The harm or damage caused by the intoxicated patron is a foreseeable event.

Julie's engagement to her ex-boyfriend, shoots Julie to try to kill her. The former girlfriend is an intervening intentional or criminal human force. The man driving the car is liable for Julie's injuries, but he is not liable for the injuries sustained at the hands of the former girlfriend.

An intervening cause becomes a superseding cause when the harm caused by the intervening force is outside the scope of the foreseeable risk originally created by the defendant's unreasonable acts or omissions and/or when the harm caused by the intervening cause is considered highly unusual or extraordinary.

If any of the intervening causes can be classified as a superseding cause, the intervening cause will then prevent the defendant from being held liable for the harm caused to the plaintiff by the intervening cause. If the intervening cause is determined not to be a superseding cause, then the defendant will be found to have been the proximate cause of the harm sustained by the plaintiff that was a result of the intervening cause. Intervening intentional or criminal human forces are often, for the most part, considered superseding causes because they are either outside the scope of the original risk or are highly extraordinary. Julie being shot in the hospital by her fiance's former girlfriend is certainly a superseding cause.

When analyzing an intervening force of nature or an intervening negligent human force, the legal professional must inquire if the injury or damage that was sustained by the plaintiff is of the same kind as would have occurred or naturally flowed from the defendant's conduct. If so, then the defendant will still be found liable for the plaintiff's harm.

PROXIMATE CAUSE OVERVIEW

The following points are important when analyzing and determining proximate cause:

- Were the but for and substantial factor tests applied?
- Was the evidence determined to be sufficient to establish that the defendant's conduct was a substantial factor in the plaintiff's injury?
- Was the injury sustained by the plaintiff foreseeable at the time the defendant acted or failed to act?
- Did the plaintiff have a particular vulnerability that was aggravated by the defendant's conduct?
- Was it a foreseeable harm that occurred in an unforeseeable manner?
- Was there a third party that contributed to the plaintiff's injury?
- Was there an act of God that contributed to the plaintiff's injury?
- Was the plaintiff's injury or the way in which the plaintiff was injured highly extraordinary or unusual in light of the defendant's conduct?

SURF'S UP

Many states have extended the liability for damages to other people who serve an intoxicated person alcohol in social situations such as at business parties, social events, and other types of social activities that do not involve the sale of alcohol by a business enterprise. One organization that is very involved in lobbying for the enactment of laws that prevent drunk driving is Mothers Against Drunk Driving. This organization is dedicated to reducing the number of deaths related to driving under the influence. Check out MADD's political activity by going to its website: www.madd.org.

Summary

Whether or not a defendant caused the plaintiff's injuries and damages is a question of fact. The legal question is whether or not the defendant's conduct was the cause in fact of the damages and injuries sustained by the plaintiff.

The but for test is one of the tests the courts use to determine whether or not the defendant was the cause in fact of the plaintiff's injury or damages. The but for test is used when there is only one defendant who is suspected of being the cause of the injury. The but for test asks the following question: Is it more likely than not that "but for" the defendant's unreasonable conduct, the injury or damages would not have been suffered by the plaintiff?

When a plaintiff is attempting to attach liability to the defendant using the but for test, the plaintiff has the burden of proof to demonstrate that the defendant caused the plaintiff's harm. However, the plaintiff does not have to prove with absolute certainty that the defendant was the cause of the harm. The plaintiff only has to prove that it is *probable* that the defendant's actions caused the harm sustained by the plaintiff.

The substantial factor test is more widely used than the but for test. The test is simple: if the defendant's conduct was a substantial factor in bringing about the injuries or damages to the plaintiff, then proximate cause can be established. The substantial factor test is used when there is more than one possible causal individual or entity. The question that needs to be asked in the substantial test is: Is it more likely than not that the defendant's unreasonable acts or omissions were a substantial factor in producing the injury suffered by the plaintiff?

The substantial factor is particularly useful when two or more events have occurred and each one by itself could have been enough to damage or harm the plaintiff. For each of the events, the substantial factor is used to determine whether or not it could have caused the harm. If so, then that event is determined to be a cause in fact of the harm. If it is determined that one of the events could have not have brought harm to the plaintiff by itself, then that event or that defendant will not be found to be a substantial factor, and liability to the defendant will not attach.

In circumstances in which numerous manufacturers may have caused the injuries to the plaintiff, and it is difficult to determine that any one manufacturer could have caused the injury to the plaintiff, then all of the manufacturers involved may be forced to pay a portion of the plaintiff's award that is proportional to each manufacturer's market share in the industry. This type of market share determination is typically found in cases that involve products. Good examples of these types of cases have involved breast implants and tobacco. Typically the courts will look for the products of the defendant manufacturers to be identical or very similar. In addition, a large number of manufacturers must be sued by the plaintiff or plaintiffs so that it can be said that they constitute a significant or substantial share of the market in the industry.

The determination that needs to be made as to when liability will attach to a defendant is that the injury to the plaintiff must be the foreseeable consequence of the original risk created by the defendant's unreasonable acts or omissions. If the injuries are the foreseeable consequences of the original risk created by defendant, then the defendant will be determined to be the proximate cause of all of plaintiff's injuries, and liability will attach. The plaintiff must take reasonable steps to mitigate any additional injury or harm that could be consequences of the original injury caused by the defendant.

If it is foreseeable that defendant's unreasonable conduct will result in any force on the plaintiff's body, and if this force to the plaintiff does occur, then the defendant will be liable for the foreseeable as well as the unforeseeable injuries sustained by the plaintiff. If it was foreseeable that the defendant's conduct would cause injuries to the plaintiff, then the defendant will be liable for unforeseeable injuries that follow from any foreseeable force that occurred to the plaintiff. If the defendant's conduct was unreasonable or intentional, the defendant will be held liable for the plaintiff's injuries. It will not matter if the plaintiff has a particular vulnerability to injury and therefore might be injured to a greater extent than a person who does not possess the same vulnerabilities as the plaintiff. A plaintiff who has particular vulnerabilities is known as an eggshell skull plaintiff. The defendant will still be held liable for the foreseeable and unforeseeable injuries sustained by the plaintiff that resulted from the defendant's actions.

There are circumstances in which the defendant will be absolved of liability for a plaintiff's injuries in a particular situation. This principle is known as intervening causes. An intervening cause is a force or an act by a third person that produces the injury or harm to the plaintiff after the defendant's unreasonable action or failure to act (omission) has occurred.

An intervening cause becomes a superseding cause when the harm caused by the intervening force is outside the scope of the foreseeable risk originally created by the defendant's unreasonable acts or omissions, and/or the harm caused by the intervening cause is considered highly unusual or extraordinary.

Key Terms

Act of God
Burden of proof
"But for" test
Cause in fact
Eggshell skull
Intervening cause

Intervening force
Mitigate
Proximate cause
Substantial factor
Supersede

Review Questions

1. What is proximate cause?
2. What is an eggshell skull plaintiff?
3. List five acts of God?
4. Why is the "but for" test important?
5. Why is the substantial factor test important?
6. What is the difference between the but for and substantial factor tests?
7. What is an intervening cause?
8. What is the difference between an intervening act of a third person and the intervening criminal act of a third person? Give examples of how each is different.
9. What is the burden of proof in a proximate cause matter?
10. What is actual cause?
11. What is cause in fact?

12. How are actual cause and cause in fact different?

13. Give an example of an eggshell skull plaintiff.

14. Does an intervening act always limit the defendant's liability? Why or why not?

15. What happens if an intervening cause is foreseeable?

Exercises

1. Sarah is going to drive to visit her grandmother in Anytown, USA. Sarah tells her friend, Benny, about the trip. Benny asks Sarah if she will deliver a package to a friend in Anytown. Sarah agrees and takes the package from Benny and puts it on the backseat of her car. Unbeknownst to Sarah, the package contains chemicals that will cause burning to the skin. Sarah is also taking her two cousins with her to visit her grandmother. Lila, who is six years old, sits in the backseat next to the package. While on the way to their grandmother's, the package on the backseat begins to leak. Some of the chemicals get on Lila and burn her. If Lila's mother brings a negligence action against Sarah, what will happen?
   a. Sarah could not have known or anticipated that the contents of the package would cause harm to her cousin, so she is not liable.
   b. Sarah should have known that the contents of the package might be harmful and had a duty to protect Lila from such exposure.
   c. Benny's actions will be considered an intervening cause, and Sarah will not be held liable for the injuries sustained by Lila.

2. David was riding his bicycle very fast on the sidewalk instead of the street. While doing so he almost collides with Nancy. To avoid being struck, Nancy throws herself out into the street. Nancy is not injured by the impact with the street. However, before Nancy can get up from the street, she is struck by Patricia, who is driving her car too fast and not paying attention to the road. Nancy's leg is seriously injured. Nancy chooses to bring a lawsuit against David. Will David be found liable, and will Nancy be able to recover an award for her damages and injuries?

3. Vivian is walking across the street. Dwayne is driving on the street dangerously fast. Dwayne sees Vivian but is unable to come to a complete stop and strikes her lightly, knocking her to the ground. Vivian sustains some minor cuts and bruises. However, Vivian now has nightmares concerning the accident and is unable to sleep. She is afraid to cross streets by foot. Vivian sues Dwayne not only for her bruises, but also for her emotional distress arising out of the accident. Will she recover damages?

4. Carco is a manufacturer of motor vehicles. Since a federal regulation mandates that all motor vehicles be equipped with seat belts, Carco equipped all of its vehicles with safety belts provided by a company called Safeco. Jake is injured when his vehicle is involved in an accident. Jake sues Safeco, alleging that the safety belts were the proximate cause of the accident. What does Jake need to prove in order to show that Safeco was the proximate cause of his injuries?

5. Assuming the same facts as above, what does Safeco need to prove in order to show that it was not the cause of Jake's injuries?

6. Wanda hired professional painters to paint her house. After a long day's work, the painters packed up their equipment and left for the day. However, the painters failed to remove a ladder that was positioned along the side of the house. Late that same night, a burglar used the ladder to enter the home and steal property. Wanda has sued the painters, alleging that they were negligent in leaving the ladder unattended. Will Wanda prevail in her claim against the painters?

7. Tony hires Lawyer to represent him in an employment suit against Tony's former employer. Tony has a valid claim against his former employer, but Lawyer has let the statute of limitations expire, and Tony is not allowed to proceed with the suit. Using the "but for" test, in addition to proving negligence, what does Tony need to establish to successfully prevail against Lawyer?

8. Daniel negligently struck Peter with his vehicle as Peter was riding his bike. Peter had a pre-existing back injury that was re-aggravated by the collision. Will Peter be able to recover for damages that were a result of his pre-existing condition?

 PORTFOLIO ASSIGNMENT

Interview the person at your insurance company who handles risk management and/or appraising and ask him or her how the notions of cause in fact, proximate cause, but for test, substantial factor test, foreseeability, and superseding and intervening causes can all play a part in assessing a claim, especially when involving car accidents. Report your findings.

Vocabulary Builders

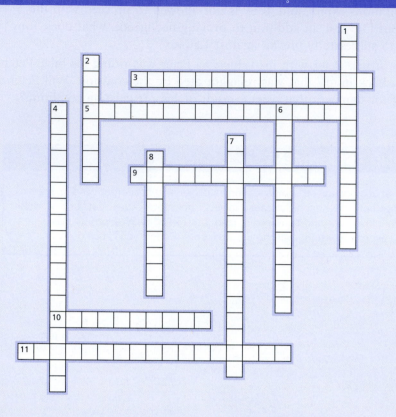

Instructions

Use the key terms from this chapter to fill in the answers to the crossword puzzle.

NOTE: When the answer is more than one word, leave a blank space between words.

ACROSS

3. The defendant's actions are the nearest cause of the plaintiff 's injuries.
5. An independent cause that intervenes between the original wrongful act or omission and the injury, turns aside the natural sequence of events, and produces a result that would not otherwise have followed and that could not have been reasonably anticipated.
9. If the complained-of act had not occurred, no injury would have resulted.
10. An act occasioned exclusively by forces of nature without the interference of any human agency.
11. An act that actively operates in producing harm to another after an actor's negligent act or omission.

DOWN

1. A person who is particularly vulnerable or susceptible to damage or injury as a result of a pre-existing condition or weakness that afflicts a particular person.
2. To make less severe or intense.
3. A material and active contributing activity or event that led to the plaintiff's injuries or damages.
5. The particular cause that produces an event and without which the event would not have occurred.
7. Standard for assessing the weight of the evidence.
8. To set aside, render unnecessary, suspend, or stay.

Pesca v. City of New York
SUPREME COURT OF NEW YORK, APPELLATE DIVISION, FIRST DEPARTMENT
298 A.D.2d 292; 749 N.Y.S.2d 26; 2002 N.Y. App. Div. LEXIS 10202
October 29, 2002, Decided
October 29, 2002, Entered

CASE SUMMARY

PROCEDURAL POSTURE: Plaintiffs, workers, sued defendants, contractors, in the Supreme Court, Bronx County (New York), for injuries suffered when a worker prevented himself from falling from a ramp and concerning the alleged improper construction of the ramp. The trial court denied the contractors' summary judgment motions, as well as the workers' partial summary judgment motion, and all appealed.

OVERVIEW: The appellate court held the trial court properly declined to dismiss the workers' claim under *N.Y. Lab. Law* § 240(1) as there was a triable issue as to whether the ramp's railing was an adequate safety device and, if not, whether it proximately caused the injury. Although the worker did not fall from the ramp, his injuries in preventing himself from falling could be compensable under § 240(1) if they resulted from a failure to provide a proper safety device. The workers' *N.Y. Lab. Law* § 241(6) claim was properly dismissed as the violation of a specific Industrial Code regulation was not alleged. Given evidence that the slope of the ramp was too steep, the motion to dismiss the workers' common-law negligence claim for negligent construction of the ramp was correctly denied. The workers' *N.Y. Lab. Law* § 200(1) claim against a contractor was reinstated as the evidence showed a worker, at the time of the accident, was directly supervised by that contractor's employees.

OUTCOME: The trial court's judgment was modified by reinstating the workers' claim against one contractor and by dismissing the workers' common-law negligence claim against another contractor premised upon the alleged defective or dangerous condition of a railing, and, as modified, was affirmed.

JUDGES: Concur—Williams, P.J., Tom, Mazzarelli, Sullivan, Gonzalez, JJ.

OPINION

Order, Supreme Court, Bronx County (Paul Victor, J.), entered on or about August 9, 2001, which, to the extent appealed and cross-appealed from as limited by the briefs, denied the cross motions of defendants City of New York, A.J. Contracting Co., and Regional Scaffolding & Hoisting Co. insofar as such cross motions sought summary judgment dismissing plaintiffs' *Labor Law* § 240 (1) claim, denied plaintiffs' motion for partial summary judgment upon their *Labor Law* claims, and granted aforementioned defendants' cross motions for summary judgment to the extent of dismissing plaintiffs' claims under *Labor Law* §§ 200 and 241 (6) and plaintiffs' claim for common-law negligence as against defendant Regional Scaffolding, unanimously modified, on the law, to deny defendant A.J. Contracting's cross motion to the extent that such cross motion seeks dismissal of plaintiffs' *Labor Law* § 200 (1) claim and to reinstate such claim against A.J. Contracting only, and to grant defendant Regional Scaffolding's cross motion to the extent of dismissing plaintiffs' common-law negligence cause against it insofar as such cause is premised upon the alleged defective or dangerous condition of the railing, and otherwise affirmed, without costs.

Summary judgment dismissing plaintiffs' *Labor Law* § 240 (1) claim was properly denied since the record discloses the existence of a triable issue of fact as to whether the railing of the construction site ramp upon which plaintiff's accident occurred constituted an adequate safety device, and, if it did not, whether such failure was the **proximate cause** of plaintiff's injury (*see Labor Law* § 240 [1]; *McCann v Central Synagogue*, 280 AD2d 298). Although plaintiff did not fall from the ramp, the injuries he allegedly sustained in preventing himself from falling may be compensable under *Labor Law* § 240 (1) if shown to have resulted from a failure to provide a proper safety device in accordance with the requirements of that statute (*see Dominguez v Lafayette-Boynton Hous. Corp.*, 240 AD2d 310; *Gramigna v Morse Diesel*, 210 AD2d 115).

Plaintiffs' *Labor Law* § 241 (6) claim was, however, properly dismissed by reason of plaintiffs' failure to allege as the requisite predicate for such claim defendants' violation of a sufficiently specific Industrial Code regulation (*see Ross v Curtis-Palmer Hydro-Elec. Co.*, 81 NY2d 494, 505).

The motion court properly declined to dismiss plaintiffs' common-law negligence claim as against Regional Scaffolding for negligent construction of the ramp to the extent that there is evidence that the slope of the ramp was too steep. There is, however, no showing to support any other theory of negligence against Regional.

Finally, plaintiffs' *Labor Law* § 200 (1) cause of action against A.J. Contracting should be reinstated since the evidence establishes that plaintiff, at the time of the alleged accident, was directly supervised by that defendant's employees (*see, e.g., Crespo v Triad, Inc.*, 294 AD2d 145).

Concur—Williams, P.J., Tom, Mazzarelli, Sullivan and Gonzalez, JJ.

Chapter 7

Negligence: Defenses

CHAPTER OBJECTIVES

Upon completion of this chapter, you will be able to:

- Understand the defense of contributory negligence.
- Evaluate the last clear chance doctrine.
- Explain the defense of comparative negligence.
- Discuss the defense of assumption of the risk.

As in an intentional tort matter, in a negligence action, it is up to plaintiffs to prove their case against defendants. Once the plaintiff has established a prima facie case of negligence against the defendant, it is the defendant's opportunity to defend against the plaintiff's allegations. This chapter focuses on the various types of defenses that are available to a defendant who is involved in a cause of action for negligence.

CONTRIBUTORY NEGLIGENCE

Remember that a defense is a legal justification or excuse. The concept of a defense means that if a defendant committed a tort or a violation, he may not be held liable for his actions because he may have a legal justification to the action. One of the defenses that a defendant can raise in an action for negligence is contributory negligence. The plaintiff's own conduct is considered when asserting this defense to a negligence action. If the plaintiff's conduct falls below a reasonable standard of care in order to safeguard her own protection, then the defendant may assert the plaintiff's unreasonable conduct as a defense to his own conduct.

contributory negligence
The plaintiff played a large part in causing the injury; thus, fundamental fairness precludes assigning liability to the defendant.

The heart of the defense of **contributory negligence** is that a plaintiff who does not take reasonable care of her own safety and exhibits negligence that contributes to her own peril cannot recover damages from the defendant. Contributory negligence is a strict rule because a plaintiff who is even 1 percent negligent is barred from recovering as a matter of law. Contributory negligence acts as a complete defense to the plaintiff's negligence action against the defendant as it totally bars the plaintiff from recovering from the defendant. If the plaintiff was unreasonable in avoiding risks for her own safety, and if this unreasonableness was a substantial factor in producing the plaintiff's own injury, the defendant is not liable for the plaintiff's injuries or damages, even though the defendant may have also acted negligently by unreasonably creating risks for the plaintiff's safety. Contributory negligence comes into play even though the defendant's unreasonableness also was a substantial factor in producing the plaintiff's injury.

Contributory negligence focuses on the conduct of plaintiffs and imposes a duty on them to safeguard their own safety. The *Restatement (Second) of Torts,* section 463, defines contributory negligence as follows:

> Contributory negligence is conduct on the part of the plaintiff which falls below the standard to which he should conform for his own protection, and which is a legally contributing cause co-operating with the negligence of the defendant in bringing about the plaintiff's harm.

In all states, the defendant bears the burden of proof when it comes to contributory negligence. The defendant must specifically plead the defense. If the defendant cannot support this defense with specific evidence, then it will not apply. In a defense of contributory negligence, the plaintiff is held to the same standard of care as the defendant. That standard of care is the reasonable person standard. The plaintiff needs to take reasonable actions to safeguard his or her own safety, actions that an ordinary, reasonable person would take in the same or similar circumstances.

The defense of contributory negligence leaves the plaintiff to bear the full loss of her injury. The contributory negligence of the plaintiff will prevent liability attaching to the defendant primarily when the defendant has committed ordinary negligence with his conduct. If the defendant's negligence falls into the category of willful, wanton, or reckless conduct, the plaintiff's contributory negligence will not prevent the liability from attaching to the defendant. Also, contributory negligence is never a defense to any of the intentional torts that the defendant might commit.

Contributory negligence must be pled and proved by a preponderance of the evidence by the defendant. The two major elements that must be established for a defense of contributory negligence are (1) the plaintiff's negligence and (2) cause in fact.

LEGAL RESEARCH MAXIM

Remember, the basis for this defense is that the plaintiff must not take unreasonable risks of injuring himself. The plaintiff will be contributorily negligent only if the risk that he created to his own safety was unreasonable and was the same risk that led to his injury.

Cause in Fact

It will be determined that the plaintiff caused his own injury if it is determined that he was a substantial factor in producing that injury. If the plaintiff acted unreasonably regarding his own safety, and this unreasonableness was a substantial factor in producing that injury, then the cause in fact element for contributory negligence is established.

Once a prima facie case has been proved by the plaintiff and then the defense of contributory negligence is established, the plaintiff's contentions are defeated. Contributory negligence is a complete bar to a negligence action by the plaintiff.

The defense of contributory negligence assumes that the plaintiff has knowledge of the peril that she faces. However, if the plaintiff can demonstrate that she had no knowledge of that peril and could not have anticipated the danger, contributory negligence will not be established.

RESEARCH THIS

The defense of contributory negligence was first established in England in the case of *Butterfield v. Forrester,* 103 Eng. Rep. 926 (K.B. 1809). It is a judge-made law. In this case, the defendant had partially blocked the road with a pole. The plaintiff was riding his horse at a rapid rate of speed at dusk and ran into the pole. The court held that the plaintiff was barred from recovery. Locate the case and read the rationale that the judge used to establish this important defense of contributory negligence.

LAST CLEAR CHANCE

last clear chance
Permits the plaintiff in a negligence action to recover, notwithstanding his or her own negligence, on a showing that the defendant had the last clear chance to avoid the accident.

The doctrine of **last clear chance** is a form of mitigation that is attributed to the plaintiff. The doctrine allows the plaintiff to recover for his injuries even if he contributed to them if the defendant had a last clear chance to avoid injuring the plaintiff and failed to do so.

The last clear chance doctrine acts to offset the impact of a defense of contributory negligence. It is a doctrine that is to the plaintiff's benefit only, and it comes into play after the defendant establishes the plaintiff's contributory negligence. The plaintiff can still recover, if it can be determined that the defendant had the opportunity to prevent or avoid the injury to the plaintiff but failed to do so. In such a case, the plaintiff would recover for her injuries or damages even though the plaintiff was contributorily negligent.

For example, suppose the plaintiff negligently parked her vehicle so that it stuck out into the street. The defendant, driving around the corner at a rapid rate of speed, ran into the plaintiff's car. The defendant will be held liable because the plaintiff lost the opportunity to avoid the accident at the time that it occurred because she had left the vehicle and the defendant could have avoided the accident if he had taken the opportunity to do so, by driving more slowly and being more cautious.

There are four situations in which the last clear chance doctrine may be successfully asserted. These situations are fashioned by combining the plaintiff's ability to avoid any danger and the defendant's knowledge. The four situations are:

- Helpless plaintiff and the defendant discovers danger.
- Helpless plaintiff with an inattentive defendant.
- Inattentive plaintiff with an aware defendant.
- Inattentive plaintiff and an inattentive defendant.

Helpless Plaintiff, Defendant Discovers

The plaintiff's contributory negligence has placed him in a dilemma from which he cannot extricate himself. Even if the plaintiff now uses reasonable care, he could not get out of the danger. If the defendant discovered the plaintiff in helpless danger and had an opportunity to avoid the accident but failed to do so, then the plaintiff's contributory negligence will not bar recovery. The reason that recovery will not be barred is that the defendant had—and failed to take—the last clear chance to avoid the injury to the plaintiff.

The *Restatement (Second) of Torts*, section 479, addresses this situation as follows:

> A plaintiff who has negligently subjected himself to a risk of harm from the defendant's subsequent negligence may recover for harm caused thereby if, immediately preceding the harm,
> a. the plaintiff is unable to avoid it by the exercise of reasonable vigilance and care, and
> b. the defendant is negligent in failing to utilize with reasonable care and competence his then existing opportunity to void the harm, when he
> (i) knows of the plaintiff's situation and realizes or has reason to realize the peril involved in it or
> (ii) would discover the situation and thus have reason to realize the peril, if he were to exercise the vigilance which it is then his duty to the plaintiff to exercise.

Helpless Plaintiff, Inattentive Defendant

Again, in this scenario, the plaintiff's contributory negligence has placed him in a situation that he could get himself out of by the use of reasonable care, but the plaintiff remains negligently unaware of the danger up to the time of the accident. If the defendant does not discover the plaintiff in inattentive peril even though he or she could have discovered it, and had a reasonable opportunity to avoid the accident but did not take it, had the defendant not negligently failed to pay attention will not bar the plaintiff from recovery. The reason is that the defendant had—and failed to take—the last clear chance to avoid the injury.

The *Restatement (Second) of Torts*, section 480, defines the inattentive plaintiff as follows:

> *A plaintiff who, by the exercise of reasonable vigilance, could discover the danger created by the defendant's negligence in time to avoid the harm to him, can recover if, but only if, the defendant*
> a. *knows of the plaintiff's situation, and*
> b. *realizes or has reason to realize that the plaintiff is inattentive and therefore unlikely to discover his peril in time to avoid the harm, and*
> c. *thereafter is negligent in failing to utilize with reasonable care and competence his then existing opportunity to avoid harm.*

Inattentive Plaintiff, Aware Defendant

In another situation, the plaintiff may be inattentive or careless as to the danger that she might be in, and negligently fail to remove herself from that danger. If the defendant discovers the plight of the plaintiff and fails to respond, then the plaintiff could recover under the last clear chance doctrine. If the defendant does not know or has reason to know of the plaintiff's inattentiveness, the defendant will not be liable because of this lack of knowledge.

Inattentive Plaintiff, Inattentive Defendant

The last scenario involves a situation where both the plaintiff and the defendant are inattentive and are unaware of the danger. In this scenario, the last clear chance doctrine cannot apply because it is unclear as to whether or not there was an opportunity to avoid the danger as both parties were inattentive and unaware.

Imputed Contributory Negligence

Contributory negligence will be **imputed** in certain three-party situations. That is, because of some relation between A and B, B's suit against C might be defeated because of A's contributory negligence, "imputed" to B. The most common situations of **imputed negligence** occur with drivers and passengers, and with family members.

With drivers and passengers, for example, a driver's negligence could be imputed to his passenger so as to prevent the passenger from recovering against the driver of another vehicle whose negligence contributed to a collision between the two cars.

Similarly, with family members, a husband's negligence was frequently imputed to his wife, and vice versa. And a parent's negligence was imputed to his or her child. For example, Father fails to supervise Child. Child runs in the street and is hit by D. Traditionally, D could defend by saying, "Father negligently failed to supervise, and his negligence should be imputed to Child, thus giving me a complete defense."

imputed
To ascribe to or charge (a person) with an act or quality because of the conduct of another over whom one has control or for whose acts or conduct one is responsible.

imputed negligence
Places upon one person responsibility for the negligence of another.

COMPARATIVE NEGLIGENCE

The defense of contributory negligence has been criticized as being overly harsh because it bars plaintiffs from recovering anything for their injuries and damages even if they are found to have contributed only slightly to the accident. Contributory negligence does not measure the plaintiff's conduct in degrees but bars recovery altogether. Many states began to become dissatisfied with the defense of contributory negligence and began to apportion fault between the two parties. The apportionment of fault between the parties is known as **comparative negligence**.

comparative negligence
Applies when the evidence shows that both the plaintiff and the defendant acted negligently.

Comparative negligence rejects the all-or-nothing approach taken in contributory negligence and acts to apportion the damages between the plaintiff and the defendant. Comparative negligence applies only to a state that has abolished contributory negligence partially or completely. In comparative negligence states, the contributory negligence of the plaintiff does not act as a complete bar to the plaintiff's action if the elements of the comparative negligence theory have been established. The total amount of damages suffered by the plaintiff are determined and then apportioned according to fault of each of the parties. The plaintiff's recovery is reduced by a proportion equal to the ratio of his or her own negligence and the total negligence that caused the incident.

A comparative negligence defense requires the establishment of the following elements:

- a determination of negligence by the defendant that caused harm to the plaintiff;
- a negligent act by the plaintiff that contributed to his or her injury;
- a measurement of the percentage of the **contribution** of the negligence of both parties; and
- an award of damages to the plaintiff that is reduced by a percentage of his or her own negligence.

contribution
Payment of a share of an amount for which one is liable as a shared payment of a judgment by joint tortfeasors, especially according to proportional fault.

Pure Comparative Negligence

When the plaintiff sues the defendant for negligence and the defendant asserts that the plaintiff's negligence contributed to the injury, a court will decide the percentage by which each side is deemed to be negligent. The plaintiff's recovery is limited to that percentage of the award that was due to the defendant's negligence. For example, suppose that the judge determined that the plaintiff's own negligence contributed to approximately 25 percent of the total negligence of the accident. If the plaintiff is awarded $100,000 in damages, the award will be reduced by 25 percent, or $25,000, to account for the plaintiff's negligent conduct. Under this defense, the plaintiff will always recover something if the injury was caused by the negligence of both parties, even if the plaintiff's fault is determined to be greater than the defendant's.

Modified Comparative Negligence

In modified comparative negligence, if it is determined that the plaintiff and the defendant are equally negligent, the plaintiff will recover nothing for his harm. If the plaintiff is determined to be 51 percent negligent and the defendant is determined to be 49 percent negligent, then the plaintiff will recover nothing. The plaintiff must be 49 percent or less negligent in order to recover.

For example, using the automobile accident described earlier, suppose that the court determined that the plaintiff contributed to the accident. However, the court that heard the case is in a state that applies comparative negligence instead of contributory negligence. The court determines that the plaintiff was 30 percent negligent by parking her car so that it stuck out into the street. The defendant was found to be 70 percent liable for driving too fast and striking the vehicle. The plaintiff will still recover because her liability is less than 50 percent and the defendant's negligence is still great than the plaintiff's negligence. The plaintiff's award will be reduced by 30 percent to account for her portion of fault.

Additionally, modified comparative negligence jurisdictions are split as to when there are multiple defendants. Some states apply what is called the "unit rule" in dealing with multiple defendants. Under the "unit rule," the plaintiff's negligence is compared with the combined negligence of all defendants.

CASE FACT PATTERN

Here is an example with multiple defendants in a modified comparative negligence jurisdiction:

Jeff suffers $50,000 damages and is 40 percent at fault. Donald is 10 percent at fault and Thomas is 50 percent at fault.

In a "pure" comparative negligence jurisdiction, Jeff (plaintiff) may recover. However, in a "modified" comparative negligence jurisdiction, there is a split of authority. In some states where multiple defendants are involved, the plaintiff's negligence is compared with that of each individual defendant. By applying this rule, in a suit by Jeff against Donald there would be no recovery since Jeff's degree of fault exceeds Donald's. Conversely, in an action by Jeff against Thomas, there would be recovery since Jeff would be less at fault.

In a "unit rule" state, Jeff would be entitled to recover $30,000 from either Donald or Thomas because Jeff's negligence would be less than the combined negligence of both defendants. In the event that Jeff did recover $30,000 from Donald, then Donald would be entitled to contribution from Thomas.

ASSUMPTION OF THE RISK

Assumption of the risk is another defense used in negligence actions. If the plaintiff knowingly and voluntarily assumes the risk of being harmed by the negligence of the defendant, then the defendant will not be liable for the injury he negligently caused to the plaintiff. (For example, think of the guy who says, "Go ahead . . . hit me in the stomach!") Assumption of the risk acts as a complete defense to the plaintiff's negligence action against the defendant and bars the plaintiff from recovering for his injuries. It is based on the premise that the plaintiff is responsible for his own choice and chose to accept the risk.

A defense of assumption of the risk requires two elements:

- Voluntary assumption of a known risk by the plaintiff.
- Full knowledge of the danger inherent in the risk.

Assumption of the risk is determined by a subjective standard. The standard is whether this plaintiff knowingly and voluntarily assumed the risk of the defendant's conduct.

The risk should have been known and understood by the plaintiff before it can be said that the plaintiff voluntarily assumed the risk. In addition, she must know or should have known the danger that is inherent in the risk.

Assumption of the risk applies in two situations. These two situations are express assumption and implied assumption.

Express Assumption

Express assumption is when the plaintiff and defendant expressly agree to limit the liability. It must be clear that the parties agree to such limitations or withholding of liability. The law will not hold up the agreement if the bargaining positions between the parties are unbalanced. The law is concerned that the weaker of the parties did not voluntarily agree to assume the risk but may have been coerced. As a matter of public policy, the law will invalidate these agreements to protect the public.

For an assumption of the risk defense to be asserted, two elements need to be established:

- The agreement to the risk must be given freely.
- The agreement must be for a particular risk that led to the injury.

An example of express assumption occurs often with contracts. Under the terms of a contract, the parties can agree under the terms of the contract to limit liability. They may agree to limit the liability to a certain dollar figure or agree that each party

assumption of the risk
The doctrine that releases another person from liability for the person who chooses to assume a known risk of harm.

express assumption
A directly and clearly stated act or agreement of assuming or taking upon one's self.

public policy
The principle that injury to the public good or public order constitutes a basis for setting aside, or denying effect to, acts or transactions.

will bear his or her own risk. Professor Keeton speaks to this situation in *Prosser and Keeton on the Law of Torts*, section 68 at 483–84 (5th ed. 1984), when he states:

> *"If an express agreement exempting the defendant from liability for this negligence is to be sustained, it must appear that its terms were brought home to the plaintiff; and if he did not know of the provision in his contract, and a reasonable person in his position would not have known of it, it is not binding upon him, and the agreement fails for want of mutual assent. It is also necessary that the expressed terms of the agreement be applicable to the particular misconduct of the defendant, and the courts have strictly construed the terms of exculpatory clauses against the defendant who is usually the draftsman."*

Implied Assumption

Most cases that involve assumption of the risk deal with implied and not express assumption. The **implied assumption** is usually implied from the plaintiff's conduct. If a plaintiff who fully understands a risk of harm to himself or his things that could be caused by the defendant's conduct and nonetheless voluntarily chooses to remain in the area of that risk, his conduct demonstrates the plaintiff's willingness to accept the risk. By accepting the risk, the plaintiff is not entitled to recover for harm that flows from the risk.

implied assumption
An inference from the plaintiff's conduct that demonstrates that the person is accepting the risk involved in the activity or event.

Two elements need to be met in order to assert a defense of assumption of the risk:

- The plaintiff must have known of the risk in question.
- The plaintiff must have demonstrated that he or she voluntarily consented to bear the risk.

An objective standard is used when determining whether or not the plaintiff knew of the risk involved. The standard is if the plaintiff actually knew of the risk and not what one ought to have known. Again, Professor Keeton gives insight into knowledge of the risk in *Prosser and Keeton on the Law of Torts*, section 68 at 487 (5th ed. 1984):

> *"Knowledge of the risk is the watchword of assumption of risk. Under ordinary circumstances the plaintiff will not be taken to assume any risk of either activities or conditions of which he has no knowledge. Moreover, he must not only know of the facts which create the danger, but he must comprehend and appreciate the nature of the danger he confronts."*

The plaintiff must also have assumed a risk that would seem to be reasonable under the circumstances. If the risk is unreasonable, the courts may look at whether or not the plaintiff actually knew of the risk involved or if she agreed to the risk under some type of duress.

A DAY IN THE LIFE OF A REAL PARALEGAL

Many people you encounter each day, friends and family in particular, probably do not know or realize how many defenses to negligence a defendant can use, depending on jurisdiction. Assumption of the risk may be the one defense that a number of people have heard of and understand to some degree. The buying of a ticket at an amusement park for the roller coaster is an example that many people recognize as assumption of the risk should something happen to the ride. Remember also that many clients may not know the defenses that are available in the jurisdiction you work in; therefore, it is important to understand the defenses that are available in your area.

YOU BE THE JUDGE

Hairco is a dandruff shampoo manufacturer. On its shampoo's box cover there is a warning label that states a small percentage of the population may be allergic to the chemicals contained in the product. Hairco recommends that its users test a small amount of the product on a portion of their hair to see if they are in fact allergic to the shampoo.

Jane buys the product and reads the warning; however, she fails to test the product on a small portion of her hair before applying it to her entire head. After using the product, Jane experiences irritation and discomfort because of an allergic reaction to the shampoo. If Jane brings suit against Hairco, what is the likely result, and why?

SPOT THE ISSUE

Patrick loves baseball. He and his friends know all the members of their local minor league base-ball team, and they love to go to games. Patrick likes to sit as close to the action as possible. When Patrick's team makes the finals, he buys tickets to go to the game. Patrick wants to view the game from a clear vantage point, so he purchases tickets that are in the front row right beside third base.

Patrick and his friends go to the game. They are having a great time. The count is 3-2 for Patrick's favorite player, and the game is tied at 2-2 in the top of the eighth inning. Patrick is standing up yelling at the batter. The batter swings a line drive foul ball right up the third field line, and it hits Patrick in the head. Patrick sustains a severe concussion and is taken to the hospital.

Patrick sues the ball park for negligence.

What issue may be present on behalf of the defendant, the baseball park?

EYE ON ETHICS

Each state has its own laws concerning de-fenses to actions brought in negligence. Some states assert a contributory negligence theory where the plaintiff will be barred from recovery. Some use a comparative theory of negligence, and almost all recognize an assumption of the risk defense. It is very important to know and understand what defenses to negligent actions are recognized for your jurisdiction. The types of defenses available to defendants will seriously influence the direction to take in preparing a plaintiff's case.

SURF'S UP

To learn more about the various defenses that are available for negligence actions, some of the following websites can be helpful:

- www.findlaw.com
- www.referenceforbusiness.com
- www.nationalpersonalinjuryattorneys.com
- www.megalaw.com
- www.lawguru.com

Summary

The heart of the defense of contributory negligence is that plaintiffs who do not take reasonable care of their own safety and exhibit negligence that contributes to their own peril cannot recover damages from a defendant. Contributory negligence acts as a complete defense to the plaintiff's negligence action against the defendant as it totally bars the plaintiff from recovering from the defendant. If the plaintiff was unreasonable in avoiding risks for her own safety, and if this unreasonableness was a substantial factor in producing the plaintiff's own injury, the defendant is not liable for the plaintiff's injuries or damages even though the defendant may have also acted negligently by unreasonably creating risks for plaintiff's safety. Contributory negli-gence comes into play even though the defendant's unreasonableness also was a sub-stantial factor in producing the plaintiff's injury.

In all states, the defendant bears the burden of proof when it comes to contribu-tory negligence. The defendant must specifically plead the defense. If the defendant cannot support this defense with specific evidence, then it will not apply. In a defense of contributory negligence, the plaintiff is held to the same standard of care as the defendant. That standard of care is the reasonable person standard. The plaintiff needs to take reasonable actions to safeguard her own safety as would an ordinary reasonable person in the same or similar circumstances.

The defense of contributory negligence leaves the plaintiff to bear the full loss of his injury. The plaintiff's contributory negligence will prevent liability attaching to the defendant primarily when the defendant has committed ordinary negligence with his conduct. If the defendant's negligence falls into the category of willful, wanton, or reckless conduct, the plaintiff's contributory negligence will not prevent the liability from attaching to the defendant. Also, contributory negligence is never a defense to any of the intentional torts that the defendant might commit.

Contributory negligence must be pled and proved by a preponderance of the evidence by the defendant. The two major elements that must be established for a defense of contributory negligence are (1) the plaintiff's negligence and (2) cause in fact.

The doctrine of last clear chance is a form of mitigation that is attributed to the plaintiff. The doctrine allows the plaintiff to recover for his injuries even if he contributed to them if the defendant had a last clear chance to avoid injuring the plaintiff and failed to do so.

The defense of contributory negligence has been criticized as being overly harsh because it bars plaintiffs from recovering anything for their injuries and damages even if they are found to have contributed only slightly to the accident. Contributory negligence does not measure the plaintiff's conduct in degrees, but bars recovery altogether. Many states began to become dissatisfied with the defense of contributory negligence and began to apportion fault between the two parties. The apportionment of fault between the parties is known as comparative negligence.

When the plaintiff sues the defendant for negligence and the defendant asserts that the plaintiff's negligence contributed to the injury, a court will decide the percentage by which each side is deemed to be negligent. The plaintiff's recovery is limited to that percentage of the award that was due to the defendant's negligence.

In modified comparative negligence, if it is determined that the plaintiff and the defendant are equally negligent, the plaintiff will recover nothing for his harm. If the plaintiff is determined to be 51 percent negligent and the defendant is determined to be 49 percent negligent, then the plaintiff will recover nothing. The plaintiff must be 49 percent or less negligent in order to recover.

Assumption of the risk is another defense employed in negligence actions. If the plaintiff knowingly and voluntarily assumes the risk of being harmed by the defendant's negligence, then the defendant will not be liable for the injury he negligently caused to the plaintiff. Assumption of the risk acts as a complete defense to the plaintiff's negligence action against the defendant and bars the plaintiff from recovering for his injuries. It is based on the premise that the plaintiff is responsible for his own choice and chose to accept the risk.

Express assumption is when the plaintiff and defendant expressly agree to limit the liability. It must be clear that the parties agree to such limitations or withholding of liability. The law will not hold up the agreement if the bargaining positions between the parties are unbalanced. The law is concerned that the weaker of the parties did not voluntarily agree to assume the risk but may have been coerced. As a matter of public policy, the law will invalidate these agreements in order to protect the public.

Most cases that involve assumption of the risk deal with implied and not express assumption. The implied assumption is usually implied from the plaintiff's conduct. Thus, if a plaintiff who fully understands a risk of harm to herself or her things that could be caused by the defendant's conduct and who nonetheless voluntarily chooses to remain in the area of that risk, then by her actions, she demonstrates her willingness to accept the risk. By accepting the risk, the plaintiff is not entitled to recover for harm that flows from the risk.

Key Terms

Assumption of the risk
Comparative negligence
Contribution
Contributory negligence
Express assumption

Implied assumption
Imputed
Imputed negligence
Last clear chance
Public policy

Review Questions

1. Define contributory negligence.
2. What does a defense of contributory negligence do to the plaintiff's claims for recovery?
3. If the plaintiff is not aware of the peril involved, how does that lack of knowledge affect the defense of contributory negligence?
4. What is comparative negligence?
5. How does comparative negligence differ from contributory negligence?
6. What are the elements necessary for comparative negligence?
7. What is assumption of the risk?
8. What are the elements necessary to assert a defense of assumption of the risk?
9. What is express assumption of the risk? Give an example.
10. What is implied assumption of the risk? Give an example.

Exercises

1. Julie lives in a state that recognizes contributory negligence as a defense. Julie was walking downtown shopping. She noticed a dress shop across the street that had a particularly beautiful dress in the window. Julie decided to cross the street and look at the dress. From between two parked cars and not in a crosswalk, Julie stepped out into the street to cross to the other side. Harry was traveling down the street. He was late for his dentist appointment and was speeding, significantly above the speed limit. Harry never saw Julie until it was too late. Harry struck Julie, who sustained severe injuries. In a negligence suit against Harry by Julie, who will prevail and why?

2. Research your state's case law concerning negligence and defenses for negligence. Using the scenario above between Julie and Harry, write an answer to the complaint for Harry. What are the appropriate defenses that he would assert in such an action? Make sure that you research the proper format for such a response with the court. Some courts use court forms, and others require typewritten documentation. Research which is used in your jurisdiction and prepare the proper documentation as if you were preparing it for your supervising attorney for filing with the court. Remember, you are representing Harry.

3. Bert was driving east on Maple Street. As he approached the intersection of Maple and Elm Street, he noticed that the traffic light was red for him. Bert prepared to stop, but his brakes were not working properly. Bert could not stop and continued into the intersection against the red light. Jane was driving north on Elm Street. She saw Bert go through the red light. Because the light was green for Jane, she did not stop and continued into the intersection as well. Jane believed that she could steer clear of Bert and avoid an accident. However, that was not the case. The two vehicles collided. Bert's car sustained minimal damage; however, Jane's car was so severely damaged that it was declared a total loss.

The jurisdiction has a statute that prohibits entering an intersection against a red traffic signal and another statute that adopts the all-or-nothing rule of contributory negligence. In an action by Jane against Bert, the court should find for:

a. Bert, since Jane had the last clear chance to avoid the accident.

b. Bert, if it was unreasonable for Jane to enter the intersection when she did.

c. Jane, if Bert's violation of statute was a substantial factor in producing the damage.

d. Jane, since Bert's conduct was negligence per se.

4. Driver and Passenger were driving to work in Driver's automobile one evening. As they traveled at a speed of 25 miles per hour (the posted speed limit), Passenger suddenly pointed to an overturned vehicle along the side of the road and said "Hey, look at that car." Driver turned around to look at the vehicle. As he did so, he failed to see an abandoned vehicle about 200 feet in front of his own vehicle. Seconds later, Driver crashed into the vehicle. The jurisdiction where the parties reside is a comparative negligence jurisdiction. If Driver asserts a claim against the owner of the abandoned auto, what is the likely result and why?

5. On a foggy morning, Harry started walking down the street. At one point he decided to walk in the middle of the street against oncoming traffic. The traffic on the morning was light and Harry failed to see any approaching vehicles. However, shortly thereafter, Tom appeared 100 feet from Harry's location. Harry failed to see Tom's vehicle approaching. Tom noticed Harry but decided not to stop or swerve his vehicle out of the way. As a result Tom struck Harry with his vehicle. If the parties reside in a contributory negligence jurisdiction that recognize the last clear chance doctrine, what is the likely result of a suit by Harry against Tom, and why?

6. In the course of trial for negligence, it is shown that Mike, the plaintiff was 55 percent responsible for the accident occurring. Danny, the defendant is shown to have been 45 percent responsible. The amount of damages to Mike is $50,000. If the parties reside in a contributory negligence jurisdiction, how much is Mike going to receive, and why?

7. Assume the same facts as above, except that the parties reside in a pure comparative negligence jurisdiction. How much is Mike going to recover and why?

PORTFOLIO ASSIGNMENT

As there are a number of defenses to the claim of negligence, which one is utilized more often in your state's courts? Check the states that are adjacent to your state. Which defenses are used in those states?

Vocabulary Builders

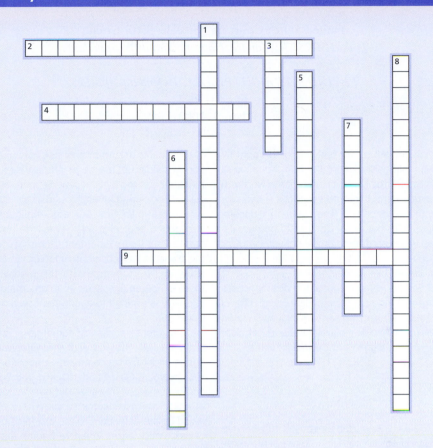

Instructions

Use the key terms from this chapter to fill in the answers to the crossword puzzle.

NOTE: When the answer is more than one word, leave a blank space between words.

ACROSS

2. The doctrine that releases another person from liability for the person who chooses to assume a known risk of harm.
6. The principle that injury to the public good or public order constitutes a basis for setting aside, or denying effect to, acts or transactions.
9. An inference from the plaintiff's conduct that demonstrates that the person is accepting the risk involved in the activity or event.

DOWN

1. The plaintiff played a large part in causing the injury; thus, fundamental fairness precludes assigning liability to the defendant.
3. To ascribe to or charge (a person) with an act or quality because of the conduct of another over whom one has control or for whose acts or conduct one is responsible.
4. Applies when the evidence shows that both the plaintiff and the defendant acted negligently.
5. A directly and clearly stated act or agreement of assuming or taking upon one's self.
7. Payment of a share of an amount for which one is liable as a shared payment of a judgment by joint tortfeasors, especially according to proportional fault.
8. Permits the plaintiff in a negligence action to recover, notwithstanding his or her own negligence, on a showing that the defendant had the last clear chance to avoid the accident.

United States Court of Appeals, Sixth Circuit
Dale HANSEN; Sandra Hansen, Plaintiffs-Appellants,
v.
FLYING J TRAVEL PLAZA, Defendant-Appellee.
No. 01-3624
Jan. 9, 2003

In personal injury action against motor fuel vendor, brought by truck driver who was allegedly injured when he slipped on spilled fuel, the United States District Court for the Northern District of Ohio, James G. Carr, J., granted vendor's motion for summary judgment. Driver appealed. The Court of Appeals, Kennedy, Circuit Judge, held that under doctrine of primary assumption of risk, vendor had no duty to protect driver.

Affirmed.

KENNEDY, Circuit Judge.

Plaintiffs Dale and Sandra Hansen appeal the district court's grant of summary judgment in favor of Defendant Flying J Travel Plaza in this diversity action seeking recovery for injuries suffered by Dale Hansen at defendant's fueling plaza. For the reasons set forth below, we AFFIRM the judgment of the district court.

I.

On February 8, 1999, Dale Hansen (Hansen) pulled into a Flying J Travel Plaza (Flying J) in Perrysburg, Ohio, to refuel his semi-truck. When Hansen entered the fueling plaza, he noticed "a lot of diesel fuel" spilled in the stall he was approaching. Rather than use that stall, Hansen waited to use another stall that had "less diesel fuel" on the ground around it. Hansen informed a station attendant that "the place was a mess" and asked "why wasn't there sand or something on the ground for the spills."

Before refueling his truck. Hansen changed out of his driving shoes and into rubber soled shoes that had a waffle-iron tread that provided better traction in slippery conditions. Hansen then proceeded to refuel his truck, walking around the truck to put hoses in both the driver and passenger side fuel tanks despite the "very slippery" conditions. While the truck was being refueled, Hansen washed his windshield using his own cleaning fluid and squeegee. Usually Hansen opened the hood of his truck and stood on the tires to reach the windshield. On this occasion, Hansen decided to stand with one foot on the truck step tread and hang from his mirror in order reach the windshield. When Hansen began to dismount from his position on the truck, his foot slipped, causing him to lose his balance and fall to the ground. As a result of this fall, Hansen suffered a broken leg, which required surgery and continues to cause him pain, as well as interfere with his activities.

II.

Hansen asserts two challenges to the district court's grant of summary judgment. First, Hansen argues that the district court erred when it granted summary judgment based on a finding of reasonable assumption of risk because reasonable assumption of risk is not a type of primary assumption of risk, a defense recognized by Ohio law. Second, Hansen argues that the district court erred when it found as a matter of law that Hansen was more than fifty percent negligent under comparative negligence principles. We review de novo the district court's grant of summary judgment. Summary judgment is proper "if the pleadings, depositions, answers to interrogatories, admissions on file, together with the affidavits, if any, show that there is no genuine issue as to any material fact and the moving party is entitled to a judgment as a matter of law." Fed. R. Civ. P. 56(c).

The defense of assumption of risk, with two exceptions, has been judicially merged with the defense of contributory negligence under Ohio's comparative negligence statute. *Anderson v. Ceccardi,* 6 Ohio St.3d 110, 451 N.E.2d 780, 783 (1983). The doctrinal merger, however, did not include primary assumption of risk, "which concerns cases where there is a lack of duty owed by the defendant to the plaintiff." or express assumption of risk, which arises when "a person expressly contracts with another not to sue for any future injuries that may be caused by that person's negligence." The *Anderson* court, thus, preserved assumption of risk rules that pose questions of law (whether a defendant owed a plaintiff a duty and whether a plaintiff had expressly waived by contract any duty owed by a defendant) as absolute bars to recovery for a plaintiff's injuries.

Reasonable assumption of risk, which entails a reasonable and voluntary exposure to obvious or known danger, has been characterized as a form of primary assumption of risk based on its conceptual equivalency to express assumption of risk. *Siglow v. Smart,* 43 Ohio App.3d 55, 539 N.E.2d 636, 640–41 (1987).

Reasonable assumption of risk, entailing a reasonable and voluntary exposure to an obvious or known danger, sounds in waiver and consent-not fault. A plaintiff who reasonably chooses to proceed in the face of a known risk is deemed to have relieved defendant of any duty to protect him.

In so characterizing reasonable assumption of risk, the *Siglow* court extended the assumption of risk exceptions to include cases where the plaintiff's conduct impliedly waived any duty owed by the defendant. *Id.* at 640. The *Siglow* court's doctrinal extension has been criticized by another state appeals court. *Borchers v. Winzeler Excavating Co.,* 83 Ohio App.3d 268, 614 N.E.2d 1065, 1069 (1992). The *Borchers'* opinion characterizes the *Anderson* court's primary assumption of risk exception as presenting a policy question of whether the courts should impose liability for risks inherent or frequently associated with certain activities, rather than a legal question regarding the existence or absence of a *216 duty. *Id.* at 1070. We disagree and find that *Siglow* is consistent with *Anderson.*

In setting forth Ohio's primary assumption of risk doctrine, the district court used language and cited precedent associated with the reasonable assumption of risk doctrine. While finding that the defense of primary assumption of risk barred recovery, the district court concluded that "the duty of ordinary care which defendant owed to plaintiff because of his invitee status was discharged" when "plaintiff chose to expose himself to injury when he climbed on his truck to wash the windshield" despite his knowledge that his shoes had been exposed to spilled diesel fuel and the slippery nature of that fuel and, hence, the primary assumption of the risk exception provided an absolute bar to recovery in this case.

Hansen was a business invitee at the time of his injury. A property owner/occupier owes a business invitee "a duty of ordinary care in maintaining the premises in a reasonably safe condition so that its customers are not unnecessarily and unreasonably exposed to danger." *Pashal v. Rite Aid Pharmacy, Inc.*, 18 Ohio St.3d 203, 480 N.E.2d 474, 475 (1985). Because a property owner/occupier is not an insurer of the customer's safety, a property owner/occupier is under no duty to protect a business invitee from dangers " 'which [1] are known to such invitee or [2] are so obvious and apparent to such invitee that he may reasonably expect to discover them and protect himself against them.' " *Id.* (quoting *Sidle v. Humphrey,* 13 Ohio St.2d 45, 233 N.E.2d 589 (1968)). We agree with the District Court that this case falls within the primary assumption of risk exception defined by the Ohio Supreme Court. In his deposition. Hansen admitted that he knew that spilled diesel fuel created slippery conditions, that such slippery conditions existed around his truck at the time of his injury, and that such conditions posed a risk of injury in case he fell while servicing his truck. Flying J, therefore, had no duty to protect Hansen from the known dangers posed by washing his truck windshield in the precarious manner he chose.

Hansen's primary assumption of risk is analogous to that assumed by a baseball spectator. A baseball spectator assumes the risk of injury because it is common knowledge that hard balls may be thrown or batted at great speed into the stands. *Anderson,* 451 N.E.2d at 784 (citing *Cincinnati Base Ball Club Co. v. Eno,* 112 Ohio St. 175, 147 N.E. 86 (1925)). Just as a baseball spectator assumes the risk of injuries from known dangers, Hansen assumed the risk of injury from a fall caused by the slippery conditions he knew to be associated with the spilled diesel fuel. Hansen's primary assumption of risk, therefore, bars recovery from Flying J and Flying J is entitled to summary judgment as a matter of law.

In view of our disposition of Hansen's first challenge to the district court's judgment, we need not address his second challenge.

III.

For the foregoing reasons, the judgment of the district court is AFFIRMED.

Source: WESTLAW Dale HANSEN v. FLYING J TRAVEL PLAZA. Reprinted with permission from Westlaw.

Chapter 8

Damages

CHAPTER OBJECTIVES

Upon completion of this chapter, you will be able to:

- Explain compensatory damages.
- Identify other types of damages.
- Understand a plaintiff's duty to mitigate.
- Discuss joint tortfeasors.

The practice of awarding damages to an injured party has been handed down for centuries, first in England and then in the United States. The theory behind the awarding of damages is that an injured party should receive **redress** for any wrong caused to him and that the wrongdoer should provide the redress. Damages are not intended to compensate the plaintiff for the costs that he incurs from pursuing a lawsuit. They are a **remedial** measure; that is, they are intended to make up for the wrong the plaintiff suffered. Various types of damages are available for different types of civil wrongs. This chapter discusses the various types of damages that may be awarded to a plaintiff in a civil tort action.

redress
Relief from distress; compensation for a loss or injury.

remedial
Intended as a remedy.

COMPENSATORY DAMAGES

Damages are an essential element of most torts. Without damages, the plaintiff does not have a tort action. Damages are **pecuniary** compensation in the form of a money award to the plaintiff for a civil wrong. Damages are considered a legal remedy.

Compensatory damages are the most common type of damages awarded in a tort action. Compensatory damages are awarded in an effort to make a plaintiff whole, to compensate her for her loss or injury. In a negligence action, the plaintiff must show actual injury in order to bring a cause of action. The court's motive for awarding monetary damages is that, through a money payment, the plaintiff is returned to the position that she was in before the injury; or, alternatively, an effort is made to return her to her former status through this payment. An attempt is also made to provide a money payment for non-economic losses, such as pain and suffering. A defendant will be liable to the plaintiff for all the natural and direct consequences that result from the defendant's action, and compensatory damages will be awarded for the injuries and harm the plaintiff sustained from that act.

However, if the consequences from the defendant's actions are considered remotely caused by the wrong, the remote consequences will not be considered in determining compensatory damages, since they do not naturally flow from the wrongdoing. For

pecuniary
Consisting of money or that which can be valued in money.

compensatory damages
A payment to make up for a wrong committed and return the nonbreaching party to a position where the effect or the breach has been neutralized.

example, if a man is liable for a woman's injuries in a car accident, he is not liable for her not paying her house payment.

In a personal injury action, a plaintiff is to be compensated for all of his damages. Those damages can include past, present, and future damages. Types of compensatory damages that can be recovered in a personal injury matter are medical expenses, loss of earnings, and **loss of earning capacity**. Out-of-pocket losses are recovered as long as they are derived from the injury. These types of injuries are known as economic losses.

Compensatory damages are typically classified into two categories: *special damages* and *general damages*. **General damages** are those compensatory damages that generally result from the kind of conduct caused by the defendant. General damages usually and naturally flow from such conduct as that engaged in by the defendant. In most states, the plaintiff does not have to initially allege general damages with specificity upon the filing of the lawsuit, but can allege them generally. The law will presume that general damages resulted from the wrong that the plaintiff sustained. Often, the plaintiff may not be aware of the total amount of the damages that she has sustained at the time of the filing of the lawsuit. For instance, the plaintiff may still be receiving medical treatment so the total amount of damages may not be able to be determined until the plaintiff completes medical treatment. General damages are known as **direct damages** because they stem directly from the injury to plaintiff.

Compensatory damages are not just limited to tort actions. For example, in a breach of contract cause of action, the plaintiff may be entitled to compensatory damages for such items as reasonable expenses that resulted from relying on the terms of the contract, interest lost by the plaintiff, or the cost of transporting or storing goods as called for by the contract.

Special damages are those compensatory damages that are peculiar to the particular plaintiff. Special damages must usually be pled in the initial filing of a lawsuit and cannot be speculated or estimated like general damages. For example, suppose a plaintiff is unable to work as a result of injuries that she sustained from the defendant's actions. How long the plaintiff remains off work and the total amount of wages that she has lost are peculiar to that particular plaintiff. Other examples of special damages are medical bills and property damage. These types of damages are also known as **consequential damages** because they are consequential to the wrong that the plaintiff suffered.

Plaintiffs are entitled to recover damages for actual pain and mental suffering sustained by them. Damages for pain and suffering usually consist of the following:

- Actual pain
- Fright
- Humiliation
- Fear and anxiety
- Loss of companionship
- Unhappiness
- Depression or other forms of mental illness

loss of earning capacity
Damage to one's ability to earn wages in the future and recoverable as an element of damage in tort actions.

general damages
Those that normally would be anticipated in a similar action.

direct damages
Damages that arise naturally or ordinarily from an injury, breach of contract, or breach of duty.

special damages
Those damages incurred beyond and in addition to the general damages suffered and expected in similar cases.

consequential damages
Damages resulting from the breach that are natural and foreseeable results of the breaching party's actions.

CASE FACT PATTERN

John was crossing the street at Main and Central when a car driven by Mary swerved into him, *negligently*, right as John was crossing the street, and hit John, causing injuries to his back. Although John had a job at the time, he nonetheless has no medical insurance or insurance of any kind to help him. John will be out of work for almost one full year. He sues the driver of the car for compensatory damages, general and special. John wins his case and is awarded both forms of damages. He is awarded general damages to help him with medical bills and special for his loss of work.

The amount recovered for pain and suffering by a plaintiff will depend on the amount of time such pain and suffering was experienced and the intensity of the experience. Also the age and condition of the plaintiff will be considered when determining an award for damages of this type.

OTHER TYPES OF DAMAGES

Hedonic Damages

hedonic damages
Damages awarded in some jurisdictions for the loss of enjoyment of life.

Hedonic damages are compensatory damages that cover the victim's loss of pleasure or enjoyment, or loss of ability to enjoy life. Some jurisdictions treat hedonic damages as separate and distinct from damages for pain and suffering and award them separately. However, some jurisdictions believe that hedonic damages are an extension of pain and suffering and consider them when awarding an amount for pain and suffering. Many courts have determined that a person must be conscious of her loss of enjoyment before an award of hedonic damages is permitted. In other words, a person cannot be in a coma and be awarded hedonic damages, because she is not aware of her loss of enjoyment of life.

RESEARCH THIS

Research your state's laws and determine if your state allows an award of hedonic damages separately and apart from an award of pain and suffering, or if your state considers hedonic damages as a part of a pain and suffering award.

LEGAL RESEARCH MAXIM

John loves to run and enjoys running marathons. John is involved in an automobile accident that Brian caused. John is severely injured, and his back is broken. For many months, it is believed that John would never walk again, let alone run. Although John recovers the use of his legs, he can no longer run. John has lost the ability to enjoy his life with running. John may be awarded hedonistic damages.

Nominal Damages

nominal damages
A small amount of money given to the nonbreaching party as a token award to acknowledge the fact of the breach.

Nominal damages consist of a small amount of money that is awarded when the defendant has committed a tort that has resulted in little or no damage to the plaintiff. Nominal damages are awarded to demonstrate that a wrong was technically committed by the defendant even though no actual damages were sustained. Nominal damages can never be awarded in a negligence action since the plaintiff must have sustained actual damages as an element of negligence. Nominal damages are awarded in intentional and strict liability cases when the tort has been committed, and there has been no actual harm other than the defendant's commission of the tort.

For example, John trespasses on Jane's property on his way to the bus stop. John does not cause any damage to Jane's property, yet he has committed an intentional tort by trespassing on her land. If Jane brings a cause of action for the tort of trespass to land, a court may rule that she was injured in the sense that John did commit the trespass, but the court may award her only a symbolic, nominal sum—often $1—since there were no damages or injuries.

Liquidated Damages

Liquidated damages are damages that two parties agree upon when they enter into a contract. The agreed-upon sum is to be paid by the party that breaches the contract. Liquidated damages are typically agreed to when the assessment of damages for actual harm could be difficult to determine or prove. The amount agreed upon should characterize a reasonable estimate of what actual damages might be should the contract be breached. If the liquidated damages assessed in the terms of the contract appear to be unreasonable, it may not be enforced by the courts.

Property Damages

If a plaintiff's property is destroyed, then the measure of damages is typically determined as the **fair market value** of the property at the time of the destruction of the property.

If the plaintiff's property is damaged, but not destroyed, then the typical measure of damages is the difference between the fair market value of the property before the damage was done and its fair market value after the damage.

In addition, if the plaintiff's property is damaged, but not destroyed, the court could also award damages as measured by the cost to repair the property. However, as just mentioned, the typical type of damages awarded is the difference between the fair market value of the property before the damage was done and its fair market value after the damage.

If the plaintiff is deprived of the use of his property, then the usual measure of damage is the fair market value of the use of the property during the time the plaintiff was wrongfully deprived of its use by the defendant. For example, in the case of the theft of an auto, the award would be the fair market value of the automobile.

If the plaintiff is deprived of the temporary use of his property, then the usual measure of damage is the fair market value of the use of the property during the time the plaintiff was wrongfully deprived of its use by the defendant. For example, in the case of the temporary theft of an auto, the award would be the fair market rental value of the automobile.

Loss of Consortium

Loss of consortium is the loss of companionship of a spouse due to injury. Loss of consortium can include loss of sexual relations between the spouses, loss of companionship, loss of earnings outside the home, and loss of the ability of the injured spouse to care for the home, to name just a few. Loss of consortium can be awarded to either the husband or the wife for injuries sustained to the other. Depending on the jurisdiction, parents or children could also seek loss of consortium for their loss.

PUNITIVE DAMAGES

Punitive damages are considered noncompensatory damages. That is, they are not designed to repay a plaintiff for losses that the person incurred. This form of damage is awarded to the injured party in order to *punish* the defendant and to deter similar conduct by others. Punitive damages are awarded when the defendant has acted with actual malice, ill will, or conscious disregard for others. They are awarded when the defendant's conduct is considered particularly outrageous. Punitive damages are also known as *exemplary damages*.

Punitive damages are intended to be so burdensome to defendants that they will be unlikely to repeat the offense. An example of this type of action is civil actions against tobacco companies for harm caused to smokers.

Punitive damages are found commonly in product liability cases where the defendant manufactures and sells a product to the public that the defendant knows is

---

liquidated damages
An amount of money agreed upon in the original contract as a reasonable estimation of the damages to be recovered by the nonbreaching party. This amount is set forth in the contract so the parties have a clear idea of the risk of breach.

fair market value
The amount that a willing buyer would pay for an item that a willing seller would accept.

loss of consortium
A claim filed, made by the plaintiff's spouse, for the loss of companionship in the marriage caused by the injuries.

punitive damages
An amount of money awarded to a nonbreaching party that is not based on the actual losses incurred by that party, but as a punishment to the breaching party for the commission of an intentional wrong.

SPOT THE ISSUE

Debbie was injured when her automobile was struck by Ken. As a result of the accident, Debbie broke her arm, leg, and three ribs. Her medical bills total $50,000, and she has been unable to work for three months. What types of damages could Debbie recover from Ken? Assume the same facts and recall the loss of consortium discussion. Are there any claims that Debbie's husband may assert against Ken?

defective. As a result, the defective product injures, damages, or otherwise harms the plaintiff or plaintiffs. For example, Evon Corporation manufactures medical rods and screws that doctors and surgeons use to plate and bolt together broken bones so that they may heal faster. However, during the testing process for the products before they were released to the public, company officers discovered that the metal used to manufacture the rods and bolts can rust and cause severe damage and disease. The officers decided that to change the material utilized in the products would cost too much to make them cost effective to manufacture. With the knowledge that these products could cause severe injury or harm, the officers decided to continue to manufacture the products, sell them in the marketplace, and allow them to be used in injured people. Evon made millions of dollars on the products for the next two years. However, slowly people began to experience severe injuries and harm as a result of the defective metal. A **class action** lawsuit was brought against Evon. During the lawsuit it was discovered that the officers of the company knew that the metal was defective and, recklessly and wantonly, without care for the damage caused, decided to manufacture the products and release them for sale and use. In a court award, the court awarded punitive damages to the plaintiffs in the sum of $30 million in an effort to punish the defendants for their outrageous conduct.

The *Federal Rules of Civil Procedure,* which mandates class actions, states that for a class action to be proper, certain prerequisites need to be meet. These are (1) the class is so numerous that joinder of all members is impracticable, (2) there are questions of law or fact common to the class, (3) the claims or defenses of the representative parties are typical of the claims or defenses of the class, and (4) the representative parties will fairly and adequately protect the interests of the class. *See Federal Rules of Civil Procedure,* Rule 23.

class action
A lawsuit involving a large group of plaintiffs who have been certified by a court as having mutual interests, common claims, and a representative plaintiff who will pursue the action on the basis of the entire group.

MITIGATION

Once a plaintiff has been injured, he must take reasonable steps to avoid sustaining any further damage or injury to himself or his property. The defendant will not be liable for any damages that could have reasonably been avoided by the plaintiff. That is, plaintiffs have a duty to **mitigate** their damages. For example, a plaintiff cannot recover for any harm or injuries that would have been avoided had he sought adequate medical care. The burden of proof is on the defendant to demonstrate that the plaintiff did not act reasonably and suffered additional damages or injuries as a result. This duty to mitigate is also known as the doctrine of avoidable consequences.

When a person is injured or dies, the plaintiff may receive funds or services from a variety of sources other than the defendant. Some of these sources may be:

mitigate
To lessen in intensity or amount.

also Know as.
avoidable
Consequences
doctrine

- The plaintiff's own medical or life insurance.

- Company insurance.

- Veteran's benefits.

YOU BE THE JUDGE

Jack, a factory worker, works at a factory that handles various biohazardous materials. While working, Jack is injured due to a machine malfunction. He sustains various injuries, including a deep cut to his forearm. Jack is suing the factory, claiming the factory negligently maintained the machine that malfunctioned. The cut to Jack's forearm became infected. Although Jack was aware of the infection, he refused to seek medical attention. The infection became severely worse. Jack now seeks to recover damages from the factory for costs related to the infection. What may the factory assert as a defense to being liable for the infection?

- Social Security.
- Wage continuation plans.
- Plaintiff's own automobile insurance.
- Free medical care provided by a relative.

These sources are known as *collateral sources*. They are sources of funds that the defendant did not contribute. The **collateral source rule** states that the defendant should not be given the benefit of the plaintiff's good luck or resourcefulness in being able to collect or receive other benefits that do not involve the defendant. The defendant must still pay the plaintiff as if the plaintiff had never received any funds from any other sources. The plaintiff may be required, however, to reimburse the collateral source. For example, if a plaintiff is injured in an accident, and her insurance company pays medical bills, the plaintiff may have to reimburse the insurance company for awards received from the defendant for those medical expenses.

> **collateral source rule**
> A rule of evidence that allows the jury to be informed about the plaintiff's other sources of compensation, such as insurance, worker's compensation, and so forth.

JOINT TORTFEASORS

When more than one person is liable to the plaintiff for damages or injuries sustained by their actions or the actions of their agent, those responsible are called **joint tortfeasors**. The significance of being a joint tortfeasor is that each joint tortfeasor has **joint and several liability** for the entire harm suffered by the plaintiff. This means that the plaintiff can sue any individual joint defendant for the entire harm or can join them all together in order to recover for the entire harm. It does not mean that the plaintiff receives a multiple recovery. The plaintiff only receives one award. However, the plaintiff can elect to sue one defendant or all the defendants together. If the plaintiff sues only one defendant but is unable to collect the full judgment, the plaintiff can sue the remaining tortfeasors until the full amount of the damages is recovered.

> **joint tortfeasors**
> Two or more persons jointly or severally liable in tort for the same injury to the plaintiff or the plaintiff's property.

> **joint and several liability**
> Shared responsibility, apportioned between all of the defendants, but in no case can the plaintiff recover more than 100 percent of the damages awarded.

Persons acting in concert to produce the negligent or intentional wrong are known as joint tortfeasors, and hence are jointly and severally liable for the harm they caused while on their joint venture. There must be an express agreement or a tacit understanding that each defendant will participate in the activity that produces the wrong to the plaintiff. To be a joint tortfeasor, the defendant must cooperate in the wrong, encourage it, or otherwise be an active participant. Someone who approves or ratifies the wrong after it is done for his or her benefit can also be a joint tortfeasor. For example, consider a scenario in which one partner in a two-partner firm falsifies bank records. Although the second partner was not involved in the falsification, he goes along after the fact to avoid having to pay back the money. The second partner is a joint tortfeasor.

When persons are not acting in concert, the defendants act independently of one another and produce a single indivisible result; however, there is no joint venture and no agreement or participation together in the activity. Each defendant is a substantial factor in producing harm to the plaintiff that is indivisible in that it comes from a single impact that cannot be divided. For example, in the case of illness caused by breast implants leaking silicone, the manufacturer, the distributor, and the doctor might all be held liable.

If the harm cannot practically be divided, the defendants will be held jointly and severally liable. If the harm can be divided, the defendants will not be joint tortfeasors, and each defendant will be responsible for his or her portion of the harm.

Release

release
A discharge from the parties' performance obligations that acknowledges the dispute but forgoes contractual remedies.

A **release** is the giving up of a claim. If satisfaction has been received from one joint tortfeasor, the plaintiff can no longer sue the others. This may be done gratuitously or for some type of **consideration**. In most states, the release of one joint tortfeasor automatically releases the others. Other states have statutes that prevent the automatic release of the remaining joint tortfeasors. In this instance, the plaintiff signs a release that is essentially making a **covenant** not to sue that particular joint tortfeasor, but he can sue the remaining joint tortfeasors.

consideration
A recompense or payment; compensation.

Contribution

covenant
The promise upon which the contract rests.

In some states, if the plaintiff collects the entire amount of the award from one of the joint tortfeasors, then that joint tortfeasor can ask the remaining joint tortfeasors to contribute to the award. Typically, **contribution** is made in proportional payments divided among the remaining joint tortfeasors.

contribution
Payment of a share of an amount for which one is liable as a shared payment of a judgment by joint tortfeasors, especially according to proportional fault.

Indemnity

Indemnity is where one party who has paid the plaintiff can force another party to reimburse him or her for the full amount paid. This sometime is known as **subrogation**. For example, suppose you are in an automobile accident where your car is rear-ended while stopped at a stop sign. It is obviously the defendant's fault. However, you carry collision insurance on your vehicle, and your insurance company proceeds to pay for the repairs to the damages sustained by your vehicle. Once the total amount of the damages is known, your insurance company goes after the defendant's insurance for reimbursement. The act of getting the reimbursement from the defendant's insurance company is known as subrogation.

indemnity
Compensation for damage, loss, or injury suffered.

subrogation
The right to sue in the name of another.

Summary

Damages are an essential element of most torts. Without damages, the plaintiff does not have a tort action. Damages are compensation in the form of a money award to the plaintiff for a civil wrong. Damages are considered a legal remedy.

Compensatory damages are the most common type of damages awarded in a tort action. Compensatory damages are awarded in an effort to make a plaintiff whole, to compensate her for her loss or injury. In a negligence action, the plaintiff must show actual injury in order to bring a cause of action. The court's motive for awarding monetary damages is that through a money payment, an effort is made to place the plaintiff in the position that she was in before the injury. An attempt is also made to provide a money payment for non-economic losses, such as pain and suffering.

A defendant will be liable to the plaintiff for all the natural and direct consequences that result from the defendant's action, and compensatory damages will be awarded for the injuries and harm sustained by the plaintiff from that act. However, if the consequences from the defendant's actions are considered remotely caused by the wrong, the remote consequences will not be considered in determining compensatory damages as they do not naturally flow from the wrongdoing.

Compensatory damages are typically classified into two categories: special damages and general damages. General damages are those compensatory damages that generally result from the kind of conduct caused by the defendant. Special damages are those compensatory damages that are peculiar to the particular plaintiff.

The amount recovered for pain and suffering by the plaintiff will depend on the amount of time such pain and suffering was experienced and the intensity of the experience. Also the age and condition of the plaintiff will be considered when determining an award for damages of this type.

Hedonic damages are compensatory damages that cover victims' loss of pleasure or enjoyment or their loss of ability to enjoy life. Some jurisdictions treat hedonic damages as separate and distinct damages from pain and suffering and award them separately.

Nominal damages consist of a small amount of money that is awarded when the defendant has committed a tort that has resulted in little or no damages to the plaintiff. Nominal damages are awarded to demonstrate that the defendant technically committed a wrong even though no actual damages were sustained. Nominal damages can never be awarded in a negligence action since the plaintiff must have sustained actual damages as an element of negligence. Nominal damages are awarded in intentional and strict liability cases when the tort has been committed, and there has been no actual harm other than the defendant's commission of the tort.

Liquidated damages are damages that two parties agree upon when they enter into a contract. The agreed-upon sum is to be paid by the party that breaches the contract. The amount agreed upon should characterize a reasonable estimate of what actual damages might be should the contract be breached. If the liquidated damages assessed in the terms of the contract appear to be unreasonable, it may not be enforced by the courts.

Loss of consortium is the loss of companionship of a spouse due to injury. Loss of consortium can include loss of sexual relations between the spouses, loss of companionship, loss of earnings outside the home and loss of the ability of the injured spouse to care for the home, just to name a few. Loss of consortium can be awarded to either the husband or the wife for injuries sustained to the other.

Punitive damages are considered noncompensatory damages. This form of damage is awarded to the injured party in order to punish the defendant and to deter similar conduct by others. Punitive damages are awarded when the defendant has acted with actual malice, ill will, or conscious disregard for others. They are awarded when the defendant's conduct is considered particularly outrageous. Punitive damages are also known as exemplary damages.

Once the plaintiff has been injured, he must take reasonable steps to avoid sustaining any further damage or injury to himself or his property. Defendants will not be liable for any damages that plaintiffs could have reasonably avoided. Thus, plaintiffs have a duty to mitigate their damages. The burden of proof is on the defendant to demonstrate that the plaintiff did not act reasonably and suffered additional damages or injuries as a result. This duty to mitigate is also known as the doctrine of avoidable consequences.

When more than one person is liable to the plaintiff for damages or injuries sustained by their actions or the actions of their agent, they are called joint tortfeasors. Each joint tortfeasor is jointly and severally liable for the entire harm suffered by the plaintiff. The plaintiff can elect to sue one defendant or all the defendants together. If the plaintiff sues only one defendant, but is unable to collect the full judgment, the plaintiff can sue the remaining tortfeasors until the full amount of the damages is recovered.

A release is the giving up of a claim. If the satisfaction has been received from one joint tortfeasor, the plaintiff can no longer sue the others. This may be done gratuitously or for some type of consideration. In most states, the release of one joint tortfeasor automatically releases the others. Other states have statutes that prevent the automatic release of the remaining joint tortfeasors. In this instance, the plaintiff signs a release that is essentially making a covenant not to sue that particular joint tortfeasor, but he or she can sue the remaining joint tortfeasors.

Key Terms

Class action	Joint tortfeasors
Collateral source rule	Liquidated damages
Compensatory damages	Loss of consortium
Consequential damages	Loss of earning capacity
Consideration	Mitigate
Contribution	Nominal Damages
Covenant	Pecuniary
Direct damages	Punitive damages
Fair market value	Redress
General damages	Release
Hedonic damages	Remedial
Indemnity	Special damages
Joint and several liability	Subrogation

Review Questions

1. What is a joint tortfeasor?
2. What is joint and several liability?
3. List types of damages that are considered compensatory?
4. Who could sue for loss of consortium?
5. What are special damages?
6. What are general damages?
7. What are pecuniary damages?
8. What is mitigation and why is it important?
9. What does a release do?
10. How does subrogation work?

11. Give a scenario where punitive damages may be awarded to the plaintiff?
12. What are liquidated damages?
13. When is fair market value applied as a tort damage?
14. What is a class action lawsuit?
15. When might nominal damages be awarded? Give an example.

1. A famous damage case in the United States occurred in 1986. The case is *United States Football League v. National Football League*, 644 F. Supp. 1040 (S.D.N.Y. 1986). Look up the case and brief it. Make sure that your brief answers what type of damages were awarded and why they were awarded in the manner in which they were. What other issues do you spot in this case that may or may not be related to the issue of damages?

2. Research the case of *McDougald v. Garber*, 536 N.E.2d 372 (N.Y. 1989). Brief the case. What are the issues of the case? How did the court handle the issue of damages? What types of damages were awarded? Do you agree with the ruling? Why or why not?

3. Releases are very important in the settlement of personal injury cases. Research various legal sources and write your own release with the following elements included:
   a. The plaintiff will receive $25,000 for medical expenses.
   b. The plaintiff will receive pain and suffering damages in the amount of $100,000.
   c. The plaintiff agrees not to pursue the defendant in any further legal action.
   d. The plaintiff is John Smith. The defendant is Brenda Sturgle. The case is an automobile accident that occurred on February 14, 2006.

4. The *Federal Rules of Civil Procedure* mandate the prerequisites for a class action to be proper. What are the prerequisites, and why are they important for class action?

5. Recently, Congress and the executive branch of the federal government have considered putting "caps," or "ceilings," on the amount of damages/awards which an injured plaintiff may recover. Should there be a cap on awards? If so, why and how much? If not, why not?

6. Does a judge have the option to limit or curtail a monetary damage award from the original amount the jury awarded? If yes, is that fair? If not, should the judge have that option?

 PORTFOLIO ASSIGNMENT

Research and brief *BMW v. Gore*, 517 U.S. 559 (1996). What did this case say in regard to punitive damages? What standard did the court set forth in determining whether a punitive damage award is excessive?

Vocabulary Builders

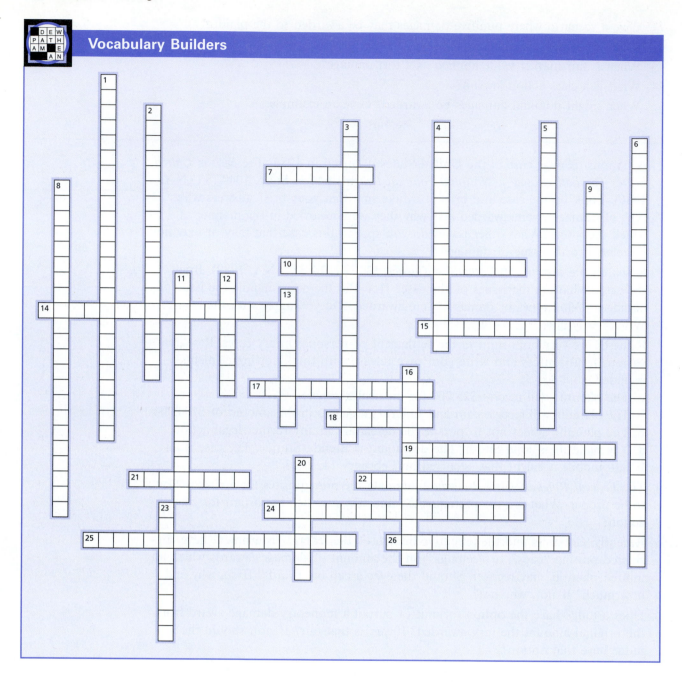

Vocabulary Builders

Instructions

Use the key terms from this chapter to fill in the answers to the crossword puzzle.

NOTE: When the answer is more than one word, leave a blank space between words.

ACROSS

7. Relief from distress; compensation for a loss or injury.

10. An amount of money awarded to a nonbreaching party that is not based on the actual losses incurred by that party, but as a punishment to the breaching party for the commission of an intentional wrong.

14. The amount that a willing buyer would pay for an item that a willing seller would accept.

15. Those that normally would be anticipated in a similar action.

17. A lawsuit involving a large group of plaintiffs who have been certified by a court as having mutual interests, common claims, and a representative plaintiff who will pursue the action on the basis of the entire group.

18. A discharge from the parties' performance obligations that acknowledges the dispute but forgoes contractual remedies.

19. Damages that arise naturally or ordinarily from an injury, breach of contract, or breach of duty.

21. Intended as a remedy.

22. The right to sue in the name of another.

24. Two or more persons jointly or severally liable in tort for the same injury to the plaintiff or the plaintiff's property.

25. An amount of money agreed upon in the original contract as a reasonable estimation of the damages to be recovered by the nonbreaching party. This amount is set forth in the contract so the parties have a clear idea of the risk of breach.

26. Payment of a share of an amount for which one is liable as a shared payment of a judgment by joint tortfeasors, especially according to proportional fault.

DOWN

1. Damage to one's ability to earn wages in the future and recoverable as element of damage in tort actions.

2. A claim filed by the plaintiff's spouse for the loss of companionship in the marriage caused by the injuries.

3. Damages resulting from the breach that are natural and foreseeable results of the breaching party's actions.

4. Damages awarded in some jurisdictions for the loss of enjoyment of life.

5. A payment to make up for a wrong committed and return the nonbreaching party to a position where the effect or the breach has been neutralized.

6. Shared responsibility, apportioned between all of the defendants, but in no case can the plaintiff recover more than 100 percent of the damages awarded.

8. A rule of evidence that allows the jury to be informed about the plaintiff's other sources of compensation, such as insurance, worker's compensation, and so forth.

9. A small amount of money given to the nonbreaching party as a token award to acknowledge the fact of the breach.

11. Those damages incurred beyond and in addition to the general damages suffered and expected in similar cases.

12. The promise upon which the contract rests.

13. Consisting of money or that which can be valued in money.

16. Parol evidence is permitted to show that the subject matter of the contract as received was not as it was bargained for.

20. To lessen in intensity or amount.

23. Compensation for damage, loss, or injury suffered.

Supreme Court of the Territory of Guam
VILLANUEVA ex rel. U.S. v. COMMERCIAL SANITATION SYSTEMS, INC
No. CVA04-005
Argued and Submitted on Oct. 27, 2004
Filed April 12, 2005

OPINION

CARBULLIDO, C.J.:

Plaintiff-Appellant Nancy A. Villanueva appeals from the trial court's Decision and Order granting partial summary judgment in favor of the Defendant-Appellee Dai-Tokyo Fire & Marine Insurance Company.

The sole issue on appeal is whether, under the Dai-Tokyo automobile liability insurance policy, Mrs. Villanueva's damages for loss of consortium are subject to the "per person" damages limit of $100,000 or whether it is subject to the "per accident" limit of $300,000. The trial court held that the damages for Mrs. Villanueva's loss of consortium are subject to the "per person" limitation clause found in the insurance policy because Mrs. Villanueva's damages for loss of consortium are a result of the bodily injury to one person, Mr. Villanueva. We affirm.

I.

Juan Villanueva was involved in a head-on collision with a truck operated by Commercial Sanitation Systems, Inc. ("Commercial Sanitation"), on March 16, 2001, on the back road to Andersen. As a result of the collision, Mr. Villanueva suffered massive head injuries. He is confined to a wheelchair for the rest of his life, is unemployable, has substantial brain damage, and requires 24-hour care. He is married to Mrs. Villanueva, and she has become his constant caretaker. In the lawsuit that arose from this incident, she asserted a claim for loss of consortium along with the Villanuevas' other claims for pain and suffering, lost wages, and compensatory damages. Defendant Dai-Tokyo Fire and Marine Insurance Co., Ltd., ("Dai-Tokyo") insured the defendant, Commercial Sanitation System. The parties filed cross-motions for summary judgment on the isolated question on appeal in this case involving the interpretation of policy language as it relates to Mrs. Villanueva's claim for loss of consortium. The matter was argued to the trial court on March 26, 2003. On June 25, 2003, the trial court entered a Decision and Order granting summary judgment in favor of defendant Dai-Tokyo on this single issue. The parties thereafter settled. The settlement allows the Villanuevas' lawyer to pursue the sole issue on appeal.

Because the parties settled, no facts were established anywhere in the record. However, to provide further background, Dai-Tokyo submitted these additional facts in briefing, to which the Villanuevas did not object. The settlement does not attribute fault to Commercial Sanitation for the collision and the Villanuevas received over $900,000.00 in other compensatory damages.

The policy language that this court is being asked to interpret is as follows: OUR LIMIT OF LIABILITY is changed to read:

Bodily Injury Liability:	$100,000.	Each Person
	$300,000.	Each Accident
Property Damage Liability:	$100,000.	Each Accident

A. Regardless of the number of covered autos, insureds, claims made or vehicles involved in the accident, our limit of liability is as follows:

1. The most we will pay for all damages resulting from bodily injury to any one person caused by any one accident is the limit of Bodily Injury Liability shown in this endorsement for "Each Person."
2. Subject to the limit for "Each Person" the most we will pay for all damages resulting from bodily injury caused by any one accident is the limit of Bodily Injury Liability shown in this endorsement for Each Accident.

Appellant's Excerpts of Record (ER), p. 23 (Dai-Tokyo Business Auto Policy).

The term "bodily injury" is defined in the policy as follows: " 'Bodily Injury' means bodily injury, sickness or disease including death resulting from any of these." Appellant's ER, p. 14 (Dai-Tokyo Business Auto Policy).

The Villanuevas argue that $300,000 policy limit for "all damages resulting from bodily injury caused by any one accident" is applicable under the facts of this case. Specifically, the Villanuevas argue that because Mrs. Villanueva's injury is a separate injury from Mr. Villanueva's bodily injury, the term "*all damages* resulting from bodily injury" must include her loss of consortium. In other words, the Villanuevas contend that the term "all damages resulting from bodily injury" comes into play when more than one person suffers injury from one accident.

Dai-Tokyo submits that because only Mr. Villanueva suffered bodily injury, under the language of the insurance policy, the $100,000 "per person" limitation applies. Dai-Tokyo argues that the $300,000 "per accident" limitation does not apply in this case, because the only person to suffer bodily injury in the accident is Mr. Villanueva. Mrs. Villanueva's loss of consortium is not a separate bodily injury resulting from the accident. Therefore, Dai-Tokyo argues that, although the policy language covers "all damages resulting from bodily injury" up to the amount of $300,000, because the "bodily injury" is suffered only by Mr. Villanueva, the $100,000 "per person" limitation applies.

[Sections II and III omitted]

II.

The isolated issue on appeal is whether a claim for loss of consortium is included in the policy's "per person" damages limitation of $100,000, or whether it is a separate claim from the "per person" damages limit, and therefore separately compensable under the policy's "per accident" limit of $300,000. If Mrs. Villanueva's damages for loss of consortium is a result of bodily injury sustained by one person in one accident, then her loss of consortium claim is bundled with all of Mr. Villanueva's claims and together they cannot recover more than the $100,000 limit. However, if the loss of consortium claim is not a result of bodily injury sustained by one person in one accident, then it is not limited to the "per person" cap, but rather, the Villanuevas may recover more because the damages would be subject to a different damages limit, specifically, the "per accident" limit of $300,000.00.

The Villanuevas rely entirely on the case of *Abellon v. Hartford Insurance Co.*, 212 Cal.Rptr. 852 (Ct.App.Dist. 1985), a California appellate court case with a controversial legacy, which found that a spouse's loss of consortium claim is subject to the "per accident" limitation. The court held:

> Loss of consortium is a distinct and individual injury. By merging [the wife's] injury with that of her husband, her injury, in effect, becomes derivative and noncompensable under the terms of the insurance contract, thus effectively negating public policy . . . [she] has suffered an independent, nonparasitic personal injury as a result of an automobile accident negligently caused by [the defendant's] insured . . . [therefore] she is a second person injured by the accident.

The court in *Abellon* was faced with the following policy language:

1. The most we will pay for all damages resulting from bodily injury to any one person caused by any one accident is the ['each person' limit.]
2. Subject to the limit for each person the most we will pay for *all damages resulting from bodily injury caused by any one accident* is the ['each accident' limit.]

The Villanuevas argue that this is identical policy language to their policy with Dai-Tokyo. We agree that the policy language is the same. Nonetheless, we must examine the reasons to follow *Abellon* or to depart from it. Thus, the debate here is essentially whether to follow a minority California case interpreting identical language, or whether to follow a majority of courts, including many in California, which, for one reason or another, have refused to follow *Abellon,* and for reasons which will be discussed below, have held that a spouse's claim for loss of consortium is subject to the "per person" limitation.

The facts in *Abellon* are similar to the case at bar: the wife, Jeanne Abellon, suffered a loss of consortium due to her husband's catastrophic injuries. The *Abellon* court states early in its deliberations that it would be unfair not to compensate Jeanne's separate injuries for loss of consortium because her loss of consortium was a distinct and individual injury, and that merging her injuries with that of her husband rendered her injury noncompensable, "thus effectively negating public policy."

We find that the *Abellon* court's rationale is not entirely accurate. The problem is not that Jeanne does not get compensated, it is that the compensation limit is reached before her injury is added to it. Without a compensation limit, Jeanne's injuries could be compensated together with her husband's pain and suffering. But the *Abellon* court interpreted the insurance contract in such a way that Jeanne would be compensated for what it deemed was a separate injury, thereby allowing Jeanne access to higher policy limits.

Abellon's holding is that "[the wife] is simply a foreseeable plaintiff to whom [the defendant] owes a separate duty of care." 212 Cal.Rptr. at 855. This holding relies on *Rodriguez v. Bethlehem Steel*, 115 Cal.Rptr. 765, 780 (Cal. 1974), where the court held that "[consortium rights] are her rights, not his." Therefore, based on *Rodriguez,* the *Abellon* court concluded that "[Jeanne] is a second person injured in the accident." *Id.* Because Jeanne's injuries were separate, they could be compensated under the "per accident" limit, but only so long as the injuries were "bodily injuries." The *Abellon* court stated that whether Jeanne sustained a "bodily injury" is a question of fact, which in turn "involves a medical or psychological problem of proof." *Id.* The court eventually concluded that Jeanne's loss of consortium had a physical component, and therefore was "bodily injury" and therefore compensable under the separate "per accident" limit.

The Villanuevas urge this court to follow the reasoning and the conclusion of *Abellon* and hold that Mrs. Villanueva's injuries are separately compensable bodily injuries, and therefore are subject to the "per accident" limit. The Villanuevas argue that the *Abellon* case did not turn on the issue of whether loss of consortium does or does not constitute bodily injury, but rather on the court's construction of specific policy language. On the contrary, the *Abellon* court simply found that the policy language was ambiguous because loss of consortium was not placed into one damage category or another. *Id.* at 858–859. Relying on case law instructing that all ambiguous policy language must be construed against the insurer, *Government Employees Insurance Co. v. Kinyon*, 173 Cal.Rptr. 805 (Ct.App. 1981), the *Abellon* court found that loss of consortium was a separately compensable bodily injury.

Dozens of cases have distinguished *Abellon,* though usually because of different policy language. Some examples of grounds that cases have used to reject *Abellon* include that used in *Lepic v. Iowa Mut. Insurance Co.*, 402 N.W.2d 758 (Iowa 1987), where the court reasoned that loss of consortium is not bodily injury. Other cases have departed from *Abellon* because the element of damages known as "loss of consortium" or "loss of services" is specifically addressed in the policy, which makes it easier to categorize loss of consortium. *See Nationwide Mut. Ins. v. Moya*, 837 P.2d 426, 430 (Nev. 1992). Other cases rely on their respective state's loss of consortium laws to distinguish *Abellon. See McGovern v. Williams*, 741 S.W.2d 373, 375–76 (Tex. 1987).

Reviewing these other cases, the result is the same. The *Abellon* case stands out from most other cases with this issue, such as *Moya*, which held that there was one injury, which caused many losses. *Moya*, 837 P.2d at 430 ("The Moyas did not suffer bodily injuries *in* the accident; their claims arose *as a result* of the injuries Mrs. Moya suffered *in* the accident . . .")

The court in *Medley v. Frey,* 660 N.E.2d 1079, 1081 (Ind.Ct. App. 1996) expressed the point this way: "[one spouse]'s claim for loss of services is not an independent 'bodily injury,' but rather arises out of the 'bodily injury' sustained by [the other spouse], for which [the insurance provider] has paid the $100,000 per person limit of coverage." In *Shepard v. State Farm Mutual Automobile Insurance Co.,* 545 So.2d 624, 628 (La.Ct.App. 1989), the court said that since the derivative claim of "loss of consortium does not come into existence until someone else is injured, that loss of consortium claims are included within the definition of bodily injury . . . However, any loss of consortium claim is only derivative, . . . [and] therefore restricted to the monetary limits placed in the policy, to a per person total."

Legal commentary is in accord. The court in *Moore v. State Farm Mutual Insurance Co.,* 710 S.W.2d 225, 226 (Ky. 1986), relied on W.E. Shipley, *Annotation, Construction and Application of Provision in Liability Policy Limiting the Amount of Insurer Liability to One Person,* 13 A.L.R.3d 1228, 1234 (1967), where it is stated:

> Under policies fixing a maximum recovery for "bodily" injury to one person, the limitation [is] applicable to all claims of damage flowing from such bodily injury, and that therefore it is immaterial that some part of the damages may be claimed by a person other than the one suffering the bodily injuries. In other words, all damage claims, direct and consequential, resulting from injury to one person, are subject to the limitation.

The court in *Moore* quoted this language and concluded that the limit of liability had already been paid on Mr. Moore's claim. 710 S.W.2d at 226. His wife's loss of consortium claim exceeded the company's limit of liability; thus, she was precluded from recovery under the policy.

The Villanuevas nonetheless urge this Court to adopt the *Abellon* case holding, arguing that though it is criticized and distinguished, it is still good law. While it is true that *Abellon* has not been overturned, it is poor precedent. The California Supreme Court has not resolved the conflict among its own judicial divisions, but most California appellate divisions except for the fourth (*Abellon*) have rejected the reasoning of *Abellon.* The case of *United Services Automobile Association v. Warner,* 135 Cal.Rptr. 34 (Ct.App. 1976) is instructive.

In *Warner,* the Court of Appeal for the Fourth District of California, Second Division, was faced with slightly different policy language in that the policy itself included a definition of "per person" and it included "loss of services." *Id.* at 36. The policy stated, "the limit . . . to 'each person' . . . include[es] damages for care and loss of services." *Id.* The court in *Warner* held that loss of consortium claims come out of the "per person" limit rather than the "per occurrence" limit. *Id.* at 38. It reasoned that "loss of consortium does not arise out of a bodily injury to the spouse suffering the loss; it arises out of the bodily injury to the spouse who can no longer perform the spousal functions." *Id.* In this way, the *Warner* case represents the contrary view to *Abellon*—that loss of consortium properly comes out of the "per person" limit because it is derived from the injury to one person. It is not derived from two separate injuries. *Abellon* rejected the *Warner* reasoning on the basis that the policy language in *Warner* was different—*Warner's* "per person"

limit defined all damages as including loss of services. But taking this logic to its natural conclusion, *Abellon* would have *Warner* mean that if a policy did not define its "per person" limit to include all conceivable derivative claims, then any and all derivative claims are converted into additionally covered parties with access to the larger $300,000 limit, rather than the smaller $100,000.00 limit. Under this analysis, if the harm is not defined in the "per person" limit, then any party suffering harm resulting from one person's accident can be compensated from the $300,000 limit rather than the $100,000.00 limit. We find this illogical and arbitrary.

This court declines to follow *Abellon's* restrictive reading of *Warner.* If "per person" damages are not defined in the policy, this court is not required to find that Mrs. Villanueva's loss is a separately covered injury. Mrs. Villanueva was not present at the accident. She was not injured in the accident. She suffers a loss that is derived from her husband's covered injuries. We reject *Abellon's* distinction and interpretation of the *Warner* case, and are persuaded by later cases applying *Warner,* which recognize the principle that derivative claims fall within the "per person" rather than "per accident" claim.

Other appellate districts in California have reasoned likewise. The Court of Appeal for the Second District of California, when faced with a choice between *Abellon* and *Warner,* said, "[w]e think that *Warner* not only represents the majority view, but is the better-reasoned case." *Mercury Ins. Co. v. Ayala,* 11 Cal.Rptr.3d 158, 162 (Ct.App. 2004). *See also State Farm Mut. Auto. Ins. Co. v. Ball,* 179 Cal.Rptr. 644 (Ct.App. 1981) (Second District relying on *Warner* to reject wife's loss of consortium claim). Though analyzing different policy language, the court of appeal for the Third District of California also rejected *Abellon* in favor of the rule that loss of consortium is part of the insured/injured person's per person limit. *Hauser v. State Farm Mut. Auto Ins. Co.,* 252 Cal.Rptr. 569 (Ct.App. 1988).

We recognize that there are a small number of other cases that, for one reason or another, have held that a loss of consortium claim is a separately compensable claim. *See* Jane M. Draper, *Annotation, Consortium Claim of Spouse, Parent or Child of Accident Victim as Within Extended "Per Accident" Coverage Rather Than "Per Person" Coverage of Automobile Liability Policy,* 46 A.L.R. 4th 735 (1986). However, these cases are in the minority, and for the policy reasons articulated herein, we decline to follow them. In addition to the many features that distinguish *Abellon* from most other cases, *Abellon* contains a logical flaw. As pointed out, Jeanne Abellon's loss of consortium injury was compensable under the "bodily injury" limit, but for the fact that the policy limits were exhausted before she could be compensated.

Abellon also stands for the principle that because loss of consortium is separate but inchoate, a court or jury must look at the fact issues underlying a loss of consortium claim to see if it is a "bodily injury." This principle directs litigants and judges to develop evidence on the physical manifestations of a loss of consortium claimant. If bodily injury is established, then loss of consortium can be a separately compensable claim. If, however, bodily injury is not established (only mental or emotional injury), then loss of consortium is not compensable. Thus, the *Abellon* case is harsher than first meets the eye, because under *Abellon,* unless there are physical manifestations for loss of consortium, there is no compensable injury. The alternative approach allows recovery for loss of consortium without testing whether or not the injury is "physical." Under the latter approach, recovery is often restricted, but only by policy limits, such as was the result in *Warner*.

In this way, *Abellon* promotes an awkward distinction—it compels courts to distinguish between, for instance, plaintiffs who have physical symptoms of grief from plaintiffs with mere emotional suffering so that the damage can be counted as bodily injury. This is unnecessary when the loss of consortium is simply an element of damage from the insured's "bodily injury." When a party suffers a bodily injury, which in turn causes damages, including loss of consortium, it is not necessary to contrive a test for physical versus non-physical bodily injury, because the analysis does not include the remotely injured person. The only "bodily injury" that matters under the policy is that sustained in the accident (in this case, Mr. Villanueva).

In conclusion, this court concurs with the reasoning expressed in the dissent in *Abellon:*

> [Defendant] negligently caused one accident. That accident caused only one person, Mr. Abellon, bodily injuries. As a result of the bodily injuries to Mr. Abellon, Mrs. Abellon, who was not present at the accident, suffered a loss of consortium. The issue here is not whether Mrs. Abellon has suffered a compensable loss, nor whether she had her own claim against [Defendant], nor whether her loss was foreseeable, nor whether [Defendant] should compensate her. Neither is the issue here whether loss of consortium is the type of loss covered by the policy. It is covered, and Hartford does not claim otherwise. The issue here is rather how much insurance coverage [Defendant] bought to cover all the claims of Mr. and Mrs. Abellon. *Abellon,* 212 Cal.Rptr. at 860 (Lewis, J., dissenting).

Similarly, in this tragic accident, one person was injured, Mr. Villanueva. As a result of Mr. Villanueva's bodily injuries, Mrs. Villanueva, who was not present at the accident, suffered a loss of consortium. The issue here is not whether Nancy Villanueva suffered a compensable loss, nor whether loss of consortium is a bodily injury, nor whether Dai-Tokyo should compensate her, nor whether loss of consortium is the type of loss covered by the policy. It is covered, and Dai-Tokyo does not claim otherwise. But unfortunately, the policy language limits the payment of damages resulting from the bodily injury sustained by Mr. Villanueva, including all collateral injuries created by his injuries, to the amount of $100,000. In other words, Mrs. Villanueva's loss of consortium is covered by the policy, but is not payable under the $300,000 "per accident" provision found in the insurance policy, because such provision is "subject to the limit of 'Each Person.'" Appellant's ER, p. 23 (Dai-Tokyo Business Auto Policy Endorsement BAP-E9 (A)(2)). Thus, because her damages resulted from bodily injury to one person, Mr. Villanueva, in one accident, the most that Dai-Tokyo must pay for the combined injuries of Mr. and Mrs. Villanueva is $100,000.

A catastrophic injury to one person typically affects many people. When an insurance company includes a "per person"

limit in its policy language, it is reasonable to take this to mean the damages flowing from only the injuries of the person who was injured in the covered accident. It is not reasonable to assume that an insurance company will compensate every collateral injury to every new person, so long as there is a physical manifestation that arises from one person's injury, as such an interpretation would mean that anyone in the close circle of people around the injured person would have a chance to assert an independent claim under the policy. We find this result unreasonable because it expands the circle of covered people to an almost unidentifiable number of claimants.

In conclusion, this court holds that there are sound reasons to reject *Abellon,* even though it interprets the same policy language. First, *Abellon* encourages litigants to make the difficult distinction between injuries with physical manifestations and non-physical manifestations in order to arrive at "bodily injury." Acceptance that loss of consortium as simply an element of the "per person" "bodily injury" obviates the need for this contrivance. Second, it is the more logical result. As most cases hold, there is one injury covered by the policy. That injury may cause many kinds of suffering, but those are all logically compensated under the "per person" limit because the accident of the "person" is insured, not all losses. Finally, the problem is not that loss of consortium is an uncompensated loss; rather, the problem is that the policy limit is usually reached before the value of the loss is added to the other inchoate losses.

One person suffered injury in an accident that was covered by insurance. This is not an ambiguous or confusing proposition, so there is no reason to resort to rules of construction. The holding in *Abellon* is isolated, and it has not been followed since, even among its sister district appellate courts. *See Ayala,* 11 Cal.Rptr.3d 158; *Hauser,* 252 Cal.Rptr. 569. The parties have presented no persuasive reason why this jurisdiction should adopt it. On the contrary, the dissenting justice, interpreting identical policy language in *Abellon,* has put forth the better logic to depart from the *Abellon* majority, and we adopt it.

We therefore adopt the reasoning laid out in the *Abellon* dissent and hold, consistent with other cases that depart from *Abellon,* that a loss of consortium claim is included within the definition of bodily injury, and that the distinction between physical manifestations of psychological injury is irrelevant. Further, we hold that because any such loss of consortium claim is derivative, it is restricted to the monetary limit placed in the insurance policy to a per person total. *See, e.g., Shepard v. State Farm Mut. Auto Ins. Co.,* 545 So.2d 624 (La.Ct. App. 1989).

III.

The trial court held that the damages for Mrs. Villanueva's loss of consortium are subject to the "per person" limitation clause found in the insurance policy because Mrs. Villanueva's damages for loss of consortium are a result of the bodily injury to one person, Mr. Villanueva. We AFFIRM.

Source: Villanueva ex rel. U.S. v. Commercial Sanitation Systems, Inc. 2005 WL 901056 Guam Terr., 2005. Reprinted with permission from Westlaw.

Chapter 9

Vicarious Liability

CHAPTER OBJECTIVES

Upon completion of this chapter, you will be able to:

- Discuss the doctrine of vicarious liability.
- Understand the employer/employee relationship.
- Explain the distinction between an independent contractor and an employee.
- Identify a joint enterprise.
- Explain automobile consent statutes.
- Discuss the family purpose doctrine.

The concept of who is responsible for a person's damage or injury permeates throughout torts. There are certain cases in tort law in which a person other than the one who actually committed the wrong is held liable for the damages and injuries suffered by the plaintiff. This chapter deals with several principles by which one person may become liable to the plaintiff for the wrongful acts someone else committed.

LEGAL RESEARCH MAXIM

The trier of fact has the exclusive obligation to make findings of fact and can be either a jury, or a judge in a jury-waived trial. The trier of law on the other hand is always the judge deciding on rulings of law.

vicarious liability
One person, or a third party, may be found liable for the act of another or shares liability with the actor.

VICARIOUS LIABILITY

The principle of **vicarious liability** deals with situations in which one person will be found liable solely because someone else acted unreasonably toward the plaintiff; the term "vicarious" means the substitution of one person for another. The unreasonableness of one person is assigned to another person even though the latter did nothing wrong. Typically, the doctrine of vicarious liability arises when there is a special relationship between the person found liable and the

SPOT THE ISSUE

Rachel, Anne, and David develop a business in which they offer various adventure vacations to tourists. One day, David took out a group of customers white-water rafting. Unfortunately David was negligent in checking the condition of the raft. As a result, four of the customers were injured when the raft crashed into rocks. The injured customers seek to sue David, Rachel, and Anne under what theory of vicarious liability?

wrongdoer. To be found vicariously liable, the trier of fact must apply some distinct tests to determine if liability will attach; these are similar to the tests that are conducted for negligence. In fact, vicarious liability is based on the principles of negligence. These tests will be discussed later.

EMPLOYER-EMPLOYEE RELATIONSHIP

Vicarious liability is commonly found in situations involving the commission of a tortious act by an employee, where, under certain circumstances, liability attaches to the employer. This type of liability is also known as **respondeat superior**. The employer–employee relationship is also referred to as **master/servant** or **principal/agent**. An *agent* is someone who agrees to do something on behalf of and under the authority of another. A *principal* is the person on whose behalf the agent is acting. (See Figure 9.1 for an example of a flowchart showing how a principal can be responsible for an agent's or employee's acts.)

The rationale behind vicarious liability has been formed by various theories. Some of these theories are as follows:

- The employer has control over the actions of an employee.
- The origination of the process that caused the tortious conduct was caused by the employer.
- The employer delegated certain duties to the employee, and the employee's actions while doing those duties caused the injury.
- When an employer hires an employee, he assumes certain responsibilities for the employee's conduct through the privilege of hiring.
- The employer has deep pockets (i.e., extensive financial resources), so she will be more able to compensate the injured plaintiff.

See Figure 9.2 which shows the theories behind vicarious liability.

Many courts justify the doctrine of vicarious liability based on the principle of **allocation of risk**. The plaintiff wants to go after the party with the deepest pockets. Usually the employer is the party who has the most money from which a negligence judgment can be satisfied, and employees are frequently judgment proof. In addition, the employer probably carries insurance policies that can essentially spread the cost of the liability throughout the community.

In some instances, the employer will sue a third party for damages the employer suffered that arose out of an accident in which the employee was also negligent. The contributory negligence of the employee will be attributed to the employer in the employer's negligence lawsuit against the third party as long as the accident occurred in the normal course and scope of the employee's employment. This principle is known as **imputed negligence**.

For example, Jeb works for Soda Co. He drives the company truck and makes deliveries of Soda Co. products to various supermarkets in the city. One day, while making his routine deliveries, the truck blows a front tire. Jeb is unable to maintain control of the vehicle and slams into Marci's vehicle. Marci is severely injured. Marci's sues Soda Co. for her damages and injuries. In the course of investigating the accident,

respondeat superior
A master is liable in certain circumstances for the wrongful acts of his servants and a principal for those of his agent.

master
An individual or entity (as a corporation) having control or authority over another.

servant
A person in the employ and subject to the direction or control of an individual or company.

principal
The source of authority.

agent
A person or entity (as an employee or independent contractor) authorized to act on behalf of and under the control of another in dealing with third parties.

allocation of risk
Assignment of uncertainty to another party.

imputed negligence
Places upon one person responsibility for the negligence of another.

Employee, agent, or servant acts unreasonably toward the plaintiff.	Plaintiff is injured as a result of employee's, agent's, or servant's actions.	Employer, principal, or master is held liable to the plaintiff.

FIGURE 9.1
Responsibility of Principal for an Agent's or Employee's Acts

FIGURE 9.2 **Theories Behind Vicarious Liability**

it is discovered that the front tire failed due to a manufacturing defect by Tirestone, the manufacturer of the tire. In fact, Tirestone issues a product recall of those particular tires as a result of the investigation of this accident. Soda Co. sues Tirestone for the damages that it incurred or may incur as a result of the accident and the lawsuit brought by Marci.

Scope of Employment

scope of employment

The activities in which an employee engages in carrying out the employer's business that are reasonably foreseeable by the employer.

The major principle used to determine whether or not an employer is vicariously liable for the torts of an employee is if the employee was acting within the **scope of his or her employment** at the time of the tortious conduct. Professor Keeton in *Prosser and Keeton on the Law of Torts,* section 70 at 502 (5th ed. 1984), defines scope of employment as follows:

> *As in the case of the existence of the relation itself, many factors enter into the question: the time, place and purpose of the act, and its similarity to what is authorized; whether it is one commonly done by such servants; the extent of departure from normal methods; the previous relations between the parties; whether the master had reason to expect that such an act would be done.*

Scope of employment means those tasks employees perform that are foreseeable by the employer or under the employer's specific or general control. Scope of employment is not determined by what the employer has authorized an employee to do. Usually, employees' conduct is considered as being in the scope of their employment if it serves the employer's purposes. If an employee's conduct furthers the interest of the employer, then liability for any tortious conduct the employee committed will attach to the employer. Whether an employee was acting in the scope of his or her employment is a question of fact. In determining the scope of employment, courts will look to (a) the employee's job description and assigned duties, (b) the time, place, and purpose of the employee's acts, (c) the similarity of the employee's conduct to the things that person was hired to do, or which are commonly done by such employees, and (d) the foreseeability of the employee's acts. After reviewing these various factors as applied to the employee, a court will determine whether the employee was acting within the scope of his or her employment, imputing liability to the employer. See Figure 9.3 showing the elements of scope of employment.

Most courts hold that if an employee is involved in an accident on her way to and from work, she is not acting within the scope of her employment. The rationale is that the employer has no control of the employee during her commute to work and that she does not usually officially start work until arriving at the job.

Frolic and Detour

Sometimes, while an employee is on a trip for his employer, he makes a short side trip or detour. The detour is for the employee's own purposes and not to further

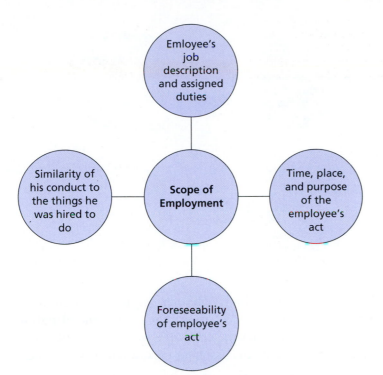

FIGURE 9.3
Factors Used in
Determining If an
Employee Was Acting
Within the Scope of
Employment

the interests of the employer. The question becomes whether or not the employee's side trip constitutes a **frolic or detour**, which depends largely on the character of the employee's actions. There is no vicarious liability if the employee committed a negligent act while he was on a frolic of his own. An employer is held vicariously liable for torts committed during an employee's detour, but not those committed during frolics. A main feature of a frolic and detour is that employees are acting primarily for their own purposes rather than for the employer's business.

A frolic occurs when the employee departs from the course and scope of employment to a significant degree. Most often, the employee departs from the normal course and scope of her employment in pursuit of her personal interests, and not those interests of the employer. An employee's detour is a less serious deviation from the course and scope of the employment. An employee's detour will typically

frolic
To engage in recreation.

detour
A deviation from a direct course of action.

A DAY IN THE LIFE OF A REAL PARALEGAL

Mary has two years of experience working as a paralegal for a firm that handles vicarious liability issues for casinos in Las Vegas. One night at the Lost Wages casino, a cleaning lady named Carol, an employee of the casino, injured a patron of the casino, Nancy, by knocking into her, which resulted in Nancy falling down two flights of stairs, paralyzing her from the waist down. Nancy has now sued Lost Wages casino and Carol for injuring her. The casino has asked you to defend them. The casino has not extended indemnification to Carol.

Regarding vicarious liability issues, Mary must now conduct an investigation and sort through the following questions: Is Carol an employee or independent contractor? Was Carol on any kind of detour or frolic when the incident occurred? Was Carol under the influence of any substance? Did Carol get training and, if yes, what kind? Was Carol negligent or did she commit an intentional tort?

Can you think of any questions you would ask should this very possible scenario happen to you in the workplace?

FIGURE 9.4
Factors Used to Determine Frolic and Detour

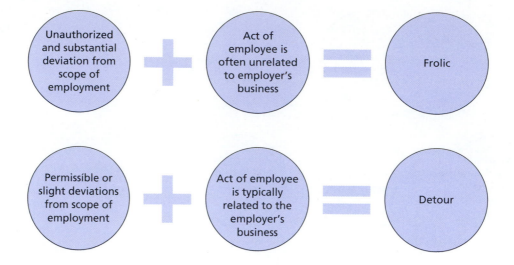

relate to the employer's business. In determining whether an act is a detour or frolic, courts inquire whether or not the conduct was of the same general nature as, or was incident to, the kind of activity that the employee was hired to perform. If the tortious conduct was characteristic of the assigned task, a court is less likely to find a frolic.

A frolic is deemed finished when the employee's own business is completed, and the employee returns to the business of the employer. In such case, the employer will be deemed liable for the employee's tortious acts if the frolic is finished. For example, an employer will be considered liable if its employee is involved in an accident while taking a different route to a delivery, even if the employer did not authorize the alternative route. However, under a frolic theory, an employer would not be held liable to a third party if the accident occurred while the employee traveled five hours off the delivery path to visit a friend. See Figure 9.4 which shows the differences between a frolic and a detour.

YOU BE THE JUDGE

Joe, an employee of Transride Inc., drives a truck across the United States as part of his job with Transride. On Joe's latest cross-country trip, as he was driving though Utah, he decided to go four hours off his designated route in order to drop in for a visit to one of his girlfriends. After about three hours off Joe's designated route, he collided with a vehicle owned by Jill. Jill was injured in the accident and now seeks to sue Transride for vicarious liability, for Joe's alleged negligence. Will Jill likely succeed in her claim?

CASE FACT PATTERN

Mary works for JP Consulting. Mary is to drive from Richmond, Virginia, to Baltimore, Maryland, for a business trip for JP Consulting. Instead of driving straight to Baltimore, Mary decides to drive out of her way to go to Washington, D.C., to visit the Smithsonian Institute first. After visiting the Smithsonian, Mary gets back on the road and heads toward Baltimore. While en route to Baltimore, just outside the city limits of Washington, D.C., Mary begins to get tired and occasionally nods off. During one of these episodes, her vehicle crosses the divider and goes into the lanes of opposing traffic. Mary collides with another vehicle, severely injuring the occupants and totaling their vehicle. Mary is also injured in the accident. The court will probably determine that Mary's trip to Washington, D.C., was a frolic and detour of her own as it was a substantial deviation from her path. Mary went to a completely different city for her own purposes before going to Baltimore for business. Mary's trip to Washington, D.C., was not for any purposes of her employer.

EMPLOYER'S LIABILITY BASED ON OWN NEGLIGENCE

The theories of vicarious liability discussed earlier deal with employers' liability based on the acts of their employees. Keep in mind, however, that an employer may be directly liable for torts committed by an employee based on the employer's own negligence or conduct. The employer may be held liable for negligently selecting, instructing, or supervising the employee.

Negligent Selection

Negligent selection holds employers liable solely on account of their hiring of employees. For negligent selection liability to apply, it must be shown that an employer should have known that the selection of the employee would lead to the injury. The most relevant issue with negligent selection is what the employer knew or should have known when the employee was hired.

For example, if a company hires a driver with numerous citations and accidents, it may be held liable for negligent selection if the driver is involved in an accident while working. The company is held liable because it should have known that the employee had a history of traffic violations and accidents, yet it hired him as a company driver.

Keep in mind however, that the alleged poor quality in the employee must be related to the employee's job duties. For example, an employee's poor driving record would not be relevant unless the scope of the employment involved the employee driving for the employer.

Negligent Instruction

A employer will be considered liable for the tortious acts of his employee if the injury resulted from the employer's lack of instruction to the employee. Under a negligent instruction theory, the plaintiff asserts that the employer failed to properly give the employee instructions, and as a result the injury to the plaintiff occurred.

For example, an employee works for an amusement park as an operator of one of the park's rides. After being hired, the employee attended two mandatory one-hour instruction classes, designed to teach the employee how to properly operate the ride. The plaintiff sustains injury after he is thrown from the ride. It is later determined that the employee accidentally released the lock of the plaintiff's chair, causing his injuries. In addition to a vicarious liability theory of liability, the plaintiff may allege that the amusement park should be held liable for not adequately instructing the employee.

Negligent Supervision

An employer will be held liable for her own negligence relating to an employee's tortious acts if the injury resulted from the employer's negligent supervision of the employee. Negligent supervision holds that employers have a duty to properly supervise their employees. Employers are perceived as having control over their employees, and as such, must properly supervise the employees' actions. As already mentioned, control over an employee by an employer is one the main theories supporting vicarious liability. The influence of control over the employee is the key theory behind negligent supervision.

For example, Susan is the manager and owner of a car dealership. She has a staff of seven salespeople. At any one time, up to five salespeople roam the car lot to help customers. Susan lets her salespeople manage themselves, and she spends the majority of the day in her back office. Tony, a customer, is injured after he is punched by a salesperson. Tony claims that the salesperson became angry after Tony refused the salesperson's price for a vehicle. Susan was in her office when the altercation took place. Negligent selection offers Tony the ability to hold Susan liable for failing to properly

FIGURE 9.5

Employer Liability for Employee Acts Due to Employer Negligence

Situations in Which an Employer Is Liable for the Acts of Employee Based on Employer's Own Negligence

Negligent Selection	Negligent Instruction	Negligent Supervision
• An employer is liable for the acts of her employee, if the employer knew or should have known that the employee had a propensity to cause the type of injury that occurred.	• An employer is liable for the acts of her employee if the injury resulted from the employer not providing proper instruction to the employee.	• An employer is liable for injuries that result from the acts of her employee if the injury resulted in the employer not properly supervising the employee.

supervise her employee. See Figure 9.5 which describes situations in which an employer is liable for the acts of employees based on the employer's own negligence.

INDEPENDENT CONTRACTOR

independent contractor
One who, in exercise of an independent employment, contracts to do a piece of work according to his own methods and is subject to his employer's control only as to the end product or final result of his work.

The courts look at certain factors to determine whether or not an employer–employee relationship exists if the person working for the employer is an **independent contractor**. Some of the factors that the court may look at are:

- The degree to which the employer may establish the details of the person's work.
- The nature of the job.
- The custom in the industry or community.
- The skill required by the person to do the job.
- Who supplied the tools or other instruments necessary to do the job.
- The period of employment.
- The manner in which the person is paid.

If the person employed in a position is found to be an independent contractor, then vicarious liability will probably not attach because the special relationship of employer–employee does not exist. The *Restatement (Second) of Torts,* section 409, speaks to this situation as follows:

> [T]he employer of an independent contractor is not liable for physical harm caused to another by an act or omission of the contractor or his servants.

See Figure 9.6 regarding factors for determining if an employee is an independent contractor.

Some of the distinguishing characteristics between an employee and an independent contractor are:

- The employer has less control over the independent contractor than over the employee.
- The independent contractor has a great deal more discretion over the way the job is done than an employee.
- The employee is on the payroll of the employer while the independent contractor is hired primarily to produce a certain product or result.

See Figure 9.7 for the elements of what makes a worker an independent contractor versus an employee.

FIGURE 9.6
Factors Used to
Determine Whether a
Worker Is Employee
or Independent
Contractor

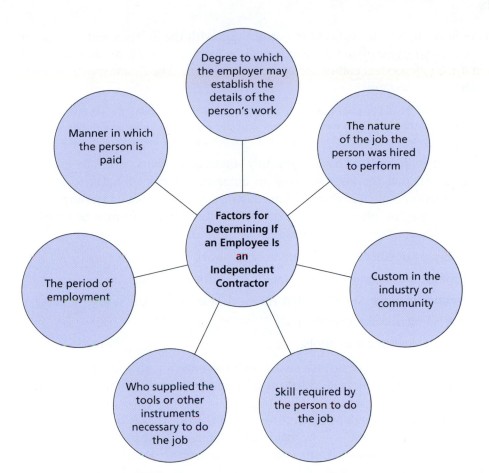

Usually, an employer is not held vicariously liable for the torts of an independent contractor except when:

- The employer himself is negligent.
- The employer was negligent in her selection of the independent contractor.
- The independent contractor is performing certain non-delegable duties of the employer.
- The independent contractor is performing inherently dangerous work for the employer.

FIGURE 9.7   **Using Independent Contractors Versus Employees**

If an employer herself is negligent in her dealings with the independent contractor or does not exercise due care in the direction of the work, the employer may be found liable even if the independent contractor performed the work. The *Restatement (Second) of Torts,* section 410, states:

> *The employer of an independent contractor is subject to the same liability for physical harm caused by an act or omission committed by the contractor pursuant to order or direction negligently given by the employer, as though the act or omission were that of the employer himself.*

The employer is deemed to have negligently directed the work when he knew or should have known that the work involved an unreasonable risk of harm to another person. This situation is often encountered in construction cases when an employer gives a subcontractor defective plans or specifications. The following items may be reviewed to determine if the employer was negligent:

- Giving orders or directions concerning how the work is to be performed.
- Hiring a competent independent contractor to perform the job.
- Taking precautions take to ensure that the work was performed safely.
- Performing his own duties and work.
- Supervising the equipment or tools.

If the employer is negligent or fails to act with reasonable care with regard to any of the preceding, he may be held vicariously liable for the acts of his independent contractor.

If an employer hires an independent contractor for work that is considered *inherently dangerous,* the employer will be held liable for any damages or injuries that result from the work the independent contractor performed. Remember, inherently dangerous activities usually come under the tort theory of strict liability in which the defendant engaging in these activities is held strictly liable for any resulting damages or injuries. The employer will be held strictly liable when engaged in inherently dangerous activities even if the independent contractor caused the injuries or damages. A few examples of inherently dangerous activities are construction of dams and reservoirs, installation of electrical wires, excavations near a public highway, and exhibition of fireworks.

As a matter of public policy, an employer is held liable for inherently dangerous activity that an independent contractor performed on behalf of the employer. If liability did not attach to the employer, employers would have the benefit of liability release by simply contracting out all their dangerous work to independent contractors. Holding an employer liable for injuries that result from inherently dangerous activities ensures that employers will more carefully select and supervise the independent contractors they hire.

For example, a city hires an independent contractor to construct a dam in the city. If third persons are injured as a result of the independent contractor's negligence in constructing the dam, the city will be held liable. The inherently dangerous character of constructing a dam will hold the city liable, even though the dam was constructed by independent contractor.

An employer will not be held liable in most jurisdictions if the independent contractor's own employees are injured.

non-delegable duties
An obligation imposed by law or contract that may not be passed to another.

An employer also can be found liable for an independent contractor's actions if the employer delegated a **non-delegable duty** to the independent contractor. Sometimes these duties are created by contract, statute, or common law. For example, the owner of a common carrier has a duty to transport people in a safe manner. He cannot delegate that duty; therefore, if the independent contractor fails to take care and harms a passenger, then the employer will be held liable.

Other examples of non-delegable duties include a city's duty to keep streets in safe repair, a landlord's duty to maintain common passageways, and a business owner's duty to keep the premises safe for customers.

For example, Peter owns a supermarket. When the supermarket recently underwent renovations, Peter hired an independent contractor to plaster the market's ceiling. On the first day of opening, a piece of plaster falls from the roof and injures a customer. Although the independent contractor may have been negligent in his plastering of the roof, Peter would also be liable for the customer's injuries.

Some courts have held that the employee's detour may be considered under the scope of the employee's business if such a deviation is reasonably foreseeable. For example, if an accident occurs while an employee is smoking or walking to the restroom, those activities are reasonably foreseeable detours, so the employer would be found vicariously liable. In addition, the premise upon which vicarious liability and respondeat superior is built is one in which employers are liable despite their own negligence. Having said that, if the employee engages in some type of activity that the employer has expressly forbidden and someone is hurt, the employer will still be liable.

For example, suppose Joe owns a gun store. He hires Bill. Joe expressly tells Bill that it is strictly forbidden to show a customer a loaded gun. Melissa comes into the store to buy a gun. While Bill is showing Melissa a particular gun, she inquires about the process for loading the ammunition. Bills knows that Joe has forbidden anyone from showing a loaded gun, but Bill thinks Melissa is attractive and wants to assist her, so he directly disobeys Joe. Bill loads the ammunition into the gun and then proceeds to show the gun to Melissa while it is loaded. Melissa is handling the gun when it goes off, striking another customer. Even though Joe had strictly forbidden Bill from showing a loaded gun and Bill directly disobeyed him, Joe will still be held liable for the customer's injuries.

INTENTIONAL TORTS

The theory of respondeat superior also applies to the intentional torts committed by employees as long as they happened within the scope of their employment. If an employee is acting in some way to further the employer's business, then the employer will be found liable for those intentional acts. Professor Keeton addresses this situation in *Prosser and Keeton on the Law of Torts*, section 70 at 506 (5th ed. 1984), when he states:

> *Thus he will be held liable where his bus driver crowds a competitor's bus into a ditch, or assaults a trespasser to eject him from the bus, or a salesman makes fraudulent statements about the product, or where the servant resorts to false imprisonment or malicious prosecution for a like purpose. Thus a railway ticket agent who assaults, arrests or slanders a passenger, in the belief that he has been given a counterfeit bill for a ticket is within the scope of his employment.*

However, if the employee commits an intentional action purely for his own purposes and not for the purposes of the employer, that act will not be considered to be in the course and scope of his employment, and many courts will not hold the employer liable

 EYE ON ETHICS

It is very important for paralegals to know their state law as well as the law that governs their jurisdiction. The law governing non-delegable duties is typically mandated by state law. Therefore, if a situation such as one of those described in the preceding text is encountered, it is important to thoroughly research your state and local laws to determine what duties may not be delegated by an employer.

for the employee's actions in this circumstance. For example, if an employee sexually assaults a customer, the employer may not be held liable. Keep in mind, however, that an employer may still be held liable under another theory. For example, if the employer in the previous example knew that employee had a history of, and a predisposition toward, sexual assault, then the employer may be held liable for negligent selection or supervision.

JOINT ENTERPRISE

joint enterprise
The joint prosecution of a common purpose under such circumstances that each has authority expressed or implied to act for all in respect to control, means, or agencies employed to execute such common purpose.

A **joint enterprise** is when a group of people come together to carry out a business purpose. For parties to be engaged in a joint enterprise, the following elements must be present:

- An express or implied agreement to participate in the enterprise among the associates.
- A common purpose.
- A common monetary interest.
- An equal and mutual right to control and direct the enterprise.

A joint enterprise is like a partnership; however, it is generally formed for a short and specific purpose. Once a joint enterprise is established, each of the parties can be held vicariously liable for the actions of the other. A joint enterprise is essentially treated like a partnership in that one partner can become personally liable for the acts of all the other partners. The *Restatement (Second) of Torts*, section 491, defines a joint enterprise as follows:

1. *Any one of several persons engaged in a joint enterprise, such as to make each member of the group responsible for physical harm to other persons caused by the negligence of any member, is barred from recovery against such other persons by the negligence of any member of the group.*
2. *Any person engaged in such a joint enterprise is not barred from recovery against the member of the group who is negligent, but is barred from recovery against any other member of the group.*

AUTOMOBILE CONSENT STATUTES

Automobile consent statutes make the owners of vehicles liable for the negligence of any person to whom they entrust their vehicle. For example, if you let your neighbor drive your car and your neighbor gets into an accident, then you would be held liable for your neighbor's wrongful act while driving your car. The owner of a vehicle is held vicariously liable for any damages or injuries committed by any person who had the owner's permission to use the owner's vehicle.

The automobile consent statutes place the financial responsibility on those best able to afford insurance coverage. By using these statutes, the desired effect is to distribute the cost of automobile accidents over the large class made up of automobile owners.

FAMILY PURPOSE DOCTRINE

family purpose doctrine
Where one purchases and maintains an automobile for the comfort, convenience, pleasure, entertainment, and recreation of one's family, any member thereof operating the automobile will be regarded as an agent or servant of the owner, and the owner will be held liable for injuries sustained by a third person by reason of negligent operation of the vehicle by a family member.

The **family purpose doctrine** is a form of vicarious liability for families concerning the family automobile. Not all states that have adopted this doctrine agree on the elements that should be reviewed in order to determine liability. Generally, the elements are:

- Defendant must own, have an ownership interest in, or control the use of the vehicle.
- Defendant must make the car available for family use rather than for the defendant's business.
- The driver must be a member of the defendant's immediate household.

FIGURE 9.8
**Elements of the Family
Purpose Doctrine**

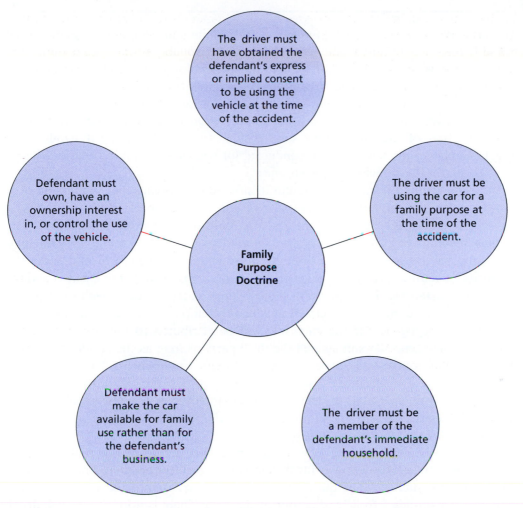

- The driver must be using the car for a family purpose at the time of the accident.
- The driver must have obtained the defendant's express or implied consent to be using the vehicle at the time of the accident.

See Figure 9.8 for the elements of the family purpose doctrine.

The defendant does not have to be the traditional head of the household and does not have to be in the car at the time of the accident in order for liability to attach.

RESEARCH THIS

Paralegals can be independent contractors as well as employees. When a paralegal commits a tort, is the attorney vicariously liable? Also, what would be considered within the scope and course of employment for a paralegal? Using whatever sources are available to you, research the profession that you are considering entering. When will your boss, the attorney, be held vicariously liable for your torts, and what tasks are considered within the scope of your employment in order for liability to attach to your boss?

SURF'S UP

To learn more about vicarious liability, research the following websites:

- www.onlinelawyesource.com
- www.findlaw.com
- www.megalaw.com

Summary

The principle of vicarious liability deals with situations in which one person will be found liable solely because someone else acted unreasonably toward the plaintiff; the term "vicarious" means the substitution of one person for another. The unreasonableness of one person is assigned to another person even though the latter did nothing wrong. Typically, the doctrine of vicarious liability arises when there is a special relationship between the person found liable and the wrongdoer. To be found vicariously liable, the trier of fact must apply some distinct tests to determine if liability will attach, similar to the tests that are conducted for negligence. In fact, vicarious liability is based on the principles of negligence.

Vicarious liability is commonly found in situations involving the commission of a tortious act by an employee, where, under certain circumstances, liability attaches to the employer. This type of liability is also known as respondeat superior. The employer–employee relationship is also referred to as master/servant or principal/agent. An agent is someone who agrees to do something on behalf of and under the authority of another. A principal is the person on whose behalf the agent is acting.

In some instances, the employer will sue a third party for damages the employer suffered that arose out of an accident in which the employee was also negligent. The contributory negligence of the employee will be attributed to the employer in the employer's negligence lawsuit against the third party as long as the accident occurred in the normal course and scope of the employee's employment. This principle is known as imputed negligence.

The major principle used to determine if an employer is vicariously liable for the torts of his employee is if the employee was acting within the scope of his or her employment at the time of the tortious conduct.

Sometimes, while the employee is on a trip for her employer, she makes a short side trip or detour. The detour is for the employee's own purposes and not to further the employer's interests. The question becomes whether or not the side trip of the employee constitutes a frolic and detour of her own. There is no vicarious liability if the employee's negligent act was committed while she was on a frolic or detour of her own. A main feature of a frolic and detour is that employees are acting primarily for their own purposes rather than for the employer's business.

The theory of respondeat superior also applies to intentional torts employees commit, as long as they happen within the scope of their employment. If the employee is acting in some way to further the employer's business, then the employer will be found liable for those intentional acts.

If the person employed in a position is found to be an independent contractor, then vicarious liability will probably not attach, because the special relationship of employer–employee does not exist. If employers themselves are negligent in their dealings with independent contractors or do not exercise due care in the direction of the work, employers may be found liable even if the work is performed by an independent contractor.

A joint enterprise is like a partnership; however, it is generally formed for a short and specific purpose. Once a joint enterprise is established, each of the parties can be held vicariously liable for the actions of the others. A joint enterprise is essentially treated like a partnership in that one partner can become personally liable for the acts of all the other partners.

Automobile consent statutes make vehicle owners liable for the negligence of any person to whom they entrust the vehicle. The automobile consent statutes place the financial responsibility on those best able to afford insurance coverage. By using these statutes, the desired effect is to distribute the cost of automobile accidents over the large class made up of automobile owners.

The family purpose doctrine is a form of vicarious liability for families concerning the family automobile. States that have adopted the doctrine attach liability when certain elements have been met. When the elements are satisfied, the owner of the vehicle may become vicariously liable to an injured third party.

Agent
Allocation of risk
Detour
Family purpose doctrine
Frolic
Imputed negligence
Independent contractor
Joint enterprise

Master
Non-delegable duty
Principal
Respondeat superior
Scope of employment
Servant
Vicarious liability

1. What is vicarious liability?
2. What is imputed negligence?
3. What is respondeat superior?
4. What is allocation of risk?
5. List the criteria that determine what is an employee in the employer–employee relationship.
6. What is (are) the difference(s) between an employee and an independent contractor?
7. When are employers held liable for the intentional torts of their employees?
8. What is a non-delegable duty, and why can liability attach to an employer because of a delegation?
9. What are the elements that determine a joint enterprise?
10. Why is an automobile consent statute important?
11. What is the purpose of the family purpose doctrine?
12. Explain when an employer is held liable for the torts of an independent contractor.
13. Is an employer liable for injuries sustained by an independent contractor's employees?
14. List the elements that are reviewed to determine if someone is acting within the scope of his or her employment.
15. Define a frolic and detour.

1. South Coast Collectors, Inc. runs a debt collection company. All employees of South Coast Collectors are instructed that they should never use violence or threats of violence when attempting to collect a debt. Darrel, one of the employees of South Coast Collectors, was attempting to collect a $10,000 debt owed by Peter to South Coast Collectors. Peter refused to pay even though Peter had the financial capability to do so. Ignoring the warnings of his employer, Darrel threatened to send someone over to Peter's residence to "rough him up." Peter paid the money. Peter has now brought suit against South Coast Collectors for assault and intentional infliction of emotional distress under the theory of respondeat superior. Can Peter recover?

2. Analyze the following situations and determine, based on what you have studied in this chapter, whether or not the employees were acting within the scope of their employment at the time of the incident. In each instance, the plaintiff is suing the employer based on the theory of respondeat superior. Will the plaintiff prevail?

    a. The employee works for a dry cleaner. The employee is smoking, and some of the ashes from his cigarette fall onto the plaintiff's fur coat, causing the coat to catch fire and causing substantial damage. The plaintiff sues for negligence.

    b. While making a delivery in a company truck, the employee drives three miles out of her way to visit her sick mother. She stays for approximately three hours. On her way back to the company plant to return the truck, the employee runs a stop sign and injures the plaintiff in a traffic accident. The plaintiff sues for negligence.

    c. The employee is a door-to-door salesperson. At one house, the employee gets into an argument with the plaintiff. The plaintiff curses at the employee. The employee takes a swing and strikes the plaintiff in the face. The plaintiff is now suing for battery.

3. Molly and Paul are husband and wife. They are on their way to sign up for a real estate training class in which couples are taught how to open their own real estate business. The car is in the names of both Molly and Paul, and Molly is driving. An accident occurs. The plaintiff sues Paul for negligence. How would you determine if there is a joint enterprise?

4. California Homes, Inc. contracts homes to be built. It receives bids by independent contractors for various house building projects. One such bid was submitted by Vista, an independent contractor. California Homes accepted Vista's bid and contracted for Vista to build four houses. One of the houses built by Vista was built negligently. What factors would a court look to in deciding whether or not California Homes should be held liable for Vista's negligence?

5. Jack bought a new luxury vehicle for his family to enjoy. Jack has a wife and three kids, ranging in age from 17 to 26. Jack bought the vehicle in celebration of his business's recent success. The vehicle was purchased solely for his family's use and enjoyment. Mike, Jack's 22-year-old son, borrowed the vehicle, with Jack's permission, to go out with friends, and to run a few errands for Jack. While out driving, Mike negligently collided with Janet as she was riding her bike. Janet was injured and now seeks to sue Jack, asserting vicarious liability against him. Is Janet likely to succeed on her claim against Jack? If so, under what theory(s) of vicarious liability?

6. Bouncer Bill works as a doorman for a popular downtown nightclub called Hotspot. As part of Bill's job, he often kicks rowdy patrons out of the club. On Saturday night, a fight broke out between a group of patrons at the club. Bill mistakenly took Thomas as one of the individuals involved in the altercation, although Thomas had nothing to do with the fight. Bill grabbed Thomas by the back of the neck and violently dragged him out of the club. As a result, Thomas suffered a neck injury. He is now suing the owner of Hotspot for Bill's actions. Will Thomas likely succeed? Under which theory(s) of vicarious liability?

 PORTFOLIO ASSIGNMENT

Reflect upon the job you currently have or a job that you have recently held. List five examples of detours that happened at your place of employment by either you or another, and list five frolics that either you or another have committed. Explain how and why you categorized the selection as you did.

Vocabulary Builders

Instructions

Use the key terms from this chapter to fill in the answers to the crossword puzzle.

NOTE: When the answer is more than one word, leave a blank space between words.

ACROSS

6. A person or entity (as an employee or independent contractor) authorized to act on behalf of and under the control of another in dealing with third parties.
7. The source of authority.
10. A person in the employ of, and subject to, the direction or control of an individual or company.
11. To engage in recreation.
12. An individual or entity (as a corporation) having control or authority over another.
13. The activities in which an employee engages in carrying out the employer's business that are reasonably foreseeable by the employer.
14. Assignment of uncertainty to another party.
15. Where one purchases and maintains an automobile for the comfort, convenience, pleasure, entertainment, and recreation of one's family, any member thereof operating the automobile will be regarded as an agent or servant of the owner, and the owner will be held liable for injuries sustained by a third person by reason of negligent operation of the vehicle by a family member.

DOWN

1. One who, in exercise of an independent employment, contracts to do a piece of work according to his own methods and is subject to his employer's control only as to end product or final result of his work.
2. One person, or a third party, may be found liable for the act of another or shares liability with the actor.
3. A master is liable in certain circumstances for the wrongful acts of his servants and a principal for those of his agent.
4. Places upon one person responsibility for the negligence of another.
5. An obligation imposed by law or contract that may not be passed to another.
8. A deviation from a direct course of action.
9. The joint prosecution of a common purpose under such circumstances that each has authority expressed or implied to act for all in respect to control, means, or agencies employed to execute such common purpose.

David *MEYER, individually and in his capacity as President and Designated Officer/Broker of Triad, Inc., etc., Petitioner, v. Emma Mary Ellen HOLLEY, et vir, et al.*

537 U.S. 280

Supreme Court of the United States

No. 01-1120.

Argued Dec. 3, 2002

Decided Jan. 22, 2003

Prospective home buyers, an interracial married couple, sued sole shareholder and president of real estate corporation, seeking to hold him vicariously liable for corporate employee's alleged violation of Fair Housing Act in preventing them from buying house. The United States District Court for the Central District of California, Wm. Matthew Byrne, Jr., Senior District Judge, dismissed action. The Court of Appeals for the Ninth Circuit, Procter Hug, Jr., Circuit Judge, 258 F.3d 1127, reversed. Certiorari was granted. The United States Supreme Court, Justice Breyer, held that: (1) Fair Housing Act imposed vicarious liability on principal or employer in accordance with traditional agency principles, and (2) authority of shareholder and president to control conduct of employee did not create principal/agent or employer/employee relationship under traditional agency principles.

Vacated and remanded.

Justice BREYER delivered the opinion of the Court.

The Fair Housing Act forbids racial discrimination in respect to the sale or rental of a dwelling. 82 Stat. 81, 42 U.S.C. §§ 3604(b), 3605(a). The question before us is whether the Act imposes personal liability without fault upon an officer or owner of a residential real estate corporation for the unlawful activity of the corporation's employee or agent. We conclude that the Act imposes liability without fault upon the employer in accordance with traditional agency principles, i.e., it normally imposes vicarious liability upon the corporation but not upon its officers or owners.

I

For purposes of this decision we simplify the background facts as follows: Respondents Emma Mary Ellen Holley and David Holley, an interracial couple, tried to buy a house in Twenty-Nine Palms, California. A real estate corporation, Triad, Inc., had listed the house for sale. Grove Crank, a Triad salesman, is alleged to have prevented the Holleys from obtaining the house—and for racially discriminatory reasons.

The Holleys brought a lawsuit in federal court against Crank and Triad. They claimed, among other things, that both were responsible for a fair housing law violation. The Holleys later filed a separate suit against David Meyer, the petitioner here. Meyer, they said, was Triad's president, Triad's sole shareholder, and Triad's licensed "officer/broker." They claimed that Meyer was vicariously liable in one or more of these capacities for Crank's unlawful actions.

The District Court consolidated the two lawsuits. . . .

The District Court certified its judgment as final to permit the Holleys to appeal its vicarious liability determinations. The Ninth Circuit reversed those determinations. The Court of Appeals recognized that "under general principles of tort law corporate shareholders and officers usually are not held vicariously liable for an employee's action," but, in its view, "the criteria for the Fair Housing Act" are "different." That Act, it said, "specified" liability "for those who direct or control or have the right to direct or control the conduct of another"—even if they were not at all involved in the discrimination itself and even in the absence of any traditional agent/principal or employee/employer relationship, Meyer, in his capacity as Triad's sole owner, had "the authority to control the acts" of a Triad salesperson. Meyer, in his capacity as Triad's officer, "did direct or control, or had the right to direct or control, the conduct" of a Triad salesperson. And even if Meyer neither participated in nor authorized the discrimination in question, that "control" or "authority to control" is "enough . . . to hold Meyer personally liable." The Ninth Circuit added that, for similar reasons, Meyer, in his capacity as Triad's license-related officer/broker, was vicariously liable for Crank's discriminatory activity.

Meyer sought certiorari. We granted his petition, to review the Ninth Circuit's holding that the Fair Housing Act imposes principles of strict liability beyond those traditionally associated with agent/principal or employee/employer relationships. We agreed to decide whether "the criteria under the Fair Housing Act . . . are different, so that owners and officers of corporations" are automatically and "absolutely liable for an employee's or agent's violation of the Act"—even if they did not direct or authorize, and were otherwise not involved in, the unlawful discriminatory acts.

The Fair Housing Act itself focuses on prohibited acts. It says nothing about vicarious liability. . . .

Nonetheless, it is well established that the Act provides for vicarious liability. This Court has noted that an action brought for compensation by a victim of housing discrimination is, in effect, a tort action. And the Court has assumed that, when Congress creates a tort action, it legislates against a legal background of ordinary tort-related vicarious liability rules and consequently intends its legislation to incorporate those rules.

It is well established that traditional vicarious liability rules ordinarily make principals or employers vicariously liable for acts of their agents or employees in the scope of their authority or employment. "The principal is liable for the acts and negligence of the agent in the course of his employment, although he did not authorize or did not know of the acts complained of"); see *Rosenthal & Co. v. Commodity Futures*

Trading Comm'n, 802 F.2d 963, 967 (C.A.7 1986). And in the absence of special circumstances it is the corporation, not its owner or officer, who is the principal or employer, and thus subject to vicarious liability for torts committed by its employees or agents. 3A W. Fletcher, *Cyclopedia of the Law of Private Corporations* § 1137, pp. 300–301 (rev. ed. 1991–1994); 10 id., § 4877 (rev. ed. 1997–2001). The Restatement § 1 specifies that the relevant principal/agency relationship demands not only control (or the right to direct or control) but also "the manifestation of consent by one person to another that the other shall act on his behalf, and consent by the other so to act." A corporate employee typically acts on behalf of the corporation, not its owner or officer.

The Ninth Circuit held that the Fair Housing Act imposed more extensive vicarious liability—that the Act went well beyond traditional principles. The Court of Appeals held that the Act made corporate owners and officers liable for the unlawful acts of a corporate employee simply on the basis that the owner or officer controlled (or had the right to control) the actions of that employee. We do not agree with the Ninth Circuit that the Act extended traditional vicarious liability rules in this way.

For one thing, Congress said nothing in the statute or in the legislative history about extending vicarious liability in this manner. . . .

Where Congress, in other civil rights statutes, has not expressed a contrary intent, the Court has drawn the inference that it intended ordinary rules to apply. *See, e.g., Burlington Industries, Inc.,* supra, at 754–755, 118 S.Ct. 2257 (deciding an employer's vicarious liability under Title VII based on traditional agency principles);

This Court has applied unusually strict rules only where Congress has specified that such was its intent. *See, e.g., United States v. Dotterweich,* 320 U.S. 277, 280–281, 64 S.Ct. 134, 88 L.Ed. 48 (1943).

For another thing, the Department of Housing and Urban Development (HUD), the federal agency primarily charged with the implementation and administration of the statute, 42 U.S.C. § 3608, has specified that ordinary vicarious liability rules apply in this area. And we ordinarily defer to an administering agency's reasonable interpretation of a statute

When it adopted the similar predecessor to this regulation (then codified at 24 CFR § 105.13, *see* 53 Fed.Reg. 24185 (1988)), HUD explained that it intended to permit a "respondent" (defined at 42 U.S.C. § 3602) to raise in an administrative proceeding any defense "that could be raised in court." 53 Fed. Reg., at 24185. It added that the underscored phrase was designed to make clear that "a complaint may be filed against a directing or controlling person with respect to the discriminatory acts of another only if the other person was acting within the scope of his or her authority as employee or agent of the directing or controlling person." HUD also specified that, by adding the words "acting within the scope of his or her authority as employee or agent of the directing or controlling person," it disclaimed any "intent to impose absolute liability" on the basis of the mere right "to direct or control."

Finally, we have found no convincing argument in support of the Ninth Circuit's decision to apply nontraditional vicarious liability principles—a decision that respondents do not defend and in fact concede is incorrect. . . .Taken as a whole, the regulation, in our view, says that ordinary, not unusual, rules of vicarious liability should apply.

[Text omitted]

The Ninth Circuit further referred to an owner's or officer's "non delegable duty" not to discriminate in light of the Act's "overriding societal priority." And it added that "[w]hen one of two innocent people must suffer, the one whose acts permitted the wrong to occur is the one to bear the burden."

"[A] nondelegable duty is an affirmative obligation to ensure the protection of the person to whom the duty runs." *General Building Contractors Assn., Inc. v. Pennsylvania,* 458 U.S. 375, 396, Such a duty imposed upon a principal would "go further" than the vicarious liability principles we have discussed thus far to create liability "although [the principal] has himself done everything that could reasonably be required of him," and irrespective of whether the agent was acting with or without authority. The Ninth Circuit identifies nothing in the language or legislative history of the Act to support the existence of this special kind of liability—the kind of liability that, for example, the law might impose in certain special circumstances upon a principal or employer that hires an independent contractor. In the absence of legal support, we cannot conclude that Congress intended, through silence, to impose this kind of special duty of protection upon individual officers or owners of corporations—who are not principals (or contracting parties) in respect to the corporation's unlawfully acting employee.

Neither does it help to characterize the statute's objective as an "overriding societal priority." 258 F.3d, at 1132. We agree with the characterization. But we do not agree that the characterization carries with it a legal rule that would hold every corporate supervisor personally liable without fault for the unlawful act of every corporate employee whom he or she has the right to supervise. Rather, which "of two innocent people must suffer," *ibid.,* and just when, is a complex matter. We believe that courts ordinarily should determine that matter in accordance with traditional principles of *291 vicarious liability—unless, of course, Congress, better able than courts to weigh the relevant policy considerations, has instructed the courts differently. *Cf., e.g.,* Sykes, The **832 Economics of Vicarious Liability, 93 Yale L.J. 1231, 1236 (1984) (arguing that the expansion of vicarious liability or shifting of liability, due to insurance, may diminish an agent's incentives to police behavior). We have found no different instruction here.

III

A

Respondents, conceding that traditional vicarious liability rules apply, argue that those principles themselves warrant liability here. For one thing, they say, California law itself creates what amounts, under ordinary common-law principles, to an employer/employee or principal/agent relationship between (a) a corporate officer designated as the broker under a real estate license issued to the corporation, and (b) a corporate employee/salesperson Insofar as this argument rests solely upon the corporate broker/officer's right to control the employee/salesperson, the Ninth Circuit considered and accepted it. But we must reject it given our determination in Part II that the "right to control" is insufficient by itself, under traditional agency principles, to establish a principal/agent or employer/employee relationship.

B

The Ninth Circuit did not decide whether other aspects of the California broker relationship, when added to the "right to control," would, under traditional legal principles and consistent with "the general common law of agency," *Burlington Industries, Inc. v. Ellerth,* 524 U.S., at 754, But in the absence of consideration of that matter by the Court of Appeals, we shall not consider it.

Respondents also point out that, when traditional vicarious liability principles impose liability upon a corporation, the corporation's liability may be imputed to the corporation's owner in an appropriate case through a " 'piercing of the corporate veil.' " The Court of Appeals, however, did not decide the application of "veil piercing" in this matter either. It falls outside the scope of the question presented on certiorari. And we shall not here consider it.

The Ninth Circuit nonetheless remains free on remand to determine whether these questions were properly raised and, if so, to consider them.

The judgment of the Court of Appeals is vacated, and the case is remanded for further proceedings consistent with this opinion.

It is so ordered.

[Footnotes omitted]

Source: Reprinted with permission from Westlaw.

Chapter 10

Premises Liability and The Doctrine of Nuisance

CHAPTER OBJECTIVES

Upon completion of this chapter, you will be able to:

- Discuss the duties of a landholder.
- Explain the liability of a landholder in regard to a trespasser.
- Understand the concept of a licensee.
- Identify duties owed to an invitee.
- Examine the liability of lessors and lessees toward a person entering the land.
- Discuss liability of a landholder to vendors and vendees.
- Understand the concept of nuisance.
- Analyze private nuisance.
- Identify the nature of a public nuisance.

Common law throughout history has been influenced by agrarian and rural lifestyles and economies, first of England and then of the United States. Historically, landowners' rights have been protected under the law. However, with the privilege of ownership rights, landholders owe a duty of due care to persons who enter their property. The doctrine of nuisance deals with property issues as well: the interference with one's property ownership rights. This chapter will discuss all of the rights, duties, and obligations that are associated with property ownership.

DUTIES OF A LANDOWNER

The term **premises** refers to any real property and those things attached to or growing from it. The **landholder** faces different types of exposure to liability that are derived from his or her ownership interest in property. **Premises liability** deals with these types of exposure.

Outside the Land

As has been seen in other torts, whenever a defendant's acts or omissions create a foreseeable risk of injury or damage to a person, a duty of reasonable care arises to take precautions to prevent such injury or damage. Premises liability operates in much the same manner.

premises
Any real property, buildings that are attached to the property, grounds, facilities, structures, and other things that are attached to the land or growing from it.

landholder
Someone who is in rightful possession of the land.

premises liability
The liability that landholders may be exposed to in connection with their use and enjoyment of real property.

149

Landholders are considered to be in the best position to know or discover any condition that exists upon their land that could cause damage or injury to another. With regard to a **natural condition** that exists upon the land, a landholder owes no duty of care to prevent injury to persons outside the land who might be injured by natural conditions that exist on the landholder's property. However, there are exceptions. For example, if a landholder owns trees in an urban area, she owes a duty of reasonable care to inspect those trees and make sure that they are safe to persons outside the land. So, if a tree is unreasonably bushy, enough to cause it to topple and cause injuries or damages to someone outside the boundary of the landholder's land, then the landholder has a duty to have that tree trimmed so that the likelihood of that occurring is reduced.

> **natural condition**
> A condition upon the land that has been untouched or influenced by humans.

The *Restatement (Second) of Torts,* section 329, handles natural conditions as follows:

1. *Except as stated in Subsection (2), neither a possessor of land, nor a vendor, lessor, or other transferor, is liable for physical harm caused to others outside of the land by a natural condition of the land.*

2. *A possessor of land in an urban area is subject to liability to persons using a public highway for physical harm resulting from his failure to exercise reasonable care to prevent an unreasonable risk of harm arising from the condition of trees on the land near the highway.*

Artificial Condition

> **artificial condition**
> A man-made condition that exists on the land.

When an **artificial condition** is present on the landholder's land, the landholder owes a duty of reasonable care to prevent injury to persons outside the land who might be injured by the artificial condition. A landholder has a duty to prevent injuries to persons outside the property that might exist from man-made structures and shrubs that have been planted on the property, as well as from changes caused by the landholder working on the property, such as doing excavation or building.

If the landholder is conducting business or personal activities on the land, then the landholder owes a duty of reasonable care to prevent injuries or damages to persons outside the land.

Entry upon Land

Once a person has entered a landholder's property, the duties of care required of the landholder change, depending on the status of the person entering the property. The law has established three broad categories to identify the status of persons entering the property of another. These categories are trespasser, licensee, and invitee. All three categories will be addressed in greater detail later in this chapter.

A person who enters the property of the landholder is afforded more protection than those who are outside the boundaries of the land. Professor Keeton in *Prosser and Keeton on the Law of Torts,* section 58 at 393 (5th ed. 1984), defines the entry upon land as follows:

> *Those who enter upon land are divided unto three fixed categories: trespassers, licensees, and invitees, and there are subdivided duties as to each. They make out, as a general pattern, a rough sliding scale, by which, as the legal status of the visitor improves, the possessor of the land owes*

YOU BE THE JUDGE

As the result of snow and rain that had occurred earlier in the day, B&B Railroad had a platform that was covered with ice. B&B promptly posted a sign that stated "Watch your step—platform is icy." However, B&B did not remove the ice from the platform, which could have been done reasonably. Patrick, who was late, was running to catch his commuter train. As he ran up the platform, Patrick slipped on the ice and received a concussion in a fall. Patrick has sued B&B for damages. Can Patrick recover?

him more of an obligation of protection. This system has long made legal writers, and some of the courts, quite unhappy because of its arbitrary and sometimes unreasonable character, and there has been some recent movement toward abolishing the distinctions, at least between invitees and licensees. But the traditional entrant classification scheme is well entrenched in the great majority of jurisdictions, and so the categories must be carefully considered one by one.

TRESPASSERS

People who enter land without the permission of the landholder are called **trespassers**. They have neither consent nor privilege to be on the land. The general rule is that the landholder owes no duty of care to a trespasser to make the land safe, to warn of dangers that are on the land, to avoid carrying out dangerous activities on the land, or to protect the trespasser in any way.

trespassers
Uninvited guests on the property of the landowner.

The *Restatement (Second) of Torts,* section 333, speaks to the liability to a trespasser as follows:

> [A] possessor of land is not liable to trespassers for physical harm caused by his failure to exercise reasonable care
> a. to put the land in a condition reasonably safe for their reception, or
> b. to carry on his activities so as not to endanger them.

However, there are a number of exceptions to the general rule. If a trespasser falls into one of the exception categories, then he or she may be afforded more protection from the landholder.

Discovered Trespasser

A known trespasser is owed a duty of reasonable care by the landholder. Reasonable care does not mean that the landholder must make the land safe for the trespasser. It simply means that once the trespasser is discovered, the landholder must use reasonable care to avoid injuring the trespasser. A landholder cannot commit any intentional harm on a known trespasser except in self-defense, defense of another, or some other recognized privilege of using such force.

Constant Trespasser

An exception to the general rule occurs when a landholder has reason to know that trespassers enter his land frequently. The area that is trespassed must be limited, such as a path, and the trespassing must be constant. Under this circumstance, the landholder has a duty of reasonable care to discover and protect trespassers who frequently enter this limited area of his land. The landholder does not have a duty to inspect his land in order to make it injury proof.

If a landholder is carrying on an activity that may subject a person to death or serious bodily harm, the landholder has a greater duty to protect the constant trespasser from this activity. The *Restatement (Second) of Torts,* section 334, identifies the landholder's responsibility in this regard to frequent trespassers by stating:

> A possessor of land who knows, or from facts within his knowledge should know, that trespassers constantly intrude upon a limited area thereof, is subject to liability for bodily harm there caused to them by his failure to carry on an activity involving a risk of death or serious bodily harm with reasonable care for their safety.

 EYE ON ETHICS

There are many exceptions to the general rule of landholders and the extent of care that they owe a trespasser. Most of these exceptions are driven by state law. As always, it is very important for paralegals to know their state law as well as the law that governs their jurisdiction.

For example, suppose that there are railroad tracks between the parking lot for Soda Co. and its factory. Every day, the workers of Soda Co. cross over the tracks to get to and from the building. The railroad should be aware of this situation, and it is under the duty to prevent injury and damage to the workers that could result from a passing train. The railroad would therefore be held liable should one of the workers sustain an injury.

Child Trespassers

As might be expected, children are given special protection. A child is usually defined as someone too young to appreciate the dangers that could be involved in a given situation. There is no age limit that sets the boundary line for the level of immaturity that is required. The *Restatement (Second) of Torts,* section 339, talks about dealing with trespassing children in pure negligence terms:

> *A possessor of land is subject to liability for physical harm to children trespassing thereon caused by an artificial condition upon the land if*
> a. *the place where the condition exists is one upon which the possessor of land knows or has reason to know that children are likely to trespass, and*
> b. *the condition is one of which the possessor knows or has reason to know and which he realizes or should realize will involve an unreasonable risk of death or serious bodily harm to such children, and*
> c. *the children because of their youth do not discover the condition or realize the risk involved in intermeddling with it or in coming within the area made dangerous by it, and*
> d. *the utility to the possessor of maintaining the condition and the burden of eliminating the danger are slight as compared with the risk to children involved, and*
> e. *the possessor fails to exercise reasonable care to eliminate the danger or otherwise to protect the children.*

attractive nuisance doctrine
The doctrine that holds a landowner to a higher duty of care even when the children are trespassers, because the potentially harmful condition is so inviting to a child.

The special protection is embodied in the **attractive nuisance** doctrine, which says a duty of reasonable care is owed to prevent injury when:

- A trespassing child *unable to appreciate the danger* is on the land,
- Where an *artificial condition* or activity exists on the land,
- To which the child can be expected to be attracted.

The foreseeability of serious injury to the child is measured or weighed against what the landholder was trying to accomplish by having the artificial condition on the property. The burden or inconvenience on the landholder is weighed against the duty to protect the child against this condition. For example, Timmy is a six-year-old boy who frequently trespasses on George's land. If there is a dangerous dump site on George's land, George has a duty to make this site safe. The duty of reasonable care is usually not applied when the child is injured by natural conditions on the land unless the defendant has significantly altered these conditions through some means or process.

LICENSEES

licensee
One known to be on the premises but whose presence gives no benefit to the property owner.

A **licensee** is someone who is on the land with the express or implied permission of the landholder. A licensee is present for her own purposes and not for any business purpose or any other purpose except by permission of the landholder. People who can be considered licensees are the following:

- Persons entering the land for their own interests.
- Members of the family or household.
- Social guests.

Landholders owe licensees the same duty of care that they owe to trespassers. That is, a landholder has a duty to warn the licensee of dangerous natural or artificial conditions for which the landholder has actual knowledge. A possessor of land is subject to liability to his licensees from physical harm caused to them by his failure to carry on his activities with reasonable care for their safety if, but only if, he should expect that they will not discover or realize the danger, and they do not know or have reason to know of the possessor's activities and of the risk involved. For example, Mike has a license to enter onto Adrian's land to swim in his pond. Unknown to Mike, Adrian has been sinking rocks into his lake to dispose of them. Adrian must warn Mike of the presence of the rocks in the pond. Mike would not be expected to discover that Adrian has been sinking rocks into his pond, and he would have no reason to know of Adrian's activities. As such, Adrian would be considered to have a duty to Mike in such a circumstance, even though he is a licensee. If the condition is extremely dangerous, the landholder's duty may be to take active, reasonable precautions to protect the licensee. The landholder will also have liability toward a licensee for any intentional, willful, or wanton conduct on the property.

The landholder is not under any duty to inspect the premises to discover any hidden dangers that might injure the licensee. Individuals become licensees when they exceed the bounds of the relationship that would make them invitees.

INVITEES

Invitees are essentially visitors who enter the land for the economic purposes of the landholder. Landholders owe invitees the highest degree of care. There must be an element of invitation by the landholder. An invitation is much stronger than mere permission or consent. The invitation is an implied or direct statement of the landholder's desire that the person be present on the property. A greater standard of care is owed to the invitee because the invitation leads the invitee to believe that the premises are safe.

invitees
People wanted on the premises for a specific purpose known by the landowner."

A person is considered an invitee if:

- He enters the property by the express or implied invitation of the landholder.
- His entry is concerned with the nature of the landholder's business.
- There is a mutual benefit for both the person invited and the landholder.

The *Restatement (Second) of Torts,* section 332, defines an invitee as a business or public visitor:

> 1. An invitee is either a public invitee or a business visitor.
> 2. A public invitee is a person who is invited to enter or remain on land as a member of the public for a purpose for which the land is held open to the public.
> 3. A business visitor is a person who is invited to enter or remain on land for a purpose directly or indirectly connected with business dealings with the possessor of the land.

The duty of care owed by a landholder to an invitee is as follows:

- The occupier owes the invitee at least the same standard of care owed to a trespasser.
- The landholder owes the invitee at least the same standard as that of a licensee.
- The landholder owes the invitee a duty of reasonable care to inspect and discover dangerous artificial conditions on the land, dangerous natural conditions on the land, and dangerous activities on the land.
- Depending on the extent of the danger of the condition or activity, the landholder must either warn the invitee or make the condition or activity safe.

The landholder is under no obligation to protect the invitee against the invitee's own negligence; however, the landholder has a duty not to conduct herself negligently toward the invitee and to warn the invitee of any known dangers. For example, Kerry owns a retail store in Los Angeles, California. Kerry displays various items on shelves in the store. In one area of the store, the shelves are unstable and have the potential of collapsing. The danger posed by these unstable shelves is not noticeable. If Kerry does not fix the shelves, and Sharon, a customer, is injured when they collapse, Kerry will be liable to Sharon for her injuries. The *Restatement (Second) of Torts*, section 343, affirms this position:

> A possessor of land is subject to liability for the physical harm caused to his invitees by a condition on the land if, but only if, he
> a. knows or by the exercise of reasonable care would discover the condition, and should realize that it involves an unreasonable risk of harm to such invitees, and
> b. should expect that they will not discover or realize the danger, or will fail to protect themselves against it, and
> c. fails to exercise reasonable care to protect them against the danger.

RESEARCH THIS

Many states have elected to reject the categories of trespasser, licensee, and invitee. Instead, these states have elected to adopt the principle that a landholder owes a reasonable duty to anyone to protect him or her against the probability of injury or damage. California led the way with the case of *Rowland v. Christian*, 443 P.2d 561 (Cal. 1968). Research this case and find out what other states have adopted this broader standard of care to all persons who enter a landholder's property. Yours might be one of those states.

LESSORS AND LESSEES

lessor
One who grants a lease or rental of a property to another.

lessee
One who rents property from another.

The **lessor–lessee** relationship centers on a legal status that involves the premises. Normally, the lessor is not entitled to possession of the land, but has a reversionary (ability to take back) interest in the land that comes into effect after the tenancy has terminated. As a result, the general rule is that the lessee or tenant assumes all liability for injuries caused by conditions or activities on the land as he is the one who has current possession of the land. The lessor will be liable to the lessee and third parties for injuries caused by any latent dangerous conditions that existed on the land at the time of the lease, but only if the lessor had actual knowledge or has reason to believe a latent dangerous condition existed. A lessor will also be responsible for common areas such as the pool area in an apartment building.

As indicated, there are some circumstances in which the lessor has a special duty. Those circumstances involve the following:

- The lessor is under an obligation to disclose any concealed or latent dangerous conditions.

- The lessor has continuous liability to third persons for any dangerous conditions that are on the property.

- The lessor is responsible and under a duty of reasonable care with regard to any common areas.

- Most jurisdictions hold that a lessor is responsible for repairs that are not made in a timely manner.

VENDORS AND VENDEES

vendor
The person who transfers property or goods by sale.

vendee
A purchaser or buyer.

When land is sold, the general rule is that the seller, or **vendor**, has no tort liability for injuries that occur on the land either to the buyer, known as the **vendee**, or to a third person. As a general rule, the vendor transfers all responsibility for the property to the vendee at the time the property is sold. The buyer, under the theory of **caveat emptor**, takes the land as she finds it, or "as is." Buyers are expected to make an inspection of the premises before purchasing. A seller will not be liable if a buyer is injured by a condition on the land, even if the condition was present when the land was sold. Third parties injured by such conditions must look to the vendee for satisfaction.

The *Restatement (Second) of Torts*, section 353, places the responsibility for any defects on the vendor if the vendee had no reason to know of the defect and the vendor failed to disclose them:

1. *A vendor of land who conceals or fails to disclose to his vendee any condition, whether natural or artificial, which involves unreasonable risk to persons on the land, is subject to liability to the vendee and others upon the land with the consent of the vendee or his sub-vendee for physical harm caused by the condition after the vendee has taken possession, if*
   a. *the vendee does not know or have reason to know of the condition or the risk involved, and*
   b. *the vendor knows or has reason to know of the condition, and realizes or should realize the risk involved, and has reason to believe that the vendee will not discover the condition or realize the risk.*

2. *If the vendor actively conceals the condition, the liability stated in Subsection (1) continues until the vendee discovers it and has reasonable opportunity to take effective precautions against it. Otherwise the liability continues only until the vendee has had reasonable opportunity to discover the condition and to take such precautions.*

If there is a hidden or latent condition on the land that is dangerous and that is known to the vendor, the vendor has a duty to either warn the vendee of the condition or repair it before turning the land over to the vendee. The vendor is under no obligation to inspect the premises in order to discover such defects. The vendor is only obligated to correct them if she knows about the dangerous condition or has reason to believe that one is present.

LEGAL RESEARCH MAXIM

The law revolving around premises liability and nuisance is not negligence per se, but both classifications of law have many similarities to note. Varying duties owed to certain types/groups of people, the breach or breaking of the particular duty, and the entering/exiting of land/property are but a few to keep in mind when studying negligence, premises liability, and nuisances.

NUISANCE

A **nuisance** usually refers to any harm caused by the use of one's property that interferes with another person's interest. Conduct or activities that cause annoyance, discomfort, or inconvenience; that affect the use or enjoyment of property; or that can endanger the health life or decency of a person could be classified as nuisances. A nuisance can be determined by the following:

- Any activity that is harmful or annoying to others.
- Any harm that is caused by a condition or conduct.
- Any combination of harm or conduct that produces a liability.

The tort of nuisance has been divided into two categories: private and public.

Private Nuisance

A **private nuisance** is an unreasonable interference with the use and enjoyment of an individual's private land. The *Restatement (Second) of Torts*, section 821D, defines a private nuisance as ". . . a nontrespassory invasion of another's interest in the private use and enjoyment of land." An individual's use and enjoyment may include the following:

- Physical condition.
- Comfort and convenience.

nuisance
That activity that arises from unreasonable, unwarranted, or unlawful use by a person of his own property; working obstruction or injury to right of another, or to the public; and producing such material annoyance, inconvenience, and discomfort that the law will presume resulting damage.

private nuisance
A thing or activity that substantially and unreasonably interferes with a plaintiff's use and enjoyment of her land.

- Peace of mind.
- Tranquility.
- Freedom from threat of future injury.

A nuisance is different from trespass in that it protects the individual property owner's right to the use and enjoyment of her land, not the entry thereof. For example, because Amanda works the graveyard shift at her job, she sleeps from nine in the morning until six in the afternoon. Her neighbor Axel rehearses with his band from one in the afternoon until about ten in the evening. The band practices in the garage, with the door open. Amanda has repeatedly asked Axel to turn down the volume or practice elsewhere. Axel has refused. Amanda may have a claim of private nuisance against Axel. The *Restatement (Second) of Torts,* section 831F, speaks to this right:

> There is liability for a nuisance only to those to whom it causes significant harm, of a kind that would be suffered by a normal person in the community or by property in normal condition and use for a normal purpose.

In a tort brought in nuisance, the plaintiff must have suffered an actual harm. Trespass does not require a harm to have been committed. A plaintiff can only sue for the tort of private nuisance if he or she possesses an interest in land. An interest in land does not mean that the plaintiff has to own the property. A tenant or lessee can bring an action for nuisance. The requirements that must be present in order to recover under nuisance tort theory are:

- The defendant must have committed an intentional act.
- The amount and extent of the interference with the use and enjoyment did not have to be anticipated.
- There must have been a substantial harm.
- There must have been an unreasonable invasion.

Interferences can be created by some of the following:

- Negligence.
- Abnormally dangerous conditions or activities that impose strict liability.
- Intentional acts.
- Violation of a statute.

Factors that are considered when determining reasonableness of an invasion are:

- The gravity and character of the harm.
- The social value of the use that the plaintiff is making of his or her land.
- The character of the locality.
- The extent of the burden on the plaintiff of avoiding or minimizing the interference.
- The motive of the defendant.
- The social value of the defendant's conduct that led to the interference.
- The extent of the burden on the defendant of avoiding or minimizing the interference.

The interference must be substantial. An objective standard is used to determine if the interference is grave. The test is how substantial a normal person in that locality would view the interference as being.

The following uses of property are considered quite valuable: use as a residence, use for business purposes, and use for recreational purposes. If a plaintiff is using his property for one of those things, then the plaintiff's use will be considered to have social value.

The character and locality of a property is considered important in determining the reasonableness or unreasonableness of the interference. Zoning ordinances are one measure of suitability. The court will review whether or not the plaintiff's use of her land is suitable to the locality. For example, if a neighborhood is zoned as residential and a person opens a store that sells pornography, that use would not be considered suitable to the locality.

Courts are unwilling to find that the defendant's interference is unreasonable if the burden on the plaintiff of avoiding or minimizing the interference is not substantial. The plaintiff has an obligation to avoid the consequences of the defendant's interference when it is realistic.

If the motives of the defendant are born out of spite or a desire to harm the plaintiff, then the courts will probably find that the interference is unreasonable. However, if the interference is as a result of the defendant's pursuit of his own interest, it will be harder for the plaintiff to establish unreasonableness.

Conduct can have social utility even if the defendant is acting in her own best interest. Social value concerns the general good of the public. The test is whether the social value or utility of the defendant's conduct outweighs the hardship of the interference the plaintiff is suffering.

Damages can be awarded for the harm caused by the private nuisance. The measure of damages is usually the difference between the value of the land before the harm and its value after the harm. Additional compensatory damages can be awarded. The additional compensatory damages include the loss in the rental value of the land, the loss of personal use of the land, and an amount to compensate the injured party for any discomfort or annoyance that the person has endured. Sometimes a monetary award is not enough and an **injunction** is issued. The plaintiff can also seek the remedy of **abatement**.

Public Nuisance

A **public nuisance** is an unreasonable interference with a right common to the general public. In order to have a public nuisance, not every member of the public has to actually be affected by it. A public nuisance can encompass the following:

- An intentional act.
- Failure to perform a legal duty.
- Harm that endangers the public health, safety, and welfare.

A public nuisance affects the public at large and not just a private person. The *Restatement (Second) of Torts,* section 821B, defines a public nuisance as:

1. *A public nuisance is an unreasonable interference with a right common to the general public.*

2. *Circumstances that may sustain a holding that an interference with the public right is unreasonable include the following:*
   a. *whether the conduct involves a significant interference with the public health, the public safety, the public peace, the public comfort or the public convenience, or*
   b. *whether the conduct is proscribed by a statute, ordinance or administrative regulation, or*
   c. *whether the conduct is of a continuing nature or has produced a permanent or long-lasting effect, and, as the actor knows or has reason to know, has a significant effect upon the public right.*

The unreasonableness of the interference to the public is often determined by statute. However, a test of the extent of the effect of the interference on the public comfort and convenience can also be utilized. A public official can bring either a civil action against the defendant or prosecute the person in the criminal courts for interference with the public comfort and convenience.

injunction
A court order that requires a party to refrain from acting in a certain way to prevent harm to the requesting party.

abatement
The suspension or cessation, in whole or in part, of a continuing charge.

public nuisance
An unreasonable interference with a right common to the general public.

A private person can sue for nuisance only when he or she has suffered in a way that is different from every other member of the public affected by the public nuisance. The plaintiff must have suffered special or particular injury or damage. The harm must be different in kind than that sustained by the public.

When a public official brings the public nuisance action, the remedies often include a fine or imprisonment. The government may also be able to collect damages in the form of fines or penalties for nuisances that may have been committed to public property.

DEFENSES TO NUISANCE

Like other tort actions, nuisance offers a defendant various defenses. When a nuisance results from the defendant's negligent conduct, the contributory negligence of the plaintiff is a defense to the same extent as in other actions founded on negligence.

However, when the harm is intentional or the result of recklessness, contributory negligence is not a defense.

The defense of *coming to the nuisance* may also be available to the defendant in defending a nuisance claim. For example, if a landowner buys property located near a factory, and builds a home on that property, the landowner may be unsuccessful in a suit against the factory claiming that fumes from the factory are a nuisance. The fact that the landowner purchased the property after a nuisance will not by itself prevent his claim, but it is a factor to be considered in determining whether the nuisance is actionable.

Summary

The term *premise* refers to any real property and those things attached to or growing from it. Landholders face different types of exposure to liability that are derived from their ownership interest in property. Premises liability deals with these types of exposures.

Landholders are considered to be in the best position to know of or discover any condition that exists upon their land that could cause damage or injury to another. With regard to a natural condition that exists upon the land, the landholder owes no duty of care to prevent injury to persons outside the land who might be injured by natural conditions that exist on the landholder's property.

A trespasser is someone who enters the land without the landholder's permission. Trespassers have neither consent nor privilege to be on the land. The general rule is that the landholder owes no duty of care to a trespasser to make the land safe, to warn of dangers that are on the land, to avoid carrying out dangerous activities on the land, or to protect the trespasser in any way.

A known trespasser is owed a duty of reasonable care by the landholder. Reasonable care does not mean that the landholder must make the land safe for the trespasser. It simply means that once the trespasser is discovered, the landholder must use reasonable care to avoid injuring the trespasser. A landholder cannot commit any intentional harm on a known trespasser except in self-defense, defense of another, or some other recognized privilege of using such force.

An exception to the general rule occurs when a landholder has reason to know that trespassers enter his land frequently. The area that is trespassed must be limited, such as a path, and the trespassing must be constant. Under this circumstance, the landholder has a duty of reasonable care to discover and protect trespassers who frequently enter this limited area of his land. The landholder does not have a duty to inspect his land in order to make it injury proof.

The attractive nuisance doctrine says that a duty of reasonable care is owed to prevent injury when a trespassing child unable to appreciate the danger is on the land, there is an artificial condition or activity on the land, and the child can be expected to be attracted to the artificial condition or activity.

The foreseeability of serious injury to the child is measured or weighed against what the landholder was trying to accomplish by having the artificial condition on the property. The burden or inconvenience on the landholder is weighed against the duty to protect the child against this condition. The duty of reasonable care is usually not applied when the child is injured by natural conditions on the land unless the defendant has significantly altered these conditions through some means or process.

A licensee is someone who is on the land with the express or implied permission of the landholder. A licensee is present for her own purposes and not for any business purpose or any other purpose except by permission of the landholder. The landholder owes the licensee the same duty of care that she owes to a trespasser. The landholder has a duty to warn the licensee of dangerous natural or artificial conditions for which the landholder has actual knowledge. If the condition is extremely dangerous, the landholder's duty may be to take active, reasonable precautions to protect the licensee. Landholders will also have liability toward licensees for any intentional, willful, or wanton conduct on the property.

An invitee is essentially a visitor who enters the land for the economic purposes of the landholder. Invitees are owed the highest degree of care by a landholder. There must be an element of invitation by the landholder. An invitation is much stronger than mere permission or consent. The invitation is an implied or direct statement of a desire by the landholder that the person be present on the property. A greater standard of care is owed to the invitee because the invitation leads the invitee to believe that the premises are safe.

The lessor–lessee relationship centers on a legal status that involves the premises. Normally, a lessor is not entitled to possession of the land but has a reversionary (ability to take back) interest in the land that comes into effect after the tenancy has terminated. As a result, the general rule is that lessees, or tenants, assume all liability for injuries caused by conditions or activities on the land as they are the ones who have current possession of the land. The lessor will be liable to the lessee and third parties for injuries caused by any latent dangerous conditions that existed on the land at the time of the lease, but only if the lessor had actual knowledge or has reason to believe a latent dangerous condition existed. A lessor is also responsible for common areas such as the pool area in an apartment building.

When land is sold, the general rule is that the seller, or vendor, has no tort liability for injuries that occur on the land either to the buyer, known as the vendee, or to a third person. As a general rule, the vendor transfers all responsibility for the property to the vendee at the time the property is sold. The buyer, under the theory of caveat emptor, takes the land as he finds it, or "as is." The buyer is expected to make an inspection of the premises before purchasing. The seller will not be liable if the buyer is injured by a condition on the land even if the condition was present when the land was sold. Third parties injured by such conditions must look to the vendee for satisfaction.

A nuisance usually refers to any harm caused by the use of one's property that interferes with the interest of another person. Conduct or activities that cause annoyance, discomfort, or inconvenience; that affect the use or enjoyment of property; or that can endanger the health, life, or decency of a person could be classified as nuisances.

A private nuisance is an unreasonable interference with the use and enjoyment of an individual's private land.

A public nuisance is an unreasonable interference with a right common to the general public. In order to have a public nuisance, not every member of the public has to actually be affected by it.

Key Terms

Abatement
Artificial condition
Attractive nuisance doctrine
Caveat emptor
Injunction
Invitees
Landholder
Lessee
Lessor
Licensee

Natural condition
Nuisance
Premises
Premises liability
Private nuisance
Public nuisance
Trespassers
Vendee
Vendor

Review Questions

1. Define premises liability.
2. What is the general duty of a landholder?
3. What duty of care does a landholder have regarding a natural condition?
4. What is an attractive nuisance?
5. What duty of care does a landholder have to persons outside the property?
6. What is a trespasser?
7. What is a licensee?
8. What is an invitee?
9. Describe the similarities and differences among a trespasser, a licensee, and an invitee.
10. What duty does a vendor owe a vendee?
11. Define a private nuisance.
12. What is a public nuisance?
13. When can an individual sue for a public nuisance?
14. What is an injunction?
15. What is abatement?

Exercises

1. The Pestco insecticide factory is located on the edge of Anytown, USA. When the wind blows from the west, a foul-smelling gas comes from Pestco's chimneys and blows over Anytown. The gas causes most residents of Anytown to experience burning in the eyes and throat. Dick is a resident of Anytown. If Dick seeks an injunction against Pestco by asserting a claim on the theory of public nuisance, which of the following would be Pestco's most effective argument as a defense?
   a. Dick has not sustained a harm different from that of the general public.
   b. A private citizen may not seek an injunction against environmental polluters.
   c. A private citizen may not sue on a theory of public nuisance.
2. Marty was driving her car down Calle Street in the rain. She rounded the bend just as a deer ran out in front of her vehicle. Marty jammed on her brakes, which caused her vehicle to skid off the road and onto Paxel's property. Paxel had been in the process of installing a drainage system and had dug a trench across his yard for the pipes. Marty's car hit the trench and stopped abruptly, and Marty was thrown through the windshield of the vehicle. Marty sustained severe injuries. In an action by Marty against Paxel for negligence, will a court decide that Paxel owed Marty a duty of reasonable care?
   a. Yes, if it was foreseeable that persons driving on Calle Street might lose control of their vehicles and skid into Paxel's yard.

    b. Yes, if, but only if, the deer was in the road because of some conduct by Paxel.

    c. No, because it was not unreasonable for Paxel to dig a trench on his own land.

    d. No, because Marty was a trespasser.

3. Patricia runs a facility for people who need peace and quiet. She does her best to create a peaceful environment for her clients. Andy, her next-door neighbor, has five younger children who run around in the front yard and make a lot of noise. If Patricia sues Andy for a private nuisance, will she succeed? Why or why not?

4. John owns Tavern Hill, a large property. He uses the land to hike, to picnic, and to watch the sunset over the city at nights. John knows that Fred likes to hike up Tavern Hill to admire the view. Although John knows of Fred's activities, he has never given him permission to do so. John keeps as an animal on the property, a raging bull. John knows that the bull has a tendency to attack people. Does John owe a duty to Fred to warn him about the presence of the bull? Why or why not? Does John have a duty to fence the bull to keep it from coming in contact with Fred or other trespassers?

5. Moe owns a six-acre property in a small town in Nebraska. Moe is aware that children often trespass onto his property to play in his large backyard. Moe is an avid collector of old cars. He often keeps these old, rusted-out cars in his backyard. Susie was injured after she slipped on the roof of one of the rusted vehicles and broke her arm. Will Moe be held to be liable to Susie for her injuries? Why?

6. Thomas has recently decided to sell his house. In preparation for the sale, he renovates his kitchen. The contractor, in the course of renovating the property, discovers that the wires in the kitchen are faulty and may cause a fire to break out in the home. The only way that the defect was noticed was that the contractor removed a piece of the kitchen wall when performing the renovations. The contractor tells Thomas about the faulty wiring and that it would cost $5,000 to rewire the kitchen. Thomas refuses to change the wiring. The contractor repatches the wall in the kitchen and finishes the renovation. Would Thomas be liable to a purchaser of the home if the home caught fire? What duties does Thomas have to potential purchasers of his home?

 PORTFOLIO ASSIGNMENT

Make a list of possible attractive nuisances that may be found on someone's property. Then, observe your own property, home, or apartment complex and list any possible attractive nuisances that you think are present on the property. If none, ask your neighbor if you could walk the area of his or her property to see if you think any attractive nuisances are present there. Compare your first possible list of attractive nuisances with the list for your property or your neighbor's property.

Vocabulary Builders

Instructions

Use the key terms from this chapter to fill in the answers to the crossword puzzle.

NOTE: When the answer is more than one word, leave a blank space between words.

ACROSS

1. The liability that landholders may be exposed to in connection with their use and enjoyment of real property.
5. Any real property, buildings that are attached to the property, grounds, facilities, structures, and other things that are attached to the land or growing from it.
6. One who rents property from another.
7. That activity that arises from unreasonable, unwarranted, or unlawful use by a person of his own property; working obstruction or injury to right of another; or to the public; and producing such material annoyance, inconvenience, and discomfort that the law will presume resulting damage.
10. People wanted on the premises for a specific purpose known by the landowner.
11. One who grants a lease or rental of a property to another.
13. The suspension or cessation, in whole or in part, of a continuing charge.
14. Someone who is in rightful possession of the land.

15. A man-made condition that exists on the land.
16. A condition upon the land that has been untouched or influenced by humans.
17. A purchaser or buyer.

DOWN

2. A court order that requires a party to refrain from acting in a certain way to prevent harm to the requesting party.
3. One known to be on the premises but whose presence gives no benefit to the property owner.
4. The doctrine that holds a landowner to a higher duty of care even when the children are trespassers, because the potentially harmful condition is so inviting to a child.
8. The person who transfers property or goods by sale.
9. Let the buyer beware.
12. Uninvited guests on the property of the landowner.

James M. BIGLANE and Nancy K. Biglane v. UNDER THE HILL CORPORATION
949 So.2d 9
Supreme Court of Mississippi
Feb. 8, 2007

Background: Neighbors brought action against a saloon, claiming the saloon was a private nuisance. Saloon counterclaimed, alleging that neighbors had tortiously interfered with its business by blocking nearby parking lots. After bench trial, the Chancery Court, Adams County, George Ward, Chancellor, found that saloon was a private nuisance, imposed equitable conditions upon the saloon's continued operation, and awarded saloon $500 in nominal damages for neighbors' tortious interference. Neighbors appealed, and saloon cross-appealed.

Holdings: The Supreme Court, Diaz, J., held that:

1. saloon was a private nuisance to the neighbors;
2. chancery court's placement of conditions on the saloon's continued operation was a proper equitable response to the private nuisance;
3. neighbor's action in blocking off parking lot that he owned in whole could not constitute tortious interference; and
4. neighbor's action in blocking off parking area that he partially owned was not tortious interference with saloon's business, in absence of showing that saloon suffered actual damages as a result.

Affirmed in part; reversed in part; rendered in part.
DIAZ, Justice, for the Court.

In this case we are asked two questions. First, was the noise coming from a local saloon such that it constituted a private nuisance to the residents of an apartment next door? Second, were the actions of the neighbor of the saloon a tortious interference with business relations? After a review of the case, we conclude there was a nuisance, but no tortious interference with business relations.

FACTS

[Text omitted]

In 1967 Nancy and James Biglane purchased a dilapidated building at 27 Silver Street that had been built in the 1840s, and opened the lower portion of the building as a gift shop in 1978. In 1973, Andre Farish, Sr., and Paul O'Malley purchased the building directly next door, at 25 Silver Street, which had been built in the 1830s; in 1975 they opened the Natchez Under the Hill Saloon. Eventually the Saloon would come to be run by the children of Mr. Farish, Melissa and Andre, Jr.

The Biglanes began converting the upper floors of 27 Silver Street into a large apartment, which they moved into in 2002.

Despite installing insulated walls and windows, locating their bedroom on the side of the building away from the Saloon, and placing their air conditioner unit on the side nearest the Saloon, the Biglanes quickly realized they had a problem: the raucous nature of the Saloon kept them wide awake at night.

Specifically, it was live music, a hallmark of the Saloon. During the summertime the un-air conditioned Under the Hill opened its windows and doors to lessen the heat inside, and music echoed up and down Silver Street. While the music was easier on Mr. Biglane, who had lost his hearing over the years, it was particularly difficult on Mrs. Biglane, who was frustrated by the constant rock and roll, conversation, and the clack of pool balls.

The Biglanes contacted the Saloon and asked that the music be turned down, and it was: Mr. Farish got rid of Groove Line, the band that seemed to trouble the Biglanes the most, and installed thick windows to block noise. He also purchased a sound meter by which bands could measure their output in decibels, and forbade them from going over a certain point.

Still dissatisfied, the Biglanes blocked off two nearby parking lots that served the Saloon, using a cable over the entrance of one and crafting a metal gate over another. Ultimately this classic neighborly dispute spilled into the Chancery Court of Adams County, prompted by a complaint from the Biglanes.

The couple alleged private nuisance, among other causes of action, and Under the Hill counterclaimed, alleging that the Biglanes had tortiously interfered in its business (by blocking the nearby parking lots) and defamed them (by sending a letter of complaint to the City Attorney)....

The chancellor determined that Under the Hill was a private nuisance to the Biglanes, and enjoined the Saloon from leaving open any doors or windows when music was playing, and ordered it to prevent patrons from loitering in the streets. The trial court also found that the Biglanes had tortiously interfered with the business relations of Under the Hill. Although no damages were actually shown, the trial court assessed nominal and punitive damages because of the intentional character of the conduct. . . .

Aggrieved, the Biglanes appealed, arguing that damages were improperly awarded, and Under the Hill cross-appealed, arguing that its business was not a private nuisance. . . .

DISCUSSION

I. Is the Under the Hill Saloon a Private Nuisance to the Biglanes?

"A private nuisance is a nontrespassory invasion of another's interest in the use and enjoyment of his property." *Leaf River Forest Prods., Inc. v. Ferguson*, 662 So.2d 648, 662 (Miss. 1995). "One landowner may not use his land so as to unreasonably annoy, inconvenience, or harm others."

An entity is subject to liability for a private nuisance only when its conduct is a legal cause of an invasion of another's interest in the private use and enjoyment of land and that invasion is either (a) intentional and unreasonable, or (b) unintentional but otherwise provides the basis for a cause of action for negligent or reckless conduct or for abnormally dangerous conditions or activities.

The trial court proceeded under the first path of liability—whether the conduct complained of was intentional and unreasonable. . . .

Ultimately the trial court weighed the fact that the Biglanes knew or should have known that there was going to be some sort of noise associated with living "within five feet of a well established saloon which provides live music on the weekends."

We have examined similar issues before. An important Mississippi case regarding private nuisance based on the actions of a neighbor is *Alfred Jacobshagen Co. v. Dockery*, 243 Miss. 511, 139 So.2d 632 (1962). . . .

The general rule is that "[a] business, although in itself lawful, which impregnates the atmosphere with disagreeable and offensive odors and stenches, may become a nuisance to those occupying property in the vicinity, where such obnoxious smells result in a material injury to such owners." This same rule extends to a situation where a lawful business injects loud music into the surrounding neighborhoods. For "[a] reasonable use of one's property cannot be construed to include those uses which produce obnoxious [noises], which in turn result in a material injury to owners of property in the vicinity, causing them to suffer substantial annoyance, inconvenience, and discomfort."

Accordingly, even a lawful business—which the Under the Hill Saloon certainly is—"may become . . . a nuisance" by interfering with its neighbors' enjoyment of their property." We recognize that "[e]ach [private nuisance] case must be decided upon its own peculiar facts, taking into consideration the location and the surrounding circumstances." Ultimately, "[i]t is not necessary that other property owners should be driven from their dwellings," because "[i]t is enough that the enjoyment of life and property is rendered materially uncomfortable and annoying."

In *Dockery* we deferred greatly to the chancery court and determined that it "had the power to enjoin such future operations of the rendering plant as constituted in fact a nuisance," and that it also "had the lesser power to permit continued operation of the plant, subject to certain stated conditions and requirements." 243 Miss. at 517, 139 So.2d at 634.

In the case at hand, the trial court exercised its power to permit continued operation of the Saloon while setting conditions to its future operation. Namely, it found that the Saloon could not "operat[e] its business with its doors and windows opened during any time that amplified music is being played inside the saloon." The chancery court found "that such a limitation is reasonable in that it should help contain the noise within the saloon, and should discourage the bar patrons from congregating or loitering in the streets outside of the saloon." . . .

Accordingly, we agree that the Saloon was a private nuisance to the Biglanes and affirm the trial court's equitable conditions placed upon its continued operation.

II. Was There a Tortious Interference with Business Relations?

In response to the Biglanes' assertion that the Saloon was a private nuisance, the bar counterclaimed, arguing that its neighbors had interfered with the operation of their business. "There are four elements necessary to prove a claim of tortious interference with a business relationship: (1) The acts were intentional and willful; (2) The acts were calculated to cause damage to the plaintiffs in their lawful business; (3) The acts were done with the unlawful purpose of causing damage and loss, without right or justifiable cause on the part of the defendant (which constitutes malice); (4) Actual damage and loss resulted." *MBF Corp. v. Century Business Comms., Inc.*, 663 So.2d 595, 598 (Miss. 1995). In this case the Biglanes essentially concede the presence of the first two prongs, but urge that neither the third nor the fourth factors were satisfied. If any of the factors are not met, there cannot be a finding of tortious interference with business.

A. "Without Right or Justifiable Cause."

Mr. Biglane, or corporations of which he has substantial control, owns much of the property surrounding the Under the Hill Saloon, including multiple parking areas around the Saloon. After the tensions escalated between the Biglanes and the Saloon, Mr. Biglane caused the two parking areas in his control to be blocked, one with a cable gate after 6:00 p.m. and the other by an iron gate. It is undisputed that Mr. Biglane controls the former lot outright, but the ownership of the second lot—the so-called Water Street area—is more complicated.

Ownership of the property is important because it speaks to the third factor of the tort—that the allegedly tortious acts must be performed without right or justifiable cause. It is a basic tenet of property law that a landowner or tenant may use the premises they control in whatever fashion they desire, so long as the law is obeyed. *See generally Ewing v. Adams*, 573 So.2d 1364, 1367–68 (Miss. 1990). This leads to the logical conclusion that a landowner or valid tenant may forbid any other persons from using their property. This ideal is protected in our law to the point that there are both civil and criminal prohibitions against trespassing. *See Alexander v. Brown*, 793 So.2d 601, 605 (Miss. 2001) .

Generally speaking, it cannot be malicious for a person to refuse access to others to their private property. Accordingly, blocking off the parking lot he owned in whole was not tortious conduct by Mr. Biglane.

The property comprising the area called Water Street is a different matter. . . .

Part of Water Street is a parking lot, and the city engineer testified that roughly two parking spaces, or portions of the spaces, were owned by the city. Another portion of Water Street is a boat ramp owned by Mr. Biglane. The city has a permanent easement to use the ramp, but of late it is basically only used by riverboat traffic. Previously the only access to the city's portions of Water Street were through Mr. Biglane's parcel, and the city engineer testified that blocking the city's right of way was impermissible, as the city no longer had use and access to the property they owned or had access to its easement because of the gate. There was also testimony that there had been a city-owned sign advertising the area as parking for the public that was later taken down. The city ultimately acquiesced to the placement of the gate and the blocking of its own property.

It is undisputed that Mr. Biglane erected an iron gate blocking Water Street. The chancellor found that part of the property blocked by the iron gate was owned by the city;

that the gate itself partially rested upon city property; and that two of the parking spaces blocked by Mr. Biglane were city property. In light of this evidence, the trial court found that the third factor required for tortious interference with business was present—that Mr. Biglane did not have the right to block property which he did not own from public access.

Substantial evidence provided at trial and in the record supported the detailed and extensive findings of fact provided by the trial court. Accordingly, we defer to the chancellor's findings and conclude that the Biglanes acted without right in blocking the Water Street property. Yet our inquiry does not end there.

B. "Actual Damage and Loss Resulted."

Next we must consider whether the Under the Hill Saloon was damaged by the actions of the Biglanes. To satisfy this tort, we require "actual" damages, which are synonymous with "compensatory" damages; they are substantial, rather than nominal. *ACI Chems., Inc. v. Metaplex, Inc.,* 615 So.2d 1192, 1202 (Miss. 1993).

This does not mean that an exact dollar value must be set before we can find actual damages....

In the case at hand, Under the Hill conceded that it could not demonstrate a loss of income from the lack of parking. In fact, business had slightly increased after the parking lots were blocked by Mr. Biglane, which was attributed by Mr. Farish to more riverboats docking in Natchez. There was evidence that one server at the Saloon had worked less than she had in years, but no receipts or other evidence was presented by the Saloon to demonstrate any sort of a loss. In its amended order the trial court found that punitive damages were not warranted under these facts, and accordingly declined to assess attorney's fees against the Biglanes. . . .

The trial court assessed a damages award of $500 for "nominal damages" because it determined the Biglanes' conduct was intentional. The trial court based this finding upon the basic legal concept that nominal damages can be awarded for intentional torts. *See Williams v. Wiggins,* 285 So.2d 163, 164–65 (Miss. 1973) ("nominal damages . . . can only be granted in the absence of actual injury in cases of intentional tort," and not in cases involving negligence). The situation at hand is different. Unlike intentional torts such as trespass or battery, "actual damage and loss" is a required component of the tort of interference with business relations. As noted *supra,* this factor can be met in differing ways, but it must be met. The Under the Hill Saloon admitted it had suffered no actual damage or loss. Nominal damages do not satisfy a finding of the tort of intentional interference with business relations. In this type of case, there must be actual damages. Because the fourth factor was not met, there cannot be a tortious interference with business and the award of nominal damages must be reversed.

CONCLUSION

This is a classic case of a dispute between two neighbors. We reaffirm our position that a finding of tortious interference with business relations must be based upon a finding of actual damages, and also that a landowner may not use its property in such a fashion as to unreasonably deprive another of the use or enjoyment of their property. We therefore affirm the chancery court's judgment finding a private nuisance but reverse the award of $500 in damages against the Biglanes for tortious interference with business relations.

[Footnotes omitted]

Source: Reprinted with permission from Westlaw. *James M. BIGLANE and Nancy K. Biglane v. UNDER THE HILL CORPORATION,* 949 So.2d9.

Chapter 11

Strict Liability

CHAPTER OBJECTIVES

Upon completion of this chapter, you will be able to:

- Understand the concept of strict liability.
- Discuss strict liability with respect to wild animals.
- Identify when strict liability is asserted with respect to domesticated animals.
- Explain how strict liability is applied to abnormally dangerous conditions.

In discussing the three types of torts—intentional torts, strict liability, and negligence—one should keep in mind that there is often overlap among the three, and it is not always black and white into which specific category a tort should fall. That is why tort litigation exists. However, dividing the types of torts into three general categories provides a guide or a place to begin when a tortious situation arises.

This chapter is concerned with the second of the three types of torts; the tort of strict liability or liability without fault. Product liability is often categorized under strict liability; however, product liability will be discussed in a later chapter in more detail. This chapter focuses on other strict liability torts.

STRICT LIABILITY

The general meaning of **strict liability** is liability without fault, also called *absolute liability*. What that means is that laws exist that determine the defendant to be liable for injuries or damages sustained by the plaintiff even if the defendant was neither at fault nor negligent. Liability is not based on the relationship between the plaintiff and the defendant, but rather on the defendant's act itself.

The source for strict liability is that defendants who engage in certain types of activity must do so at their own peril and must be responsible for all damages that stem from that activity. Strict liability is based on the premise that if the defendant engages in a certain kind of conduct that causes harm to the plaintiff, then liability will result, irrespective of intent, negligence, or innocence. Certain types of conduct are thought to be inherently dangerous and, therefore, any harm that results from these types of activities will result in liability being assessed to the defendant.

The strict liability torts are considered of such a nature that social policy dictates that defendants engaged in certain designated dangerous activities will be liable for damages ensuing from those activities. The public policy concerns can also be seen as compelling strict liability. Often the defendants involved in strict liability actions are large corporations. Due to the large size of many of these businesses, the potential

strict liability
The defendant is liable without the plaintiff having to prove fault.

A DAY IN THE LIFE OF A REAL PARALEGAL

Brenda was excited about her new position with the strict liability department of her firm. For the past two years, she had been working in the personal injury department and had requested a change. She was settling in well with her new department and was just given a big assignment. It seems as though the firm had taken on "ABC TNT CO." as a client. ABC had won the contract to help build a new dam in the state, blasting mountain areas so that water from the "Last Chance" river would be diverted to the state's 13 million inhabitants. The dam was necessary, as state reservoirs had dried up due to the last six years of drought. When the project first got started, ABC blew out part of the mountain *so much so* that 230 homes were destroyed in the process. Thankfully, no one died but many were injured. Brenda was given the assignment of contacting all claimants whose property or person was damaged and/or injured. She also had the task of preparing deposition questions. This task was seemingly not too difficult, until Brenda found out that 412 claims were levied for approximately 240 people.

to cause harm to a large number of people is increased. Strict liability seeks to ensure that these corporations will adhere to the highest level of care to avoid injury to potential plaintiffs.

Some examples of these activities include owning a wild animal, storing hazardous chemicals, or possessing explosives.

ANIMALS

Wild Animals

wild animal
An animal of an untamable disposition or that is in a state of nature.

inherent
Part of the essential character of something; by nature.

A **wild animal** is an animal that has not been domesticated. Wild animals may include lions, tigers, monkeys, boa constrictors, and a host of other animals that are usually found in zoos. Most states recognize that such animals need particular care and that care should be taken so the public is not exposed to the danger that exists from such animals. Anyone who owns a wild animal will be held strictly liable for any damages that animal caused. It does not matter whether the owner knew the animal was dangerous or not. Nor does it matter how much care was taken to protect people from the animal or how much training the wild animal received. Keeping wild animals is considered to be an **inherently** dangerous activity. Therefore, it doesn't matter how careful the owner of the animal is; if the animal causes damages or injury, the owner will be found liable.

Strict liability does not attach to all injuries caused by a wild animal. Strict liability is limited to harm that results from a dangerous propensity that is a characteristic of the wild animal. If the injury sustained by the wild animal is not typical or attributable to the kind of injury that usually is associated with the animal, then strict liability will not apply. Keep in mind, however, that that injured party may likely sue under other tort theories. See Figure 11.1 for strict liability regarding wild animals.

For example, Steve owns an 18-foot-long boa constrictor named Lucy. Steve loves Lucy and allows her to have free rein in his apartment. One day, Steve forgets to close

FIGURE 11.1
Strict Liability for Wild Animals

the screen door to the apartment's patio. He goes out to the store, and while he is gone, Lucy escapes. Lucy finds her way to the apartment across the lawn where a small dog lives. Being hungry, Lucy squeezes the small dog to death and proceeds to eat it. When the dog's owner comes home, he finds Lucy on his patio with a big bulge in her body where the dog is being digested. Steve will be liable for the damages caused by Lucy eating the dog because boa constrictors are considered wild animals.

Domesticated Animals

A **domesticated animal** is an animal that is accustomed to living with humans. Such animals include dogs, cats, and horses, to name a few. Typically, owners of domesticated animals are not necessarily strictly liable for injury and damages caused by their animals unless two elements exist. Those two elements are:

domesticated animal
An animal accustomed to living with humans.

- The owner knows that the animal has a specific propensity to cause injury or damage.
- The harm caused to the plaintiff was due to the specific propensity of the animal.

Normally, an owner of a domesticated animal needs to know or should have known that the animal possessed dangerous propensities. If the owner is unaware of the animal's dangerous propensities, she may not necessarily be held strictly liable. Sometimes an owner is unaware of the dangerous propensities of her animal until it attacks someone. At that time, then the owner will be held strictly liable for any further injuries or damages that animal causes. See Figure 11.2 regarding strict liability for domestic animals.

As mentioned above, an owner of a domestic animal would not be held strictly liable if the owner was unaware of the animal's dangerous propensity. A dog owner, for example, would not be liable for strict liability if her dog bit another person, if it was the dog's first bite.

Strict Liability Is Proper

| Domestic Animal | • Owner knows that the animal has a specific propensity to cause damage or injury.
 • Harm caused to the plaintiff due to the specific propensity of the animal. |

FIGURE 11.2
Strict Liability for Domestic Animals

| Domestic Animal | • Owner is unaware and has no reason to know that animal has a specific propensity to cause damage or injury.
 * Unless state has abolished "one free bite" rule. |

Strict Liability Is Not Proper

For example, Dawn owned a pit bull named Daisy. Dawn believed Daisy to be very sweet and often said Daisy "would never hurt anyone." However, one day while Dawn was at work, Daisy got out. She roamed the neighborhood until she came upon a little boy. The little boy began to throw rocks at Daisy. Daisy attacked the little boy, causing him to be severely injured, requiring over 100 stitches to his body. Dawn now knows that Daisy has dangerous propensities. Once she knows that the animal is dangerous, she will be held strictly liable for any further attacks. However, Dawn would not be held liable to the boy in the example because she did not know of any dangerous propensity of Daisy at the time the attack occurred. If a subsequent attack occurs, however, Dawn would be held liable because she now has knowledge of Daisy's dangerous tendency.

Many states, however, have abolished the so-called "one free bite" rule. The states that have abolished this exception to strict liability typically hold owners strictly liable for all injuries caused by their animals. In these jurisdictions, it is irrelevant whether the owner knew, or had reason to know, that the animal was dangerous.

Liability to Third Parties

A possessor of a wild animal or a domestic animal with known dangerous propensities will be liable in strict liability for injuries that animal caused to a *licensee* or an *invitee*. As mentioned before, a **licensee** is someone who comes onto the defendant's property for the person's own benefit. The most common example of a licensee is a social guest. **Invitees** are those persons who enter the defendant's land for the defendant's benefit. This may be a customer or business partner of the defendant. In terms of strict liability for animals, whether wild or dangerous domestic, the distinction between licensee and invitee is irrelevant. The owner of the animal is held strictly liable for injuries caused by the animal.

Strict liability for animals holds that a trespasser may not recover in strict liability for such animal-inflicted injuries. A possessor of land does not owe a duty to trespassers to protect them from harm from either a wild animal or a dangerous domestic animal. For example, Lisa owns a salvage car lot where customers can pick out used parts for their vehicles. Lisa closes the lot at 6 p.m. and locks all the gates. Lisa keeps two pit bull guard dogs on the property for security. Although no one has ever burglarized Lisa's lot, she feels better with the dogs present. If a burglar is attacked by the dogs after the person has attempted to gain access to the lot, Lisa would not be held strictly liable for the burglar's injuries.

However, keep in mind that a trespasser may recover in negligence where the landowner knows of the trespasser's presence and fails to post warning signs. Although a trespasser would be able to recover in negligence, the strict liability rules do not apply to a trespasser injured by an animal. In the preceding example, Lisa could reduce her liability to the burglar by posting signs warning of the guard dogs' presence.

licensee
One known to be on the premises but whose presence gives no benefit to the property owner.

invitees
People wanted on the premises for a specific purpose known by the landowner.

LEGAL RESEARCH MAXIM

In common law, domesticated dogs were *allowed* one bite before the owner would be fined and/or the animal put down. It was referred to as the "one bite rule." Domesticated animals generally include cats, dogs, sheep, cows, horses, and goats.

SURF'S UP

Some cities in the United States have declared pit bulls to be inherently dangerous. Using the Internet, see if you can research some cities in the United States that deem pit bulls to be dangerous animals.

SPOT THE ISSUE

Mike owns a small toy poodle. The poodle is six years old. Two years ago, the dog attacked a neighbor. Mike contends that his dog is the sweetest, gentlest animal, and that the only reason the poodle attacked the neighbor was because the neighbor was hostile to Mike. If the dog attacks another person, what will happen?

Livestock

Most jurisdictions have provisions that hold the owner of livestock liable for damages and injuries caused by that animal if it is trespassing on another's property. The *Restatement (Second) of Torts*, section 504, states the following about trespassing livestock:

1. *Except as stated in Subsections (3) and (4) a possessor of livestock intruding upon the land of another is subject to liability for the intrusion although he has exercised the utmost care to prevent them from intruding.*

2. *The liability stated in Subsection (1) extends to any harm to the land or to its possessor or a member of his household, or their chattels, which might reasonably be expected to result from the intrusion of the livestock.*

3. *The liability stated in Subsection (1) does not extend to harm*
   a. *not reasonably to expected from the intrusion;*
   b. *done by animals straying onto abutting land while driven on the highway; or*
   c. *brought about by the unexpected operation of a force of nature, action or another animal or intentional, reckless or negligent conduct of a third person.*

4. *A possessor of land who fails to erect and maintain a fence required by the applicable common law or by statute to prevent the intrusion of livestock, can not recover under the rule stated in Subsection (1).*

The theory behind strict liability for livestock comes from the position that the keeper of the livestock is in the best position to adequately contain them. However, in the western United States, where roaming livestock is more common, strict liability in not applied. As civilization slowly encroaches on grazing lands, each jurisdiction has had to deal with the issue of roaming livestock statutorily.

Strict liability for damage done by livestock is not all encompassing. Liability is limited to recovery for the kind of harm expected from intrusion by livestock. If the damage caused to the plaintiff or his property is uncommon or unusual, strict liability will not apply. Additionally, strict liability will not apply to damage caused by livestock if the damage was caused by a natural force, another animal, or conduct of a third person. See Figure 11.3 for exceptions to strict liability for livestock.

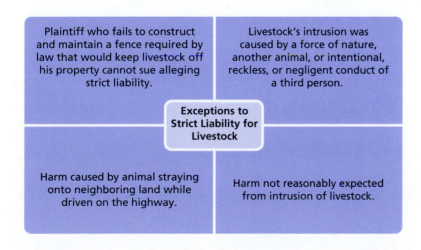

FIGURE 11.3
Exceptions to Strict Liability for Livestock

Exceptions to Strict Liability for Livestock

Plaintiff who fails to construct and maintain a fence required by law that would keep livestock off his property cannot sue alleging strict liability.

Livestock's intrusion was caused by a force of nature, another animal, or intentional, reckless, or negligent conduct of a third person.

Harm caused by animal straying onto neighboring land while driven on the highway.

Harm not reasonably expected from intrusion of livestock.

ABNORMALLY DANGEROUS ACTIVITIES

abnormally dangerous activity
A non-natural or unusual activity that creates a substantial likelihood of great harm to persons or property that cannot be eliminated by reasonable care by the defendant.

Defendants who engage in **abnormally dangerous activities** are held strictly liable for injuries and damages resulting from those activities. This tort was established to protect a person's right to be free from harm caused by abnormally dangerous conditions or activities. The elements for this tort are:

- The *existence of an abnormally dangerous condition or activity.*
- *Knowledge* by the defendant of the condition or activity.
- *Damages.*
- *Causation.*

See Figure 11.4 for factors for abnormally dangerous activities.

The *Restatement (Second) of Torts* codifies the rule of strict liability for abnormally dangerous activities. The *Restatement* at section 520 provides for the following factors to exist in order to establish strict liability for an abnormally dangerous condition:

- The "existence of a high degree of risk of some harm to the person, land or chattel of others";
- The "likelihood that the harm that results from it will be great";
- The "inability to eliminate the risk by the exercise of reasonable care";
- The "extent to which the activity is not a matter of common usage";

FIGURE 11.4
Abnormally Dangerous Activities

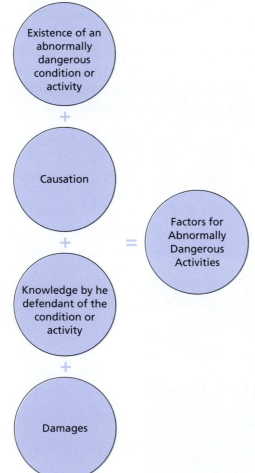

FIGURE 11.5
Factors Used
to Establish Strict
Liability for
an Abnormally
Dangerous Condition

Likelihood that the harm that results from it will be great

A high degree of risk of some harm

Extent to which the activity is not a matter of common usage

Inappropriateness of the activity to the place where it is carried on

Inability to eliminate the risk by the exercise of reasonable care

Extent to which its value to the community is outweighed by its dangerous attributes

- The "inappropriateness of the activity to the place where it is carried on"; and
- The "extent to which its value to the community is outweighed by its dangerous attributes."

See Figure 11.5 for factors present to establish strict liability for an abnormally dangerous condition.

RESEARCH THIS

The law surrounding strict liability for engaging in abnormally dangerous activities takes it roots from an English case, *Rylands v. Fletcher,* L.R. 3H.L.330 (1868). Look up the *Rylands* case and prepare a brief of the case. Also, include a section in your brief on how that case applies to what you read in this chapter.

What is an abnormally dangerous activity or condition? A key requirement in determining whether or not an activity is abnormally dangerous is that it cannot be carried out safely even if the defendant takes reasonable care to do so. The environment in which the activity is conducted will have a bearing on whether an activity is declared abnormally dangerous. Some activities that are considered abnormally dangerous are:

- Storing and using explosives.
- Blasting in a residential area.
- Storing large quantities of flammable liquid such as gasoline.
- Operating nuclear reactors.
- Crop dusting or spraying.
- Storage and transport of toxic chemicals.

See Figure 11.6 for common activities that are considered abnormally dangerous.

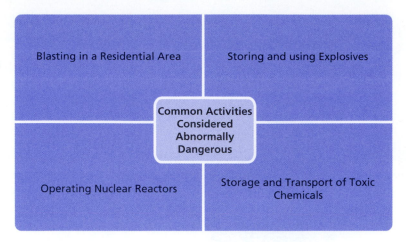

Strict liability for abnormally dangerous activities exists to ensure that defendants engaged in such activity exercise the utmost care. Although strict liability often attaches to even the most careful and cautious defendant, the laws are in place to encourage such care on the part of the defendant. The law recognizes that some dangerous activity is necessary and unavoidable. In the interests of public policy, strict liability for abnormally dangerous activities seeks to balance the need for the activity against the potential harm created. Absolute liability for abnormally dangerous conditions discourages reckless behavior and needless loss by forcing potential defendants to take every possible precaution to make sure the activity is as safe as possible.

Strict liability will not be imposed on a defendant who is unaware of an abnormally dangerous activity or condition. An example of this would be a house built over a long-abandoned mine shaft, which later caves in. It is the plaintiff's burden to establish that the defendant had knowledge of the abnormally dangerous condition or activity. In addition, the harm sustained by the plaintiff must be as a result of the defendant's abnormally dangerous condition or activity.

DEFENSES TO STRICT LIABILITY

As mentioned previously, defendants will be held liable in a strict liability action regardless of whether they were negligent or not. Defendants will not be able to assert that they are not liable because they exercised due care in their activities. Defendants in a strict liability action are limited to the defense of assumption of risk.

As mentioned in previous chapters, assumption of risk states that a plaintiff who voluntarily assumes a risk of harm cannot recover for such harm from the defendant. The plaintiff's assumption of risk of harm bars her recovery in a strict liability action. The defendant does not need to show that the plaintiff expressly assumed the risk. The assumption of risk may be implied by the plaintiff's actions and the surrounding circumstances.

For example, employees working for an employer whose business consists of abnormally dangerous activities cannot sue the employer under a theory of strict liability if they become injured. Although the employees may be able to sue under a different tort theory of recovery, a strict liability argument would not succeed. Employees are deemed to have assumed the risk of getting injured by working in a profession where the activities carried on are considered abnormally dangerous. The enhanced compensation benefits and training these employees receive charge them with having assumed the risk of injury.

YOU BE THE JUDGE

Russ is the captain of an oil tanker owned by Zelon Oil Company. He is transporting crude oil from Alaska southward to some California refineries. During the course of the trip, the seas become very foggy, making it difficult for Russ and his crew to navigate the large tanker along the coast. All of a sudden, the boat is struck by something massive. The boat has either hit or been hit by a large iceberg. The iceberg has ripped a large, gaping hole in the ship, and crude oil is dumping into the ocean. By the time the oil leak has been stopped, thousands of gallons of crude oil have been dumped into the ocean and are showing up along the beaches in a five-square-mile area of Alaska. Birds and wildlife have been affected. Will Russ or Zelon be held strictly liable for the accident? What facts suggest that they will prevail in a strict liability suit brought against them? What facts suggest that they will be held liable in a strict liability action?

EYE ON ETHICS

Just because a defendant is engaging in an abnormally dangerous activity does not mean that a plaintiff can automatically recover for damages or injuries sustained from that activity. In the case of *Foster v. Preston Mill Co.*, 268 P.2d 645 (Wash. 1954), a plaintiff owned a mink farm and one of the minks had killed her young as a result of being frightened by blasting operations conducted by the defendant more than two miles from the farm. The court in *Foster* held that the minks had an abnormally sensitive disposition and that the theory of strict liability did not extend to "harms incident to the plaintiff's extraordinary and unusual use of the land." It is important to examine the harm or damage caused to the plaintiff before applying a strict liability cause of action.

The contributory negligence of the plaintiff is not a defense in a strict liability action. The exception to this rule is the plaintiff's contributory negligence in knowingly and unreasonably subjecting himself to the risk of harm from the defendant's activity. A defendant who conducts activities that are abnormally dangerous will not be held strictly liable for the injuries of a plaintiff who recognizes the danger of the harm and still subjects himself to the harm. In such a circumstance, the plaintiff's contributory negligence would be considered a defense to strict liability. This kind of contributory negligence, which consists of voluntarily and unreasonably encountering a known risk, is called either contributory negligence or assumption of risk. See Figure 11.7 for defenses to strict liability.

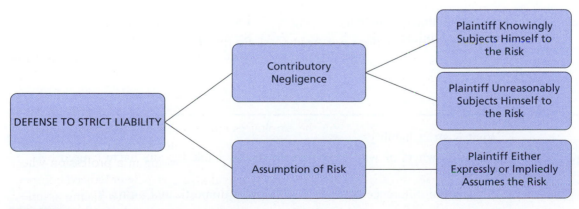

FIGURE 11.7   **Defenses to Strict Liability**

Summary

The general meaning of *strict liability* is liability without fault, also called absolute liability. What that means is that laws exist that determine the defendant to be liable for injuries or damages sustained by the plaintiff even if the defendant was neither at fault nor negligent. Liability is not based on the relationship between the plaintiff and the defendant, but rather on the defendant's act itself.

The source for strict liability is that defendants who engage in certain types of activity must do so at their own peril and must be responsible for all damages that stem from that activity. Strict liability is based on the premise that if the defendant engages in a certain kind of conduct that causes harm to the plaintiff, then liability will result irrespective of intent, negligence, or innocence. It is thought that certain types of conduct are inherently dangerous and, therefore, any harm that results from these types of activities will result in liability being assessed to the defendant.

A wild animal is an animal that has not been domesticated. Wild animals may include lions, tigers, monkeys, boa constrictors, and a host of other animals that are usually found in zoos. Anyone who owns a wild animal will be held strictly liable for any damages caused by that animal. It does not matter whether the owner knew the animal was dangerous or not. It does not matter how much care was taken to protect people from the animal or how much training the wild animal has received.

Normally, an owner of a domesticated animal needs to know or should have known that the animal possessed dangerous propensities. If the owner is unaware of the animal's dangerous propensities, he or she may not necessarily be held strictly liable. Sometimes, an owner is unaware of the dangerous propensities of his animal until it attacks someone. At that time then, the owner will be held strictly liable for any further injuries or damages caused by that animal.

Defendants who engage in abnormally dangerous activities are held strictly liable for injuries and damages resulting from those activities. This tort was established to protect a person's right to be free from harm caused by abnormally dangerous conditions or activities.

A key requirement in determining whether or not an activity is abnormally dangerous is that it cannot be carried out safely even if the defendant takes reasonable care to do so. The environment in which the activity is conducted will have a bearing on whether an activity is declared abnormally dangerous.

A defendant in a strict liability action may assert that the plaintiff assumed the risk of the danger from the defendant's activities. This kind of contributory negligence, which consists of voluntarily and unreasonably encountering a known risk, is the only defense available to the defendant.

Key Terms

Abnormally dangerous activity	Licensee
Domesticated animal	Strict liability
Inherent	Wild animal
Invitees	

Review Questions

1. What is strict liability?
2. Why are owners of wild animals held strictly liable for any harm caused by them?
3. What is the difference between a wild and a domesticated animal?
4. When can an owner of a domesticated animal be held strictly liable?

5. Are owners of livestock held strictly liable?

6. What is the leading case that is the origin of the tort of strict liability?

7. What is the reasoning behind the tort of strict liability?

8. What is an "abnormally sensitive" activity?

9. List five activities that could be considered abnormally dangerous, and why.

10. Are defendants held strictly liable if they are unaware of the abnormally dangerous activity?

Exercises

1. Look in your local newspapers and locate an article that involves a person or entity conducting some type of abnormally dangerous activity. Prepare a memorandum concerning the article and include your rationale as to why you believe this activity is abnormally dangerous and describe the harm, damage, or injury that could arise from such an activity.

2. Maynor Blasting Company is blasting a hill in the town of Orosco in order to clear land for a housing development. Surrounding the blasting site are residential communities. Maynor Blasting Company takes all precautions necessary to conduct the blasting safely and, in fact, blasts on four separate occasions without mishap. On the fifth blasting episode, Polly Plaintiff asserts a claim for damages to her house, stating that she has sustained cracks to the walls and foundation as a result of the blasting. Polly's house is located one mile from the blasting site. Will Maynor Blasting Company be liable to Polly Plaintiff for the damages that she sustained to her dwelling? Explain.

3. Blastco is a manufacturer of explosive devices. The company tests its products on its factory site, in an outdoor testing area. Blastco built the factory over 30 years ago at a location chosen because of its remoteness. However as a result of the growth of the nearby city, homes have been built near the factory's testing grounds. Will the factory be held to be strictly liable for damage that occurs as a result of their activities? What factors will the court look to in determining Blastco's liability?

4. Assume the same facts as above. Tom, a 30-year-old man living near Blastco's facility, often enters Blastco's outdoor testing facility because he likes the way the explosions look. On one particular occasion, Tom was observing the testing of a new explosive. The workers testing the explosive were unaware of Tom's presence. As a result of an explosive blast, Tom is injured by a piece of shrapnel. If Tom sues Blastco in strict liability, what defense(s) can Blastco assert? What is the likely success of these defenses by Blastco?

5. What are the policy reasons behind strict liability? How does absolute liability for abnormally dangerous activities further these interests?

PORTFOLIO ASSIGNMENT

Research cases from your jurisdiction. Locate a case for each of the three different areas of strict liability listed below and brief the cases:

1. Wild animals.

2. Domesticated animals.

3. Abnormally dangerous condition or activity.

Vocabulary Builders

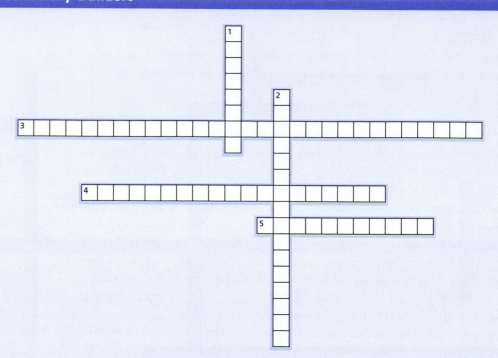

Instructions

Use the key terms from this chapter to fill in the answers to the crossword puzzle.

NOTE: When the answer is more than one word, leave a blank space between words.

ACROSS

3. A non-natural or unusual activity that creates a substantial likelihood of great harm to persons or property that cannot be eliminated by reasonable care by the defendant.
4. An animal accustomed to living with humans.
5. An animal of an untamable disposition or that is in a state of nature.

DOWN

1. Part of the essential character of something; by nature.
2. The defendant is liable without the plaintiff having to prove fault.

In re Hanford Nuclear Reservation Litigation
United States District Court,
E.D. Washington
No. CV-91-3015-WFN
Nov. 3, 2004

Background: Individuals allegedly exposed to radioactive emissions from federal nuclear facility used to produce plutonium for atomic weapons brought action under the Price-Anderson Act against entities that operated the facility under contract with the United States. Plaintiffs moved for partial summary judgment on the issue of whether defendants were engaged in an abnormally dangerous activity and thus were strictly liable for plaintiffs' alleged thyroid disease.

Holdings: The District Court, Nielsen, Senior District Judge, held that:

1. under Washington law, the chemical separation process that occurred in the production of plutonium was an "abnormally dangerous activity," even though defendants may have exercised all reasonable care;
2. the public duty exception to strict liability was not applicable to defendants; and
3. the Washington strict liability standard was not preempted by federal safety regulations.

Motion granted.

ORDER RE: PLAINTIFFS' MOTION FOR SUMMARY JUDGMENT—ABNORMALLY DANGEROUS ACTIVITY
NIELSEN, Senior District Judge.

I. DISCUSSION

The Plaintiffs' Motion requires the Court to determine whether the chemical separation that occurred in the Hanford plutonium production process is an abnormally dangerous activity. The chemical separation created radioactive I-131 that was released into the air by Defendants DuPont and General Electric and allegedly caused thyroid disease in the Plaintiffs. If the activity is abnormally dangerous then the Defendants may be held strictly liable for Plaintiffs' damages, regardless of whether Defendants exercised the utmost care in the conduct of their activities at Hanford.

Here the parties are in agreement that the question of whether Defendants were engaged in an abnormally dangerous activity is a question of law for the court. They also agree that the facts upon which the Court must make its legal determination are not facts that a jury must decide. Thus, since the material facts are generally not disputed, and disagreement is over the inferences to be drawn from the facts, the Court is permitted to draw the inferences and reach a legal conclusion. If factual disputes exist, the Court is permitted to weigh the facts. The Court will construe all facts in favor of the Defen-

dants as the non-moving party and all justifiable inferences will also be drawn in their favor.

The Defendants argue that summary judgment should not be granted because the record is not complete. The Court disagrees. Both parties had sufficient opportunity to present a complete factual record on this dispositive motion. Further, both parties submitted significant documentary evidence in support of their statement of facts. There is enough evidence in the record for the Court to determine the issue.

Abnormally Dangerous Activity. . . . In Washington, [the] court has adopted the *Restatement (Second) of Torts* [*Restatement*] §§ 519, 520 (1977).

Section 519 of the Restatement provides:

> One who carries on an abnormally dangerous activity is subject to liability for harm to the person, land, or chattels of another resulting from the activity, although he has exercised the utmost care to prevent the harm.

This strict liability is limited to the kind of harm the possibility of which makes the activity abnormally dangerous.

Restatement, § 519, p. 34. Section 520 of the *Restatement* lists the factors to be considered in determining whether an activity is abnormally dangerous:

(a) existence of high degree of risk of some harm to the person, land, or chattels of others;
(b) likelihood that the harm that results from it will be great;
(c) inability to eliminate the risk by the exercise of reasonable care;
(d) extent to which the activity is not a matter of common usage;
(e) inappropriateness of the activity to the place where it is carried on; and
(f) extent to which its value to the community is outweighed by its dangerous attributes.

In determining whether an activity is abnormally dangerous, the Court is to consider all of the factors, but all do not have to weigh equally in favor of characterizing an activity as abnormally dangerous in order for the Court to determine that the activity is subject to strict liability. However, one factor alone is not necessarily sufficient for a finding that the activity is abnormally dangerous. "The essential question is whether the risk created is so unusual, either because of its magnitude or because of the circumstances surrounding it, as to justify the imposition of strict liability for the harm which results from it, even though it is carried on with all reasonable care." After a review of all the factors which will be discussed infra, this Court concludes that this essential question must be answered in the affirmative. Even though the Defendants may have exercised all reasonable care in the chemical separation activity, which was necessary to the production of plutonium for the World War II atomic weapons, the risk of harm to the downwind population was so unusual that under Washington law strict liability should be imposed for harm that resulted from the activity.

[Text omitted]

Based upon these facts, the Court concludes that Defendants were engaged in an unusual activity that caused significant early releases of I-131 which in turn created a risk of some harm in the form of illnesses to exposed humans. Whether the risk was very high (as Plaintiffs state) or not very high (as Defendants urge) is immaterial as the potential harm was very serious as will be discussed infra so a lower risk is sufficient. *Restatement,* § 520, comment g, p. 38.

Public Duty. Defendants, assert that they may not be held strictly liable because they acted pursuant to a public duty. Defendants cite, inter alia, *Restatement (Second) of Torts* § 521. Plaintiffs counter that Washington has never adopted § 521 and even if it had, the Defendants would not fit within the plain terms of the section because they are not public officers or employees or common carriers.

Restatement § 521 provides:

> The rules as to strict liability for abnormally dangerous activities do not apply if the activity is carried on in pursuance of a public duty imposed upon the actor as a public officer or employee or as a common carrier. *Restatement* § 521, p. 46.

A justifiable inference may be drawn that Defendants were fulfilling a "public duty." It is not disputed that the plutonium production by Defendants was at the direct request of the government and was important, if not critical, to the nation's defense. Still, the fact that Defendants were engaged in a public duty does not necessarily mean that the public duty exception to strict liability would be applicable here.

[Text omitted]

Preemption of State Standard. Defendants also argue that the Washington strict liability standard is preempted by federal regulations. Defendants assert that all federal circuits that have addressed the issue have concluded that the P-AA (Price Anderson Act) preempts states from imposing nonfederal duties in tort for alleged injuries arising from nuclear incidents and that federal, not state, law provides the liability standard for claims arising under the Act. Plaintiffs respond first that there were no federal regulations at the time of the Defendants' releases at issue in this case, only tolerance doses that the operators consulted for practical guidance. Second, Plaintiffs assert that the cases cited by the Defendants from other circuits were wrongly decided as explained by Judge Kane in *Cook v. Rockwell Int'l Corp.*, 273 F.Supp.2d 1175 (D.Colo.2003).

[Text omitted]

The Court concludes that no federally-established regulations existed in the early years of Hanford emissions of I-131. Thus no standards would exist to test the Plaintiffs' claims against if the Washington law of strict liability was preempted. Here, from a purely practical standpoint federal law does not preempt state strict liability standards.

From a legal standpoint the Court also concludes that even if the tolerance doses were construed as federal regulations they would not preempt the Washington standard of strict liability. . . .

IT IS ORDERED that Plaintiffs' Motion for Summary Judgment—Abnormally Dangerous Activity, filed September 9, 2004, Ct. Rec. 1564, is GRANTED.

[Footnotes omitted]

Source: Reprinted with permission from Westlaw. In re Hanford Nuclear Reservation Litigation, United States District Court, E.D. Washington.

Chapter 12

Product Liability

CHAPTER OBJECTIVES

Upon completion of this chapter, you will be able to:

- Explain the tort of product liability.
- Understand the theory of negligence as it relates to product liability.
- Discuss the concept of warranty and strict liability in product liability.
- Understand design defects.
- Explain failure to warn.

The tort of product liability centers on the sale and use of manufactured goods and products. Within the tort of product liability, many of the tort theories that you have learned so far come into play. Those theories are negligence, strict liability, and statutory liability. You will also learn about a new tort theory that applies to product liability cases—the theory of warranty. All of these theories of tort law are applied in product liability to allow an injured plaintiff to recover for injuries sustained due to an unreasonably dangerous product. Today, state statutory laws may dictate strict liability laws for products. In these states, the product liability statutes are often the exclusive remedy for recovery. This chapter discusses the common law principles of negligence, warranty, and strict liability related to product liability.

PRODUCT LIABILITY

The tort of **product liability** centers on the liability of a seller who sells a defective **chattel** that causes injury to the plaintiff. Product liability describes an entire area of potential liability for injury caused by products that have been placed on the market. It is perhaps one of the fastest-growing areas in tort law. When injured by a defective or dangerous product, the plaintiff can bring a cause of action under various theories of tort law that are associated with product liability.

Some of the product liability causes of action involve a product that is considered to be defective. A defective product has something wrong with it that makes the product dangerous. Because the product is defective, an injury or damage to person or property is caused by the defective product. There are three categories of defects:

- Manufacturing defects—With a manufacturing defect, the defective product does not conform to its design. Something went wrong in the manufacturing or distribution process that made the product become dangerous. The defective product is different from the other similarly manufactured products.

product liability
Refers to the legal liability of manufacturers and sellers to compensate buyers, users, and even bystanders for damages or injuries suffered because of defects in goods purchased.

chattel
Tangible personal property or goods.

- Design defects—The product does conform to the design; however, the design of the product itself is defective. During the planning stage of the product when the manufacturer was designing how to make the product, the design itself was flawed so that every product made under that design would be dangerous. The defective product is exactly like all the other products that are made with that same design. Something is wrong with all of them because of the defectiveness inherent in the very design of the product.

- Warning defects—There are no effective instructions or warnings that accompany the product to direct the user how to safely use the product. The lack of warning makes the product defective and dangerous. The design of the product is otherwise reasonable, and there are no manufacturing flaws in it, but the consumer should have been told certain details regarding the use of the product and the limitations of the product's use. If the manufacturer improperly or inadequately labeled the product, the product could be considered defective and dangerous.

NEGLIGENCE

When a plaintiff brings a negligence claim alleging a defective product, the plaintiff must first establish the same elements of negligence that are required for other types of negligence actions. These elements are:

- Duty
- Breach of duty
- Proximate cause
- Damages

privity
A relationship between the parties to the contract who have rights and obligations to each other through the terms of the agreement.

A defendant who brings a product on the market for sale is under a duty to use reasonable care to see that the product does not cause injury to anyone. Historically, only those people who actually bought the defective product from the seller could sue the seller. This was called **privity**. If privity did not exist, then there was no duty required of the defendant to an injured party. However, the landmark case of *MacPherson v. Buick,* 111 N.E. 1050 (N.Y. 1916) changed the privity rule. As a result of *MacPherson,* a duty of reasonable care is now owed to all foreseeable users of a defective product whenever it can be anticipated that substantial harm to a person or property will result.

A breach of duty is considered to have occurred when it is determined that the defendant acted unreasonably when a serious injury was foreseeable and the defendant did not take precautions to avoid the injury. The possibility of serious injury outweighs the burden or inconvenience of trying to avoid the accident. If defendants fail to go through that burden or inconvenience and serious injury occurs, then they have breached their duty of due care.

A defendant does not have to produce a product that is considered safe, but only has a duty to produce a product that is *reasonably* safe. That is, the defendant only has to take reasonable steps to avoid defects in a product. He does not have to produce a product that has no defects. If a defendant has taken all reasonable precautions to produce a safe product, liability based on negligence will not attach to the defendant.

Manufacturer

A manufacturer of a product is the person or entity that is most likely to have been negligent where a product is concerned. A manufacturer's duty of care includes the following considerations:

- To design a product that is reasonably safe.
- To establish manufacturing procedures that are free from errors.

- To perform reasonable inspections and tests of the finished product.
- To package and ship the product in a reasonably safe manner.
- If component parts are used to assemble a product, to inspect those component parts and to purchase them from a reliable source.

A manufacturer will be held to the standard of an expert in product manufacturing. Reasonable care needs to be taken to discover and correct manufacturing defects before a product is released to the consumer. Inspection and testing are necessary. Reasonable care also must be used in the training of employees who are on the assembly lines as well as those who operate machinery. Defects that are discovered or should have been discovered must be identified.

A manufacturer of products acts reasonably when she provides adequate instructions on a product's use to the consumer and warns against dangers that may not be obvious. Whether or not the design of a product is defective must be looked at in terms of other types of similar products that are being manufactured.

Retailer

A retailer who sells a product either wholesale or by retail directly to the consumer can also be liable for negligence when a defective product causes injury. However, a retailer is less likely to be found negligent than the manufacturer. The fact that the retailer sold a defective product is not enough to attach liability to the retailer. The retailer may not have a duty to inspect the product. The major issue in a negligence case against a retailer is whether or not the injury was foreseeable. To determine foreseeability from a retailer's perspective, one must look at the following:

- Complaints—If a merchant has received complaints of injury from customers, then the retailer may have had warning that a product is defective.

- Reputation of the manufacturer—A reasonable retailer who deals with a reputable manufacturer has less concern over the safety of the product being manufactured than when he deals with a manufacturer who has had a history of problems or is relatively new to manufacturing this type of product.

- Packaging—A reasonable retailer is less likely to be concerned about packaged products than those that are sold without packaging. Packaging assists in the prevention of damage to a product. A retailer cannot be expected to open every package to inspect each product in order to ensure that there are no defects.

- Custom in the trade—The custom in the trade should also be taken into consideration when determining what is reasonable conduct for a retailer.

In a product liability case based on negligence, liability will be on any seller of a defective product. Professor Keeton in *Prosser and Keeton on the Law of Torts*, section 100 at 704 (5th ed. 1984), explains negligence as it relates to product liability as follows:

> *So far as liability for negligence is concerned, there is no longer any doubt that it attaches to any seller of a product, including the maker of a component part of the final product, and an assembler of parts supplied by others, or even a mere processor under contract with the maker. It applies to dealers, whether at wholesale or retail, and to a second-hand dealer who reconditions automobiles for sale. It is obvious that less in the way of care may be required of some of these sellers than of others; but if reasonable care has not been exercised, there may be liability.*

Defenses

It is considered contributory negligence for a plaintiff to fail to discover a defect in a product if a reasonable person in the plaintiff's position in the same or similar circumstances would have discovered it. If the plaintiff does discover the defect in the product and understands the danger it poses and continues to use the product under such circumstances, then the plaintiff assumes the risk of injury. Assumption of the risk is a complete defense to any cause of action in a product liability case. However, the plaintiff must have actual knowledge of the danger and voluntarily use the product.

strict liability
The defendant is liable without the plaintiff having to prove fault.

warranty
A promise or representation by the seller that the goods in question meet certain standards.

Uniform Commercial Code
A collection of modernized, codified, and standardized laws that apply to all commercial transactions with the exception of real property.

WARRANTY AND STRICT LIABILITY

A **warranty** is an assurance in a commercial transaction by one party to another party and that party relies on that assurance. A warranty action is a form of **strict liability**. If a defendant commits a breach of the warranty, then liability will attach, and it will not matter whether the defendant acted intentionally, negligently, or innocently. As with other strict liability torts, the plaintiff does not have to demonstrate that the defendant was negligent or acted intentionally in order to recover damages. Warranties come in two types: express and implied. These will be discussed below.

The **Uniform Commercial Code** (U.C.C.) addresses the area of warranties. The U.C.C. is a model code created by legal scholars to provide model regulations concerning the dealings between merchants and the sale of goods. It is not law, but many states have adopted it or some version of it as their state law. Currently, the only state that has not adopted the U.C.C. is Louisiana.

YOU BE THE JUDGE

Johnny had both of his hands blown off when he ignited fireworks in his backyard on the July 4th holiday. The doctors were unable to reattach his hands. The purchase, sale, and possession of any type of fireworks is prohibited by state law. Does Johnny have a claim of defective product against the manufacturer of the fireworks? Does Johnny have a claim against the merchant that sold the fireworks? Would a claim fall under the theory of strict liability, regarding inherently dangerous material, or does he have a claim of product liability? Does he have a claim at all against anyone? You be the judge.

A DAY IN THE LIFE OF A REAL PARALEGAL

Theresa loves working at the firm she has been with for four years. The firm is primarily a personal injury firm representing injured parties. To bring more work and clients into the fold, Theresa's supervising attorney would like to begin representing clients on strict liability and products liability issues. Her supervising attorney has given her an assignment to research all aspects of the U.C.C. and to give a presentation on the U.C.C. to the partners of the firm and its associate attorneys.

EYE ON ETHICS

Although the U.C.C. provides guidance by providing a model code, many states have adopted their own versions of it. In addition, case law in various states has not followed the model provided by the U.C.C. Remember that each state has its own laws. It is always important to know what the state law states in the particular jurisdiction where the incident occurred. Also, the U.C.C. is considered a secondary resource and cannot be cited as a primary source in a legal argument.

Express Warranty

An **express warranty** is a statement, either written or oral, made by the seller that expressly represents that the goods being sold have certain qualities. Uniform Commercial Code section 2-313 governs express warranties. The section points out that express warranties are confirmations of fact or promises about goods that produce reliance on that by the plaintiff. The warranty is supposed to be part of the basis of the deal. A plaintiff will have a cause of action for a breach of express warranty under the following circumstances:

express warranty
A written representation by the seller as to the nature of the goods to be sold.

- A statement of fact that is false.
- Made with the intention or expectation that the statement will reach the plaintiff.
- Reliance on the statement by the plaintiff.
- Damages.
- Causation.

The first element of a breach of express warranty cause of action is that a false statement of fact has been made about the product. The statement must be reasonably understood as a fact. Statements of opinion are not statements of fact, nor are statements a seller makes that fall into the category of "puffing," or seller's talk. The creation of the express warranty does not require the use of the words *warranty* or *guarantee*. Any words used to describe the product can be sufficient as long as the words communicate statements of fact regarding the product. An express warranty can also be created by showing the plaintiff a model or sample. In showing the plaintiff a sample or model, the defendant is essentially stating that the product will conform to the model or sample. The plaintiff does not have to prove that the statement was false. The plaintiff also does not have to show that the defendant acted negligently or intentionally in communicating the false statement, just that it was communicated. For example, if a salesperson showed a consumer a vacuum cleaner, and displayed all the various features and qualities, the salesperson would have to provide the buyer with a cleaner of the same kind and quality of the sample shown.

The false statement of fact must be made to the plaintiff. If the statement is made to the public, such as in an advertisement or commercial, the defendant must reasonably expect that the statement will be communicated to someone like the plaintiff.

The plaintiff must demonstrate that she saw or heard the false statement and that she relied on the false statement. Reliance means the plaintiff either bought or used the product based on the statement.

The reliance on the false statement of fact must have been the cause of the plaintiff's damage or injury. The plaintiff must demonstrate that if it had not been for the statements made by the defendant, the damage or injury would not have occurred; that is, the statement was a substantial factor in producing the damage or injury.

A cause of action for breach of warranty usually applies to the sale of goods and not to services. Sales of products must be made by **merchants**. Sales of products between individuals who are not merchants are not covered under warranty provisions.

merchants
Businesspersons who have a certain level of expertise dealing in commercial transactions regarding the goods they sell; persons who regularly deal in goods of the kind specified in the agreement. They hold themselves out as having special knowledge in their area.

A seller making a representation of fact that is the basis of the bargain, involving more than mere puffing, will be liable on the contract to the plaintiff. Regardless of fault, the seller will be liable to the plaintiff upon breach of that warranty.

Implied Warranty

A warranty can be implied simply because the seller offers the product for sale. **Implied warranties** are imposed by law and not through agreements or statements. Implied warranties are established in the statutory codes of each state. The breach of the two implied warranties (merchantability and fitness of purpose) imposes strict liability on

implied warranty
An unwritten representation that is normally and naturally included by operation of law that applies to the goods to be sold.

the defendant. The plaintiff does not have to demonstrate that the defendant intended to breach the warranty. The plaintiff also does not have to establish that the defendant was negligent in breaching the warranties.

The U.C.C. provides for several implied warranties as a matter of law. Perhaps the most important of these implied warranties is the warranty of **merchantability**. U.C.C. section 2-314 (1) says that warranties regarding a product's merchantability are an implied part of the contract for its sale if the seller is a merchant, under law, of those goods. The elements of a breach of an implied warranty of merchantability are:

merchantability
The article sold shall be of the general kind described and reasonably fit for the general purpose for which it shall have been sold, and where the article sold is ordinarily used in but one way.

- The sale of goods.
- By a merchant of goods of that kind.
- The goods are not merchantable.
- Damage.
- Causation.

The first element in a breach of implied warranty involves the sale of goods. Services are not covered by these implied warranties. The implied warranty of merchantability does not apply to someone who occasionally sells goods. The defendant must be a merchant in the business of selling goods of the kind in question.

Goods are merchantable when they are fit for the ordinary purposes for which the goods are used. The plaintiff does not have to prove that he or she actually relied on the merchantability of the goods before purchase in order for this element to be satisfied. The reliance on merchantability is assumed from the sale. If the product has obvious defects, which a reasonable inspection of the goods would reveal to the typical consumer, then no implied warranty with respect to such defects exists as long as the consumer had full opportunity to inspect the goods prior to purchase.

fitness for a particular purpose
Where the seller at the time of contracting has reason to know any particular purpose for which the goods are required and that the buyer is relying on the seller's skill or judgment to select or furnish suitable goods, there is, unless excluded or modified, an implied warranty that the goods shall be fit for such purpose.

The plaintiff's damage or injury must be caused by the fact that the goods were not fit for their ordinary purpose. U.C.C. section 2-315 covers the implied warranty of **fitness for a particular purpose**. This implied warranty occurs when the seller knows that the buyer wants to buy the goods for a particular purpose, but the buyer relies on the seller's judgment to recommend a product that is suitable. The implied warranty is that the recommended goods are suitable for the purpose intended by the plaintiff.

The elements for the breach of the implied warranty of fitness for a particular purpose are:

- Sale of goods.
- The seller has reason to know the buyer's particular purpose in buying the goods.

CASE FACT PATTERN

Bob is planning to go mountain climbing at Mt. Hood. He decides that he needs a new pair of mountain boots that have very good traction. Bob is not a professional climber. In fact, he has only been on a couple of easy hikes through the local mountains prior to his attempting this arduous climb of Mt. Hood. He goes to Mountain Climbing 'R Us to buy a new pair of boots. At the store, Bob asks the clerk, Danny, to assist him with his purchase of his new mountain boots. Bob explains that he is an amateur climber and that he needs new boots with better traction. Danny gets commissioned on his sales. He steers Bob away from mountain boots that would suit his purpose and, instead, directs him to a pair of walking boots that have very little traction but are much more expensive. Danny tells Bob that these walking boots will not only be comfortable on the long hike, but that they have great traction and will enable him to climb without slipping. Danny knows of the specific purpose for which Bob wants the boots and knows that the walking boots are not fit for the particular purpose that Bob needs. Relying on Danny's apparent expertise in the area of climbing, Bob purchases the walking boots and wears them on his hike up Mt. Hood. The boots prove to have little or no traction, and during the hike Bob falls and breaks his leg. In a lawsuit against Mountain Climbing 'R Us for breach of the implied warranty of fitness for a particular purpose, Bob will prevail because Danny knew the particular purpose for which Bob was purchasing the boots and made statements of fact that were untrue about the fitness for that purpose of the walking boots.

- The seller has reason to know that the buyer is relying on the seller's skill or judgment in buying the goods.
- The goods are not fit for the particular purpose.
- Damage.
- Causation.

Defenses to Warranty Actions

Once the plaintiff has established a product liability case against the defendant, it is the defendant's turn to offer up defenses that may absolve him or her of liability. While some of the defenses that have been discussed previously can be used for product liability cases that stem from the defendant's negligence, there are a few defenses that are typically seen in breach of warranty cases. Typical defenses that may be available to a defendant in a product liability action for breach of warranty are discussed below.

Disclaimer

Under the U.C.C., a seller can make a written **disclaimer** of the warranty of merchantability. The disclaimer must be conspicuous and unambiguous so that it is clearly communicated to the buyer. For example, the disclaimer usually has to be printed in bold print and capital letters as opposed to small print on the back of a standardized contract form. When goods are sold **as is**, an implied disclaimer is given by selling the goods in the condition that they are in and the buyer accepting those goods in that condition with full knowledge of their condition.

disclaimer
A term which limits claim or denial.

as is
A sale of goods by sample "as is" requires that the goods be of the kind and quality represented, even though they may be in a damaged condition.

RESEARCH THIS

Federal law has placed limits on what can be disclaimed in a written warranty. The case of Magnuson-Moss Federal Trade Commission Improvement Act of 1974, 15 U.S.C. §2301, *et seq.* states that if a manufacturer provides a written warranty to a consumer, there can be no disclaimer of implied warranty. A manufacturer does not have to give a written warranty, but if the company does have a written warranty, an implied warranty of merchantability will be considered to be included in the warranty.

Notice

Notice is a defense to a warranty action in which the injured plaintiff failed to give notice within a reasonable time to the defendant that a breach of the warranty exists. The notice needs to be given within a reasonable time after the plaintiff discovered or should have discovered the breach. U.C.C. section 2-607(3) points out that purchasers

notice
Intelligence of a fact communicated to another.

SPOT THE ISSUE

Thomas is looking to buy a used car. He goes to Shady Sam's Used Car Lot to purchase a vehicle. After looking at Sam's inventory, Thomas decided to buy a 1997 Toyota. As Thomas was looking at the vehicle, Sam was telling him what an amazing car it was, what wonderful features it had, and how well the car handled. Sam also mentioned that the car was being sold "as is." After Thomas bought the vehicle, he drove it down to the beach. As he was driving on the freeway, the car stalled to a stop, and the engine blew. What claims does Thomas have against Sam? What are Sam's potential defenses to Thomas's claims?

must notify sellers of any breaches of warranty within a reasonable time period after the discovery of the breach.

Assumption of the Risk

Assumption of the risk is a defense to a breach of warranty action. The defendant must show that the plaintiff had actual knowledge of the danger and yet voluntarily and unreasonably proceeded to use the product. For example, if the defendant can demonstrate that the plaintiff misused the product or used it for an abnormal use, this may be a defense to product liability. *Abnormal use* is using a product for some purpose other than the use intended by the defendant. For example, suppose the plaintiff uses the microwave to wash his clothes. The microwave catches the house on fire, and the plaintiff is injured. The plaintiff used the microwave for an abnormal use, since its proper use is to cook and heat food. *Misuse* is when the plaintiff handles the product in a careless or inappropriate way. For example, the plaintiff elects to install tires that are too big for his car. The tires come off, and the plaintiff is injured. The product was intended to be used on a different vehicle, for which they are a fit.

The elements of a strict liability product liability cause of action are as follows:

- There must be a seller.
- There must be a defective product that is unreasonably dangerous.
- There must be a consumer.
- Physical harm.
- Causation.

The defendant must be considered a seller of goods. A seller is any person engaged in the business of selling products for use or consumption. An occasional seller of a product who is not engaged in selling as part of her business is not covered under this theory of liability. The following would be considered sellers of goods:

- Manufacturer of entire product.
- Supplier.
- Assembler.
- Distributor.
- Wholesaler.
- Retailer.
- Operator of a restaurant.

The product must be both defective and unreasonably dangerous. The plaintiff need not prove that the defendant was negligent in producing these defects. A defendant who sold a defective product can be held strictly liable even if the defendant used all reasonable care.

A product is unreasonably dangerous when it is dangerous to an extent beyond that which would be contemplated by the ordinary consumer who purchased it. An ordinary consumer is one who possesses ordinary knowledge common to the community as to characteristics of the product.

A manufacturer can be held liable if the product turns out to be defective when it is used for its intended purpose. The intended use of a product is that use for which the manufacturer intended the product. It is the reason the product was built and placed on the market.

A manufacturer can also be held strictly liable if the product injures someone who is using it for a foreseeable use. A foreseeable use is a use for which the manufacturer anticipates or should be able to anticipate that the product will be used. A foreseeable use may not be the intended use. An ordinary consumer would expect the product to be reasonably safe for all purposes, including any of its intended purposes. It is not considered misuse of a product to use it for a purpose that the defendant should have anticipated or foreseen as a possible use. Manufacturers will not be held liable for unforeseeable misuses of their products.

The plaintiff does not have to be the actual purchaser of the product. The plaintiff only has to be a consumer of the product. Strict liability covers actual damage to the plaintiff. If no such damage has occurred, and the plaintiff has suffered economic damage only, most courts do not allow recovery under strict liability. The plaintiff must show that the product was defective at the time it left the hands of the defendant and that this defect actually caused the physical harm.

Sellers are not liable if they deliver products in a safe condition, and then they are mishandled, or, for some other reason, they are defective by the time they reach the consumer. If the injury results from abnormal handling, then the seller is not liable under strict liability.

Strict liability in a product liability action avoids many potential problems for recovery by the plaintiff. For example:

- The plaintiff does not have to prove the negligence of the defendant. It is presumed.

- The plaintiff does not have to prove that the defendant knew of the defect.

- The plaintiff does not have to establish privity.

- The defendant cannot disclaim the obligation of safety.

- The plaintiff has no duty to notify the defendant after the injury caused by the product.

DESIGN DEFECTS

To prove that a manufacturer is liable to the plaintiff for manufacturing an unreasonably dangerous product, the plaintiff must prove that the product was defective. There are two basic types of product defects. The first type is a manufacturing defect that involves a product with characteristics that are different from other products of this type that have been manufactured. Something went wrong with the manufacturing process, and the product causes damage or injury because of it. The second type is a design defect—all the products manufactured by the defendant have the same feature, making them all unreasonably dangerous. Thus, a flaw in the actual design of the product makes the product dangerous.

Remember, the plaintiff must prove the defect. The courts use two methods to determine if the product has a design flaw. These methods are:

- Consumer contemplation test—A product is considered to be defectively dangerous if it is dangerous to an extent beyond that which would be contemplated by an ordinary consumer who purchased it with ordinary knowledge common to the community. The defect is defined in terms of consumer expectations and using the product for reasonably foreseeable uses.

- Risk-utility test—A product is considered to be unreasonably dangerous if the magnitude of the danger outweighs the utility of the product. This test looks at how reasonable it was for the manufacturer to place the product on the market. Was there a need for the product? What is the likelihood that the product may cause an injury, and how severe will the injury be? Is there another design or an alternative design available for the product?

DUTY TO WARN

A plaintiff can prove liability against a manufacturer if the manufacturer knew or should have known that the product was defective and failed to warn the public. Duty to warn cases are often found in the pharmaceutical industry. They involve failure to warn the public as to the side effects or dangers of using or misusing a particular drug.

SURF'S UP

Product liability cases are becoming more prevalent in recent years. One notable recent case involved a tire company whose tires caused vehicles to flip over and injure and kill consumers. In another, the tobacco industry was hit with a significant lawsuit for failing to properly warn consumers of the dangers of smoking. Products are recalled all the time because of design defects. If you would like to research various products that have been recalled because of design defects or other dangerous conditions, check out the following websites:

www.warrantyguide.com

www.recalls.gov

www.cpsc.gov

www.wxyz.com

www.consumerreports.org

Summary

The tort of product liability centers on the liability of a seller who sells a defective chattel that causes injury to the plaintiff. Product liability describes an entire area of potential liability for injury caused by products that have been placed on the market. When injured by a defective or dangerous product, the plaintiff can bring a cause of action under various theories of tort law that are associated with product liability.

A defendant who brings a product on the market for sale is under a duty to use reasonable care to see that the product does not cause injury to anyone. Historically, only those people who actually bought the defective product from the seller could sue the seller. This was called privity. If privity did not exist, then there was no duty required of the defendant to an injured party. However, the landmark case of *MacPherson v. Buick,* 111 N.E. 1050 (N.Y. 1916) changed the privity rule. As a result of *MacPherson,* a duty of reasonable care is now owed to all foreseeable users of a defective product whenever it can be anticipated that substantial harm to a person or property will result.

A breach of duty is considered to have occurred when it is determined that the defendant acted unreasonably when a serious injury was foreseeable and the defendant did not take precautions to avoid the injury. The possibility of serious injury outweighs the burden or inconvenience of trying to avoid the accident. If defendants fail to go through that burden or inconvenience and serious injury occurs, then they have breached their duty of due care.

A defendant does not have to produce a product that is considered safe. but only has a duty to produce a product that is *reasonably* safe. The defendant only has to take reasonable steps to avoid defects in a product. He does not have to produce a product that has no defects. If a defendant has taken all reasonable precautions to produce a safe product, liability based on negligence will not attach to the defendant.

A warranty is an assurance in a commercial transaction by one party to another party. A warranty action is a form of strict liability. If a defendant commits a breach of the warranty, then liability will attach, and it will not matter whether the defendant acted intentionally, negligently, or innocently. As with other strict liability torts, the plaintiff does not have to demonstrate that the defendant was negligent or acted intentionally in order to recover damages.

The first element of a breach of express warranty cause of action is that a false statement of fact has been made about the product. The statement must be reasonably understood as a fact. Statements made by a seller that fall into the category of puffing, or seller's talk, are not considered to be statements of fact. The creation of the express warranty does not require the use of the words *warranty* or *guarantee*. Any words used to describe the product can be sufficient as long as the words communicate statements of fact regarding the product. An express warranty can also be created by showing the plaintiff a model or sample. The defendant is essentially stating that the product will conform to the model or sample. The plaintiff does not have to prove that the statement was false; the statement basically must be false. The plaintiff also does not have to show that the defendant acted negligently or intentionally in communicating the false statement, just that it was communicated.

A warranty can be implied simply because the seller offers the product for sale. Implied warranties are imposed by law and not through agreements or statements. Implied warranties are established in the statutory codes of each state. The breach of the two implied warranties (merchantability and fitness of purpose) imposes strict liability on the defendant. The plaintiff does not have to demonstrate that the defendant intended to breach the warranty. The plaintiff also does not have to establish that the defendant was negligent in breaching the warranties.

The Uniform Commercial Code provides for several implied warranties as a matter of law. Perhaps the most important of these implied warranties is the warranty of merchantability. U.C.C. section 2-314 (1) states that warranties regarding a product's merchantability are an implied part of the contract for its sale if the seller is a merchant, under law, of those goods.

Goods are merchantable when they are fit for the ordinary purposes for which the goods are used. Plaintiffs do not have to prove that they actually relied on the merchantability of the goods before purchase in order for this element to be satisfied. The reliance on merchantability is assumed from the sale. If there are obvious defects in the product, which a reasonable inspection of the goods would reveal to the typical consumer, then no implied warranty with respect to such defects exists as long as the consumer had full opportunity to inspect the goods prior to purchase.

The plaintiff's damage or injury must be caused by the fact that the goods were not fit for their ordinary purpose. U.C.C. section 2-315 covers the implied warranty of fitness for a particular purpose. This implied warranty occurs when the seller knows that the buyer wants to buy the goods for a particular purpose, but the buyer relies on the seller's judgment to recommend a product that is suitable. The implied warranty is that the recommended goods are suitable for the purpose the plaintiff intended.

Under the U.C.C., a seller can make a written disclaimer of the warranty of merchantability. The disclaimer must be conspicuous and unambiguous so that it is clearly communicated to the buyer. For example, the disclaimer usually has to be printed in bold print and capital letters as opposed to small print on the back of a standardized contract form. When goods are sold "as is," an implied disclaimer is given by selling the goods in the condition that they are in and the buyer accepting those goods in that condition with full knowledge of their condition.

Notice is a defense to a warranty action where the injured plaintiff failed to give notice within a reasonable time to the defendant that a breach of the warranty exists. The notice needs to be given within a reasonable time after the plaintiff discovered or should have discovered the breach. U.C.C. section 2-607(3) points out that purchasers must notify sellers of any breaches of warranty within a reasonable time period after the discovery of the breach.

To prove that a manufacturer is liable to the plaintiff for manufacturing an unreasonably dangerous product, the plaintiff must prove that the product was defective. There two basic types of product defects. The first type is a manufacturing defect that involves a product that has characteristics that are different from other products of this type that have been manufactured. Something went wrong with the manufacturing process, and the product causes damage or injury because of it. The second type is a design defect, which is where all the products manufactured by the defendant have the same feature that makes them unreasonably dangerous. A flaw in the actual design of the product makes the product dangerous.

A plaintiff can prove liability against a manufacturer if the manufacturer knew or should have known the product was defective and failed to warn the public. Some of the most common duty to warn cases can be found in the pharmaceutical industry. They involve failure to warn the public as to the side effects or dangers of using or misusing a particular drug.

Key Terms

As is	Merchantability
Chattel	Notice
Disclaimer	Privity
Express warranty	Product liability
Fitness for a particular purpose	Strict liability
Implied warranty	Uniform Commercial Code
Merchants	Warranty

Review Questions

1. What is product liability?
2. What is privity?
3. Discuss the concept of warranty?
4. What does the term "unreasonably dangerous" mean?
5. What is an express warranty?
6. What is an implied warranty?
7. What are some of the defenses to breach of warranty?
8. What is a design defect?
9. What is a duty to warn?
10. What is the consumer expectation test?
11. What is the risk-utility test?
12. Explain strict liability as it pertains to product liability.
13. What is the U.C.C., and why is it important?
14. What does "merchantability" mean?
15. What does "fitness for a particular purpose" mean?

Exercises

1. Peter purchased a generic box of cereal from Super Market. While eating the cereal, Peter broke a tooth on a stone that was in the cereal. The generic cereal is provided to Super Market by three different companies: Branch, Mullen, and Ace. Each sells approximately equal quantities of cereal to Super Market. In addition, all the companies package their product in identical wrappers so that it is impossible to tell which of the companies furnished the box of cereal that Peter purchased. Although the companies compete with each other, at Super Market's request they worked together to design the product wrapper. If Peter is successful in an action for damages against Super Market, it will probably be because:
   a. Super Market, Branch, Mullen, and Ace were involved in a concerted action in the manufacture and marketing of the product.
   b. Super Market, Branch, Mullen, and Ace established standards on an industry-wide basis, which made identification of the product's manufacturer impossible.

    c. The negligence of Mullen, Branch, or Ace resulted in harm to Peter under circumstances such that it was impossible to tell which of them caused the harm.

    d. One of the three companies, Mullen, Branch, or Ace, manufactured a defective product, and Super Market sold that product while it was in a defective condition.

2. Dan, who was 12 years old, received a sled manufactured by Rosebud from his aunt as a Christmas present. Since he already had a better sled, Dan sold the Rosebud sled to his neighbor Willie. Willie was riding the Rosebud sled down a snow-covered hill when one of the bolts that held it together broke, causing the sled to turn over and severely injuring Willie. The bolt broke because of a crack that was in the sled when it left the Rosebud factory but that was too small to be discovered by reasonable inspection. If Willie brings an action against Rosebud, the court should find for:

    a. Willie, if the cracked bolt was a defect.

    b. Willie, but only if Dan did not use the sled before selling it to Willie.

    c. Rosebud, since the sale by Dan was outside the regular course of business.

    d. Rosebud, because the crack was too small to be discovered upon reasonable inspection.

3. The theories upon which a product liability case can be brought include:

    a. negligence.

    b. an intentional act on the part of the defendant.

    c. strict liability in tort.

    d. all of the above.

    e. only a and c.

4. Through online research, find a recent recall of a consumer product made by the manufacturer. What was this product used for? Did the manufacturer or seller of this product make any express or implied warranties to the consumer? What is the liability of the seller and manufacturer for the defect in the product? (Note: if you need help with finding a product recall, research Firestone Tires or Peter Pan Peanut Butter.)

5. John has a 1964 Chevy Impala. He often works on the vehicle and performs many of the automotive repairs himself. Every other weekend John goes to the auto supply store to pick up parts and talk about his vehicle with the owner, Owen. Owen is aware that John owns a 1964 Impala. John goes to the shop and asks to purchase an engine gasket. Owen sells John a gasket for a Corvette. The gasket is in perfectly fine condition. After installing the gasket and driving it, John's vehicle catches fire. Under what theory will John be able to recover from Owen?

6. On a Saturday afternoon, Julie receives a knock on the door. A door-to-door salesperson who is selling cookware appears at the door. The salesperson shows Julie the complete set of the cookware and describes the features and "good quality" of the product. Julie purchases a set of the cookware, to be delivered to her by mail. Three weeks later, the cookware arrives at her house. However, the cookware delivered is different in size, shape, and quality from the product the salesperson showed her. Under what theories of product liability can Julie recover from salesperson?

 PORTFOLIO ASSIGNMENT

Research online. What are the state statutory laws regarding product liability in your state? If your state does not currently have statutory laws regarding product liability, research neighboring states for their product liability laws. How are these laws different, and how are they the same as the common law rules mentioned in this chapter?

Vocabulary Builders

Instructions

Use the key terms from this chapter to fill in the answers to the crossword puzzle.
NOTE: When the answer is more than one word, leave a blank space between words.

ACROSS

4. A written representation by the seller as to the nature of the goods to be sold.
8. Businesspersons who have a certain level of expertise dealing in commercial transactions regarding the goods they sell; persons who regularly deal in goods of the kind specified in the agreement. They hold themselves out as having special knowledge in their area.
10. A sale of goods by sample "as is" requires that the goods be of the kind and quality represented, even though they may be in a damaged condition.
13. Where the seller at the time of contracting has reason to know any particular purpose for which the goods are required and that the buyer is relying on the seller's skill or judgement to select or furnish suitable goods, there is, unless excluded or modified, an implied warranty that the goods shall be fit for such purpose.
14. A promise or representation by the seller that the goods in question meet certain standards.

DOWN

1. Tangible personal property or goods.
2. The article sold shall be of the general kind described and reasonably fit for the general purpose for which it shall have been sold, and where the article sold is ordinarily used in but one way.
3. Refers to the legal liability of manufacturers and sellers to compensate buyers, users, and even bystanders for damages or injuries suffered because of defects in goods purchased.
5. A collection of modernized, codified, and standardized laws that apply to all commercial transactions with the exception of real property.
6. A term which limits claim or denial.
7. An unwritten representation that is normally and naturally included by operation of law that applies to the goods to be sold.
9. Intelligence of a fact communicated to another.
11. The defendant is liable without the plaintiff having to prove fault.
12. A relationship between the parties to the contract who have rights and obligations to each other through the terms of the agreement.

Supreme Court, Appellate Division, Second Department, New York

Zoila GODOY, Plaintiff, v. ABAMASTER OF MIAMI, INC., Defendant-Appellant, Mike's Restaurant Equipment Corporation, Defendant, Carfel, Inc., Defendant-Respondent (and a Third-Party Action)

754 N.Y.S.2d 301

Jan. 21, 2003

In this product liability action, the issue, which appears to be one not previously presented to this court, is whether the distributor of a defective product is entitled to indemnification from an importer/distributor of the product which is higher in the chain of distribution, where both are strictly liable in tort to the plaintiff.

The plaintiff commenced this action to recover damages for the loss of all four fingers on her right hand, an injury sustained while she was operating a manually fed, electrically-powered commercial meat grinder. The plaintiff commenced the instant action against the retailer that sold the meat grinder, Mike's Restaurant Equipment Corp. (hereinafter Mike's Restaurant Equipment), Abamaster of Miami, Inc., and Abamaster, Inc. (hereinafter collectively referred to as Abamaster), a wholesale distributor of restaurant equipment in Miami, Florida, that sold the meat grinder to Mike's Restaurant Equipment, and Carfel, Inc. (hereinafter Carfel), an importer/distributor, also based in Miami, that sold the meat grinder to Abamaster.

Abamaster and Carfel interposed separate answers denying the plaintiff's allegations and asserting affirmative defenses and cross claims against one another. Abamaster cross-claimed for contribution and indemnification, while Carfel sought only contribution from Abamaster. A default judgment on the issue of liability was entered against Mike's Restaurant Equipment. It is Abamaster's cross claim against Carfel for indemnification which is the subject of this appeal.

Carfel attempted to commence a third-party action against, inter alia, Aroma Taiwan Machinery Company, the manufacturer of the meat grinder. Carfel was not able to obtain jurisdiction over the third-party defendants. Thus, the manufacturer is not a party to this action. Carfel settled with the plaintiff before trial for the sum of $350,000.

[Text omitted]

At the close of the plaintiff's case, the defendant Carfel, which had previously settled with the plaintiff, made an application to dismiss Abamaster's cross claim for indemnification. The Supreme Court deferred decision on the application until the close of the proof and subsequently, until the verdict was rendered on the issue of liability.

[Text omitted]

After the verdict, Abamaster sought a determination of its cross claim for common-law indemnification against Carfel, and Carfel renewed its application to dismiss the cross claim. Carfel argued that the jury's assignment of 50% of the fault in the happening of the accident to Abamaster, and only 10% to it, reflected that the jury found Abamaster more culpable than Carfel, and that Carfel should not be compelled to indemnify the more culpable defendant. Abamaster argued, on the other hand, that the proof presented in the case allowed only one conclusion, that the product was designed and manufactured

by a Taiwanese company not a party to this action and that both Carfel and Abamaster were mere sequential distributors who passed the product along the distribution chain without knowledge of the defect. The Supreme Court ruled that Abamaster was not entitled to indemnification because Abamaster and Carfel were found by the jury to be joint tortfeasors.

In strict product liability, a manufacturer, wholesaler, distributor, or retailer who sells a product in a defective condition is liable for injury which results from the use of the product "regardless of privity, foreseeability or the exercise of due care" *Gebo v. Black Clawson Co.*, 92 N.Y.2d 387. The plaintiff need only prove that the product was defective as a result of either a manufacturing flaw, improper design, or a failure to provide adequate warnings regarding the use of the product and that the defect was a substantial factor in bringing about the injury (see *Codling v. Paglia*, 32 N.Y.2d 330). Distributors and retailers may be held strictly liable to injured parties, even though they may be innocent conduits in the sale of the product, because liability rests not upon traditional considerations of fault and active negligence, but rather upon policy considerations which dictate that those in the best "position to exert pressure for the improved safety of products" bear the risk of loss resulting from the use of the products (*Sukljian v. Charles Cross & Son, Inc.*, supra at 95, 511 N.Y.S.2d 821. Strict product liability is not vicarious liability, but like vicarious liability, it creates an exception to the usual rule which limits one's liability to one's own wrongdoing (see *Mondello v. New York Blood Ctr.-Greater N.Y. Blood Program*, 80 N.Y.2d 219).

Here, the jury was charged solely on strict product liability. The answers on the verdict sheet indicate that it found that the meat grinder was defectively designed and/or manufactured by Aroma Taiwan Machinery Corp., a nonparty, and that the defect was a substantial factor in bringing about the plaintiff's injury. As to Carfel and Abamaster, the jury expressly found that each was a distributor of the defectively-designed meat grinder. Indeed, the proof presented at trial did not support the conclusion that either defendant was anything more than an innocent conduit in the sale of the defective product. There was no proof to support a finding that either Carfel or Abamaster was actively negligent in designing the meat grinder, or that they committed any independent tort which caused or contributed to the plaintiff's injury.

[Text omitted]

Here, both Carfel and Abamaster are liable to the plaintiff, not because they were negligent, but "only by imputation of law" Where, as here, liability is not based upon culpability, the appropriate concept is indemnification, rather than contribution.

One who is liable for an injury "by imputation of law may seek common-law indemnity from a person primarily liable for the injury" (23 N.Y. Jur 2d, Contributions, Indemnity and Subrogation § 90; see *Bellevue S. Assocs. v. HRH Constr. Corp.*,

78 N.Y.2d 282) . . . Where an entity "has discharged a duty which is owed by [it] but which as between [it] and another should have been discharged by the other" a contract to reimburse or indemnify is implied by law (*McDermott v. City of New York*, 50 N.Y.2d 211. Thus, it is well settled that a seller or distributor of a defective product has an implied right of indemnification as against the manufacturer of the product (*see McDermott v. City of New York, supra;* In the instant case, both Carfel and Abamaster have the benefit of the implied right of indemnification as against the manufacturer of the defectively-designed meat grinder. Unfortunately, the manufacturer is not amenable to the jurisdiction of the Supreme Court. In the absence of the manufacturer, we must determine whether, as Abamaster contends, the importer/distributor, Carfel, as the party closest to the negligent manufacturer, should indemnify the distributor lower in the commercial chain of distribution of the product.

Although we have not previously considered this question, the Supreme Court of New Jersey had occasion to address it in *Promaulayko v. Johns Manville Sales Corp.*, 116 N.J. 505. In Promaulayko, where the producer of the product causing the harm was located in the former Soviet Union and was not a party to the action, the issue on appeal was whether an intermediate distributor should indemnify the distributor below it in the chain of distribution where both were held strictly liable in tort to the injured plaintiff. The court held that it should, based upon the policy considerations underlying the concept of strict liability in tort. The court stated that "the effect of requiring the party closest to the original producer to indemnify parties farther down the chain is to shift the risk of loss to the most efficient accident avoider" and "[p]assing the cost of the risk up the distributive chain also fulfills, as a general rule, the goal of distributing the risk to the party best able to bear it." The court reasoned that the distributor at the top of the distribution chain can generally spread the risk among a greater number of customers than the smaller distributor at the lower end of the chain. Moreover, the distributor at the top of the chain is closer to the producer or manufacturer, and thus, is in a better position to pressure it to make the product safe.

We find the reasoning in *Promaulayko* to be persuasive. In New York, strict product liability evolved as an exception to the usual rule limiting liability to one's own wrongdoing for policy reasons related to the allocation of the risk of loss and deterrence. *See Mondello.* Manufacturers are in the best position to know when products are suitably designed and properly made, *see Sukljian*, as well as to diffuse the cost of safety in design and production. *See Codling.* The rule imposing strict liability upon retailers and distributors advances the policy of encouraging improved product safety because, by reason of their continuing relationships with manufacturers, sellers and distributors are in a position to exert pressure on them to produce safe products. *See Sukljian.* Of those in the chain of distribution, the distributor or importer closest to the manufacturer (at the top of the chain of distribution) is in the best position to further the public policy considerations underlying the doctrine of strict product liability. Here, the upstream distributor, Carfel, selected the Taiwanese manufacturer and dealt exclusively with it through Carfel's offices in Taiwan. Carfel is in a better position to exert pressure on the Taiwanese manufacturer to make a safer product and, thus, to eliminate the danger posed by the meat grinder at issue in this case. Carfel is also in a better position to seek indemnification from the Taiwanese manufacturer for the loss, thereby shifting the cost of the loss to the entity best able to distribute the cost to all users of the product. Thus, the Supreme Court should have granted judgment as a matter of law to Abamaster on its cross claim for indemnification.

[Text omitted]

Accordingly, the amount that Carfel will be required to pay Abamaster on the indemnification claim, which shall be determined by the Supreme Court after a trial on the issue of damages, in the event one has not been held, shall be reduced by the sum paid to the plaintiff pursuant to the settlement.

[Text omitted]

Accordingly, the order is reversed, on the law, with costs, judgment is granted as a matter of law to the defendant Abamaster of Miami, Inc., on its cross claim for indemnification as against Carfel, Inc., and the matter is remitted to the Supreme Court, Westchester County, for further proceedings consistent herewith, including a trial on the issue of damages, in the event one has not been held, and a determination of the amount to be paid by the defendant Carfel, Inc., on the cross claim of the defendant Abamaster of Miami, Inc., for indemnification.

[Text omitted]

ORDERED that the order is reversed, on the law, with costs, judgment is granted as a matter of law to the defendant Abamaster of Miami, Inc., on its cross claim for indemnification as against Carfel, Inc., and the matter is remitted to the Supreme Court, Westchester County, for further proceedings consistent herewith, including a trial on the issue of damages, in the event one has not been held, and a determination of the amount to be paid by the defendant Carfel, Inc., on the cross claim of the defendant Abamaster of Miami, Inc., for indemnification.

Source: Used with permission from Westlaw. Zoila GODOY v. ABAMASTER OF MIAMI, INC., Mike's Restaurant Equipment Corporation, Carfel, Inc., 754 N.Y.S.2d 301.

Chapter 13

Other Torts

CHAPTER OBJECTIVES

Upon completion of this chapter, you will be able to:

- Understand medical malpractice.
- Discuss legal malpractice.
- Explain the tort of survival.
- Identify the elements of the tort of wrongful death.
- Understand business torts.

Malpractice as a tort occurs when a professional, under a duty to act, fails to follow generally accepted professional standards, and that breach of duty is the cause of damage to the plaintiff. Malpractice in general involves a standard of care from someone who has superior ability or knowledge. As such, people who possess such superior ability or knowledge are held to a higher standard of care than those who do not.

MEDICAL MALPRACTICE

A doctor is not required to accept every patient who walks through his door. He can reject patients. The physician–patient relationship arises when the doctor undertakes to render services in response to either an express or implied request for services by the patient. The physician–patient relationship does not come into existence just because the doctor has provided emergency medical care to an injured person. The relationship needs to be created out of a patient's express or implied request for medical services and the doctor's acceptance of that request.

A doctor cannot withdraw from the physician–patient relationship at will. The doctor must give the patient reasonable notice of the withdrawal so that the patient can locate a different doctor in order to obtain treatment. The patient, however, is free to end the relationship at any time. The client remains responsible for any fees for services the doctor rendered up to the time the relationship is terminated.

Typically, a doctor will not promise a particular result or cure. If such a promise is given by the doctor, then a breach-of-warranty or breach-of-contract action against the doctor can be brought if the patient does not become cured as promised. If a doctor uses language that could be construed as having rendered a promise concerning treatment and the patient is not cured, the patient could bring a breach-of-contract action against the doctor even though the doctor was not negligent when performing the services. An opinion by a doctor regarding the possible results of treatment does not constitute a promise or guarantee.

Doctors can and do make mistakes and can cause injuries while treating patients and performing medical services, but they are not always found liable for such mistakes. To attach liability to a doctor for negligence, the patient must demonstrate that the mistake was wrongful. Doctors are held to a standard of reasonable care compared with the kind of care another doctor under the same or similar circumstances would have rendered to the patient. A doctor must have the skill and learning commonly possessed by members of the profession who are considered to be in good standing.

Two standards are normally used to assess whether or not a doctor has the standard of skill normally possessed by members of the profession: national and local.

- National standard—Does the doctor have and use the equipment, knowledge, and experience that doctors have and use nationally?
- Local standard—Does the doctor have and use the equipment, knowledge, and experience that doctors have and use locally or in localities similar to the community where the doctor practices?

The standard that a professional will be held to depends on the classification of the professional. Typically, professionals will be held to the standard of those in their similar area and locale. This is referred to the local standard. However, if a professional holds herself out as a specialist, she will be held to the higher national standard of care.

Negligence does not attach because the wrong selection of treatment is made or because other doctors have used different methods of treatment. As long as the doctor is diligent and used good judgment, liability will not attach because her approach to the patient's health problem was different from an approach someone else might have used.

Doctors can commit a battery if they make physical contact with a part of the patient's body without the patient's consent. The patient must grant informed consent; she must be fully informed of the risks associated with the treatment that was rendered. If she is not fully informed, the theory of informed consent alleges that the failure to inform the patient of the risks involved prevented the patient from being able to make an intelligent decision on what treatment to seek or whether to have an operation. Doctors and hospitals often use consent forms as a way of providing information as well as avoiding liability.

A doctor sometimes can give treatment to a patient without consent. The factors the court looks at to determine if it was reasonable for a doctor to give a patient treatment without consent are:

- The seriousness of the patient's condition.
- The patient's emotional stability.
- The availability of time.
- The extent of the emergency.
- The practice in the medical community in such cases.

 SPOT THE ISSUE

Daniel lives in a rural area of Montana. The nearest hospital is over 300 miles away. When Daniel begins to feel sick, he drives himself to the local town doctor, Dr. Neb. Dr. Neb examines Daniel and determines that he has been bitten on the foot by a brown recluse spider. Dr. Neb does not have antivenom for the spider bite on hand at his small rural clinic. He treats Daniel as best he can and calls for an ambulance to drive Daniel the 300 miles to the nearest hospital. When Daniel arrives, the venom from the spider bite has spread up his leg, and by the time doctors at the hospital can administer enough antivenom to stop the spread, it is too late. Daniel's leg needs to be amputated because of the spider bite. Does Daniel have a claim against Dr. Neb in court?

Local Standard
- Expertise and skill is compared to other like professionals in the local vicinity of the doctor
- Knowledge and skill required of doctor is lower than national standard
- Typically used when the doctor does not hold himself out to be a specialist

National Standard
- Expertise and skill is compared to other like professionals throughout the nation
- Higher standard of skill and knowledge required of the doctor
- Typically used when the doctor holds himself out to be a specialist

Medical Malpractice Standard

FIGURE 13.1   Medical Malpractice Standards

- Seriousness of Patien's Condition
- Patient's Emotional Stability
- Availability of Time
- Extent of Emergency
- Practice in the Medical Community in Such Cases

FIGURE 13.2

Factors to Determine Whether It Was Reasonable for a Doctor to Provide Treatment to a Patient Without Consent

See Figure 13.1 displaying both the local and national standards of medical malpractice, and see Figure 13.2 for factors courts use to determine whether it was reasonable for a doctor to provide treatment to a patient without consent.

LEGAL MALPRACTICE

As is the case with a doctor, liability for an attorney will not be established just because the attorney makes a mistake or loses a case. Unless the attorney specifically guarantees a result to a client, the standard of care used in a **malpractice** case will be reasonableness. The American Bar Association states in its *Model Rules of Professional Conduct* that when an attorney engages in the practice of law and, by agreement, decides to pursue a case on behalf of a client, the attorney implies that:

- The attorney possesses the requisite degree of learning, skill, and ability necessary to practice his profession and that other similarly situated attorneys ordinarily possess.

- The attorney will exert his best judgment in the prosecution of the case entrusted to him.

- The attorney will exercise reasonable and ordinary care and diligence in the use of his skill and in the application of his knowledge to the client's case.

malpractice
Failure of a professional person, as a physician or lawyer, to render proper services through reprehensible ignorance or negligence, especially when injury or loss follows.

FIGURE 13.3
Standard of Care Implied to Lawyer Representing a Client

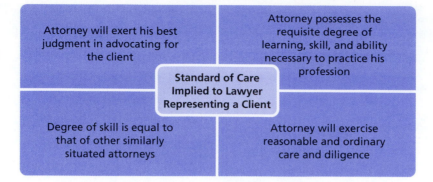

See Figure 13.3 for the standard of care implied to a lawyer representing a client.

An attorney who acts in good faith and possesses an honest belief that his advice and acts are in the best interest of his client's case will not be held liable for a mistake in judgment or on a point of law. An attorney will be responsible for any damages or loss to his client that directly results from a lack of degree of knowledge and skill ordinarily possessed by other attorneys that are similarly situated. Liability will attach from the omission by the attorney to use reasonable care and diligence or from the failure to exercise in good faith and judgment in attending to a client's matter.

An attorney in good standing who makes a *reasonable* mistake in demonstrating the skill and knowledge normally possessed by attorneys of her caliber will generally not be held liable for her mistake. An attorney who makes an *unreasonable* mistake, however, will be held liable. The test is whether the average attorney would have made the same mistake. The focus is on the attorney in good standing using the knowledge and skills normally found in attorneys of the same caliber.

There are three basic errors made by an attorney that can lead to successful negligence actions against the attorney. They are:

- Taking on too many cases.
- Failing to do more than the minimal legal research.
- Failing to consult and/or associate with more experienced attorneys when necessary.

 LEGAL RESEARCH MAXIM

Although malpractice is generally associated with the legal and medical professions, it can encompass any profession. Malpractice is any professional misconduct and/or unreasonable lack of skill in professional and fiduciary duties.

In order for negligence to attach to an attorney, the plaintiff must establish that the attorney was the cause of the damage or harm. It must be proved that, as a result of the attorney's mistake, the plaintiff was damaged or harmed.

See Figure 13.4 for the basic errors that can lead to attorney negligence.

FIGURE 13.4
Basic Errors That Can Lead to Attorney Negligence

attorney–client relationship
Attorneys have a duty to maintain a client's confidences regarding any information that the client wants kept confidential.

SURVIVAL TORT

Survival is similar to inheriting a tort action. The tort of survival deals with the situation of whether or not a tort action can survive the unconnected death of either the victim or the defendant.

Tort actions that survive the death of a victim who dies from unrelated causes have the following characteristics:

survival
Actions for personal injuries that by state statute survive the death of the injured person.

- The action is brought by the victim's estate. This type of action can be brought by the decedent's executor, court-appointed administrator, or other legal representative.
- The action is not a new or an independent action. It is the same action that the victim would have brought had he or she lived.
- The plaintiff in the action is not an heir or a relative of the victim unless the heir or relative happens to be the legal representative of the victim's estate.
- Heirs or relatives do not directly receive any benefit from a damage award in the tort action that survives the victim's death. Any benefit will come to them as beneficiaries of a will or in some other testamentary manner.
- There is no recovery for the death of the victim because the victim's death is unrelated to the tort.
- Any defenses that the defendant would have asserted against the victim had they lived are available to the defendant in the action that survives the victim's death.

Some of the torts that survive the death of the victim or the defendant are discussed next. (See Figure 13.5 for a chart setting out the tort of survival.)

Personal Tort

At common law, torts against a victim did not survive the death of either the victim or the defendant. If the victim died, the lawsuit was not allowed to be brought by the victim's estate or representative. If the defendant died, the action could not be brought against the estate or representative of the defendant.

Most states have passed survival statutes. These statutes do not apply to all torts. In some states, torts such as defamation, invasion of privacy, malicious prosecution, or

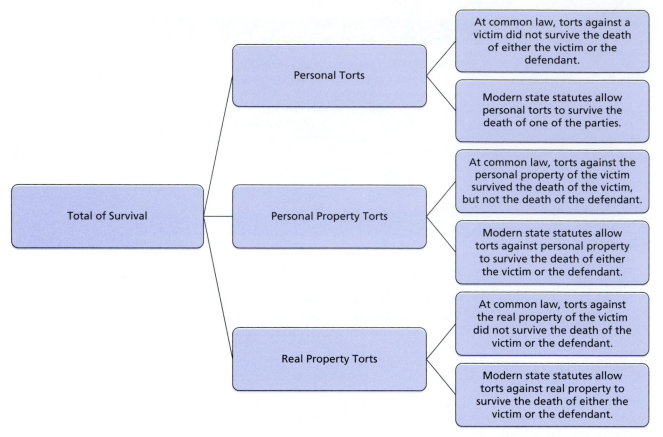

FIGURE 13.5 **Tort of Survival**

similar torts involving invasions of intangible interests do not survive the death of either the victim or the defendant. Other personal torts do survive the death of one of the parties.

Personal Property Tort

At common law, torts against the personal property of the victim survived the death of the victim but did not survive the death of the defendant. In all states today, torts against personal property survive the death of either the victim or the defendant.

Real Property Tort

At common law, torts against the real property of the victim did not survive the death of the victim or the defendant. In all states today, survival statutes have been enacted so that torts against real property survive the death of either the victim or the defendant.

WRONGFUL DEATH TORT

Wrongful death is the tortious death of a victim. At common law, no civil action for the victim's death could be initiated against the wrongdoer. If the victim died as a result of criminal conduct by the defendant, the defendant was prosecuted under criminal law and not civil law. Every state now has a civil statute for wrongful death of a victim.

In most states, the wrongful death of a victim is dealt with as follows:

- The tort action of the victim survives his death and covers damages that accrued up to the moment of the victim's death.

- Damages resulting from the victim's death can be recovered in the same survival action.

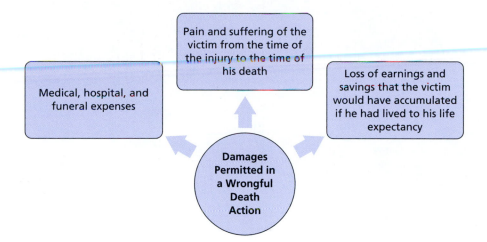

FIGURE 13.6
Damages Permitted in Wrongful Death Action

No new cause of action is generated because of the victim's death. The victim's cause of action is continued through the individual's legal representative. Any defense that would have been available to the defendant in an action had the victim lived will be available after the person's death. The damages that can be sought are:

- Pain and suffering of the victim from the time of the injury to the time of her death.
- Medical, hospital, and funeral expenses.
- Loss of earnings and savings that the victim would have accumulated if she had lived to her life expectancy.

The wrongful death action is brought by a representative of the victim for the benefit of the relatives or beneficiaries. Damages that are recoverable are limited to **pecuniary** losses. This covers the loss of economic value of the support services and contributions that the beneficiaries would have received had the victim lived to his or her life expectancy. See Figure 13.6 for damages permitted in a wrongful death action.

Under most wrongful-death statutes, the defendant can raise any defense she would have had against the victim had he lived.

pecuniary
Consisting of money or that which can be valued in money.

WRONGFUL BIRTH TORT

In addition to wrongful death actions, some states allow **wrongful birth** actions. Wrongful birth actions are medical malpractice claims brought by the parents of a child born with a birth defect. With such claims the parents allege that the physician's negligent advice or treatment deprived them of the opportunity to terminate the pregnancy or prevent the pregnancy from occurring.

In a wrongful birth action, the parents of the child born with birth defects sue for damages. The claim for damages arises out of the expenses of having to raise a child with an unexpected birth defect. Currently, over 20 states recognize the wrongful birth tort. The states that recognize the tort allow parents to recover some or all of the expenses of raising the child, if the parents can show that the physician was negligent.

BUSINESS TORT

A business can be liable for the torts committed by its employees, as was seen with vicarious liability. The following are the types of torts that can occur in the business community. (See Figure 13.7 for types of business torts.)

FIGURE 13.7
Types of Business Torts

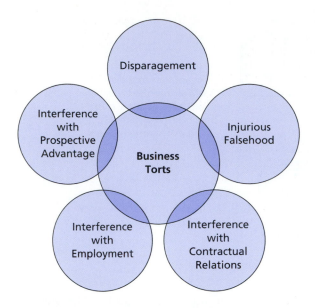

Disparagement

disparagement
A falsehood that tends to denigrate the goods or services of another party.

malign
To speak harmful or detrimental untruths about.

Disparagement is an assault made against the plaintiff's business or property. To establish the tort of disparagement, the plaintiff must first prove that a statement of fact made by the defendant was in fact false. Remember that statements that involve opinion or puffing are not actionable.

The false statement must **malign** the plaintiff's property or business. That is, the statement must throw uncertainty on the plaintiff's title to property or attribute an undesirable quality to goods that could affect the perception of their fitness for sale or other marketable use. Because of the disparaging statement, people choose not to enter into a transaction with the plaintiff or buy his goods. The defendant must intend that the statement be disparaging. A statement is also considered disparaging if people who come to know of it reasonably understand it as being disparaging, even if the defendant did not intend the statement to have a disparaging meaning.

The disparaging statement, like defamation, must be published or communicated to someone other than the plaintiff. It can be communicated intentionally or negligently.

The plaintiff must initially plead and prove special damages in order to recover. It is not enough for the plaintiff to prove that there was a general loss of business following the defendant's disparaging statements; she must show that actual economic harm was suffered. In addition, the plaintiff must demonstrate that because of the disparaging statement, the plaintiff suffered special damages. If it had not been for the defendant's disparaging statement, the plaintiff would not have suffered pecuniary losses.

SURF'S UP

Oprah Winfrey was sued in 1998 by Texas cattlemen for alleging making disparaging statements regarding the consumption of beef. After Winfrey's statements on her television show in 1996, the sales of beef dropped considerably. The Texas cattlemen brought a lawsuit against Winfrey, alleging that economic damages were sustained as a result of the drop in beef sales, which they attributed directly to Winfrey's on-the-air statements. To learn more about this case, go to www.google.com, www.msn.com, www.yahoo.com, or a search engine of your choice and conduct a search of Oprah Winfrey and beef.

Injurious Falsehood

An **injurious falsehood** can consist of a statement of fact that injures someone economically in some other manner than by the disparagement of goods. The plaintiff is only required to demonstrate that the statement was harmful to the interests of the plaintiff.

injurious falsehood
In the law of slander and libel, a defamation that does actual damage.

Interference with Contractual Relationships

The tort of **interference with contractual relationships** involves a situation in which the defendant intentionally interferes with a person or entity with which the plaintiff had contracted. The elements for this tort are:

- A contract must exist.
- An interference with the contract by the defendant.
- Intent.
- Damages.
- Causation.

interference with contractual relationship
The defendant's intentional procuring of a breach of the contract that an entity or person has with the plaintiff so that the plaintiff sustains damages.

The first element is that a contract must exist with which the defendant interferes. The interference can include some of the following:

- Inducing a breach of the contract.
- Inducing one party to terminate the contract even if no breach has occurred.
- Making it impossible for one party to perform the contract.
- Making it more difficult for one party to perform the contract.

The plaintiff must establish that the defendant intended to interfere with the contractual relationship of the plaintiff by inducing a breach or termination or by rendering performance of the contract impossible or burdensome. The defendant must desire this interference or know with substantial certainty that the interference will result from his actions. The negligent conduct of the defendant is not sufficient to establish this tort.

Damages for this tort can include the loss of the contract or the diminished value of its performance. In addition, damage for mental suffering and punitive damages may be recovered. An **injunction** can be sought in order to limit any continuing injuries from which the plaintiff may be suffering. See Figure 13.8 for elements necessary for interference with a contractual relationship.

injunction
A court order that requires a party to refrain from acting in a certain way to prevent harm to the requesting party.

FIGURE 13.8
Elements Necessary
for Interference with
Contractual Relations

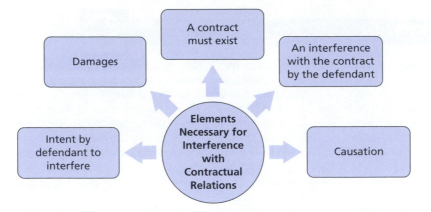

Interference with Prospective Advantage

Interference with prospective advantage is when the defendant interferes with potential or prospective advantages that may have been available to the plaintiff. No false statements of fact need to have been made, and there is no existing contract that was breached. The elements for this tort are:

- A reasonable expectation of an economic advantage.
- Interference with this expectation.
- Intent.
- Damages.
- Causation.

The defendant could have committed other torts that may have led to the interference. In business, this tort is called **unfair competition**.

Individuals have a privilege to protect their business interests by engaging in fair competitive practices but not unfair ones. Deceptive advertising constitutes unfair competition.

unfair competition
A term that is applied generally to all dishonest or fraudulent rivalry in trade and commerce, but is particularly applied to the practice of endeavoring to substitute one's own goods or products in the markets for those of another, having an established reputation and extensive sale, by means of imitating or counterfeiting the name, title, size, shape, or distinctive peculiarities of the product.

 RESEARCH THIS

Unfair competition is prevalent in the music industry, typically coupled with copyright infringement allegations. A particular problem is the smuggling of counterfeit DVDs and CDs into the United States. These counterfeit products are smuggled into the country and then sold at significantly lower prices than the original products. The sales of the original products suffer, and the music and movie industries suffer economic losses. In an effort to encourage other countries to crack down on this illegal production of products, the North American Free Trade Agreement has a provision addressing this issue. Look up this landmark agreement and read the portions concerning unfair competition.

Interference with Employment

Most people are employed in "at-will" states. The term "at will" means that the employee or the employer can terminate the relationship at any time and for any reason. If someone is employed with some type of expressed contract of employment,

---

YOU BE THE JUDGE

Bob accepts a job offer from Perkins College. The college sends Bob a contract stating that he is to work for a period of two years for a salary of $100,000 as a dean of humanities. After a year, the college fires Bob. Bob sues the college for wrongful termination. Will Bob prevail?

he or she cannot be terminated at will. Instead, the person will be employed for a predetermined period of time, and termination of the relationship within this period must comply with the terms of the employment contract. Sometimes an employer terminates an employee in retaliation for the employee's reporting information to the proper authorities; that is, whistle-blowing. This type of retaliatory termination is considered wrongful. A plaintiff **(whistle-blower)** who finds herself in this situation can attempt to establish the tort of tortious interference with employment.

Summary

Malpractice in general involves a standard of care from someone who has superior ability or knowledge. As such, people who possess such superior ability or knowledge are held to a higher standard of care than those who do not.

A doctor is not required to accept every patient that walks through her door. She can reject patients. Moreover, the physician–patient relationship does not come into existence just because the doctor has provided emergency medical care to an injured person. The relationship needs to be created out of the potential patient's express or implied request for medical services and the acceptance of that request by the doctor.

Typically, a doctor will not promise a particular result or cure. If such a promise is given by the doctor, then a breach-of-warranty or breach-of-contract action against the doctor can be brought if the patient does not become cured as promised. If a doctor uses language that could be construed as having rendered a promise concerning treatment, and the patient is not cured, the patient could bring a breach-of-contract action against the doctor even though the doctor was not negligent when performing the services. An opinion by a doctor regarding the possible results of treatment does not constitute a promise or guarantee.

Negligence does not attach because the wrong selection of treatment is made or because other doctors have used different methods of treatment. As long as the doctor is diligent and used good judgment, liability will not attach because the approach to the patient's health problem was different from the approach someone else might have used.

As is true with a doctor, liability for an attorney will not be established just because the attorney makes a mistake or loses a case. Unless the attorney specifically guarantees a result to a client, the standard of care used in a malpractice case will be reasonableness. The American Bar Association states in its model code that when an attorney engages in the practice of law and, by agreement, decides to pursue a case on behalf of a client, the attorney implies that the attorney possesses the requisite degree of learning, skill, and ability necessary to practice his profession and which other similarly situated attorneys ordinarily possess; the attorney will exert his best judgment in the prosecution of the case entrusted to him; and the attorney will exercise reasonable and ordinary care and diligence in the use of his skill and in the application of his knowledge to the client's case.

Survival is similar to inheriting a tort action. The tort of survival deals with the situation of whether or not a tort action can survive the unconnected death of either the victim or the defendant.

Wrongful death is the tortious death of a victim. At common law, no civil action for the victim's death could be initiated against the wrongdoer. If the victim died as a result of criminal conduct by the defendant, the defendant was prosecuted under criminal law and not civil law. Every state now has a civil statute for wrongful death of a victim.

Disparagement is an assault made against the business or property of the plaintiff. In order to establish the tort of disparagement, the plaintiff must first prove that a statement of fact made by the defendant was in fact false. Remember that statements that involve opinion or puffing are not actionable.

The false statement must malign the plaintiff's property or business. The statement must throw uncertainty on the plaintiff's title to property or attribute an undesirable quality to goods that could affect the perception of their fitness for sale or other marketable use. Because of the disparaging statement, people choose not to enter into a transaction with the plaintiff or buy his or her goods. The defendant must intend that the statement be disparaging. A statement is also considered disparaging if people who come to know of it reasonably understand it as being disparaging, even if the defendant did not intend the statement to have a disparaging meaning.

An injurious falsehood can consist of a statement of fact that injures someone economically in some other manner than by the disparagement of goods. The plaintiff is only required to demonstrate that the statement was harmful to the interests of the plaintiff.

The tort of interference with contractual relations involves a situation in which the defendant intentionally interferes with a person or entity with which the plaintiff had contracted.

Interference with prospective advantage is when the defendant interferes with potential or prospective advantages that may have been available to the plaintiff. No false statements of fact need to have been made, and there is no existing contract that was breached.

Most people are employed in "at-will" states. The term "at will" means that the employee or the employer can terminate the relationship at any time and for any reason. If individuals are employed with some type of expressed contract of employment, they cannot be terminated at will. Instead, the person will be employed for a predetermined period of time, and termination of the relationship within this period must comply with the terms of the employment contract. Sometimes, an employer terminates an employee in retaliation for the employee's reporting information to the proper authorities; that is, whistle-blowing. This type of retaliatory termination is considered wrongful. Plaintiffs who find themselves in this situation can attempt to establish the tort of tortious interference with employment.

Key Terms

Attorney-client relationship	Malign
Disparagement	Malpractice
Injunction	Pecuniary
Injurious falsehood	Survival
Interference with contractual relationship	Unfair competition
	Whistle-blower

Review Questions

1. What is malpractice?
2. When does the physician–patient relationship begin?
3. What does the patient have to request?
4. What standard of care is a doctor held to?
5. Define the national standard as it applies to doctors.
6. Define the local standard as it applies to doctors.
7. List the elements that are required of an attorney.
8. What are three reasons that attorneys commit malpractice?
9. Define unfair competition.
10. Give an example of at-will employment.

1. Go to the Internet and look up the website for your local state bar association. Find an article on legal malpractice. Prepare a brief of the article to present to the class on the issues that surrounded the legal malpractice in the article.

2. Suppose a psychiatrist has been treating a patient for over a year. The patient has a wide variety of psychological issues. One of these issues is that the patient is violent and often hostile. The patient tells the psychiatrist that he intends to kill his former girlfriend. Would it be a violation of privilege for the psychiatrist to warn others about the patient's threat? For a legal discussion regarding this situation, see *Tarasoff v. Regents of University of California,* 17 Cal.3d 425.

3. Assume the same facts as above, except that the psychiatrist in the hypothetical case does not warn the former girlfriend or the proper authorities about the patient's threats. The patient does in fact kill his former girlfriend. What causes of action may the family of the victim bring against the patient? Against the psychiatrist?

4. Thomas has been involved in an auto accident. He was severely injured when his car was stuck by a truck driven by Pat, who ran a red light and collided with Thomas's vehicle. Thomas hires Attorney to bring suit against Pat. The statute of limitations for such causes of action is two years in Thomas's state. The attorney unexpectedly receives more clients and cases than he anticipated. As a result he forgets to file Thomas's lawsuit before the statute of limitations expires. If Thomas brings a malpractice suit against Attorney, what does Thomas need to show in order to be successful?

5. Saleco has a valid contract with Buyco to sell various household furnishings to Buyco. Saleco spent time and money seeking out Buyco's business. After the contract between the two parties was signed, Supply Inc. contacted Buyco and informed the company that Supply Inc. could sell to Buyco the same furnishings as Saleco for a lower price, and that Saleco was known in the industry for always being late with its deliveries. Buyco now seeks to get a lower price from Saleco. If Saleco sues Supply Inc. for interference with contractual relations, what does it need to prove in order to be successful?

 PORTFOLIO ASSIGNMENT

Research the following online. What are the wrongful death statutes in your state? Does your state currently allow recovery for a wrongful birth action? Keep a list of the statutes in your portfolio.

Vocabulary Builders

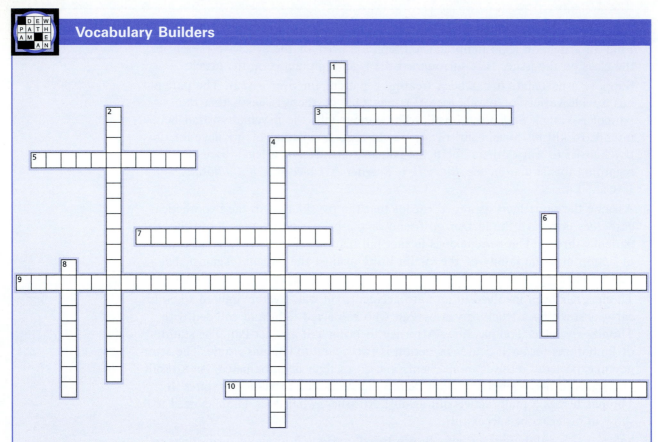

Instructions

Use the key terms from this chapter to fill in the answers to the crossword puzzle.

NOTE: When the answer is more than one word, leave a blank space between words.

ACROSS

3. A falsehood that tends to denigrate the goods or services of another party.
4. A court order that requires a party to refrain from acting in a certain way to prevent harm to the requesting party.
5. Failure of a professional person, as a physician or lawyer, to render proper services through reprehensible ignorance or negligence, especially when injury or loss follows.
7. One who reveals wrongdoing within an organization to the public or to those in positions of authority.
9. The defendant's intentional procuring of a breach of the contract that an entity or person has with the plaintiff so that the plaintiff sustains damages.
10. Attorneys have a duty to maintain a client's confidences regarding any information that the client wants kept confidential.

DOWN

1. To speak harmful or detrimental untruths about.
2. A term that is applied generally to all dishonest or fraudulent rivalry in trade and commerce, but is particularly applied to the practice of endeavoring to substitute one's own goods or products in the markets for those of another, having an established reputation and extensive sale, by means of imitating or counterfeiting the name, title, size, shape, or distinctive peculiarities of the product.
4. In the law of slander and libel, a defamation that does actual damage.
6. Actions for personal injuries that by state statute survive the death of the injured person.
8. Consisting of money or that which can be valued in money.

Supreme Court of Idaho, Twin Falls, November 2005 Term

Frank C. NEWBERRY, Plaintiff-Respondent, v. Laurence L. MARTENS, M.D., Defendant-Appellant,
and Twin Falls Clinic and Hospital, and John Doe and Jane Doe, husband and wife, I through X,
and Business Entities I through X, Defendants

127 P.3d 187

No. 30967

Dec. 30, 2005

I. FACTUAL AND PROCEDURAL BACKGROUND

One night while repairing an automobile, Newberry, who was hammering metal on metal, felt something strike his right eye. Newberry immediately felt a burning sensation and saw spots in his field of vision. He was driven to an emergency room in Twin Falls where Dr. Martens, a family practice physician, was on duty. Dr. Martens examined Newberry's eye, but was unable to locate any foreign matter. Dr. Martens determined that most likely an object struck Newberry's eye, causing a superficial laceration, but deflected away without penetrating. Dr. Martens prescribed Newberry antibiotics and sent him home with instructions to return the next day.

When Newberry returned the following day, Dr. Martens again examined his eye. Newberry reported that the spots in his vision remained but that the burning sensation was less severe. Seeing nothing of concern, Dr. Martens again sent Newberry home.

The day after this second visit, Newberry experienced extreme pain in his eye and increasing disturbances of his vision. Later that day, he lost all vision in his right eye. Newberry sought medical treatment from Dr. David Leach (Dr. Leach) an ophthalmologist. Dr. Leach located a small piece of metal deep in Newberry's eye, and sent Newberry to Salt Lake City for specialized treatment not available in Twin Falls. Doctors performed surgery on Newberry's eye, but were unable to return his vision. It was later determined that Newberry lost his eyesight due to the introduction of a virulent bacteria known as Bacillus-Cereus along with the metal shard.

Newberry sued Dr. Martens and the Twin Falls Clinic and Hospital for medical negligence and other related claims. Twin Falls Clinic and Hospital was dismissed by stipulation, but Newberry and Dr. Martens proceeded to trial. At trial, Dr. Martens objected to two jury instructions discussing proximate cause, and he also objected to the admission of expert testimony presented by Dr. Leach suggesting that Dr. Martens breached the applicable standard of care for a health care provider. After an eight-day trial, a jury returned a verdict in favor of Newberry and awarded him $250,000 in economic damages and $500,000 in non-economic damages. Following post-trial motions, the district court adjusted the economic damages from $250,000 down to $39,843.05, resulting in a total judgment of $539,843.05. Dr. Martens filed a timely appeal from that judgment which is now before this Court.

[Text omitted]

ANALYSIS

[Text omitted]

A. JURY INSTRUCTIONS

It is Dr. Martens' position that two jury instructions in particular were in error. At trial, these instructions were numbered 10 and 11, and both dealt with proximate cause. The instructions at issue were not identical to the standard pattern jury instructions, but a court may diverge from those instructions if a "different instruction would more adequately, accurately or clearly state the law." I.R.C.P. 51(a)(2). Instruction number 10 stated:

> When I use the expression "proximate cause," I mean a cause which, in natural or probable sequence, produced the damage complained of. It need not be the only cause. It is sufficient if it is a substantial factor concurring with some other cause acting at the same time, which in combination with it, causes the damage.

Instruction number 11 read:

> A cause can be a substantial contributing cause even though the injury, damage or loss would likely have occurred anyway without that contributing cause. A substantial cause need not be the sole factor, or even the primary factor in causing the plaintiff's injuries, but merely a substantial factor therein.

From Dr. Martens' perspective, the problem with these instructions is that they permitted the jury to assign liability if the plaintiff met the "substantial factor" test, rather than the arguably stricter "but for" test. . . .

At trial, Dr. Martens advanced as his theory of the case that he was not liable for Newberry's loss because Newberry would have lost his eye even without Dr. Martens' negligence. In sum, Dr. Martens argued to the jury that his alleged negligence was not a "but for" cause of Newberry's injury. Dr. Martens contends the district court erred in permitting the jury to assign liability based on the substantial factor test and that so instructing the jury precluded it from considering his theory of the case. Additionally, Dr. Martens argues the "but for" test is properly used in place of the "substantial factor" test in cases such as this where there is only one allegedly negligent cause of the plaintiff's injury.

In discussing proximate cause, it should first be noted that it contains two components. First there is actual cause, and second there is true proximate cause, sometimes known as "legal cause." Actual cause is the factual question of whether a particular event produced a particular consequence. True proximate cause "focuses upon legal policy in terms of whether responsibility will be extended to the consequences of conduct which has occurred." . . .

Under Idaho law, in a medical malpractice action where there is evidence of two or more possible causes of the plaintiff's injury, rather than using the "but for" test the jury must be instructed that the doctor's negligence "was a proximate cause of the injury if it was a substantial factor in bringing about the damage." *Fussell v. St. Clair,* 120 Idaho 591, 591, 818 P.2d 295, 295 (1991). This Court has "specifically reject[ed]" the inclusion of the "but for" test where more than one cause could have brought about the injury. "The but for instruction and the substantial factor instruction are mutually exclusive." *Le'Gall v. Lewis County,* 129 Idaho 182, 187, 923 P.2d 427, 432 (1996). . . .

In *Fussell,* the plaintiffs were the parents of a child who suffered brain damage as the result of a difficult birth. At trial, the parties presented evidence of two possible causes of the baby's injury: the parents indicated the harm was caused by the defendant doctor's negligence, and the doctor argued that the injury resulted from a prolapsed umbilical cord that occurred naturally and without negligence on anyone's part. The trial court in *Fussell* gave instructions to the jury that included the "but for" test, but because there were multiple possible causes of the baby's injury, this Court determined that instructing the jury on the "but for" test under those circumstances was reversible error.

In this case the district court determined that as in *Fussell,* more than one cause was advanced at trial as a possible cause of the Plaintiff's damages. At trial, Newberry stressed as possible causes Dr. Martens' negligence in failing to locate the metal shard and to refer Newberry to a specialist. Dr. Martens stressed causes unrelated to his alleged negligence, such as the presence of the Bacillus-Cereus bacteria. . . .

Instruction number 10 was taken from standard pattern jury instruction 2.30.2 but omitted the following language: "It is not a proximate cause if the injury, loss or damage likely would have occurred anyway." The district court explained this omission by pointing out that the excluded language was, in substance, simply a rephrasing of the "but for" test and therefore inappropriate in a multiple cause case. . . .

Faced with the rule in *Fussell,* Dr. Martens first attempts to distinguish that case by arguing that unlike in *Fussell,* here there was only one possible cause of Newberry's injury—the bacteria. The difficulty with that argument is it simply ignores evidence presented by Newberry that Dr. Martens' negligence contributed to the injury. . . . Dr. Martens cannot simultaneously point to a second cause, independent of his negligence, and at the same time maintain that this is a single cause case.

Dr. Martens next asserts that by instructing the jury on the "substantial factor" test rather than the "but for" test, the district court wrongly precluded him from arguing his theory of the case—that absent Dr. Martens' negligence Newberry was nevertheless likely to have lost sight in the affected eye. This is incorrect. Nothing prevented Dr. Martens from presenting his factual assertion that Newberry would likely have lost his sight even if there had been no negligence and that medical negligence was not a substantial factor in causing the lost eyesight. What the trial court refused to do was instruct the jury on the "but for" test as Dr. Martens urged. Although Dr. Martens correctly points out that the trial court must "instruct the jury on every reasonable theory recognized by law that is supported at trial," *Everton v. Blair,*

99 Idaho 14, 16, 576 P.2d 585, 587 (1978), in multiple cause cases instruction on the "but for" test is not "recognized by law" and consequently Dr. Martens is not entitled to such an instruction. *Le'Gall,* 129 Idaho at 186–87, 923 P.2d at 431–32. . . .

Dr. Martens next contends that even if there are multiple possible causes, the *Fussell* rule does not apply unless there are multiple defendants and multiple potential acts of negligence. Non-negligent causes, Dr. Martens argues, are not causes at all for the purpose of determining whether a case is a single or multiple cause case. . . . In *Fussell,* this Court determined the possible causes of the baby's injury were (1) the doctor's negligence, and (2) a naturally occurring prolapsed umbilical cord not attributable to the doctor's negligence. The prolapsed umbilical cord was the "second" cause that rendered *Fussell* a multiple cause case, even though the problem with the umbilical cord was not the result of negligence and even though the doctor was the only defendant. . . .

Dr. Martens also argues that there is language in *Fussell* requiring Idaho courts to use the "but for" test in cases where there is only one defendant and only one cause resulting from negligence. For this proposition, Dr. Martens quotes the following language from *Fussell*:

> Although the evidence presented by the Fussells indicated that Dr. St. Clair's negligence was the sole cause of the brain damage and death of the child, the evidence submitted by Dr. St. Clair indicated that there was a cause for which Dr. St. Clair was not responsible—an occult (hidden) prolapsed umbilical cord. Dr. St. Clair's evidence would have supported a finding by the jury that the prolapsed umbilical cord occurred without any negligence of the doctor. If the jury had accepted this evidence and yet had found that Dr. St. Clair was negligent in responding to the prolapsed cord when it was discovered, the jury might have been misled by the proximate cause instruction given by the trial court. . . .

When placed in context, the meaning of those words from *Fussell* is roughly the opposite of the meaning given to them by Dr. Martens. It should be remembered that the potentially misleading proximate cause instruction at issue in *Fussell* was the "but for" test now advocated by Dr. Martens. When this Court in *Fussell* wrote that "[t]he jury might have concluded that the doctor's negligence could not have been a proximate cause because even if the doctor had not been negligent, the brain damage and death of the child would have occurred," the Court was not, as Dr. Martens appears to suggest, promoting such reasoning as exemplary in multiple cause cases.

Finally, Dr. Martens directs our attention to a pair of policy arguments. The first of these contends that if the existence of a non-negligent possible cause alongside an allegedly negligent possible cause requires instruction on the "substantial factor" test in place of the "but for test," use of the "but for" test would be largely extinguished in medical negligence cases. This, Dr. Martens continues, is because in such cases a non-negligent possible cause can often be found in the underlying physical problem that first brought the plaintiff to seek medical attention. . . .

Dr. Martens is correct to observe that the rule in *Fussell* and *Manning* is apt to apply to medical negligence cases in many instances. The subtext of Dr. Martens' argument is that such an outcome—the widespread use of the substantial factor test in medical negligence cases—is unthinkable. It is not unthinkable, and as *Fussell* and *Manning* make clear, it has already been the rule for many years where the trial court is presented with evidence of multiple possible causes.

The second policy argument introduced by Dr. Martens contends that rejecting the "but for" test in cases where there is only a single potentially negligent defendant does not serve any valid policy objective. The reason many courts have rejected the "but for" instruction in multiple cause cases, continues Dr. Martens, is to prevent multiple potentially negligent defendants from each escaping liability by assigning blame to each other. Rejecting the "but for" test in a case lacking multiple defendants, Dr. Martens argues, is applying a solution where no problem exists.

Dr. Martens' argument on this point is a cogent one, but there exists at least one policy argument supporting the use of the substantial factor test cases involving multiple causes but only one potentially negligent defendant. The facts of the instant case present a classic "lost chance" scenario. In some other jurisdictions, Newberry would be permitted to advance the theory that even if it were likely he would have lost sight in the affected eye absent Dr. Martens negligence, that negligence robbed Newberry of whatever chance he had for timely, effective treatment. Idaho, however, has declined to adopt the doctrine of "lost chance."

We see then that this Court, when it rejected the lost chance doctrine, did so based on its confidence that the use of the substantial factor test in such circumstances "strikes a fair balance between the claimant and the defense." Here, Dr. Martens proposes that whatever hope Newberry had to recover under the substantial factor test be taken away as well. Doing so would be contrary to this Court's stated intention in *Manning* to employ the substantial factor test in place of the "but for" test in cases such as this in order to provide a fair balance between claimants and defendants. . . .

We consequently affirm their use under the facts presented.

B. ADMISSION OF TESTIMONY ESTABLISHING THE STANDARD OF CARE

Dr. Martens contends the district court erred in permitting Newberry's expert, Dr. Leach, to present testimony that Dr. Martens' conduct breached the applicable standard of care. Since Dr. Martens contends that Dr. Leach's testimony should not have been accepted, Dr. Martens argues that the case Newberry presented at trial was fatally deficient and the verdict should therefore be reversed.

[Text omitted]

Under Idaho law, the plaintiff in a medical malpractice case must offer expert testimony indicating the applicable standard of care was breached by the defendant health care provider. I.C. § 6-1013. . . . Idaho law defines the applicable standard of care as:

> (a) the standard of care for the class of health care provider to which the defendant belonged and was functioning, taking into account the defendant's training, experience, and fields of medical specialization, if any; (b) as such standard existed at the time of the defendant's alleged negligence; and (c) as such standard existed at the place of the defendant's alleged negligence.

Dr. Leach practiced in the same community, Twin Falls, and at the same time as the events that gave rise to this action. Dr. Leach is an ophthalmologist, whereas Dr. Martens is a family practice physician. Dr. Martens does not contend that Dr. Leach was unqualified to offer an opinion because they belong to different specialties—Dr. Martens correctly concedes that it is unnecessary for an expert witness to be of the same specialty as the defendant so long as the expert establishes he possesses actual knowledge of the standard of care to be applied. *See Clarke v. Prenger,* 114 Idaho 766, 769, 760 P.2d 1182, 1185 (1988).

Instead, Dr. Martens argues that Dr. Leach lacked actual knowledge of the standard of care applicable to family practice physicians because Dr. Leach did not testify that he explicitly asked a family practice physician what the standard of care was in Twin Falls. At trial, Dr. Leach testified that he learned the standard of care by practicing alongside family practice physicians in Twin Falls, by providing and obtaining referrals, and by discussing patient care with them. Dr. Martens contends that these interactions with family practice physicians were not enough to provide Dr. Leach with the statutorily required "actual knowledge" of the applicable standard of care.

It is necessary for an expert testifying as to the standard of care to "state how he or she became familiar with that standard of care." *Dulaney,* 137 Idaho at 164, 45 P.3d at 820. Inquiring with a local specialist is "[o]ne method" an expert witness may obtain such knowledge, but it is not the only method. Idaho Code § 6-1013 requires that an expert witness must possess "actual knowledge" of the standard of care, but contrary to Dr. Martens' suggestion it does not dictate that such actual knowledge must in all cases be obtained by explicitly asking a specialist in the relevant field to explain the local standard of care.

When reviewing a trial court's ruling under the abuse of discretion standard, we inquire (1) whether the trial court correctly perceived the issue as one of discretion; (2) whether the trial court acted within the outer boundaries of its discretion and consistently with the legal standards applicable to the specific choices available to it; and (3) whether the trial court reached its decision by an exercise of reason. *Sun Valley Shopping Ctr., Inc., v. Idaho Power Co.,* 119 Idaho 87, 94, 803 P.2d 993, 1000 (1991). When ruling that Dr. Leach's testimony was admissible, the district court stated its determination was an exercise of discretion. The district court used reason and acted within the boundaries of its discretion when ruling that Dr. Leach's professional interactions with family practice physicians in the Twin Falls area at the time of the events giving rise to the present suit provided Dr. Leach with the requisite actual knowledge of the applicable standard of care. We therefore affirm the district court's ruling admitting the expert testimony of Dr. Leach.

[Text omitted]

III. CONCLUSION

This Court affirms the judgment entered by the district court in all respects. Costs, but not attorney fees on appeal, are awarded to Newberry.

[Footnotes omitted]

Source: Used with permission from Westlaw. Frank C. NEWBERRY v. Laurence L. MARTENS, M.D. and Twin Falls Clinic and Hospital, and John Doe and Jane Doe, husband and wife, I through X, and Business Entities I through X, 127 P.3d 187.

Chapter 14

Immunity from Tort Liability

CHAPTER OBJECTIVES

Upon completion of this chapter, you will be able to:

- Define the principle of immunity from tort liability.
- Understand family immunity.
- Discuss the defense of charitable immunity.
- Identify sovereign immunity.
- Understand immunity for public officers.

immunity
Exemption, as from serving in an office, or performing duties that the law generally requires other citizens to perform.

Sometimes, a defendant can be immune from tort liability. For public policy or social interest reasons, under certain circumstances, a defendant can invoke a defense of immunity. In previous discussions, defendants have been able to use an excuse or a justification of their conduct as an excuse from liability. By invoking a defense of **immunity**, defendants do not have to justify or excuse their behavior. Liability does not attach to defendants who can claim immunity.

PUBLIC POLICY

Immunity is a defense to tort liability. People who claim immunity typically fall into a certain category or class. In order to claim immunity as a defense, the defendant usually falls under one of the following categories:

- Immunity is derived from the defendant's relationship with the plaintiff.
- Immunity is derived from the nature of the defendant's occupation.
- Immunity is derived from the defendant's status as a governmental or charitable entity.

Immunity enables individuals to be free of liability because they fall into one of the preceding categories and provides an absolute defense against actions brought under negligence or intentional tort theories. Courts and legislatures try to balance the interests of a plaintiff against the cost to the state. The trend in recent times is to preserve the interest of the plaintiff and let the public bear the burden of cost.

EYE ON ETHICS

As has been discussed many times throughout this text, each state possesses its own immunity laws. Individual states must be researched to establish the extent and conditions on which immunity is applied in that jurisdiction. Suffice it to say that there is wide divergence among the states regarding who is immune and the limit in the scope of the doctrine. It is always important to check your own state's codes and case law to determine the proper parameters and scope of the law in that jurisdiction.

FAMILY IMMUNITY

Family immunity is a concept that involves the premises that family members should have certain rights and protection from other family members. The driving force behind family immunity is the desire to foster better relationships between family members, and to avoid situations where family members bring suit against one another. Under common law, family immunity was delineated into two categories: interspousal immunity and parent–child immunity.

Interspousal Immunity

At common law, married couples were considered under the law as one person. Under that premise, it did not make sense for a husband or wife to bring a tort action against the other because they were legally considered to be one person. At that period in time, the husband was the primary spouse in the relationship. The wife was not allowed to own property or enter into contracts. In the late nineteenth century, the Married Women's Acts were passed, giving women the right to own property and be considered their own legal entities.

The Married Women's Acts arose in response to demands for economic and social change. Prior to the passage of these acts, unmarried women who owned property lost such ownership rights upon marriage. From a legal perspective, ownership of the property was assigned to the husband. Rights to the women's property included both personal and real property. As a result, the husband was allowed to sell, trade, or gift away any property the wife owned before marriage. Upon death, the husband was allowed to dispose of the property through his will. Such inequalities resulted in demand for change. Among the various social and legal advancements enacted on behalf of women in the late nineteenth Century, the Married Women's Acts were among the most important.

The passage of these acts also changed the immunity that husbands previously held against suit from their wives. As mentioned, upon marriage, a husband and wife were considered one person for legal purposes, disallowing a wife to sue her husband. However, as a result of the Married Women's Acts, women were now allowed to bring suits against their husbands concerning property interests.

The *Restatement (Second) of Torts,* section 895F, speaks to the doctrine of interspousal immunity as follows:

1. *A husband or wife is not immune from tort liability to the other solely by reason of that relationship.*

2. *Repudiation of general tort immunity does not establish liability for an act or omission that, because of the marital relationship, is otherwise privileged or is not tortious.*

Interspousal immunity used to exist with regard to personal injury lawsuits. A wife who was a passenger in a car that was driven negligently by her husband could not sue her husband if she was injured as a result of his negligence. A battered wife could not sue her husband for her injuries as a result of the battery. The inequality and social demand for change led to most states abolishing the immunity altogether.

SPOT THE ISSUE

Tom and his wife, Jamie, have been married for five years. When the couple first moved in together, Tom was neat and conscious of picking up after himself. However, as time has gone on, he has become more and more careless. Tom often leaves his tools lying around the house. One day, after doing some work around the house, Tom failed to put away his tools. Jamie was not paying attention and banged her foot on a hammer he left out. As a result of the accident, Jamie has broken two toes in her foot. If she brings suit against Tom in a state that has abolished interspousal immunity, will she succeed?

Most states have completely abolished interspousal immunity even in personal injury actions. With that abolition, however, the courts recognized that there are instances in which spouses should not be allowed to sue the other. For example, Jen and Mark are married. Both spouses are slobs. Mark leaves his clothes all over the floor, and Jen throws her shoes behind doors. One day, Jen trips over Mark's clothes and breaks her ankle. In a situation such as this, the courts will not permit Jen to sue Mark for personal injuries. Courts have recognized the need to protect spouses from certain harms or injuries that result from actions of their spouse. Injuries sustained by one spouse that are caused by innocent or harmless actions of the other spouse often are viewed as being immune from suit. The recognition of immunity from suit between spouses is not all encompassing, however. A spouse may bring suit against the other spouse in certain circumstances. For example, if one spouse contracts a venereal disease, then she may sue her spouse for the injury. Immunity from suit is largely dictated by the nature of the spouse's acts toward the other. Generally immunity will apply when one spouse has not intended to hurt the other, or has acted in a way not meant to be offensive to the other. Immunity will not attach, however, when the injury or harm to the spouse has resulted from bad faith or destructive actions by the other.

The rules and policy relating to interspousal immunity have been largely shaped by the court seeking to protect marriage. Immunity seeks to minimize unnecessary friction and turmoil between spouses. Permitting a spouse to sue for all harmless actions of the other spouse would potentially cause excessive friction in marriages.

Spousal Privilege

spousal privilege
Combination of two elements: (1) the right not to be compelled to testify against one's spouse, and (2) the protection of marital confidences.

In addition to immunity from suit in selected situations, spouses also are entitled to certain privileges. Like interspousal immunity, **spousal privileges** are recognized as necessary to promote better marriages. Open communication between spouses during a marriage is essential to a healthy marriage. Spousal privilege rules ensure that spouses may speak freely and openly with their respective spouse without fear that such communications may later be used against them. Spousal privilege, in the United States, comprises two separate privileges, the marital confidences privilege and the spousal testimonial privilege.

The *marital confidences privilege* protects confidential communications between a husband and a wife. The privilege applies to both criminal and civil proceedings. When applied, the court may not force one spouse to testify against the other concerning confidential communications made during marriage. The privilege attaches to the parties upon marriage and remains until the death of one of the spouses. In most instances, the privilege attaches even after divorce; however, communications conducted after divorce are no longer privileged.

FIGURE 14.1
Spousal Privilege

	Holder of the Privilege	Function of the Privilege	Exceptions
Marital Confidences Privilege	• Held by both husband and wife.	• Prevents a spouse from testifying about a confidential marital communication, made during the marriage.	• Does not apply to communications involving crimes against the other spouse or crimes against the children of either.
Spousal Testimonial Privilege	• Held by both husband and wife. • Many modern rules give the privilege to the witness spouse only.	• A criminal defendant could keep spouse from testifying against him or her in a criminal case. • Currently, most hold that only the witness spouse may refuse to testify.	• Privilege does not survive after divorce. • Currently, witness spouses may testify if they so desire.

Generally, for a communication to be considered privileged, it must not have been uttered in the presence of a third person, and the parties intended the communication to be confidential. At common law, if an **eavesdropper** or some third person intercepted the communication, he or she could testify to it. Most state statutes have eliminated a third person from testifying to the communication, if the husband and wife did not know of the person's presence and held a reasonable belief that the communication was confidential. Communications made to an attorney in the presence of the spouse are considered privileged under the attorney–client privilege, and not subject to being revealed.

Either spouse may invoke this privilege by either refusing to testify, or by preventing the other from testifying. The privilege does not apply, however, to communications involving crimes against the other spouse or crimes against the children of either. The spouse who made the communication may waive the privilege.

Spousal testimonial privilege can be used to prevent any party in a criminal case from calling the defendant's spouse to testify against the defendant about any topic. Under the former laws of most states, a criminal defendant had a privilege to keep his or her spouse from testifying against him or her in a criminal case. Although some states still retain this rule, most modern statutes and the **Federal Rules of Evidence** hold that the privilege belongs to the witness spouse instead of the defendant spouse. Witness spouses may choose to testify if they so desire. Unlike martial communications, spousal testimonial privilege does not survive after divorce. As such, there is no right to refuse to testify against a defendant ex-spouse. See Figure 14.1 for a chart on spousal privilege.

eavesdropper
A secret listener to private conversations.

Federal Rules of Evidence
Rules governing the introduction of evidence in proceedings, both civil and criminal, in federal courts. While they do not apply to suits in state courts, the rules of many states have been closely modeled after these rules.

RESEARCH THIS

The case of *Trammel v. United States*, 445 U.S. 40 (1980) is the landmark decision that established the witness spouse as holding the privilege. Locate the case online. What policy reasons does the court offer to support its ruling?

FIGURE 14.2
Family Immunity

	Holder of the Privilege	Function of the Privilege	Exceptions
Interspousal Immunity	• Held by married couple. • Held by both husband and wife.	• Abolished traditional notion that man and wife were one legal entity. • Spouse is no longer considered immune from torts against the other spouse.	• Torts resulting from innocent nonmalicious acts of the other spouse.
Parent–Child Immunity	• Held by parents and children.	• Privilege barred suit by parent or child against the other.	• Many states have eliminated the privilege, except for allowing suit regarding food and care for the child.

Parent and Child

In the United States, immunity developed between parents and children that led to a bar on legal actions between parents and children. However, many states have abolished this immunity except as it relates to providing food and care by a parent for a child and parental control of children. The *Restatement (Second) of Torts,* section 895G, states the fact that parent and child relationships are not immune from tort liability:

1. *A parent or child is not immune from tort liability to the other solely by reason of that relationship.*

2. *Repudiation of general tort immunity does not establish liability for an act or omission that, because of the parent-child relationship, is otherwise privileged or is not tortious.*

See Figure 14.2 for interspousal immunity and parent-child immunity.

CASE FACT PATTERN

Attorney Jones, a sole practitioner, is retained to represent Joe Johnson in a suit. Mr. Johnson brings a civil suit after he is involved in a traffic accident. Mr. and Mrs. Johnson are both present at a meeting with Attorney Jones. During this meeting, Mr. Johnson makes a number of statements to Attorney Jones regarding Mrs. Johnson. At a divorce proceeding between the Johnsons a few months later, Mrs. Johnson seeks to have Attorney Jones testify as to the communications made during the meeting. Mrs. Johnson correctly asserts that the communications are not privileged because the comments involve a crime perpetrated against her by Mr. Johnson. Although Attorney Jones knows that Mr. Johnson is lying about not making the comments in the meeting, he may not testify as to whether or not the comments were made. The attorney–client privilege would prevent Attorney Jones from testifying, regardless of the applicability of any spousal privileges.

A DAY IN THE LIFE OF A REAL PARALEGAL

The courts did not examine the issue of parent–child immunity until the case of *Hewellette v. George,* 68 Miss. 703, 9 So. 885 (1881). In that case, the court examined the case of a child bringing an action against the parent for false imprisonment. Your supervising attorney has asked you to look up this case and determine why the court refused to allow the child to bring a claim for personal injuries against the parents.

CHARITABLE IMMUNITY

At common law, **charitable organizations** received immunity from tort liability. The following three principal reasons existed for providing charitable organizations with immunity:

charitable organization
An organization that provides charity without obtaining a profit or gain for itself or its owners.

- Donations to charitable organizations would be curtailed if immunity was not available to organizations.

- Respondeat superior did not apply to charitable organizations.

- The beneficiary of the charity has, by his conduct, waived his right to sue in tort due to the fact that he had accepted charity.

Charities were granted immunity from tort liability to ensure charities were not using their donations to defend from constant suit for civil actions. Additionally, many advocates of charitable immunity are convinced that eliminating charitable immunity would curtail donations to charitable organizations. They reason that if donations are used to defend against a suit, rather than promote the charitable purpose, society's desire to donate will be greatly diminished. For example, imagine if one-half of all the Red Cross's donations were spent on legal fees and civil liability settlements. The number of donations and the volume of donations would likely significantly decrease. Charitable immunity acts recognize that donations are made to a charity with the implied belief that the donation is going to be used to further the charity's goal.

Under traditional charitable immunity acts, a charity's liability to a third person for an employee's tortious acts was eliminated. As discussed previously, employers are said to be responsible for the acts of their employees under the doctrine of respondeat superior. Respondeat superior holds that an employer is just as liable for an injury to a third person as the employee responsible for committing the act, if the act was committed within the course and scope of the employee's employment. Charitable immunity relieved the charitable entity from being held liable for the actions of its employees.

Charitable immunity also provided that volunteers of the charity were granted immunity from civil liability. Volunteers would usually be persons who did not receive compensation for their services beyond reimbursement for expenses incurred in volunteering for the organization. The immunity would often be attached to a person serving as a director, officer, trustee, or direct service volunteer. Allowing volunteers to enjoy immunity from suit was intended to reduce the liability exposure of such individuals. Thus, to promote charitable volunteering, and ensure a steady flow of volunteers, charitable immunity acts were enacted.

The immunity enjoyed by volunteers is limited to acts that are done in the scope and course of their duties and function in charity. As such, a charitable volunteer will not enjoy immunity from suit if the act was carried out for a purpose outside the course and scope of the charity. Moreover, immunity does not apply to acts that are willful or negligent, or acts that are done with conscious indifference or reckless disregard. (See Figure 14.3 on charitable immunity.)

For example, Terry volunteers as a carpenter for Habitat for Humanity, a charity that builds homes for underprivileged families. One day as Terry was working on a home for the charity, he took his lunch break at a diner across town. While at lunch, Terry was involved in an altercation with another man. That man now brings suit against Terry for injuries he allegedly sustained in the altercation. In this case Terry would not be immune from suit, even though he was working for the charity at the time. His actions were not performed in the scope or course of his volunteering for the charity.

Compare the following: Terry, a carpenter, volunteers for Habit for Humanity. One day he is working on the frame of a house. As he is hammering nails into the

FIGURE 14.3
Charitable Immunity

	Traditional Common Law	**Typical Modern Statutes**	**Purpose of the Immunity**
Immunity Granted to the Charity	• Charities are immune from civil liability suits. • The individual, by accepting the charity, is deemed to have waived any claim against the charity.	• Many state statutes have eliminated charitable immunity. • Immunity may be statutorily granted for certain activities.	• Traditionally, the immunity is in place to ensure the charity continues to receive donations. • States that eliminate the immunity recognize the individual's right and interest in bringing suit.
Immunity Granted to Volunteers of Charity	• Volunteers were granted immunity from suit for acts done in the scope and course of volunteering for the charity. • No immunity for reckless or negligent acts, or those acts committed outside the scope of volunteering.	• Same as traditional common law rules. • Immunity granted if not reckless or negligent, and done in scope and course of volunteering.	• To ensure charities would continue to receive adequate numbers of volunteers.
Immunity Granted to Charity for Actions of Employees	• Charities are not held responsible for acts of employees. • Respondeat superior does not attach to the charity for acts of employees.	• Charity is liable for acts of employees if the act is performed in the course and scope of the employment. • Liability of the charity may be limited.	• Traditionally, the immunity is in place to ensure the charity continues to receive donations. • States that eliminate the immunity recognize the individual's right and interest in bringing suit.

wood, he accidentally loses his grip on the hammer's handle. The hammer slips from his hand and lands on Susan's head. Susan suffers a concussion. She now seeks to bring suit against Terry. Under charitable immunity acts, Terry will be immune from suit because the accident occurred in the scope and course of his volunteer work for the charity.

Employees of charitable organizations often obtained immunity as well. An employee is an individual, including an officer or director, who is compensated for the work he or she does for the charity. The immunity given to an employee typically limits liability for tort causes of action. For example, a statute may hold that recovery for tortious acts of an employee of a charity is limited to $200,000 for personal injury and $750,000 for wrongful death. Like other charitable immunity laws, the legislation seeks to balance the charity's apparent need for immunity, and the individual's right to sue.

The *Restatement (Second) of Torts*, section 895E, states the current view of rejecting the doctrine of charitable immunity in modern law:

> One engaged in a charitable, educational, religious or benevolent enterprise or activity is not for that reason immune from tort liability.

Most states have either rejected the theory of charitable immunity or have enacted statutory modifications to limit its scope. Most states that have rejected the theory of charitable immunity re-create specific immunities for particular charitable activities or for individuals engaged in certain charitable activities. These states seek to balance the social benefit of allowing charitable immunity against an individual's right to bring suit.

SOVEREIGN IMMUNITY

Sovereign immunity means that the government is protected from lawsuits at all levels. Under the doctrine of sovereign immunity, the government cannot be held liable for the tortious acts of its employees unless the government has sanctioned the employees' actions. The government may also be sued if it waives immunity or consents to be sued. Legislatures sometimes pass private bills that allow private individuals to sue the government when the individuals would otherwise be prevented from suing due to sovereign immunity.

sovereign
A person, body, or state in which independent and supreme authority is vested.

Federal Government

Sovereign immunity holds that the federal government is not liable for certain specific activities. The legislation recognizes that in particular activities, it would be unfit to allow the federal government to be liable for suit. The main activities that are granted immunity are those activities involving tax collection, failure to deliver mail, military combat in time of war, and actions arising in foreign countries. A lack of immunity in such activities would greatly expose the federal government to liability. Imagine the overwhelming burden to the federal government that would be created if all those who are injured or lose property in a war are then able to bring suit for their injury. An absence of immunity would drastically impair a federal government's ability to govern the nation.

Sovereign immunity has been in existence since the formation of the federal government. With the enactment of the Federal Tort Claims Act in 1946, the American government could be held liable for torts according to the local law where the tort occurred under restricted circumstances. The action is brought in federal court, but state law applies. The Federal Tort Claims Act provides that the federal government can be sued as if it were a private citizen. The Federal Tort Claims Act provides for three procedural requirements for a tort action against the government:

- Jurisdiction is in the federal district courts.
- No jury trial is permitted.
- A two-year statute of limitations on claims against the government applies.

The *Restatement (Second) of Torts*, section 895A, speaks to federal government immunity:

1. *Except to the extent that the United States consents to suit and to tort liability, it and its agencies are immune to the liability.*
2. *Statutory provisions give the requisite consent to suit and liability for many types of tortious conduct.*

See Figure 14.4 on sovereign immunity.

Before a person brings a claim under the Federal Tort Claims Act, the administrative agency of the government that is involved must be given the opportunity to settle the case on its own within certain dollar limits.

FIGURE 14.4
Sovereign Immunity

Federal Government
• Federal Tort Claims Act in 1946 allowed suit against the federal government under restricted circumstances.
• Requirements:
 1) Jurisdiction in the federal courts
 2) No jury trial
 3) Two-year statute of limitations
• Administrative agency involved must be allowed to settle the case before suit is brought.

State Government
• State governments are not subject to civil liability.
• Exceptions:
 1) If a state government consents, it may be sued.
 2) Suit for acts or ommisions regarding:
  a) exercise of judicial or legislative functions, or
  b) the exercise of an administrative function involving the determination of fundamental governmental policy.

Local Government
• Local governments have partial immunity from civil suit.
• Immunity for activities associated with government functions.
• No immunity for activities that are considered proprietary in nature.
 (Examples: local government running airports, garages, utility facilities.)

There are exceptions to the Federal Torts Claims Act. For example, the federal government is not liable for any claim that springs from an intentional tort such as malicious prosecution, abuse of process, libel, slander, false imprisonment, and false arrest, to name just a few. Perhaps the most important exception to the Federal Torts Claims Act is the one that prohibits liability from attaching to the federal government for claims "based upon the exercise or performance or the failure to exercise or perform a **discretionary** function or duty on the part of a Federal agency or an employee of the Government, whether or not the discretion involved be abused." 28 U.S.C.A. §2680(a). This code section enables the federal government to conduct planning and leadership functions that are associated with the government without the fear of being sued by claims arising out of tortious conduct as a result of those activities. Discretionary functions are generally associated with planning functions while the actual carrying out of those plans are **operational** functions.

discretionary
Left to or regulated by one's own judgment.

operational
Pertaining to a process or series of actions for achieving a result.

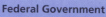

LEGAL RESEARCH MAXIM

The government may seize and take your land for fair market value under the taking clause of the Fifth Amendment to the U.S. Constitution. The government can exercise its eminent domain powers with immunity from lawsuits.

The Federal Torts Claims Act holds that the government is not liable for acts done with due care in the execution of a statute or regulation. This immunity attaches even though the statute or regulation is later deemed invalid. The most important consideration under this exception is whether the acts were done under due care and in good faith.

SURF'S UP

Using the Internet, research the case of *Berkovitz v. U.S.*, 486 U.S. 531 (1988). This case speaks to the difference between "discretionary" and "operational" functions of the government, specifically, the federal health and safety agencies. Using websites such as www.megalaw.com or www.findlaw.com, research the *Berkovitz* case. What does the court say about the work of federal health and safety agencies? What landmark case is cited in *Berkovitz*? What does the court say about an agency's failure to follow the program?

State Government

The federal government is not the only sovereign entity that enjoyed immunity from tort liability in the absence of consent. State governments also enjoyed such sovereign immunity. The *Restatement (Second) of Torts*, section 895B, speaks to state government immunity:

1. *A State and its governmental agencies are not subject to suit without the consent of the State.*

2. *Except to the extent that a State declines to give consent to tort liability, it and its governmental agencies are subject to the liability.*

3. *Even when a State is subject to tort liability, it and its governmental agencies are immune to the liability for acts and omissions constituting*
   a. *the exercise of a judicial or legislative function, or*
   b. *the exercise of an administrative function involving the determination of fundamental governmental policy.*

4. *Consent to suit and repudiation of general tort immunity do not establish liability for an act or omission that is otherwise privileged or is not tortious.*

However, most states have rejected the concept of sovereign immunity. Many states have legislation that limits the state's liability for certain governmental functions. Immunity is generally preserved for judicial and legislative acts, and for the exercise of high-level administrative discretion. States have largely followed the federal government's stance that immunity from an individual's right to sue should be limited largely to those acts necessary to ensure the proper functioning of the state government. Any state immunity that survives usually is associated with state-operated prisons, hospitals, educational institutions, and other state agencies.

Local Government

Local governments typically have partial sovereign immunity. The general rule is that municipal governments are subject to liability for **proprietary functions** and are immune from liability for **governmental functions**. The *Restatement (Second) of Torts*, section 895C, provides guidance regarding municipal governmental immunity:

1. *Except as stated in Subsection (2), a local government entity is not immune from tort liability.*

2. *A local government entity is immune from tort liability for acts and omissions constituting*
   a. *the exercise of a legislative or judicial function, and*
   b. *the exercise of an administrative function involving the determination of fundamental governmental policy.*

3. *Repudiation of general tort immunity does not establish liability for an act or omission that is otherwise privileged or is not tortious.*

Therefore, when school districts, cities, and other local governmental entities conduct activities that are governmental in nature, they will be immune from claims of tort liability. However, should those same entities perform functions that could be performed by a private company as well as by the governmental agency, then those

proprietary functions
Functions that a city or town, in its discretion, may perform when considered to be for the best interest of its citizens.

governmental functions
Functions of a municipality that are essential to its existence, in the sense of serving the public at large, that are not necessary to its existence, and that ensure the advantage of its inhabitants.

activities may be considered proprietary and subject the local governmental entity to liability. Activities of local governments that produce revenue for the government are usually considered proprietary. For example, activities such as airports, garages, and utilities are proprietary activities of local governments.

PUBLIC OFFICERS

public officer
A person who, upon being issued a commission, taking required oath, enters upon, for a fixed tenure, a position called an office where he or she exercises in his or her own right some of the attributes of sovereign he or she serves for benefit of the public.

Public officers are usually not held liable for torts that occur during the discharge of their duties. The general rule is that tort liability will not attach to a public official if it would impair the public officer's ability to effectively perform his discretionary functions. The *Restatement (Second) of Torts*, section 895D, speaks to the immunity of public officers:

1. *Except as provided in this Section a public officer is not immune from tort liability.*

2. *A public officer acting within the general scope of his authority is immune from tort liability for an act or omission involving the exercise of a judicial or legislative function.*

3. *A public officer acting within the general scope of his authority is not subject to tort liability for an administrative act or omission if*
   a. *he is immune because engaged in the exercise of a discretionary function,*
   b. *he is privileged and does not exceed or abuse the privilege, or*
   c. *his conduct was not tortious because he was not negligent in the performance of his responsibility.*

Government officers and employees are immune from tort liability when exercising a judicial or legislative function. The highest executive officers of state and federal governments are absolutely immune from suit. Immunity attaches to acts of the officers done in the scope and course of their employment. Immunity does not attach where the officer has so far exceeded the scope of her official duty as to be acting beyond the bounds of her position. Lower-level executives also enjoy immunity for the good faith exercise of responsibilities.

Legislators and judges are traditionally completely immune from tort liability as long as their actions fall with the general scope of their duties. If their actions are completely outside the jurisdiction of the official, then liability may attach.

DIPLOMATIC IMMUNITY

diplomat
A person appointed by a national government to conduct official negotiations and maintain political, economic, and social relations with another country or countries.

The need to ensure that certain government employees were allowed to freely negotiate and settle grievances in foreign countries gave rise to diplomatic immunity. As a result of this immunity, **diplomats** are viewed as immune from civil liability. Historically, diplomatic immunity developed to allow for the maintenance of government relations, including during periods of difficulties and even armed conflict. Immunity may be waived by the diplomat's home country. This waiver typically occurs if the diplomat is involved in a serious crime, unconnected to his or her diplomatic role.

YOU BE THE JUDGE

Barbara is a state senator. She is vehemently against legalizing gambling in her state. She believes that gambling establishments are corrupt, breed crime, and are run by organized crime. A bill is to go before the state senate that will legalize certain types of gambling and allow casinos to open, organize, and operate within the state. John works for a group of investors who want to open a casino in the state. The investor group is well funded and has organized a political campaign to see that the bill passes through the state legislature. When the bill is presented for debate upon the senate floor, Barbara steps to the podium. Barbara lashes out at the gambling industry. She specifically names John and his investor group. She calls them gangsters and felons and accuses them of being corrupt and laundering money. John is infuriated with these attacks against his character and his business reputation. John feels that he has been slandered and that there has been an intentional interference with his business. John decides to sue Barbara for intentional torts arising out of her conduct as a public officer. Will John prevail?

For example, a country may waive its immunity for the diplomat if the diplomat is involved in a robbery that is completely unconnected with the person's role as a diplomat. In other instances, the immunity will not be waived if the diplomat is charged with a crime and it is related to the person's diplomatic status; for example, if the diplomat is charged with spying, or seeking to purchase confidential information. In such scenarios, the home country is less likely to waive the immunity because it is connected with the diplomat's position.

Summary

Immunity is a defense to tort liability. People who claim immunity typically fall into a certain category or class. In order to claim immunity as a defense, the defendant usually falls under one of the following categories: immunity is derived from the defendant's relationship with the plaintiff; immunity is derived from the nature of the defendant's occupation; and immunity is derived from the defendant's status as a governmental or charitable entity.

Immunity enables individuals to be free of liability because they fall into one of the preceding categories and provides an absolute defense against actions brought under negligence or intentional tort theories. Courts and legislatures try to balance the interests of the plaintiff against the cost to the state. The trend in recent times is to preserve the interest of the plaintiff and let the public bear the burden of the cost.

At common law, married couples were considered under the law as one person. Under that premise, it did not make sense for a husband or wife to bring a tort action against the other because they were legally considered one person. During this time period, the husband was the primary spouse in the relationship. The wife was not allowed to own property or enter into contracts. In the late nineteenth century, the Married Women's Acts were passed, giving women the right to own property and be considered their own legal entities. Women were now allowed to bring suits against their husbands concerning property interests.

Married couples possess the privilege of not having their confidential marital communications, made during the course of the marriage, revealed by the other spouse. These communications are classified as confidential, and either spouse may prevent the other from passing on the communication. Under common law, married couples were able to prevent a spouse from testifying against them in a criminal proceeding. Today, the federal courts and most states recognize the witness spouse as the holder of the privilege.

In the United States, immunity developed between parents and children that led to a bar on legal actions between parents and children. However, many states have abolished this immunity except as it relates to providing food and care by a parent for a child and parental control of children.

At common law, charitable organizations received immunity from tort liability. Three principal reasons existed for providing charitable organizations with immunity: donations to charitable organizations would be curtailed if immunity was not available to the organization; respondeat superior did not apply to charitable organizations; and the beneficiary of the charity has, by her conduct, waived her right to sue in tort because she had accepted charity.

Sovereign immunity means that the government is protected from lawsuits at all levels. Under the doctrine of sovereign immunity, the government cannot be held liable for the tortious acts of its employees unless the government has sanctioned the employees' actions. Legislatures sometimes pass private bills that allow private individuals to sue the government when the individuals would otherwise be prevented from suing due to sovereign immunity.

Public officers are usually not held liable for torts that occur during the discharge of their duties. The general rule is that tort liability will not attach to a public official if it would impair the public officer's ability to effectively perform her discretionary functions.

Diplomats are usually not held liable for torts. Although the home country may waive the immunity, this is generally only done when the diplomat has committed a serious crime, and the crime is not connected to the person's status as a diplomat.

Key Terms

Charitable organization	Immunity
Diplomat	Operational
Discretionary	Proprietary functions
Eavesdropper	Public officer
Federal Rules of Evidence	Sovereign
Governmental functions	Spousal privilege

Review Questions

1. What is immunity?
2. Can a wife sue her husband for tort liability?
3. Can a child bring a tort action against his parents?
4. What is the status of immunity for charitable organizations in most states?
5. What is sovereign immunity?
6. What is the significance of the Federal Tort Claims Act?
7. Define a proprietary function.
8. Define a governmental function.
9. What is a public officer?
10. List two types of public officers who are completely immune from liability. Why are they immune?

Exercises

1. Locate three articles on the Internet or in some other source that demonstrate a public official who is being sued in tort for his or her conduct. What is the theory of tort liability being asserted against the government official? Why, in your opinion, is the governmental immunity not attaching to the official?

2. Under the theory of eminent domain, a governmental entity can seize the land of a private citizen for its own use. The governmental agency must pay the private citizen for the value of the land. Why is it not usually probable that the landowner will prevail in a lawsuit against the governmental entity for taking her property? What elements exist in your jurisdiction that may lead to a private citizen prevailing in this circumstance?

3. In the beating of Rodney King in Los Angeles, why was it possible to bring suit against the police officers? Why is it that immunity did not apply?

4. What are the policy reasons behind abolishing interspousal immunity? What goals are furthered by forbidding a spouse to sue the other spouse? Why are certain actions not given immunity?

5. City, a midsized suburb outside of Big City, owns and operates a recycling center. The recycling center is large and modern. City initially built the facility to encourage its citizens to recycle. After five years in operation, the recycling center

has been a success. The facility currently produces significant revenues for City. If a citizen brings suit against City for injuries he received after an accident at the facility, will City succeed in asserting that it is immune from such suits? Why?

6. Harry and Wilma have been married for seven years. One year after the couple divorced, Wilma was charged with assault and battery. Harry was present when the alleged assault and battery took place. The prosecution seeks to compel Harry to testify as to what he saw take place. Wilma seeks to prevent Harry from testifying. Will Wilma succeed? Why?

7. Vickie and her husband, Mike, have been married for four years. During their marriage, Mike often made comments to Vickie regarding his interactions with his business partners. Mike made these statements intending them to be confidential. After the pair divorced, one of Mike's business partners seeks to have Vickie testify as to what Mike told her. Vickie says she will testify if permitted. Mike seeks to prevent Vickie from testifying. Will Mike be successful? Why?

 PORTFOLIO ASSIGNMENT

Does your state recognize charitable immunity? What, if any, limitations are placed upon the application of the immunity? What policies do charitable immunity acts seek to further? List any limitations that are placed in your state and keep them in your portfolio.

Vocabulary Builders

Instructions

Use the key terms from this chapter to fill in the answers to the crossword puzzle.

NOTE: When the answer is more than one word, leave a blank space between words.

ACROSS

6. Functions of a municipality that are essential to its existence, in sense of serving the public at large, that are not necessary to its existence, and that ensure the advantage of its inhabitants.

7. A person, body, or state in which independent and supreme authority is vested.

9. A person appointed by a national government to conduct official negotiations and maintain political, economic, and social relations with another country or countries.

10. Left to or regulated by one's own judgment.

11. Exemption, as from serving in an office, or performing duties that the law generally requires other citizens to perform.

12. A person who, upon being issued a commission, taking required oath, enters upon, for a fixed tenure, a position called an office where he or she exercises in his or her own right some of the attributes of sovereign he or she serves for benefit of the public.

DOWN

1. Functions that a city or town, in its discretion, may perform when considered to be for the best interest of its citizens.

2. Rules governing the introduction of evidence in proceedings, both civil and criminal, in federal courts. While they do not apply to suits in state courts, the rules of many states have been closely modeled after these rules.

3. Pertaining to a process or series of actions for achieving a result.

4. An organization hat provides charity without obtaining a profit or gain for itself or its owners.

5. Combination of two elements: (1) the right not to be compelled to testify against one's spouse, and (2) the protection of marital confidences.

8. A secret listener to private conversations.

United States Court of Appeals, Eighth Circuit

Lamoni K. RIORDAN, *Appellee/Cross Appellant,* v. CORPORATION OF THE PRESIDING BISHOP OF THE CHURCH OF JESUS CHRIST OF LATTER-DAY SAINTS, *doing business as The Church of Jesus Christ of Latter-Day Saints, Appellant/Cross Appellee*

416 F.3d 825 Nos. 04-2304, 04-2392

Submitted: March 16, 2005

Filed: Aug. 5, 2005

I. BACKGROUND

On April 13, 1985, five-year-old Lamoni was injured in an accident involving a riding lawnmower operated by Ken while Ken was mowing at a CPB-owned facility. Because of the accident, Lamoni's foot was partially amputated. Lamoni filed suit against CPB on February 15, 2002, in Missouri state court, claiming (1) CPB was liable for Ken's negligence under the doctrine of respondeat superior, (2) CPB negligently maintained the lawnmower, and (3) CPB negligently failed to train and supervise its employees properly. CPB removed the case to the federal district court.

The district court denied CPB's motion for summary judgment on CPB's argument that the respondeat superior claim was barred by parental immunity. The court granted CPB's motion on the negligent maintenance claim. CPB moved in limine to exclude at trial all evidence regarding CPB's failure to maintain the lawnmower and to prevent Lamoni from asserting claims at trial other than the respondeat superior claim. The district court granted the motion as to evidence regarding the failure to maintain the lawnmower. The court denied the motion as to Lamoni's direct negligence claim based on negligent supervision. Thus, the district court concluded Lamoni could bring both the respondeat superior and direct negligence claims at trial.

Before trial, Lamoni's counsel sent a letter to Lamoni and sent a copy to Ken. The letter explained what Lamoni would have to prove to prevail on his claims against CPB, explained the district court's rulings in limine, instructed Lamoni and Ken that certain evidentiary matters were off limits to all witnesses, and included a list of Lamoni's allegations of fault against Ken and thereby CPB. At trial, Lamoni presented evidence about past surgeries on his foot, as well as potential future surgeries, such as a below-the-knee amputation, after which Lamoni would use energy-storing prosthetics. Following the trial, the jury found for Lamoni on the respondeat superior and direct negligence claims, awarding $80,651.73 for past medical expenses, $682,976.18 for future medical expenses, $420,000.00 for past non-economic damages, and "none" for future non-economic damages, for a total of $1,183,627.91.

Lamoni moved for a new trial on damages, arguing the verdict of "none" for future non-economic damages was contrary to law and against the weight of evidence. The district court denied the motion, concluding Lamoni did not preserve the error and, thus, waived objection to the allegedly inconsistent verdict. The court also ruled that, even if Lamoni had not waived the objection, he was not entitled to a new trial, because the jury simply may not have believed Lamoni's claims that he would have future non-economic damages. The court also concluded the total damages award fairly and reasonably compensated Lamoni for his injuries.

CPB appeals, arguing respondeat superior liability is purely derivative, i.e., because Ken cannot be liable to Lamoni due to parental immunity, CPB cannot be liable either. CPB also argues the direct negligence claim fails due to parental immunity. Further, CPB claims Ken's self-admitted negligence was an intervening cause of the injury, breaking the causal chain. In his cross-appeal, Lamoni contends the district court erred in denying the motion for a new trial, because there was evidence of future pain and suffering.

II. DISCUSSION

Exercising diversity jurisdiction, we interpret Missouri law. *Ehlis v. Shire Richwood, Inc.,* 367 F.3d 1013, 1016 (8th Cir. 2004). We review the district court's interpretation of Missouri law de novo, attempting to forecast how the Missouri Supreme Court would decide the issues presented. *Id.* We also review the grant of summary judgment de novo. *Gray v. AT & T Corp.,* 357 F.3d 763, 765 (8th Cir. 2004).

A. RESPONDEAT SUPERIOR CLAIM

CPB argues respondeat superior liability is purely derivative, so Ken's parental immunity shields CPB from liability. Thus, CPB claims the district court erred in submitting Lamoni's respondeat superior claim to the jury. CPB also contends applying parental immunity to bar Lamoni's claims is necessary to prevent collusion between Lamoni and Ken.

Although the Missouri Supreme Court has abrogated parental immunity, the doctrine still applies to causes of action accrued before December 19, 1991. *See Campbell v. Callow,* 876 S.W.2d 25, 27 (Mo.Ct.App. 1994). The parties stipulated "[p]arental immunity applies to this case and, therefore, Plaintiff's parents, Kenneth and Pearl Riordan, cannot be joined as parties to this action." We find no reason to disagree. Thus, we examine whether Ken's parental immunity shields CPB from liability.

The Missouri Supreme Court has recognized the close and analogous connection between parental immunity and spousal immunity. *Hartman,* 821 S.W.2d at 855. Missouri adopted parental immunity on "the belief that allowing children to sue their parents would disturb the unity and harmony of the family." 1. Spousal immunity also had underpinnings in notions of family unity and harmony. *See Townsend v. Townsend,* 708 S.W.2d 646, 648–50 (Mo. 1986). In the absence of authority on the applicability of parental immunity in situations like that presented here, it is appropriate for us to consider Missouri courts' rulings on spousal immunity.

In *Mullally v. Langenberg Brothers Grain Co.*, 339 Mo. 582, 98 S.W.2d 645, 645 (1936), the defendant contended, because a wife could not maintain an action against her husband for damages arising from injuries caused by the husband's negligence, the husband's employer enjoyed that derivative immunity against the wife's respondeat superior claim against the employer. After noting two lines of authority on this question, the Missouri Supreme Court concluded "legal principle and public policy [dictate] the wife has a right of action against the husband's employer." The court quoted extensively from the reasoning in *Schubert v. August Schubert Wagon Co.*, 249 N.Y. 253, 164 N.E. 42 (1928): "The disability of wife or husband to maintain an action against the other for injuries to the person is not a disability to maintain a like action against the other's principal or master." *Mullally*, 98 S.W.2d at 646 (quoting *Schubert*, 164 N.E. at 42). "The statement sometimes made that it is derivative and secondary . . . means this, and nothing more: That at times the fault of the actor will fix the quality of the act. Illegality established, liability ensues." The New York court explained why defendants attempt to hide behind the husband's immunity: "The defendant, to make out a defense, is thus driven to maintain that the act, however negligent, was none the less lawful because committed by a husband upon the person of his wife. This is to pervert the meaning and effect of the disability that has its origin in marital identity." The court reasoned, "A trespass, negligent or willful, upon the person of a wife, does not cease to be an unlawful act, though the law exempts the husband from liability for the damage. Others may not hide behind the skirts of his immunity."

According to the *Restatement (Second) of Agency*, in an action against a principal based on an agent's conduct during the course of the agent's employment, "[t]he principal has no defense because of the fact that . . . the agent had an immunity from civil liability as to the act." *Restatement (Second) of Agency* § 217 (1958). These immunities include those "resulting from the relation of parent and child and of husband and wife." Moreover, "[s]ince the Restatement, . . . the trend has been strongly to enforce the liability of the [employer]."

Other jurisdictions have rejected the argument that parental immunity bars a suit by a child against a parent's employer based on the parent's negligence during the scope of employment. Particularly instructive to our discussion is *Hooper v. Clements Food Co.*, 694 P.2d 943 (Okla. 1985). In *Hooper,* a minor child's mother brought suit against the employer of the child's father, seeking damages for injuries the child suffered due to the father's negligence while acting in the course and scope of employment. The court noted the employer's "liability for the child's injuries was predicated upon principles of respondeat superior," and "[t]he fact that the injuries of the child proximately resulted from the negligence of [the] employee while engaged in the course and scope of employment was never in dispute." The employer argued its liability to the child was derivative; thus, "its employee's parental immunity precluded any recovery against it by the child." The employer essentially "argued that inasmuch as recovery is personally precluded against the negligent employee, recovery must also be precluded against the employer." The trial court granted Clements's motion for summary judgment, concluding the doctrine of parental immunity shielded the employer from liability to the child.

The Oklahoma Supreme Court reversed, ruling the parental immunity exception to tort liability was inapplicable to the facts of the case. Noting courts generally hold an employer liable for

the torts of its employee that occur during the course and scope of employment, even when the employee is personally immune from suit, the court adopted the majority view "that the immunity of a parent is a personal immunity, and it does not, therefore, protect a third party who is liable for the tort." The court declared a "child may fully recover damages from the employer of the child's parent when the parent's negligence, proximately causing the injury to the child, occurred in the course and scope of the parent's employment." Similarly, in *Mi-Lady Cleaners v. McDaniel*, 235 Ala. 469, 179 So. 908, 911 (1938), the Alabama Supreme Court opined, "The law imputes to the [employer] the act of the [employee], and if the act is negligent or wrongful proximately resulting in injury to a third person, the negligence or wrongful conduct is the negligence or wrongful conduct of the [employer] for which he is liable, and this rule of liability is not qualified by any special immunity resulting from the domestic relation existing between the person injured and the [employee] who committed the negligent or wrongful act."

We believe the Missouri Supreme Court, if confronted with this appeal, would conclude parental immunity does not bar Lamoni's respondeat superior claim against CPB. . . .

CPB also argues application of the parental immunity doctrine is necessary to protect it from collusion between Ken and Lamoni. Claiming the evidence of collusion here is "overwhelming," CPB points to the letter from Lamoni's counsel to Lamoni, copied to Ken, before the trial. CPB asserts the Missouri Supreme Court, in *Hartman,* recognized "the danger of fraud and collusion between parent and child" as a justification for the parental immunity doctrine. Notwithstanding CPB's litigation position, the Missouri Supreme Court recognized no such justification, instead explaining "[o]ther jurisdictions have considered additional reasons for adoption of the parental immunity doctrine: . . . the danger of fraud and collusion between parent and child"; however, Missouri premised its rule adoption on the belief that such suits would "disturb the unity and harmony of the family." *Hartman,* 821 S.W.2d at 854 n. 1.

In any event, our review of the record does not convince us collusion occurred. Although the letter sent to Ken may have contained information the disclosure of which reflected poor judgment by Lamoni's counsel, the letter only set forth what Lamoni needed to prove to prevail against CPB, explained the district court's rulings in limine, informed Lamoni and Ken of certain inadmissible evidence, and attached a list of Lamoni's allegations of fault against CPB. Ken's account of the accident did not change based on the letter. Witnesses testified at trial Ken blamed himself for the accident from the moment it occurred, admitted the injury was his fault, and stated he did not realize Lamoni was behind him as he mowed. In his deposition, Ken acknowledged mowing in reverse was more dangerous. During trial, Ken recounted the events surrounding the accident. Although Ken did not state he blamed himself, his testimony clearly demonstrates he accepted the blame for the accident, again acknowledging the danger involved in mowing in reverse. Ken also admitted reading the letter before taking the stand. We agree with the district court "nothing in this letter [was] designed to any way influence the testimony of this witness." Furthermore, the letter was admitted into evidence at trial, and CPB had the opportunity to impeach Ken and to argue collusion to the jury. Thus, whatever collusion CPB claims occurred certainly was insufficient to warrant application of the now-abrogated parental immunity doctrine to bar Lamoni's respondeat superior claim against CPB.

B. DIRECT NEGLIGENCE CLAIM

CPB argues the court erred in submitting to the jury Lamoni's direct negligence claim based on negligent supervision. CPB contends this claim is inextricably intertwined with the respondeat superior claim and is barred by parental immunity, and CPB claims Ken's own negligence was an intervening cause of the injury.

"The majority view is that once an employer has admitted respondeat superior liability for [ ] negligence, it is improper to allow a plaintiff to proceed against the employer on any other theory of imputed liability." *McHaffie v. Bunch,* 891 S.W.2d 822, 826 (Mo. 1995). The rationale behind this view is that, "where the imputation of negligence is admitted, the evidence laboriously submitted to establish other theories serves no real purpose." Assuming without deciding that once course and scope of employment is admitted, a plaintiff must rely on respondeat superior liability, we conclude CPB's argument fails. CPB did not admit Ken was acting within the course and scope of his employment, alternatively contending Ken was acting as a parent in babysitting Lamoni at the time of the injury. In fact, CPB denied Ken was acting within the course and scope of employment up to and through closing argument. Further, as explained above, parental immunity does not shield CPB from liability.

In support of its contention Ken's own negligence was an efficient, intervening cause, CPB cites *Heffernan v. Reinhold,* 73 S.W.3d 659, 664 (Mo.Ct.App. 2002). In *Heffernan,* the court opined that the existence of proximate cause is normally a jury question, but the court may decide the issue when the evidence reveals "an intervening cause that eclipses the role the defendant's conduct played in the plaintiff's injury." *Heffernan,* 73 S.W.3d at 665. But a plaintiff may not recover if the defendant's negligence "did nothing more than furnish the condition or give rise to the occasion by which the injury was made possible, and there intervened between that cause and the injury a distinct, successive, unrelated and efficient cause of the injury, though the injury would not have occurred but for the condition or occasion." Liability still exists if the alleged intervening cause is "merely an act of concurring or contributing negligence." *Heffernan,* 73 S.W.3d at 665.

In this case, Ken's negligence resulted from CPB's negligent failure to train or supervise him properly. CPB's failure to train and supervise Ken properly caused Ken to operate the mower negligently. Thus, Ken's negligence cannot be considered an intervening cause of the injury. The jury verdict establishes not only the negligence and causation, but the foreseeability of the failure to train and supervise leading directly to the injury. *See, e.g., Ponticas v. K.M.S. Invs.,* 331 N.W.2d 907, 915–16 (Minn. 1983). The district court did not err in submitting both claims to the jury.

C. FUTURE DAMAGES

In his cross-appeal, Lamoni argues the district court should have granted a new trial on damages, because the evidence supports an award of future non-economic damages for pain and suffering. Under Missouri law, "a new trial should be granted on the ground that a verdict is inadequate only if the verdict is against the weight of the evidence." *Johnson v. Cowell Steel Structures, Inc.,* 991 F.2d 474, 477 (8th Cir. 1993). "When the trial court has overruled a motion for new trial alleging inadequacy of damages . . . , the jury's exercise of its discretion is conclusive unless the verdict is so shockingly inadequate as to indicate that it is the result of passion and prejudice or a gross abuse of discretion." (quoting *Havel v. Diebler,* 836 S.W.2d 501, 504 (Mo.Ct.App. 1992)). Moreover, "[a]bsent proof that the verdict was 'shockingly inadequate,' we will not disturb the trial court's decision to deny the motion for new trial." We have declared, "When 'the basis of the motion for a new trial is that the jury's verdict is against the weight of the evidence, the district court's denial of the motion is virtually unassailable on appeal.' "

In *Root,* 91 S.W.3d at 146-47, the Missouri Court of Appeals upheld a denial of a new trial motion after the jury awarded medical expenses to the plaintiffs, awarded minimal pain and suffering damages to one plaintiff, and denied the same to the other three plaintiffs. The court noted *Davidson v. Schneider,* 349 S.W.2d 908, 913 (Mo. 1961), wherein the Missouri Supreme Court affirmed the denial of a motion for new trial, but nevertheless stated the generally accepted view that awards of medical expense only, without an award for pain and suffering, are invalid and are "set aside almost as a matter of course." *See Root,* 91 S.W.3d at 146. . . .

In the present case, although Lamoni argues it is undisputed he will have future pain and suffering, the jury could have believed the trans-tibial surgery he may have in the future (for which he received future medical expenses) and the prosthetics he sought would alleviate any pain or suffering. Or the jury could have believed Lamoni simply would have no future pain and suffering with modern medications and the proposed surgery and prosthetics. The jury also may have concluded Lamoni's proposed surgeries were not medically necessary. The verdict form, to which Lamoni did not object, instructed the jury to write down a dollar amount, or the word, "none," if it found Lamoni would have no future pain and suffering.

Furthermore, Lamoni has not shown the jury's $1.18 million verdict, which incorporated no recovery for future pain and suffering, was "shockingly inadequate," "the result of passion and prejudice," or "against the weight of the evidence." Just as in *Root* and *Davidson,* "the jury may have found 'from the conflicting evidence that the [plaintiff's] complaints were all subjective' and in the end awarded [him his] 'actually established financial losses.' " *Root,* 91 S.W.3d at 147 (quoting *Davidson,* 349 S.W.2d at 913). "The ultimate test for a jury verdict is what fairly and reasonably compensates the plaintiff for the injuries sustained." Because the district court did not abuse its broad discretion in denying the new trial motion, a decision that is virtually conclusive and unassailable on appeal, and because we conclude the $1.18 million verdict fairly and reasonably compensates Lamoni for his injuries, we reject Lamoni's argument that the district court erred in denying his motion for a new trial.

III. CONCLUSION

We affirm in all respects.
[Footnotes omitted]

Source: Reprinted with permission from Westlaw. Lamoni K. RIORDAN v. CORPORATION OF THE PRESIDING BISHOP OF THE CHURCH OF JESUS CHRIST OF LATTER-DAY SAINTS, doing business as The Church of Jesus Christ of Latter-Day Saints, 416 F.3d 825.

Appendix

THE UNITED STATES CONSTITUTION

In these pages, superseded text is presented like this: *(This is superseded text.)* Added text that is not a part of the Constitution is presented like this: **(This is added text.)**

CONTENTS

Preamble

Article 1 - The Legislative Branch
- Section 1 - The Legislature
- Section 2 - The House
- Section 3 - The Senate
- Section 4 - Elections, Meetings
- Section 5 - Membership, Rules, Journals, Adjournment
- Section 6 - Compensation
- Section 7 - Revenue Bills, Legislative Process, Presidential Veto
- Section 8 - Powers of Congress
- Section 9 - Limits on Congress
- Section 10 - Powers Prohibited of States

Article 2 - The Executive Branch
- Section 1 - The President
- Section 2 - Civilian Power over Military, Cabinet, Pardon Power, Appointments
- Section 3 - State of the Union, Convening Congress
- Section 4 - Disqualification

Article 3 - The Judicial Branch
- Section 1 - Judicial Powers
- Section 2 - Trial by Jury, Original Jurisdiction, Jury Trials
- Section 3 - Treason

Article 4 - The States
- Section 1 - Each State to Honor All Others
- Section 2 - State Citizens, Extradition
- Section 3 - New States
- Section 4 - Republican Government

Article 5 - Amendment
Article 6 - Debts, Supremacy, Oaths
Article 7 - Ratification
Signatories
Amendments

- Amendment 1 - Freedom of Religion, Press, Expression
- Amendment 2 - Right to Bear Arms
- Amendment 3 - Quartering of Soldiers
- Amendment 4 - Search and Seizure
- Amendment 5 - Trial and Punishment, Compensation for Takings
- Amendment 6 - Right to Speedy Trial, Confrontation of Witnesses
- Amendment 7 - Trial by Jury in Civil Cases
- Amendment 8 - Cruel and Unusual Punishment
- Amendment 9 - Construction of Constitution
- Amendment 10 - Powers of the States and People
- Amendment 11 - Judicial Limits
- Amendment 12 - Choosing the President, Vice President
- Amendment 13 - Slavery Abolished
- Amendment 14 - Citizenship Rights
- Amendment 15 - Race No Bar to Vote
- Amendment 16 - Status of Income Tax Clarified
- Amendment 17 - Senators Elected by Popular Vote
- Amendment 18 - Liquor Abolished
- Amendment 19 - Women's Suffrage
- Amendment 20 - Presidential, Congressional Terms
- Amendment 21 - Amendment 18 Repealed
- Amendment 22 - Presidential Term Limits
- Amendment 23 - Presidential Vote for District of Columbia
- Amendment 24 - Poll Taxes Barred
- Amendment 25 - Presidential Disability and Succession
- Amendment 26 - Voting Age Set to 18 Years
- Amendment 27 - Limiting Congressional Pay Increases

THE CONSTITUTION OF THE UNITED STATES

Preamble

We the People of the United States, in Order to form a more perfect Union, establish Justice, insure domestic Tranquility, provide for the common defence, promote the general Welfare, and secure the Blessings of Liberty to ourselves and our Posterity, do ordain and establish this Constitution for the United States of America.

Article I. - The Legislative Branch

Section 1 - The Legislature

All legislative Powers herein granted shall be vested in a Congress of the United States, which shall consist of a Senate and House of Representatives.

Section 2 - The House

The House of Representatives shall be composed of Members chosen every second Year by the People of the several States, and the Electors in each State shall have the Qualifications requisite for Electors of the most numerous Branch of the State Legislature.

No Person shall be a Representative who shall not have attained to the Age of twenty five Years, and been seven Years a Citizen of the United States, and who shall not, when elected, be an Inhabitant of that State in which he shall be chosen.

*(Representatives and direct Taxes shall be apportioned among the several States which may be included within this Union, according to their respective Numbers, which shall be determined by adding to the whole Number of free Persons, including those bound to Service for a Term of Years, and excluding Indians not taxed, three fifths of all other Persons.)***(The previous sentence in parentheses was modified by the 14th Amendment, section 2.)** The actual Enumeration shall be made within three Years after the first Meeting of the Congress of the United States, and within every subsequent Term of ten Years, in such Manner as they shall by Law direct. The Number of Representatives shall not exceed one for every thirty Thousand, but each State shall have at Least one Representative; and until such enumeration shall be made, the State of New Hampshire shall be entitled to chuse three, Massachusetts eight, Rhode Island and Providence Plantations one, Connecticut five, New York six, New Jersey four, Pennsylvania eight, Delaware one, Maryland six, Virginia ten, North Carolina five, South Carolina five and Georgia three.

When vacancies happen in the Representation from any State, the Executive Authority thereof shall issue Writs of Election to fill such Vacancies.

The House of Representatives shall chuse their Speaker and other Officers; and shall have the sole Power of Impeachment.

Section 3 - The Senate

The Senate of the United States shall be composed of two Senators from each State, *(chosen by the Legislature thereof,)* **(The preceding words in parentheses superseded by 17th Amendment, section 1.)** for six Years; and each Senator shall have one Vote.

Immediately after they shall be assembled in Consequence of the first Election, they shall be divided as equally as may be into three Classes. The Seats of the Senators of the first Class shall be vacated at the Expiration of the second Year, of the second Class at the Expiration of the fourth Year, and of the third Class at the Expiration of the sixth Year, so that one third may be chosen every second Year; *(and if Vacancies happen by Resignation, or otherwise, during the Recess of the Legislature of any State, the Executive thereof may make temporary Appointments until the next Meeting of the Legislature, which shall then fill such Vacancies.)* **(The preceding words in parentheses were superseded by the 17th Amendment, section 2.)**

No person shall be a Senator who shall not have attained to the Age of thirty Years, and been nine Years a Citizen of the United States, and who shall not, when elected, be an Inhabitant of that State for which he shall be chosen.

The Vice President of the United States shall be President of the Senate, but shall have no Vote, unless they be equally divided.

The Senate shall chuse their other Officers, and also a President pro tempore, in the absence of the Vice President, or when he shall exercise the Office of President of the United States.

The Senate shall have the sole Power to try all Impeachments. When sitting for that Purpose, they shall be on Oath or Affirmation. When the President of the United States is tried, the Chief Justice shall preside: And no Person shall be convicted without the Concurrence of two thirds of the Members present.

Judgment in Cases of Impeachment shall not extend further than to removal from Office, and disqualification to hold and enjoy any Office of honor, Trust or Profit under the United States: but the Party convicted shall nevertheless be liable and subject to Indictment, Trial, Judgment and Punishment, according to Law.

Section 4 - Elections, Meetings

The Times, Places and Manner of holding Elections for Senators and Representatives, shall be prescribed in each State by the Legislature thereof; but the Congress may at any time by Law make or alter such Regulations, except as to the Place of Chusing Senators.

The Congress shall assemble at least once in every Year, and such Meeting shall *(be on the first Monday in December,)* **(The preceding words in parentheses were superseded by the 20th Amendment, section 2.)** unless they shall by Law appoint a different Day.

Section 5 - Membership, Rules, Journals, Adjournment

Each House shall be the Judge of the Elections, Returns and Qualifications of its own Members, and a Majority of each shall constitute a Quorum to do Business; but a smaller number may adjourn from day to day, and may be authorized to compel the Attendance of absent Members, in such Manner, and under such Penalties as each House may provide.

Each House may determine the Rules of its Proceedings, punish its Members for disorderly Behavior, and, with the Concurrence of two-thirds, expel a Member.

Each House shall keep a Journal of its Proceedings, and from time to time publish the same, excepting such Parts as may in their Judgment require Secrecy; and the Yeas and Nays of the Members of either House on any question shall, at the Desire of one fifth of those Present, be entered on the Journal.

Neither House, during the Session of Congress, shall, without the Consent of the other, adjourn for more than three days, nor to any other Place than that in which the two Houses shall be sitting.

Section 6 - Compensation

(The Senators and Representatives shall receive a Compensation for their Services, to be ascertained by Law, and paid out of the Treasury of the United States.) **(The preceding words in parentheses were modified by the 27th Amendment.)** They shall in all Cases, except Treason, Felony and Breach of the Peace, be privileged from Arrest during their Attendance at the Session of their respective Houses, and in going to and returning from the same; and for any Speech or Debate in either House, they shall not be questioned in any other Place.

No Senator or Representative shall, during the Time for which he was elected, be appointed to any civil Office under the Authority of the United States which shall have been created, or the Emoluments whereof shall have been increased during such time; and no Person holding any Office under the United States, shall be a Member of either House during his Continuance in Office.

Section 7 - Revenue Bills, Legislative Process, Presidential Veto

All bills for raising Revenue shall originate in the House of Representatives; but the Senate may propose or concur with Amendments as on other Bills.

Every Bill which shall have passed the House of Representatives and the Senate, shall, before it become a Law, be presented to the President of the United States; If he approve he shall sign it, but if not he shall return it, with his Objections to that House in which it shall have originated, who shall enter the Objections at large on their Journal, and proceed to reconsider it. If after such Reconsideration two thirds of that House shall agree to pass the Bill, it shall be sent, together with the Objections, to the other House, by which it shall likewise be reconsidered, and if approved by two thirds of that House, it shall become a Law. But in all such Cases the Votes of both Houses shall be determined by Yeas and Nays, and the Names of the Persons voting for and against the Bill shall be entered on the Journal of each House respectively. If any Bill shall not be returned by the President within ten Days (Sundays excepted) after it shall have been presented to him, the Same shall be a Law, in like Manner as if he had signed it, unless the Congress by their Adjournment prevent its Return, in which Case it shall not be a Law.

Every Order, Resolution, or Vote to which the Concurrence of the Senate and House of Representatives may be necessary (except on a question of Adjournment) shall be presented to the President of the United States; and before the Same shall take Effect, shall be approved by him, or being disapproved by him, shall be repassed by two thirds of the Senate and House of Representatives, according to the Rules and Limitations prescribed in the Case of a Bill.

Section 8 - Powers of Congress

The Congress shall have Power To lay and collect Taxes, Duties, Imposts and Excises, to pay the Debts and provide for the common Defence and general Welfare of the United States; but all Duties, Imposts and Excises shall be uniform throughout the United States;

To borrow money on the credit of the United States;

To regulate Commerce with foreign Nations, and among the several States, and with the Indian Tribes;

To establish an uniform Rule of Naturalization, and uniform Laws on the subject of Bankruptcies throughout the United States;

To coin Money, regulate the Value thereof, and of foreign Coin, and fix the Standard of Weights and Measures;

To provide for the Punishment of counterfeiting the Securities and current Coin of the United States;

To establish Post Offices and Post Roads;

To promote the Progress of Science and useful Arts, by securing for limited Times to Authors and Inventors the exclusive Right to their respective Writings and Discoveries;

To constitute Tribunals inferior to the supreme Court;

To define and punish Piracies and Felonies committed on the high Seas, and Offenses against the Law of Nations;

To declare War, grant Letters of Marque and Reprisal, and make Rules concerning Captures on Land and Water;

To raise and support Armies, but no Appropriation of Money to that Use shall be for a longer Term than two Years;

To provide and maintain a Navy;

To make Rules for the Government and Regulation of the land and naval Forces;

To provide for calling forth the Militia to execute the Laws of the Union, suppress Insurrections and repel Invasions;

To provide for organizing, arming, and disciplining the Militia, and for governing such Part of them as may be employed in the Service of the United States, reserving to the States respectively, the Appointment of the Officers, and the Authority of training the Militia according to the discipline prescribed by Congress;

To exercise exclusive Legislation in all Cases whatsoever, over such District (not exceeding ten Miles square) as may, by Cession of particular States, and the acceptance of Congress, become the Seat of the Government of the United States, and to exercise like Authority over all Places purchased by the Consent of the Legislature of the State in which the Same shall be, for the Erection of Forts, Magazines, Arsenals, dock-Yards, and other needful Buildings; And

To make all Laws which shall be necessary and proper for carrying into Execution the foregoing Powers, and all other Powers vested by this Constitution in the Government of the United States, or in any Department or Officer thereof.

Section 9 - Limits on Congress

The Migration or Importation of such Persons as any of the States now existing shall think proper to admit, shall not be prohibited by the Congress prior to the Year one thousand eight hundred and eight, but a tax or duty may be imposed on such Importation, not exceeding ten dollars for each Person.

The privilege of the Writ of Habeas Corpus shall not be suspended, unless when in Cases of Rebellion or Invasion the public Safety may require it.

No Bill of Attainder or ex post facto Law shall be passed.

(No capitation, or other direct, Tax shall be laid, unless in Proportion to the Census or Enumeration herein before directed to be taken.) **(Section in parentheses clarified by the 16th Amendment.)**

No Tax or Duty shall be laid on Articles exported from any State.

No Preference shall be given by any Regulation of Commerce or Revenue to the Ports of one State over those of another: nor shall Vessels bound to, or from, one State, be obliged to enter, clear, or pay Duties in another.

No Money shall be drawn from the Treasury, but in Consequence of Appropriations made by Law; and a regular Statement and Account of the Receipts and Expenditures of all public Money shall be published from time to time.

No Title of Nobility shall be granted by the United States: And no Person holding any Office of Profit or Trust under them, shall, without the Consent of the Congress, accept of any present, Emolument, Office, or Title, of any kind whatever, from any King, Prince or foreign State.

Section 10 - Powers Prohibited of States

No State shall enter into any Treaty, Alliance, or Confederation; grant Letters of Marque and Reprisal; coin Money; emit Bills of Credit; make any Thing but gold and silver Coin a Tender in Payment of Debts; pass any Bill of Attainder, ex post facto Law, or Law impairing the Obligation of Contracts, or grant any Title of Nobility.

No State shall, without the Consent of the Congress, lay any Imposts or Duties on Imports or Exports, except what may be absolutely necessary for executing it's inspection Laws: and the net Produce of all Duties and Imposts, laid by any State on Imports or Exports, shall be for the Use of the Treasury of the United States; and all such Laws shall be subject to the Revision and Controul of the Congress.

No State shall, without the Consent of Congress, lay any duty of Tonnage, keep Troops, or Ships of War in time of Peace, enter into any Agreement or Compact with another State, or with a foreign Power, or engage in War, unless actually invaded, or in such imminent Danger as will not admit of delay.

Article II. - The Executive Branch

Section 1 - The President

The executive Power shall be vested in a President of the United States of America. He shall hold his Office during the Term of four Years, and, together with the Vice-President chosen for the same Term, be elected, as follows:

Each State shall appoint, in such Manner as the Legislature thereof may direct, a Number of Electors, equal to the whole Number of Senators and Representatives to which the State may be entitled in the Congress: but no Senator or Representative, or Person holding an Office of Trust or Profit under the United States, shall be appointed an Elector.

(The Electors shall meet in their respective States, and vote by Ballot for two persons, of whom one at least shall not lie an Inhabitant of the same State with themselves. And they shall make a List of all the Persons voted for, and of the Number of Votes for each; which List they shall sign and certify, and transmit sealed to the Seat of the Government of the United States, directed to the President of the Senate. The President of the Senate shall, in the Presence of the Senate and House of Representatives, open all the Certificates, and the Votes shall then be counted. The Person having the greatest Number of Votes shall be the President, if such Number be a Majority of the whole Number of Electors appointed; and if there be more than one who have such Majority, and have an equal Number of Votes, then the House of Representatives shall immediately chuse by Ballot one of them for President; and if no Person have a Majority, then from the five highest on the List the said House shall in like Manner chuse the President. But in chusing the President, the Votes shall be taken by States, the Representation from each State having one Vote; a quorum for this Purpose shall consist of a Member or Members from two-thirds of the States, and a Majority of all the States shall be necessary to a Choice. In every Case, after the Choice of the President, the Person having the greatest Number of Votes of the Electors shall be the Vice President. But if there should remain two or more who have equal Votes, the Senate shall chuse from them by Ballot the Vice-President.) **(This clause in parentheses was superseded by the 12th Amendment.)**

The Congress may determine the Time of chusing the Electors, and the Day on which they shall give their Votes; which Day shall be the same throughout the United States.

No person except a natural born Citizen, or a Citizen of the United States, at the time of the Adoption of this Constitution, shall be eligible to the Office of President; neither shall any Person be eligible to that Office who shall not have attained to the Age of thirty-five Years, and been fourteen Years a Resident within the United States.

(In Case of the Removal of the President from Office, or of his Death, Resignation, or Inability to discharge the Powers and Duties of the said Office, the same shall devolve on the Vice President, and the Congress may by Law provide for the Case of Removal, Death, Resignation or Inability, both of the President and Vice President, declaring what Officer shall then act as President, and such Officer shall act accordingly, until the Disability be removed, or a President shall be elected.) **(This clause in parentheses has been modified by the 20th and 25th Amendments.)**

The President shall, at stated Times, receive for his Services, a Compensation, which shall neither be increased nor diminished during the Period for which he shall have been elected, and he shall not receive within that Period any other Emolument from the United States, or any of them.

Before he enter on the Execution of his Office, he shall take the following Oath or Affirmation:

"I do solemnly swear (or affirm) that I will faithfully execute the Office of President of the United States, and will to the best of my Ability, preserve, protect and defend the Constitution of the United States."

Section 2 - Civilian Power over Military, Cabinet, Pardon Power, Appointments

The President shall be Commander in Chief of the Army and Navy of the United States, and of the Militia of the several States, when called into the actual Service of the United States; he may require the Opinion, in writing, of the principal Officer in each of the executive Departments, upon any subject relating to the Duties of their respective Offices, and he shall have Power to Grant Reprieves and Pardons for Offenses against the United States, except in Cases of Impeachment.

He shall have Power, by and with the Advice and Consent of the Senate, to make Treaties, provided two thirds of the Senators present concur; and he shall nominate, and by and with the Advice and Consent of the Senate, shall appoint Ambassadors, other public Ministers and Consuls, Judges of the supreme Court, and all other Officers of the United States, whose Appointments are not herein otherwise provided for, and which shall be established by Law: but the Congress may by Law vest the Appointment of such inferior Officers, as they think proper, in the President alone, in the Courts of Law, or in the Heads of Departments.

The President shall have Power to fill up all Vacancies that may happen during the Recess of the Senate, by granting Commissions which shall expire at the End of their next Session.

Section 3 - State of the Union, Convening Congress

He shall from time to time give to the Congress Information of the State of the Union, and recommend to their Consideration such Measures as he shall judge necessary and expedient; he may, on extraordinary Occasions, convene both Houses, or either of them, and in Case of Disagreement between them, with Respect to the Time of Adjournment, he may adjourn them to such Time as he shall think proper; he shall receive Ambassadors and other public Ministers; he shall take Care that the Laws be faithfully executed, and shall Commission all the Officers of the United States.

Section 4 - Disqualification

The President, Vice President and all civil Officers of the United States, shall be removed from Office on Impeachment for, and Conviction of, Treason, Bribery, or other high Crimes and Misdemeanors.

Article III. - The Judicial Branch

Section 1 - Judicial powers

The judicial Power of the United States, shall be vested in one supreme Court, and in such inferior Courts as the Congress may from time to time ordain and establish. The Judges, both of the supreme and inferior Courts, shall hold their Offices during good Behavior, and shall, at stated Times, receive for their Services a Compensation which shall not be diminished during their Continuance in Office.

Section 2 - Trial by Jury, Original Jurisdiction, Jury Trials

(The judicial Power shall extend to all Cases, in Law and Equity, arising under this Constitution, the Laws of the United States, and Treaties made, or which shall be made, under their Authority; to all Cases affecting Ambassadors, other public Ministers and Consuls; to all Cases of admiralty and maritime Jurisdiction; to Controversies to which the United States shall be a Party; to Controversies between two or more States; between a State and Citizens of another State; between Citizens of different States; between Citizens of the same State claiming Lands under Grants of different States, and between a State, or the Citizens thereof, and foreign States, Citizens or Subjects.) **(This section in parentheses is modified by the 11th Amendment.)**

In all Cases affecting Ambassadors, other public Ministers and Consuls, and those in which a State shall be Party, the supreme Court shall have original Jurisdiction. In all the other Cases before mentioned, the supreme Court shall have appellate Jurisdiction, both as to Law and Fact, with such Exceptions, and under such Regulations as the Congress shall make.

The Trial of all Crimes, except in Cases of Impeachment, shall be by Jury; and such Trial shall be held in the State where the said Crimes shall have been committed; but when not committed within any State, the Trial shall be at such Place or Places as the Congress may by Law have directed.

Section 3 - Treason

Treason against the United States, shall consist only in levying War against them, or in adhering to their Enemies, giving them Aid and Comfort. No Person shall be convicted of Treason unless on the Testimony of two Witnesses to the same overt Act, or on Confession in open Court.

The Congress shall have power to declare the Punishment of Treason, but no Attainder of Treason shall work Corruption of Blood, or Forfeiture except during the Life of the Person attainted.

Article IV. - The States

Section 1 - Each State to Honor All Others

Full Faith and Credit shall be given in each State to the public Acts, Records, and judicial Proceedings of every other State. And the Congress may by general Laws prescribe the Manner in which such Acts, Records and Proceedings shall be proved, and the Effect thereof.

Section 2 - State Citizens, Extradition

The Citizens of each State shall be entitled to all Privileges and Immunities of Citizens in the several States.

A Person charged in any State with Treason, Felony, or other Crime, who shall flee from Justice, and be found in another State, shall on demand of the executive Authority of the State from which he fled, be delivered up, to be removed to the State having Jurisdiction of the Crime.

(No Person held to Service or Labour in one State, under the Laws thereof, escaping into another, shall, in Consequence of any Law or Regulation therein, be discharged from such Service or Labour, But shall be delivered up on Claim of the Party to whom such Service or Labour may be due.) **(This clause in parentheses is superseded by the 13th Amendment.)**

Section 3 - New States

New States may be admitted by the Congress into this Union; but no new States shall be formed or erected within the Jurisdiction of any other State; nor any State be formed by the Junction of two or more States, or parts of States, without the Consent of the Legislatures of the States concerned as well as of the Congress.

The Congress shall have Power to dispose of and make all needful Rules and Regulations respecting the Territory or other Property belonging to the United States; and nothing in this Constitution shall be so construed as to Prejudice any Claims of the United States, or of any particular State.

Section 4 - Republican Government

The United States shall guarantee to every State in this Union a Republican Form of Government, and shall protect each of them against Invasion; and on Application of the Legislature, or of the Executive (when the Legislature cannot be convened) against domestic Violence.

Article V. - Amendment

The Congress, whenever two thirds of both Houses shall deem it necessary, shall propose Amendments to this Constitution, or, on the Application of the Legislatures of two thirds of the several States, shall call a Convention for proposing Amendments, which, in either Case, shall be valid to all Intents and Purposes, as part of this Constitution, when ratified by the Legislatures of three fourths of the several States, or by Conventions in three fourths thereof, as the one or the other Mode of Ratification may be proposed by the Congress; Provided that no Amendment which may be made prior to the Year One thousand eight hundred and eight shall in any Manner affect the first and fourth Clauses in the Ninth Section of the first Article; and that no State, without its Consent, shall be deprived of its equal Suffrage in the Senate.

Article VI. - Debts, Supremacy, Oaths

All Debts contracted and Engagements entered into, before the Adoption of this Constitution, shall be as valid against the United States under this Constitution, as under the Confederation.

This Constitution, and the Laws of the United States which shall be made in Pursuance thereof; and all Treaties made, or which shall be made, under the Authority of the United States, shall be the supreme Law of the Land; and the Judges in every State shall be bound thereby, any Thing in the Constitution or Laws of any State to the Contrary notwithstanding.

The Senators and Representatives before mentioned, and the Members of the several State Legislatures, and all executive and judicial Officers, both of the United States and of the several States, shall be bound by Oath or Affirmation, to support this Constitution; but no religious Test shall ever be required as a Qualification to any Office or public Trust under the United States.

Article VII. - Ratification

The Ratification of the Conventions of nine States, shall be sufficient for the Establishment of this Constitution between the States so ratifying the Same.

Done in Convention by the Unanimous Consent of the States present the Seventeenth Day of September in the Year of our Lord one thousand seven hundred and Eighty seven and of the Independence of the United States of America the Twelfth. In Witness whereof We have hereunto subscribed our Names.

Go Washington - President and deputy from Virginia

New Hampshire - John Langdon, Nicholas Gilman

Massachusetts - Nathaniel Gorham, Rufus King

Connecticut - Wm Saml Johnson, Roger Sherman

New York - Alexander Hamilton

New Jersey - Wil Livingston, David Brearley, Wm Paterson, Jona. Dayton

Pennsylvania - B Franklin, Thomas Mifflin, Robt Morris, Geo. Clymer, Thos FitzSimons, Jared Ingersoll, James Wilson, Gouv Morris

Delaware - Geo. Read, Gunning Bedford jun, John Dickinson, Richard Bassett, Jaco. Broom

Maryland - James McHenry, Dan of St Tho Jenifer, Danl Carroll

Virginia - John Blair, James Madison Jr.

North Carolina - Wm Blount, Richd Dobbs Spaight, Hu Williamson

South Carolina - J. Rutledge, Charles Cotesworth Pinckney, Charles Pinckney, Pierce Butler

Georgia - William Few, Abr Baldwin

Attest: William Jackson, Secretary

THE AMENDMENTS

The following are the Amendments to the Constitution. The first ten Amendments collectively are commonly known as the **Bill of Rights.**

Amendment 1 - Freedom of Religion, Press, Expression. Ratified 12/15/1791.

Congress shall make no law respecting an establishment of religion, or prohibiting the free exercise thereof; or abridging the freedom of speech, or of the press; or the right of the people peaceably to assemble, and to petition the Government for a redress of grievances.

Amendment 2 - Right to Bear Arms. Ratified 12/15/1791.

A well regulated Militia, being necessary to the security of a free State, the right of the people to keep and bear Arms, shall not be infringed.

Amendment 3 - Quartering of Soldiers. Ratified 12/15/1791.

No Soldier shall, in time of peace be quartered in any house, without the consent of the Owner, nor in time of war, but in a manner to be prescribed by law.

Amendment 4 - Search and Seizure. Ratified 12/15/1791.

The right of the people to be secure in their persons, houses, papers, and effects, against unreasonable searches and seizures, shall not be violated, and no Warrants shall issue, but upon probable cause, supported by Oath or affirmation, and particularly describing the place to be searched, and the persons or things to be seized.

Amendment 5 - Trial and Punishment, Compensation for Takings. Ratified 12/15/1791.

No person shall be held to answer for a capital, or otherwise infamous crime, unless on a presentment or indictment of a Grand Jury, except in cases arising in the land or naval forces, or in the Militia, when in actual service in time of War or public danger; nor shall any person be subject for the same offense to be twice put in jeopardy of life or limb; nor shall be compelled in any criminal case to be a witness against himself, nor be deprived of life, liberty, or property, without due process of law; nor shall private property be taken for public use, without just compensation.

Amendment 6 - Right to Speedy Trial, Confrontation of Witnesses. Ratified 12/15/1791.

In all criminal prosecutions, the accused shall enjoy the right to a speedy and public trial, by an impartial jury of the State and district wherein the crime shall have been committed, which district shall have been previously ascertained by law, and to be informed of the nature and cause of the accusation; to be confronted with the witnesses against him; to have compulsory process for obtaining witnesses in his favor, and to have the Assistance of Counsel for his defence.

Amendment 7 - Trial by Jury in Civil Cases. Ratified 12/15/1791.

In Suits at common law, where the value in controversy shall exceed twenty dollars, the right of trial by jury shall be preserved, and no fact tried by a jury, shall be otherwise re-examined in any Court of the United States, than according to the rules of the common law.

Amendment 8 - Cruel and Unusual Punishment. Ratified 12/15/1791.

Excessive bail shall not be required, nor excessive fines imposed, nor cruel and unusual punishments inflicted.

Amendment 9 - Construction of Constitution. Ratified 12/15/1791.

The enumeration in the Constitution, of certain rights, shall not be construed to deny or disparage others retained by the people.

Amendment 10 - Powers of the States and People. Ratified 12/15/1791.

The powers not delegated to the United States by the Constitution, nor prohibited by it to the States, are reserved to the States respectively, or to the people.

Amendment 11 - Judicial Limits. Ratified 2/7/1795.

The Judicial power of the United States shall not be construed to extend to any suit in law or equity, commenced or prosecuted against one of the United States by Citizens of another State, or by Citizens or Subjects of any Foreign State.

Amendment 12 - Choosing the President, Vice-President. Ratified 6/15/1804. History The Electoral College

The Electors shall meet in their respective states, and vote by ballot for President and Vice-President, one of whom, at least, shall not be an inhabitant of the same state with themselves; they shall name in their ballots the person voted for as President, and in distinct ballots the person voted for as Vice-President, and they shall make distinct lists of all persons voted for as President, and of all persons voted for as Vice-President and of the number of votes for each, which lists they shall sign and certify, and transmit sealed to the seat of the government of the United States, directed to the President of the Senate;

The President of the Senate shall, in the presence of the Senate and House of Representatives, open all the certificates and the votes shall then be counted;

The person having the greatest Number of votes for President, shall be the President, if such number be a majority of the whole number of Electors appointed; and if no person have such majority, then from the persons having the highest numbers not exceeding three on the list of those voted for as President, the House of Representatives shall choose immediately, by ballot, the President. But in choosing the President, the votes shall be taken by states, the representation from each state having one vote; a quorum for this purpose shall consist of a member or members from two-thirds of the states, and a majority of all the states shall be necessary to a choice. And if the House of Representatives shall not choose a President whenever the right of choice shall devolve upon them, before the fourth day of March next following, then the Vice-President shall act as President, as in the case of the death or other constitutional disability of the President.

The person having the greatest number of votes as Vice-President, shall be the Vice-President, if such number be a majority of the whole number of Electors appointed, and if no person have a majority, then from the two highest numbers on the list, the Senate shall choose the Vice-President; a quorum for the purpose shall consist of two-thirds of the whole number of Senators, and a majority of the whole number shall be necessary to a choice. But no person constitutionally ineligible to the office of President shall be eligible to that of Vice-President of the United States.

Amendment 13 - Slavery Abolished. Ratified 12/6/1865.

1. Neither slavery nor involuntary servitude, except as a punishment for crime whereof the party shall have been duly convicted, shall exist within the United States, or any place subject to their jurisdiction.

2. Congress shall have power to enforce this article by appropriate legislation.

Amendment 14 - Citizenship Rights. Ratified 7/9/1868.

1. All persons born or naturalized in the United States, and subject to the jurisdiction thereof, are citizens of the United States and of the State wherein they reside. No State shall make or enforce any law which shall abridge the privileges

or immunities of citizens of the United States; nor shall any State deprive any person of life, liberty, or property, without due process of law; nor deny to any person within its jurisdiction the equal protection of the laws.

2. Representatives shall be apportioned among the several States according to their respective numbers, counting the whole number of persons in each State, excluding Indians not taxed. But when the right to vote at any election for the choice of electors for President and Vice-President of the United States, Representatives in Congress, the Executive and Judicial officers of a State, or the members of the Legislature thereof, is denied to any of the male inhabitants of such State, being twenty-one years of age, and citizens of the United States, or in any way abridged, except for participation in rebellion, or other crime, the basis of representation therein shall be reduced in the proportion which the number of such male citizens shall bear to the whole number of male citizens twenty-one years of age in such State.

3. No person shall be a Senator or Representative in Congress, or elector of President and Vice-President, or hold any office, civil or military, under the United States, or under any State, who, having previously taken an oath, as a member of Congress, or as an officer of the United States, or as a member of any State legislature, or as an executive or judicial officer of any State, to support the Constitution of the United States, shall have engaged in insurrection or rebellion against the same, or given aid or comfort to the enemies thereof. But Congress may by a vote of two-thirds of each House, remove such disability.

4. The validity of the public debt of the United States, authorized by law, including debts incurred for payment of pensions and bounties for services in suppressing insurrection or rebellion, shall not be questioned. But neither the United States nor any State shall assume or pay any debt or obligation incurred in aid of insurrection or rebellion against the United States, or any claim for the loss or emancipation of any slave; but all such debts, obligations and claims shall be held illegal and void.

5. The Congress shall have power to enforce, by appropriate legislation, the provisions of this article.

Amendment 15 - Race No Bar to Vote. Ratified 2/3/1870.

1. The right of citizens of the United States to vote shall not be denied or abridged by the United States or by any State on account of race, color, or previous condition of servitude.

2. The Congress shall have power to enforce this article by appropriate legislation.

Amendment 16 - Status of Income Tax Clarified. Ratified 2/3/1913.

The Congress shall have power to lay and collect taxes on incomes, from whatever source derived, without apportionment among the several States, and without regard to any census or enumeration.

Amendment 17 - Senators Elected by Popular Vote. Ratified 4/8/1913.

The Senate of the United States shall be composed of two Senators from each State, elected by the people thereof, for six years; and each Senator shall have one vote. The electors in each State shall have the qualifications requisite for electors of the most numerous branch of the State legislatures.

When vacancies happen in the representation of any State in the Senate, the executive authority of such State shall issue writs of election to fill such vacancies:

Provided, That the legislature of any State may empower the executive thereof to make temporary appointments until the people fill the vacancies by election as the legislature may direct.

This amendment shall not be so construed as to affect the election or term of any Senator chosen before it becomes valid as part of the Constitution.

Amendment 18 - Liquor Abolished. Ratified 1/16/1919. Repealed by Amendment 21, 12/5/1933.

1. After one year from the ratification of this article the manufacture, sale, or transportation of intoxicating liquors within, the importation thereof into, or the exportation thereof from the United States and all territory subject to the jurisdiction thereof for beverage purposes is hereby prohibited.

2. The Congress and the several States shall have concurrent power to enforce this article by appropriate legislation.

3. This article shall be inoperative unless it shall have been ratified as an amendment to the Constitution by the legislatures of the several States, as provided in the Constitution, within seven years from the date of the submission hereof to the States by the Congress.

Amendment 19 - Women's Suffrage. Ratified 8/18/1920.

The right of citizens of the United States to vote shall not be denied or abridged by the United States or by any State on account of sex.

Congress shall have power to enforce this article by appropriate legislation.

Amendment 20 - Presidential, Congressional Terms. Ratified 1/23/1933.

1. The terms of the President and Vice President shall end at noon on the 20th day of January, and the terms of Senators and Representatives at noon on the 3rd day of January, of the years in which such terms would have ended if this article had not been ratified; and the terms of their successors shall then begin.

2. The Congress shall assemble at least once in every year, and such meeting shall begin at noon on the 3rd day of January, unless they shall by law appoint a different day.

3. If, at the time fixed for the beginning of the term of the President, the President elect shall have died, the Vice President elect shall become President. If a President shall not have been chosen before the time fixed for the beginning of his term, or if the President elect shall have failed to qualify, then the Vice President elect shall act as President until a President shall have qualified; and the Congress may by law provide for the case wherein neither a President elect nor a Vice President elect shall have qualified, declaring who shall then act as President, or the manner in which one who is to act shall be selected, and such person shall act accordingly until a President or Vice President shall have qualified.

4. The Congress may by law provide for the case of the death of any of the persons from whom the House of Representatives may choose a President whenever the right of choice shall have devolved upon them, and for the case of the death of any of the persons from whom the Senate may choose a Vice President whenever the right of choice shall have devolved upon them.

5. Sections 1 and 2 shall take effect on the 15th day of October following the ratification of this article.

6. This article shall be inoperative unless it shall have been ratified as an amendment to the Constitution by the legislatures of three-fourths of the several States within seven years from the date of its submission.

Amendment 21 - Amendment 18 Repealed. Ratified 12/5/1933.

1. The eighteenth article of amendment to the Constitution of the United States is hereby repealed.

2. The transportation or importation into any State, Territory, or possession of the United States for delivery or use therein of intoxicating liquors, in violation of the laws thereof, is hereby prohibited.

3. The article shall be inoperative unless it shall have been ratified as an amendment to the Constitution by conventions in the several States, as provided in the Constitution, within seven years from the date of the submission hereof to the States by the Congress.

Amendment 22 - Presidential Term Limits. Ratified 2/27/1951.

1. No person shall be elected to the office of the President more than twice, and no person who has held the office of President, or acted as President, for more than two years of a term to which some other person was elected President shall be elected to the office of the President more than once. But this Article shall not apply to any person holding the office of President, when this Article was proposed by the Congress, and shall not prevent any person who may be holding the office of President, or acting as President, during the term within which this Article becomes operative from holding the office of President or acting as President during the remainder of such term.

2. This article shall be inoperative unless it shall have been ratified as an amendment to the Constitution by the legislatures of three-fourths of the several States within seven years from the date of its submission to the States by the Congress.

Amendment 23 - Presidential Vote for District of Columbia. Ratified 3/29/1961.

1. The District constituting the seat of Government of the United States shall appoint in such manner as the Congress may direct: A number of electors of President and Vice President equal to the whole number of Senators and Representatives in Congress to which the District would be entitled if it were a State, but in no event more than the least populous State; they shall be in addition to those appointed by the States, but they shall be considered, for the purposes of the election of President and Vice President, to be electors appointed by a State; and they shall meet in the District and perform such duties as provided by the twelfth article of amendment.

2. The Congress shall have power to enforce this article by appropriate legislation.

Amendment 24 - Poll Tax Barred. Ratified 1/23/1964.

1. The right of citizens of the United States to vote in any primary or other election for President or Vice President, for electors for President or Vice President, or for Senator or Representative in Congress, shall not be denied or abridged by the United States or any State by reason of failure to pay any poll tax or other tax.

2. The Congress shall have power to enforce this article by appropriate legislation.

Amendment 25 - Presidential Disability and Succession. Ratified 2/10/1967.

1. In case of the removal of the President from office or of his death or resignation, the Vice President shall become President.

2. Whenever there is a vacancy in the office of the Vice President, the President shall nominate a Vice President who shall take office upon confirmation by a majority vote of both Houses of Congress.

3. Whenever the President transmits to the President pro tempore of the Senate and the Speaker of the House of Representatives his written declaration that he is unable to discharge the powers and duties of his office, and until he transmits to them a written declaration to the contrary, such powers and duties shall be discharged by the Vice President as Acting President.

4. Whenever the Vice President and a majority of either the principal officers of the executive departments or of such other body as Congress may by law provide, transmit to the President pro tempore of the Senate and the Speaker of the House of Representatives their written declaration that the President is unable to discharge the powers and duties of his office, the Vice President shall immediately assume the powers and duties of the office as Acting President.

Thereafter, when the President transmits to the President pro tempore of the Senate and the Speaker of the House of Representatives his written declaration that no inability exists, he shall resume the powers and duties of his office unless the Vice President and a majority of either the principal officers of the executive department or of such other body as Congress may by law provide, transmit within four days to the President pro tempore of the Senate and the Speaker of the House of Representatives their written declaration that the President is unable to discharge the powers and duties of his office. Thereupon Congress shall decide the issue, assembling within forty eight hours for that purpose if not in session. If the Congress, within twenty one days after receipt of the latter written declaration, or, if Congress is not in session, within twenty one days after Congress is required to assemble, determines by two thirds vote of both Houses that the President is unable to discharge the powers and duties of his office, the Vice President shall continue to discharge the same as Acting President; otherwise, the President shall resume the powers and duties of his office.

Amendment 26 - Voting Age Set to 18 Years. Ratified 7/1/1971.

1. The right of citizens of the United States, who are eighteen years of age or older, to vote shall not be denied or abridged by the United States or by any State on account of age.

2. The Congress shall have power to enforce this article by appropriate legislation.

Amendment 27 - Limiting Congressional Pay Increases. Ratified 5/7/1992.

No law, varying the compensation for the services of the Senators and Representatives, shall take effect, until an election of Representatives shall have intervened.

Glossary

A

abatement The suspension or cessation, in whole or in part, of a continuing charge.

abnormally dangerous activity A non-natural or unusual activity that creates a substantial likelihood of great harm to persons or property that cannot be eliminated by reasonable care by the defendant.

abuse of process Using the threat of resorting to the legal system to extract agreement to terms against the other party's will.

act of God An act occasioned exclusively by forces of nature without the interference of any human agency.

agent A person or entity (as an employee or independent contractor) authorized to act on behalf of and under the control of another in dealing with third parties.

allocation of risk Assignment of uncertainty to another party.

appropriation Stealing and using someone's identity or image.

artificial condition A man-made condition that exists on the land.

as is A sale of goods by sample "as is" requires that the goods be of the kind and quality represented, even though they may be in a damaged condition.

assault Intentional voluntary movement that creates fear or apprehension of an immediate unwanted touching; the threat or attempt to cause a touching, whether successful or not, provided the victim is aware of the danger.

assumption of the risk The doctrine that releases another person from liability for the person who chooses to assume a known risk of harm.

attorney–client relationship Attorneys have a duty to maintain a client's confidences regarding any information that the client wants kept confidential.

attractive nuisance doctrine The doctrine that holds a landowner to a higher duty of care even when the children are trespassers, because the potentially harmful condition is so inviting to a child.

B

battery An intentional and unwanted harmful or offensive contact with the person of another; the actual intentional touching of someone with intent to cause harm, no matter how slight the harm.

beyond a reasonable doubt The requirement for the level of proof in a criminal matter in order to convict or find the defendant guilty. It is a substantially higher and more-difficult-to-prove criminal matter standard.

black letter An informal term indicating the basic principles of law generally accepted by the courts and/or embodied in the statutes of a particular jurisdiction.

burden of proof Standard for assessing the weight of the evidence.

but for test If the complained-of act had not occurred, no injury would have resulted.

C

capacity The ability to understand the nature and significance of a contract; to understand or comprehend specific acts or reasoning

cause in fact The particular cause that produces an event and without which the event would not have occurred.

cause of action A personal, financial, or other injury for which the law gives a person the right to receive compensation.

caveat emptor Let the buyer beware.

charitable organization An organization that provides charity without obtaining a profit or gain for itself or its owners.

chattel Tangible personal property or goods.

civil Relating to private rights and remedies sought in an action brought to enforce, redress, or protect private rights.

class action A group of people ranked together as having common characteristics that arose from a common legal position relating to the defendant.

co-defendant More than one defendant who is being sued in the same lawsuit.

collateral source rule The legal doctrine that there should be no reduction in damages due to an injured person merely because there are other sources of partial indemnity (such as insurance) for the same harm or loss. The rule prevents a tortfeasor from escaping full responsibility.

common law Judge-made law, the ruling in a judicial opinion.

comparative negligence Negligence is measured in terms of percentage, and any damages allowed are diminished in proportion to amount of negligence attributable to the person for whose injury, damage or death recovery is sought.

compensatory damages A payment to make up for a wrong committed and return the nonbreaching party to a position where the effect or the breach has been neutralized.

consent All parties to a novation (substitution of a new contract) must knowingly assent to the substitution of either the obligations or parties to the agreement.

consequential damages Damages resulting from the breach that are natural and foreseeable results of the breaching party's actions.

consideration A recompense or payment; compensation.

continuing trespass Remaining in force or being carried on without letup.

contract A legally binding agreement between two or more parties.

contribution Payment of a share of an amount for which one is liable as a shared payment of a judgment by joint tortfeasors, especially according to proportional fault.

contributory negligence The plaintiff played a large part in causing the injury; thus, fundamental fairness precludes assigning liability to the defendant.

covenant An agreement, convention, or promise of two or more parties, by deed in writing, signed, and delivered, by which either of the parties pledges himself to the other that something is either done, or shall be done, or shall not be done, or stipulates for the truth of certain facts.

conversion An overt act to deprive the owner of possession of personal property with no intention of returning the property, thereby causing injury or harm.

co-plaintiff More than one plaintiff who is involved in the same lawsuit.

crime An act that violates the penal law of the local, state, or federal government.

cyberspace Computer network consisting of a worldwide network of computer networks that use the TCP/IP network protocols to facilitate data transmission and exchange.

D

damages Money paid to compensate for loss or injury.

defamation An act of communication involving a false and unprivileged statement about another person, causing harm.

defendant The party in a lawsuit against whom an action is brought.

defense Legally sufficient reason to excuse the complained-of behavior.

defense of others A justification available when one harms or threatens another in defense of a person other than oneself.

defense of property A justification for the use of force in protecting one's property through such force as must be reasonable under all circumstances.

detour A deviation from a direct course of action.

diplomat A person appointed by a national government to conduct official negotiations and maintain political, economic, and social relations with another country or countries.

direct damages Damages that arise naturally or ordinarily from an injury, breach of contract or breach of duty.

discipline Instruction, comprehending the communication of knowledge and training to observe and act in accordance with rules and order.

disclaimer A term which limits claim or denial.

discretionary Left to or regulated by one's own judgment.

disparagement A falsehood that tends to denigrate the goods or services of another party.

domesticated animal An animal accustomed to living with humans.

dominion The perfect control in right of ownership.

duty of care Such a degree of care, precaution, or diligence as may fairly and properly be expected or required, having regard to the nature of the action, or of the subject matter, and the circumstances surrounding the transaction.

dwelling place The home or other structure in which a person lives.

E

eavesdropper A secret listener to private conversations.

eggshell skull A person who is particularly vulnerable or susceptible to damage or injury as a result of a pre-existing condition or weakness that afflicts a particular person.

elements A constituent part of a claim that must be proved for the claim to succeed.

express assumption A directly and clearly stated act or agreement of assuming or taking upon one's self.

express warranty A written representation by the seller as to the nature of the goods to be sold.

F

fair market value The amount that a willing buyer would pay for an item that a willing seller would accept.

false imprisonment Any deprivation of a person's freedom of movement without that person's consent and against his or her will, whether done by actual violence or threats.

false light An untrue and misleading portrayal of a person.

family purpose doctrine Where one purchases and maintains an automobile for the comfort, convenience, pleasure, entertainment and recreation of one's family, any member thereof operating the automobile will be regarded as an agent or servant of the owner, and the owner will be held liable for injuries sustained by a third person by reason of negligent operation of the vehicle by a family member.

Federal Rules of Evidence Rules governing the introduction of evidence in proceedings, both civil and criminal, in federal courts. While they do not apply to suits in state courts, the rules of many states have been closely modeled after these rules.

fitness for a particular purpose Where the seller at the time of contracting has reason to know any particular purpose for which the goods are required and that the buyer is relying on the seller's skill or judgment to select or furnish suitable goods, there is, unless excluded or modified, an implied warranty that the goods shall be fit for such purpose.

foreseeability The capacity for a party to reasonably anticipate a future event.

frolic To engage in recreation.

G

general damages Those that normally would be anticipated in a similar action.

governmental functions Functions of a municipality that are essential to its existence, in sense of serving the public at large, that are not necessary to its existence, and that ensure the advantage of its inhabitants.

gross negligence The intentional failure to perform a manifest duty in reckless disregard of the consequences as affecting the life or property of another.

H

hedonic damages Damages awarded in some jurisdictions for the loss of enjoyment of life.

hypothesis An assumption made especially in order to test its logical or empirical consequences.

I

immunity Exemption, as from serving in an office, or performing duties that the law generally requires other citizens to perform.

implied assumption An inference from the plaintiff's conduct that demonstrates that the person is accepting the risk involved in the activity or event.

implied warranty An unwritten representation that is normally and naturally included by operation of law that applies to the goods to be sold.

imputed To ascribe to or charge (a person) with an act or quality because of the conduct of another over whom one has control or for whose acts or conduct one is responsible.

imputed negligence Places upon one person responsibility for the negligence of another.

indemnity Compensation for damage, loss, or injury suffered.

independent contractor One who, in exercise of an independent employment, contracts to do a piece of work according to his own methods and is subject to his employer's control only as to the end product or final result of his work.

inference Arriving at a conclusion based on evidence.

inherent Part of the essential character of something; by nature.

injunction A court order that requires a party to refrain from acting in a certain way to prevent harm to the requesting party.

injurious falsehood In the law of slander and libel, a defamation that does actual damage.

integrity A standard of values having soundness or moral principle and character.

intent Having the knowledge and desire that a specific consequence will result from an action.

intentional infliction of emotional distress Intentional act involving extreme and outrageous conduct resulting in severe mental anguish.

intentional tort An intentional civil wrong that injures another person or property.

interference with contractual relationship The defendant's intentional procuring of a breach of the contract that an entity or person has with the plaintiff so that the plaintiff sustains damages.

intervening cause An independent cause that intervenes between the original wrongful act or omission and the injury, turns aside the natural sequence of events, and produces a result that would not otherwise have followed and that could not have been reasonably anticipated.

intervening force An act that actively operates in producing harm to another after actor's negligent act or omission.

intrusion Trespassing on or encroachment on the possessions of another.

invitees People wanted on the premises for a specific purpose known by the landowner.

J

joint enterprise The joint prosecution of a common purpose under such circumstances that each has authority expressed or implied to act for all in respect to control, means or agencies employed to execute such common purpose.

joint tortfeasors Two or more persons jointly or severally liable in tort for the same injury to the plaintiff or the plaintiff's property.

joint and several liability Shared responsibility, apportioned between all of the defendants, but in no case can the plaintiff recover more than 100 percent of the damages awarded.

K

knowledge Understanding gained by actual experience.

L

landholder Someone who is in rightful possession of the land.

last clear chance Permits the plaintiff in a negligence action to recover, notwithstanding his own negligence, on a showing that the defendant had the last clear chance to avoid the accident.

lessee One who rents property from another.

lessor One who grants a lease or rental of a property to another.

liable A determination of financial responsibility of the tortfeasor for tortious conduct that has resulted in some form of injury to an individual's property or person.

libel Written defamatory statement.

licensee One known to be on the premises but whose presence gives no benefit to the property owner.

liquidated damages An amount of money agreed upon in the original contract as a reasonable estimation of the damages to be recovered by the nonbreaching party. This amount is set forth in the contract so the parties have a clear idea of the risk of breach.

loco parentis Of, relating to, or acting as a temporary guardian or caretaker of a child, taking on all or some of the responsibilities of a parent.

loss of consortium A claim filed, made by the plaintiff's spouse, for the loss of companionship in the marriage caused by the injuries.

loss of earning capacity Damage to one's ability to earn wages in the future and recoverable as element of damage in tort actions.

M

malice Person's doing of any act in reckless disregard of another person.

malicious prosecution Initiating a criminal prosecution or civil suit against another party with malice and without probable cause.

malign To speak harmful or detrimental untruths about.

malpractice Failure of a professional person, as a physician or lawyer, to render proper services through reprehensible ignorance or negligence, especially when injury or loss follows.

master An individual or entity (as a corporation) having control or authority over another.

merchantability The article sold shall be of the general kind described and reasonably fit for the general purpose for which it shall have been sold, and where the article sold is ordinarily used in but one way.

merchants Businesspersons who have a certain level of expertise dealing in commercial transactions regarding the goods they sell; persons who regularly deal in goods of the kind specified in the agreement. They hold themselves out as having special knowledge in their area.

misfeasance The improper performance of some act which a person may lawfully do.

mitigate To lessen in intensity or amount.

murder The killing of a human being with intent.

mutual agreement A meeting of the minds on a specific subject, and a manifestation of intent of the parties to do or refrain from doing some specific act or acts.

N

natural condition A condition upon the land that has been untouched or influenced by man.

necessity Individuals are excused from criminal and sometimes tortious liability if they act under a duress of circumstances to protect life or limb or health in a reasonable manner and with no other acceptable choices.

negligence The failure to use reasonable care to avoid harm to another person or to do that which a reasonable person might do in similar circumstances.

negligence per se Results from statutes establishing that certain actions or omissions are impermissible under any and all circumstances; the failure to use reasonable care to avoid harm to another person or to do that which a reasonable person might do in similar circumstances.

nominal damages A small amount of money given to the nonbreaching party as a token award to acknowledge the fact of the breach.

non-delegable duties An obligation imposed by law or contract that may not be passed to another.

nonfeasance The omission of an act which a person ought to do.

notice Intelligence of a fact communicated to another.

nuisance That activity that arises from unreasonable, unwarranted or unlawful use by a person of his own property, working obstruction or injury to right of another, or to the public, and producing such material annoyance, inconvenience and discomfort that the law will presume resulting damage.

O

omission The failure to act when there exists a legal duty to do so.

objective standard A legal standard that is based on conduct and perceptions external to a particular person.

operational Pertaining to a process or series of actions for achieving a result.

P

pecuniary Consisting of money or that which can be valued in money.

person The body and clothing of an individual as well as anything attached or an extension of the body such as a purse.

personal property Movable or intangible thing not attached to real property.

plaintiff The party initiating legal action.

precedent The holding of past court decisions that are followed in future judicial cases where similar facts and legal issues are present.

premises Any real property, buildings that are attached to the property, grounds, facilities, structures, and other things that are attached to the land or growing from it.

premises liability The liability that a landholder may be exposed to in connection with his use and enjoyment of real property.

preponderance of the evidence The weight or level of persuasion of evidence needed to find the defendant liable as alleged by the plaintiff in a civil matter.

presumed damages Damages that are presumed under the law to result naturally and necessarily from an act and do not require proof.

presumption A rule of law, statutory or judicial, by which finding of a basic fact gives rise to existence of presumed fact, until the presumption is rebutted.

prima facie (Latin) "At first sight." A case with the required proof of elements in a tort cause of action; the elements of the plaintiff's (or prosecutor's) cause of action; what the plaintiff must prove; accepted on its face, but not indisputable.

principal The source of authority.

private nuisance A thing or activity that substantially and unreasonably interferes with plaintiff's use and enjoyment of her land.

privilege Reasonable expectation of privacy and confidentiality for communications in furtherance of the relationship such as attorney–client, doctor–patient, husband–wife, psychotherapist–patient, and priest–penitent.

privity A relationship between the parties to the contract who have rights and obligations to each other through the terms of the agreement.

probable cause The totality of circumstances leads one to believe certain facts or circumstances exist; applies to arrests, searches, and seizures.

product liability Refers to the legal liability of manufacturers and sellers to compensate buyers, users, and even bystanders for damages or injuries suffered because of defects in goods purchased.

proprietary functions Functions that a city or town, in its discretion, may perform when considered to be for the best interest of its citizens.

proximate cause The defendant's actions are the nearest cause of the plaintiff's injuries.

public disclosure Stated in the news or printed in a newspaper.

public nuisance An unreasonable interference with a right common to the general public.

public officer A person who, upon being issued a commission, taking required oath, enters upon, for a fixed tenure, a position called an office where he or she exercises in his or her own right some of the attributes of sovereign he or she serves for benefit of public.

public policy The principle that injury to the public good or public order constitutes a basis for setting aside, or denying effect to, acts or transactions.

punitive damages An amount of money awarded to a non-breaching party that is not based on the actual losses incurred by that party, but as a punishment to the breaching party for the commission of an intentional wrong.

R

real property Land and all property permanently attached to it, such as buildings.

reasonable care Conduct that an ordinary person would do under the same or similar circumstances.

reasonable person A hypothetical person used as a legal standard, especially to determine whether someone acted with negligence; specifically, a person who exercises the degree of attention, knowledge, intelligence, and judgment that society requires of its members for the protection of their own and of others' interests.

reasonable person test Asking whether or not an ordinary or average person would find the action offensive or harmful.

rebutt To defeat, refute, or take away the effect of something.

recapture of chattels The act of recovering personal property by a property owner.

redress Relief from distress; compensation for a loss or injury.

release A discharge from the parties' performance obligations that acknowledges the dispute but forgoes contractual remedies.

remedial Intended as a remedy.

remedy The means by which a right is enforced or the violation of a right is prevented, redressed, or compensated.

res ipsa loquitur Doctrine in which it is assumed that a person's injuries were caused by the negligent act of another person as the harmful act ordinarily would not occur but for negligence.

respondeat superior A master is liable in certain circumstances for the wrongful acts of his servants; and a principal for those of his agent.

S

scope of employment The activities in which an employee engages in carrying out the employer's business that are reasonably foreseeable by the employer.

self-defense A defendant's legal excuse that the use of force was justified.

servant A person in the employ and subject to the direction or control of an individual or company.

slander Oral defamatory statements.

slander per quod Slander that requires proof of damages.

slander per se Slander that is actionable without the plaintiff providing proof of damages.

sovereign A person, body, or state in which independent and supreme authority is vested.

special damages Those damages incurred beyond and in addition to the general damages suffered and expected in similar cases.

specific intent The mental desire and will to act in a particular way.

spousal privilege Combination of two elements: (1) the right not to be compelled to testify against one's spouse, and (2) the protection of marital confidences.

stare decisis (Latin) "Stand by the decision." Decisions from a court with substantially the same set of facts should be followed by that court and all lower courts under it; the judicial process of adhering to prior case decisions; the doctrine of precedent whereby once a court has decided a specific issue one way in the past, it and other courts in the same jurisdiction are obligated to follow that earlier decision in deciding cases with similar issues in the future.

statutory law Derived from the Constitution in statutes enacted by the legislative branch of state or federal government; primary source of law consisting of the body of legislative law.

strict liability The defendant is liable without the plaintiff having to prove fault.

subrogation The right to sue in the name of another.

substantial certainty The defendant knows that the plaintiff's damage is probably going to occur as a result of the defendant's actions.

substantial factor A material and active contributing activity or event that led to the plaintiff's injuries or damages.

supersede To set aside, render unnecessary, suspend, or stay.

survival Actions for personal injuries that by state statute survive the death of the injured person.

T

tort A civil wrongful act, committed against a person or property, either intentional or negligent.

tort litigation Legal action that involves an injury that falls under the definition of a tort.

tortfeasor Actor committing the wrong, whether intentional, negligent, or strict liability.

tortious conduct The intentional or unintentional behavior or conduct that results in harm to another person.

transferred intent doctrine The doctrine that holds a person liable for the unintended result to another person not contemplated by the defendant's actions.

trespass to land Intentional and unlawful entry onto or interference with the land of another person without consent.

trespassers Uninvited guests on the property of the landowner.

trier of fact Jury.

U

Uniform Commercial Code A collection of modernized, codified, and standardized laws that apply to all commercial transactions with the exception of real property.

unfair competition A term that is applied generally to all dishonest or fraudulent rivalry in trade and commerce, but is particularly applied to the practice of endeavoring to substitute one's own goods or products in the markets for those of another, having an established reputation and extensive sale, by means of imitating or counterfeiting the name, title, size, shape, or distinctive peculiarities of the product.

V

vendee A purchaser or buyer.

vendor The person who transfers property or goods by sale.

vicarious liability One person, or a third party, may be found liable for the act of another or shares liability with the actor.

W

warranty A promise or representation by the seller that the goods in question meet certain standards.

whistle-blower One who reveals wrongdoing within an organization to the public or to those in positions of authority.

wild animal An animal of an untamable disposition or one that is in a state of nature.

wrongful death A death attributable to the willful or negligent act of another.

Index

A

ABAMASTER OF MIAMI, INC., Mike's Restaurant Equipment Corporation, Carfel, Inc., Zoila GODOY v., 195–196
Abatement, defined, 157
Abellon v. Hartford Insurance Co., 127
Abnormal use, product liability and, 188
Abnormally dangerous activities, defined, 172–174
Absolute liability, 167. *See also* Strict liability
Abuse of process, defined, 27
ACI Chems., Inc. v. Metaplex, Inc., 166
Act, defined, 20
Act of God, defined, 92
Action
 cause of (*See* Cause of action)
 civil, 17
 criminal, 17
Activity, in foreseeability, 71, 72
ACTON, ___U.S.___ (1995), VERNONIA SCHOOL DIST. 47J v., 65–69
Adams, Ewing v., 165
Adkins v. Lester, 16
Agent, defined, 131
Airspace, 40
Alesko v. Union Pac. R. Co., 50–51
Alexander v. Brown, 165
Alfred Jacobshagen Co. v. Dockery, 165
Allocation of risk, defined, 131
Amburgy, Heidel v., 37
American Bar Association, 199
American Law Institute, 8
Anderson v. Ceccardi, 112
Andrews test, 75
Animals, 168–171
 domesticated, 169–171
 livestock as, 171
 wild, 168–169, 170
Appellate court, 5
Appropriation, defined, 30
Archdioceses of N.Y., O'Neal v., 86
Area, in foreseeability, 71, 72
Artificial condition, 150, 152
As is, defined, 187
Assault
 consent and, 55
 defense of property and, 58
 defined, 21–22
 elements of, 21–22
 harm to property and, 39
 self-defense and, 57
Assembler, product liability and, 188

Assumption of the risk
 defined, 105–106
 product liability and, 184, 188–189
 strict liability and, 174–175
At will, defined, 206
AT&T Corp., Gray v., 229
Attorney
 ethics for, 18
 legal malpractice and, 199–201
 statute of limitations and, 45
Attorney-client privilege, 217
Attorney-client relationship, defined, 201
Attractive nuisance doctrine, defined, 152
August Schubert Wagon Co., Schubert v., 230
Automobile consent statutes, 140
Ayala, Mercury Ins. Co. v., 128

B

Baldwin, Burns v., 50
Ball, State Farm Mut. Auto. Ins. Co. v., 128
Barbee v. Barbee, 51–52
Battery
 consent and, 55
 defense of property and, 58
 defined, 20
 elements of, 20
 harm to property and, 39
 as intentional tort, 19–21
 medical malpractice and, 198
 self-defense and, 57
Baxter, Ferrell v., 15
Behavior, in foreseeability, 72
Bellevue S. Assocs. v. HRH Constr. Corp., 195–196
Berkovitz v. U.S., 223
Bethel School Dist. No. 403 v. Fraser, 67
Bethlehem Steel, Rodriguez v., 127
Beyond a reasonable doubt, defined, 3
Bezenek, Thrifty-Tel, Inc. v., 42
Biswell, United States v., 67
Black Clawson Co., Gebo v., 195
Black letter, defined, 8
Blair, Everton v., 212
BMW v. Gore, 123
Borchers v. Winzeler Excavating Co., 112
Bowles v. Pro Indiviso, Inc., 50
Bramwell v. South Rigby Canal Co., 50
Breach-of-contract action, medical malpractice and, 197
Breach of duty, 74–77, 182

Breach-of-warranty action, medical malpractice and, 197
Briney, Katko v., 58
Brown, Alexander v., 165
Buick, MacPherson v., 182
Bunch, McHaffie v., 231
Burden of proof
 contributory negligence and, 101
 defined, 3, 88–89
 proximate cause and, 90
Burdens, breach of duty and, 77
Burglary, harm to property and, 39
Burlington Industries, Inc. v. Ellerth, 148
Burns v. Baldwin, 50
Business tort, 203–207
"But for" test, defined, 88–89
Butterfield v. Forrester, 101
Byerly, Graham v., 38

C

Callow, Campbell v., 229
Camp v. East Fort Ditch Company, Ltd., 50
Campbell v. Callow, 229
Capacity, defined, 54
Cardozo test, 74, 75. *See also* Zone-of-danger test
Causation
 of abnormally dangerous activities, 172
 business tort and, 205, 206
 product liability and, 185, 186, 187
 proximate cause and, 90–92
Causation in fact, 87–88
Cause in fact
 contributory negligence and, 101
 defined, 87
 proximate cause and, 90
Cause of action
 for breach of warranty, 185
 defined, 3
 elements of, 5
 intentional torts and, 6, 18
 for malicious prosecution, 26
 against property rights, 39
Caveat emptor, defined, 155
Ceccardi, Anderson v., 112
Central Synagogue, McCann v., 99
Century Business Comms., Inc., MBF Corp. v., 165
Chamberlin, Morgan v., 38
Charitable immunity, 219–221
Charitable organizations, defined, 219
Charles Cross & Son, Inc., Suklijian v., 195

Chattel
  conversion and, 44
  defined, 41–42, 181
  recapture of, 59
  trespass to (*See* Trespass to chattels)
Child, defined, 152
Child trespassers, 152
Christian, Rowland v., 154
Cincinnati Base Ball Club Co. v. *Eno,* 113
City of New York, McDermott v., 196
City of New York, Mirand v., 86
City of New York, Pesca v., 99
City of Newburgh School Dist.,
    Moores v., 86
City of Rye School Dist., Convey v., 86
Civil, defined, 1–2
Civil action, defined, 17
Civil proceedings, wrongful/unjust, 27
Class action, defined, 118
Clements Food Co., Hooper v., 230
Co-defendants, defined, 5, 6
Co-plaintiffs, defined, 5
Codling v. *Paglia,* 195
Collateral source rule, defined, 119
Coming to the nuisance defense, 159
*COMMERCIAL SANITATION
    SYSTEMS, INC, VILLANUEVA
    ex rel. U.S.* v., 126–129
*Commodity Futures Trading Comm'n,
    Rosenthal & Co.* v., 146–147
Common law
  defamation and, 28
  defined, 5
  domesticated animals and, 170
  immunity and, 215
  vicarious liability and, 138
Common sense
  in foreseeability, 71, 72
  proximate cause and, 90
Communication, immunity and, 215, 216
Comparative negligence, 103–105
Compensatory damages
  defined, 114–116
  nuisance and, 157
Complaints, product liability and, 183
CompuServe, Inc. v. *Cyber Promotions,
    Inc.,* 42
Conduct
  discipline and, 61
  intentional infliction of emotional
      distress and, 25
  proximate cause and, 91
  reasonable care and, 2
  tortious, 3
  unreasonable (*See* Unreasonable
      conduct)
Confinement, in false imprisonment, 23–24
Consent
  defined, 39, 54–55
  exceeding, 54
  express, 54
  implied, 54
  medical malpractice and, 198–199
Consequential damages, defined, 115
Consideration, defined, 120
Constant trespasser, 151–152
Constitution, United States, 232–247

Consumer contemplation test, 189
Contact
  assault and, 21
  battery and, 20
  physical, 198
Continuing trespass, defined, 41
Contract(s)
  business tort and, 205, 206
  defined, 4
  liquidated damages and, 117
  vicarious liability and, 138
Contribution, defined, 104, 120
Contributory negligence
  comparative negligence and, 103
  defined, 100–101
  ethics for, 107
  last clear chance and, 102
  nuisance and, 158–159
  product liability and, 183
  strict liability and, 175
  vicarious liability and, 131
Conversion
  consent and, 55
  defense of property and, 58
  defined, 43–46
  elements of, 44
  self-defense and, 57
Convey v. *City of Rye School Dist.,* 86
Cook v. *Rockwell Int'l Corp.,* 180
Cornell Law School Legal Information
    Institute, 8
*CORPORATION OF THE PRESIDING
    BISHOP OF THE CHURCH OF
    JESUS CHRIST OF LATTER-
    DAY SAINTS, Lamoni K. Riordan*
    v., 229–231
Covenant, defined, 120
Cowell Steel Structures, Inc., Johnson v., 231
Crespo v. *Triad, Inc.,* 99
Crime, defined, 3–4
Criminal action, defined, 17
Criminal human force, defined, 92, 93
Curtis-Palmer Hydro-Elec. Co., Ross v., 99
Custom, 79
Custom in the trade, product liability
    and, 183
*Cyber Promotions, Inc., CompuServe,
    Inc.* v., 42
Cyberspace
  defined, 42
  ethics in, 43
  trespass in, 42–43

D

Dale HANSEN; Sandra Hansen v.
    FLYING J TRAVEL PLAZA,
    112–113
Damages, 114–129
  of abnormally dangerous activities, 172
  for assault, 22
  for battery, 21
  business tort and, 204, 205, 206
  compensatory (*See* Compensatory
      damages)
  consequential, 115

Damages—*Cont.*
  for conversion, 44
  defined, 2
  direct, 115
  ethics for, 120
  exemplary, 117 (*See also* Punitive
      damages)
  in false imprisonment, 24
  general, 115
  hedonic, 116
  joint tortfeasors and, 119–120
  liquidated, 117
  mitigation and, 118–119
  nominal, 21, 116
  noncompensatory, 117 (*See also*
      Punitive damages)
  nuisance and, 157
  presumed, 28
  product liability and, 182, 185, 186, 187
  property, 117
  punitive (*See* Punitive damages)
  for slander, 29
  special, 115, 204
  in trespass to chattel, 42
  in trespass to land, 41
  in wrongful birth tort, 203
  in wrongful death tort, 202–203
Data
  historical, 72
  sensory, 71, 72
*David MEYER, individually and in his
    capacity as President and
    Designated Officer/Broker of Triad,
    Inc., etc.* v. *Emma Mary Ellen
    HOLLEY, et vir, et al.,* 146–148
Davidson v. *Schneider,* 231
Deadly force, 58
Deceit, consent and, 55
Deer Creek, Inc. v. *Hibbard,* 50
Defamation, 201–202
  consent and, 55
  defined, 27–29
  disparagement and, 204
  elements of, 27
Defamation per quod, 27
Defamation per se, 27, 29
Defamatory statement, defined, 27
Defects
  design, 182, 189
  manufacturing, 181, 183, 189
  in product liability, 181–182, 183, 189
  warning, 182
Defendant
  defined, 5
  last clear chance and, 102–103
Defense of others, defined, 57–58
Defense of property, defined, 58–59
Defense(s), 100–113
  of assumption of the risk, 105–106
  of comparative negligence, 103–104
  concept of, 53
  consent and, 54–55
  of contributory negligence, 100–101
  defined, 53, 100
  discipline and, 60–61
  justification and, 60
  necessity and, 59–60

Defense(s)—*Cont.*
of others, 57–58
product liability and, 183–184
of property, 58–59
recapture of chattels and, 59
self- (*See* Self-defense)
types of, 54–62
to warranty actions, 187–189
Delaware v. *Prouse,* 66
Deshaney v. *Winnebago County Dept. of Social Servs.,* 67
Design defects, 182, 189
Detour, defined, 132–134
Diebler, Havel v., 231
Diplomatic immunity, 224–225
Diplomats, defined, 224
Direct damages, defined, 115
Discipline, defined, 60–61
Disclaimer, defined, 187
Discovered trespasser, 151
Discretionary function/duty, 222, 223
Disparagement, defined, 204
Distributor, product liability and, 188
Dockery, Alfred Jacobshagen Co. v., 165
Domesticated animal, defined, 169–171
Dominguez v. *Lafayette-Boynton Hous. Corp.,* 99
Dominion, defined, 44
Dotterweich, United States v., 147
Dram Shop Act, 93
Duty, 74–79
breach of, 75–77, 182
defined, 74
non-delegable, 138–139
product liability and, 182
res ipsa loquitur and, 78–79
Duty of care, defined, 74
Duty to warn, in product liability, 190
Dwelling place, defined, 58

E

Easement, 41
East Fort Ditch Company, Ltd., Camp v., 50
Eavesdropper, defined, 217
Economic losses, 115
Eggshell skull, defined, 91
Ehlis v. *Shire Richwood, Inc.,* 229
Electrical Wholesale Supply Co., Inc. v. *Nielson,* 50
Elements, defined, 5
Elkins v. *United States,* 66
Ellerth, Burlington Industries, Inc., v., 148
Emma Mary Ellen HOLLEY, et vir, et al., David MEYER, individually and in his capacity as President and Designated Officer/Broker of Triad, Inc., etc. v., 146–148
Emotional distress
consent and, 55
defense of property and, 58
intentional infliction of, 24–26
self-defense and, 57
Emotions, intentional torts and, 18

Employees
business tort and, 203, 206
employer liability and, 135–136
immunity and, 219, 220, 221, 224
independent contractors and, 136–139
intentional torts and, 139–140
paralegals as, 141
Employer
business tort and, 206
immunity and, 219
independent contractor and, 136–139
intentional torts and, 139–140
Employer-employee relationship, vicarious liability and, 131–134, 136
Employer liability, 135–136
Employment, scope of, 132, 133
Eno, Cincinnati Base Ball Club Co. v., 113
Entry upon land, 150–151
Ethics
for attorney, 18
for contributory negligence, 107
in cyberspace, 43
for damages, 120
for immunity, 215
for intentional torts, 18
for legal malpractice, 201
for negligence, 81, 107
for product liability, 184
for property, 59
for proximate cause, 93
for strict liability, 175
for trespassers, 151
for vicarious liability, 139
Everton v. *Blair,* 212
Ewing v. *Adams,* 165
Exceeding consent, 54
Exemplary damages, 117. *See also* Punitive damages
Express assumption, defined, 105–106
Express consent, 54
Express warranty, defined, 185
Exxon Valdez, public nuisance and, 159

F

Fair market value, defined, 117
Fair on its face, 24
False arrest, defined, 24
False imprisonment
consent and, 55
defense of property and, 58
defined, 22–24
elements of, 22–23
self-defense and, 57
False light, defined, 31
False statement of fact, product liability and, 185
Family immunity, 215–218
Family purpose doctrine, defined, 140–141
FARR WEST INVESTMENTS v. *TOPAZ MARKETING, L.P. and MR. AND MRS. DENNIS LOWER,* 41, 49–52
Federal government, immunity and, 221–222
Federal Rules of Civil Procedure, 118

Federal Rules of Evidence, defined, 217
Federal Tort Claims Act, 221–222
Ferguson, Leaf River Forest Prods., Inc., v., 164
Ferrell v. *Baxter,* 15
First Fed. Sav. & Loan Ass'n of Boise, O'Boskey v., 50
Fitness for a particular purpose, defined, 186
Fletcher, Rylands v., 173
FLYING J TRAVEL PLAZA, Dale HANSEN; Sandra Hansen v., 112–113
Force
criminal human, 92, 93
deadly, 58
defense of others and, 57
defense of property and, 58
intervening, 92, 93
intervening intentional human, 92, 93
intervening negligent human, 92
non-deadly, 59
proximate cause and, 91
reasonable, 56, 59
self-defense and, 56–57
Foreseeability
breach of duty and, 77
defined, 71, 72
proximate cause and, 91–92
Foreseeable use, product liability and, 188–189
Forrester, Butterfield v., 101
Foster v. *Preston Mill Co.,* 175
Frank C. NEWBERRY v. *Laurence L. MARTENS, M.D. and Twin Falls Clinic and Hospital, and John Doe and Jane Doe, husband and wife, I through X, and Business Entities I through X,* 211–213
Fraser, Bethel School Disc. No. 403 v., 67
Freedom of movement, in false imprisonment, 23
Frey, Medley v., 128
Frolic, defined, 132–134
Fuhrman, Rowley v., 50
Fussell v. *St. Clair,* 212

G

Gannett Satellite Information Network, Inc., Williams v., 37
Gebo v. *Black Clawson Co.,* 195
General Building Contractors Assn., Inc. v. *Pennsylvania,* 147
General damages, defined, 115
General intent, defined, 17–18
George, Hewellette v., 218
Getchell v. *Lodge,* 14–16
Gonzales, Mitchell v., 89
Good Samaritan, duty and, 75
Goods, product liability and, 186, 187, 188
Gore, BMW v., 123
Government
federal, 221–222
immunity and, 221–224
local, 222, 223–224
state, 222, 223

Government Employees Insurance Co. v. *Kinyon*, 127
Governmental functions, defined, 223
Graham v. *Byerly*, 38
Gramigna v. *Morse Diesel*, 99
Gray v. *AT&T Corp.*, 223
Griffin v. *Wisconsin*, 66
Gross negligence, defined, 80–81

H

Hamidi, Intel Corp. v., 43
Hartford Insurance Co., Abellon v., 127
Hauser v. *State Farm Mut. Auto Ins. Co.*, 128
Havel v. *Diebler*, 231
Hazlewood School Dist. v. *Kuhlmeier*, 67
Hedonic damages, defined, 116
Hefferman v. *Reinhold*, 231
Heidel v. *Amburgy*, 37
Hewellette v. *George*, 218
Hibbard, Deer Creek, Inc. v., 50
High-stakes personal injury, 7
Historical data, in foreseeability, 72
History
     in foreseeability, 71
     proximate cause and, 90
Hooper v. *Clements Food Co.*, 230
HRH Constr. Corp., Bellevue S. Assocs. v., 195–196
Human nature, in foreseeability, 71
Humphrey, Sidle v., 113
Hurricane Katrina, property and, 60
Hutchinson v. *State of Idaho*, 52
Hypothesis, defined, 76

I

Immunity, 214–231
     charitable, 219–221
     defined, 214
     diplomatic, 224–225
     ethics for, 215
     family, 215–218
     interspousal, 215–216, 218
     parent-child, 215, 218
     public officers and, 224
     public policy for, 214
     sovereign, 221–224
Implied assumption, defined, 105, 106
Implied consent, 54
Implied warranty, defined, 185–187
Imputed, defined, 103
Imputed contributory negligence, defined, 103
Imputed negligence, defined, 103, 131
In re Hanford Nuclear Reservation Litigation, 179–180
Inconveniences, breach of duty and, 77
Indemnity, defined, 120
Independent contractor
     defined, 136–139
     paralegals as, 141

Inference, defined, 78
Ingraham, State ex rel. Bruggeman v., 38
Ingraham v. *Wright*, 67
Inherent, defined, 168
Inherently dangerous activities, 138, 168
Injunction
     business tort and, 205
     defined, 42, 157
Injurious falsehood
     business tort and, 204
     consent and, 55
     defined, 205
     self-defense and, 57
Inspection, product liability and, 183
Integrity
     battery and, 21
     defined, 19
Intel Corp. v. *Hamidi*, 43
Intent
     business tort and, 206
     defined, 6, 17–19, 71
     general, 17–18
     specific, 17
     transferred, 19, 22
Intentional infliction of emotional distress, defined, 24–26
Intentional torts
     contributory negligence and, 101
     conversion as, 43–46
     defenses to (*See* Defense(s))
     defined, 6
     elements of, 18
     harm to property as, 39
     intent in (*See* Intent)
     negligence and, 167
     against person, 17–38
     against property, 39–52
     statute of limitations and, 45
     strict liability and, 167
     transferred intent in, 19, 22
     trespass in cyberspace as, 42–43
     trespass to chattels as, 41–42
     trespass to land as, 39–41
     types of, 19–31
     vicarious liability and, 139–140
Interest in land, nuisance and, 156
Interference, 156–157. *See also* Nuisance
Interference with contractual relations, 204, 205–206
Interference with employment, 204, 206–207
Interference with prospective advantage, 204, 206
Interspousal immunity, 215–216, 218
Intervening causes, defined, 92–93
Intervening force, defined, 92, 93
Intervening intentional human force, defined, 92, 93
Intervening negligent human force, defined, 92
Intrusion
     defense of property and, 58
     defined, 29–30
Invasion of privacy, 29–31, 201–202
Invitees, defined, 153–154, 170
Iowa Mut. Insurance Co., Lepic v., 127

J

James M. BIGLANE and Nancy K. Biglane v. *UNDER THE HILL CORPORATION*, 161–166
Johns Manville Sales Corp., Promaulayko v., 196
Johnson v. *Cowell Steel Structures, Inc.*, 231
Joint and several liability, defined, 119
Joint enterprise, defined, 140
Joint tortfeasors, defined, 119–120
Judd, Joe, 31
Judge, warrants and, 24
Judgments, intentional torts and, 18
Justification, defined, 60

K

Katko v. *Briney*, 58
Keeton, W. Page, 20, 88, 106, 132, 139, 150, 183
Kennedy v. *Seaford Union Free School Dist. No. 6*, 86
Kidd Island Bay Water Users Coop. Ass'n, Inc. v. *Miller*, 50
Kinyon, Government Employees Insurance Co. v., 127
K.M.S. Invs., Ponticas v., 231
Knowledge
     of abnormally dangerous activities, 172
     defined, 73
Kuhlmeier, Hazlewood School Dist. v., 67

L

Lafayette-Boynton Hous. Corp., Dominguez v., 99
Lamoni K. Riordan v. *CORPORATION OF THE PRESIDING BISHOP OF THE CHURCH OF JESUS CHRIST OF LATTER-DAY SAINTS*, 229–231
Landholders
     defined, 149
     duties of, 149–151
     invitees and, 153–154
     licensees and, 152–153
     trespassers and, 151–152
Langenberg Brothers Grain Co., Mullally v., 230
Last clear chance, defined, 102–103
Lateral/lower courts, 5
Laurence L. MARTENS, M.D. and Twin Falls Clinic and Hospital, and John Doe and Jane Doe, husband and wife, I through X, and Business Entities I through X, Frank C. NEWBERRY v., 211–213
Law
     common (*See* Common law)
     statutory, 5
     tort (*See* Tort law)
Law enforcement officer, warrants and, 24
Law of torts, 5

Leaf River Forest Prods., Inc. v. Ferguson, 164
Legal malpractice, 199–201
Le'Gall v. Lewis County, 212
Lepic v. Iowa Mut. Insurance Co., 127
Lessee
    defined, 154
    nuisance and, 156
Lessor, defined, 154
Lessor-lessee relationship, 154
Lester, Adkins v., 16
Lewis County, Le'Gall v., 212
Liability
    employer, 135–136
    immunity from (*See* Immunity)
    joint and several, 119
    medical malpractice and, 198
    premises, 7, 149–155
    product (*See* Product liability)
    proximate cause and, 91–92
    strict (*See* Strict liability)
    of trespassers, 151
    vicarious (*See* Vicarious liability)
Liable, defined, 3
Libel, defined, 28
Licensees, 152–153, 170
Liquidated damages, defined, 117
Litigation, tort, 7
Livestock, strict liability for, 171
Local government, immunity and, 222, 223–224
Local standard, medical malpractice and, 198, 199
Location, proximate cause and, 90
Loco parentis, defined, 61
Lodge, Getchell v., 14–16
Long Island R. Co., Palsgraf v., 81
Loss of consortium, defined, 117
Loss of earning capacity, defined, 115

M

MacPherson v. Buick, 182
MADD. *See* Mothers Against Drunk Driving (MADD)
Magnuson-Moss Federal Trade Commission Improvement Act of 1974, 187
Malice, 26, 28
Malicious prosecution, 26, 201–202
Malign, defined, 204
Malpractice
    defined, 200
    legal, 199–201
    medical, 197–199
Manufacturer, product liability and, 182–183, 188–189
Manufacturing defects, 181, 183, 189
Marital confidences privilege, 216
Market share, proximate cause and, 90
Married Women's Acts, 215
Martinez-Fuerte, United States v., 66
Mass latent injury, 7
Master, defined, 131
MBF Corp. v. Century Business Comms., Inc., 165

McCann v. Central Synagogue, 99
McCartney v. Oblates of St. Francis de Sales, 37
McDaniel, Mi-Lady Cleaners v., 230
McDermott v. City of New York, 196
McHaffie v. Bunch, 231
Media
    defamation and, 28
    false light and, 31
    public disclosure and, 31
Medical malpractice, 197–199
Medley v. Frey, 128
Merchantability, 186, 187
Merchants, defined, 185
Mercury Ins. Co. v. Ayala, 128
Metaplex, Inc., ACI Chems., Inc. v., 166
Mi-Lady Cleaners v. McDaniel, 230
Michigan Dept. of State Police v. Sitz, 66
Miller, Kidd Island Bay Water Users Coop. Ass'n, Inc. v., 50
Miller v. Phillips, 15–16
Minors, reasonable person standard and, 73
Mirand v. City of New York, 86
Misfeasance, defined, 75
Misuse, product liability and, 188, 189
Misuse of legal proceedings, consent and, 55
Mitchell v. Gonzales, 89
Mitigate, defined, 91, 118
Mitigation, damages and, 118–119
Model Penal Code, 58–59
Model Rules of Professional Conduct, 199
Modified comparative negligence, defined, 104–105
Mondello v. New York Blood Ctr.-Greater N.Y. Blood Program, 195
Money
    damages as, 2, 114
    vicarious liability and, 131
Moore v. State Farm Mutual Insurance Co., 128
Moores v. City of Newburgh School Dist., 86
Morgan v. Chamberlin, 38
Morse Diesel, Gramigna v., 99
Mothers Against Drunk Driving (MADD), 94
Motive, battery and, 21
Moya, Nationwide Mut. Ins. v., 127
Mullally v. Langenberg Brothers Grain Co., 230
Murder, defined, 3
Mussell, Nampa & Meridian Irrigation Dist. v., 50–51
Mutual agreement, defined, 4
Myers v. Workmen's Auto Insurance Company, 51

N

Nampa & Meridian Irrigation Dist. v. Mussell, 50–51
National Personal Injury Attorneys website, 80
National standard, medical malpractice and, 198–199

Nationwide Mut. Ins. v. Moya, 127
Natural condition, defined, 150
Necessity, defined, 59–60
Negligence, 70–113
    assumption of the risk and, 105–106
    comparative, 103–105
    contributory (*See* Contributory negligence)
    custom/usage and, 79
    defenses for (*See* Defenses)
    defined, 6, 7, 70–71
    duty and (*See* Duty)
    elements of, 71–72
    employer liability on, 135–136
    ethics for, 81, 107
    gross, 80–81
    imputed, 103, 131
    imputed contributory, 103
    intentional torts and, 167
    interspousal immunity and, 215
    last clear chance and, 102–103
    legal malpractice and, 200
    medical malpractice and, 198
    modified comparative, 104–105
    nuisances and, 155, 156, 158
    premises liability and, 155
    presumption of, 80–81
    product liability and, 182–184, 189
    proximate cause for (*See* Proximate cause)
    pure comparative, 104–105
    reasonable person and, 73–74
    strict liability and, 167, 170
    violation of law and, 79–80
Negligence per se, defined, 80
Negligent instruction, 135, 136
Negligent selection, 135, 136
Negligent supervision, 136–137
New Jersey v. T.L.O., 66
New York Blood Ctr.-Greater N.Y. Blood Program, Mondello v., 195
New York Transit Authority, Sindle v., 60
Nielson, Electrical Wholesale Supply Co., Inc. v., 50
Nominal damages, defined, 21, 116
Non-deadly force, 59
Non-delegable duty, defined, 138–139
Noncompensatory damages, 117. *See also* Punitive damages
Nonfeasance, defined, 75
Norman v. Whiteside v. Thomas Williams et al., 29, 37–38
North American Trade Agreement, 206
Notice, defined, 187–188
Nuisance, 7, 149, 155–159
    defenses to, 158–159
    defined, 155
    private, 155–157
    public, 157–158
    trespass vs., 156

O

Objective standard, defined, 71
Oblates of St. Francis de Sales, McCartney v., 37

O'Boskey v. *First Fed. Sav. & Loan Ass'n of Boise,* 50
O'Connor v. *Ortega,* 68
Omission, defined, 6
One bite rule, 170
O'Neal v. *Archdioceses of N.Y.,* 86
Operational functions, 222, 223
Operator of a restaurant, product liability for, 188
Orenthal J. Simpson, People of the State of California v., 3
Ortega, *O'Connor* v., 68
Out-of-pocket losses, 115

P

Packaging, product liability and, 183
Paglia, Codling v., 195
Pain and suffering
    damages for, 115, 116
    hedonic damages and, 116
    wrongful death tort and, 203
Palsgraf v. *Long Island R. Co.,* 81
Paralegal
    defenses and, 54
    ethics for, 18
    immunity and, 218
    intentional torts and, 18
    malpractice and, 201
    negligence defenses and, 106
    nuisances and, 158
    premises liability and, 158
    product liability and, 184
    proximate cause and, 88
    statute of limitations and, 45
    strict liability and, 168
    tort law and, 2, 19
    trespass to land and, 41
    vicarious liability and, 133, 141
Parent-child immunity, 215, 218
Pashal v. *Rite Aid Pharmacy, Inc.,* 113
Pecuniary
    business tort and, 204
    defined, 114, 203
Pennsylvania, General Building Contractors Assn., Inc. v., 147
People, in foreseeability, 71, 72
People of the State of California v. *Orenthal J. Simpson,* 3
Person, defined, 21
Personal injury
    high-stakes, 7
    routine, 7
Personal property
    chattel and, 41, 42
    conversion and, 44
    defined, 39
Personal property tort, 202
Personal tort, 201–202
Pesca v. *City of New York,* 99
Phillips, Miller v., 15–16
Phillips, State v., 16
Physical contact, medical malpractice and, 198
Physician-patient relationship, 197

Plaintiff
    defined, 5
    last clear chance and, 102–103
Ponticas v. *K.M.S. Invs.,* 231
Precedent, defined, 5
Premises, defined, 149
Premises liability, 7, 149–155
Preparation, in foreseeability, 71, 72
Preponderance of the evidence
    contributory negligence and, 101
    defined, 3
    proximate cause and, 90
Preston Mill Co., Foster v., 175
Presumed damages, defined, 28
Presumption of negligence, defined, 80–81
Prima facie
    for assault, 22
    for battery, 20
    for contributory negligence, 101
    defined, 5
    for false imprisonment, 23
    for intentional tort, 19
Principal, defined, 131
Privacy
    consent and, 55
    invasion of, 29–31, 201–202
Private necessity, 60
Private nuisance, defined, 155–157
Privilege
    attorney-client, 217
    defamatory statements and, 29
    defined, 53
    false arrest and, 24
    spousal, 216
    spousal testimonial, 217
Privity, 182, 189
Pro Indiviso, Inc., Bowles v., 50
Probable cause, defined, 26
Product liability, 7, 167, 181–196
    defects and, 181–182, 189
    defined, 181–182
    duty to warn in, 190
    ethics for, 184
    negligence in, 182–184
    strict liability and, 184–189
    warranty and, 184–189
Promaulayko v. *Johns Manville Sales Corp.,* 196
Proof, burden of. *See* Burden of proof
Property
    defense of, 58–59
    intentional torts against, 39–52
    interspousal immunity and, 215
    personal (*See* Personal property)
    real, 39
    recapture of chattels and, 59
Property damages, defined, 117
Proprietary functions, defined, 223
Prosser and Keeton on Torts, 20, 88, 106, 132, 139, 150, 183
Prouse, Delaware v., 66
Proximate cause, 87–99
    "but for" test and, 88–89
    causation in fact and, 87–88
    defined, 71, 87
    ethics of, 93
    intervening causes and, 92–93

Proximate cause—*Cont.*
    overview of, 93
    product liability and, 182
    substantial factor and, 89–90
Public disclosure, defined, 30–31
Public figure, defined, 31
Public necessity, 60
Public nuisance, defined, 157–159
Public officers, defined, 224
Public policy
    for immunity, 214
    tort law and, 2
Publication, defined, 30
Publicity, defined, 30
Puffing, 185
Punitive damages
    conversion and, 44
    defined, 21, 117–118
    emotional distress and, 25
Pure comparative negligence, defined, 104–105

R

Railway Labor Executives' Assn., Skinner v., 66, 68
Ransom v. *Topaz Mktg.,* 49
Real property, defined, 39
Real property tort, 202
Reasonable care
    defined, 2–3
    medical malpractice and, 198
    product liability and, 183
Reasonable force, 56, 59
Reasonable mistake, legal malpractice and, 200
Reasonable person
    contributory negligence and, 101
    defined, 55
    negligence and, 73–74, 76, 77
Reasonable person test, 20, 22
Reasonableness
    breach of duty and, 75–76
    legal malpractice and, 199
Rebut, defined, 80
Recapture of chattels, defined, 59
Redress, defined, 114
Reentry onto land, 58–59
Reference for Business website, 80
Reinhold, Hefferman v., 231
Relationship
    attorney-client, 201
    employer-employee, 131–134, 136
    lessor-lessee, 154
    physician-patient, 197
Release, defined, 120
Remedial, defined, 114
Remedy, defined, 2
Res ipsa loquitur, defined, 78–79
Resources, tort law, 8
Respondeat superior, 131, 139, 219
Restatement (Second) of Torts, 7, 8
    assault and, 22
    breaking/entering and, 58
    contributory negligence and, 101
    conversion and, 43

Restatement (Second) of Torts—Cont.
discipline and, 60–61
force and, 56–57
immunity and, 215, 218, 221, 223, 224
intent and, 18
invitees and, 153, 154
last clear chance and, 102, 103
natural conditions and, 150
negligence and, 71
nuisance and, 155, 156, 157
proximate cause and, 89, 92
reasonable person and, 73
strict liability and, 171, 172–173
trespassers and, 151, 152
vendors/vendees and, 155
vicarious liability and, 136, 138, 140
Retailer, product liability and, 183, 188
Risk
allocation of, 131
assumption of the (*See* Assumption of
the Risk)
Risk-utility test, 189
Rite Aid Pharmacy, Inc., Pashal v., 113
Rockwell Int'l Corp., Cook v., 180
Rodriguez v. Bethlehem Steel, 127
*Rosenthal & Co. v. Commodity Futures
Trading Comm'n,* 146–147
Ross v. Curtis-Palmer Hydro-Elec. Co., 99
Routine personal injury, 7
Rowland v. Christian, 154
Rowley v. Fuhrman, 50
Rylands v. Fletcher, 173

S

Safety, product liability and, 189
*Samsung Electronics America, Inc,
White v.,* 30
*Schaill v. Tippecanoe County School
Corp.,* 67
Schneider, Davidson v., 231
Schubert v. August Schubert Wagon Co., 230
Scope of employment, defined, 132, 133
*Seaford Union Free School Dist. No. 6,
Kennedy v.,* 86
Self-defense
defense of others and, 57–58
defense of property and, 58
defined, 55–57
trespassers and, 151
Seller, product liability and, 188, 189
Seller's talk, 185
Sensory data, in foreseeability, 71, 72
Servant, defined, 131
Services, product liability and, 186
*Shepard v. State Farm Mutual Automobile
Insurance Co.,* 128, 129
Shire Richwood, Inc., Ehlis v., 229
Sidle v. Humphrey, 113
Siglow v. Smart, 112
Simpson, O. J., 3–4
Sindle v. New York Transit Authority, 60
Sitz, Michigan Dept. of State Police v., 66
*Skinner v. Railway Labor Executives'
Assn.,* 66, 68
Slander, defined, 29

Slander per quod, defined, 29
Slander per se, defined, 29
Smart, Siglow v., 112
South Rigby Canal Co., Bramwell v., 50
Sovereign, defined, 221
Sovereign immunity, 221–224
Special damages, 115, 204
Specific intent, defined, 17
Spousal privileges, defined, 216
Spousal testimonial privilege, 217
St. Clair, Fussell v., 212
Stare decisis, defined, 5
State ex rel. Bruggeman v. Ingraham, 38
State ex rel. Fogle v. Steiner, 38
State Farm Mut. Auto. Ins. Co. v. Ball, 128
*State Farm Mut. Auto Ins. Co.,
Hauser v.,* 128
*State Farm Mutual Automobile Insurance
Co., Shepard v.,* 128, 129
*State Farm Mutual Insurance Co.,
Moore v.,* 128
State government, immunity
and, 222, 223
State of Idaho, Hutchinson v., 52
State v. Phillips, 16
Statements of fact, product
liability and, 185
Statements of opinion, product liability
and, 185
Statute
automobile consent, 140
vicarious liability and, 138
Statute of limitations, 45
Statutory law, defined, 5
Steiner, State ex rel. Fogle v., 38
Strict liability, 138, 167–180
abnormally dangerous activities as,
172–174
for animals (*See* Animals)
defenses to, 174–175
defined, 6, 7, 167–168, 184
ethics for, 175
intentional torts and, 167
negligence and, 167
nuisance and, 156
product liability and, 184–189
warranty and, 184–189
Subrogation, defined, 120
Substantial certainty, defined, 18
Substantial factor, defined, 89–90
Subterranean space, 40
Suklijian v. Charles Cross & Son, Inc., 195
Supersede, defined, 92
Supplier, product liability and, 188
Supreme court, 5
Survival, defined, 201
Survival tort, defined, 201–202

T

Tenant, nuisance and, 156
Test
Andrews, 75
"But-for," 88–89
Cardozo, 74, 75
consumer contemplation, 189

Test—Cont.
reasonable person, 20, 22
risk-utility, 189
world-at-large, 75
zone-of-danger, 74, 75
Testing, product liability and, 183
Theft, harm to property and, 39
Theme, of tort law, 2
*Thomas Williams et al., Norman v.
Whiteside v.,* 29, 38–39
Threats, false imprisonment and, 23
Thrifty-Tel, Inc. v. Bezenek, 42
Time, proximate cause and, 90
*Tippecanoe County School Corp.,
Schaill v.,* 67
T.L.O., New Jersey v., 66
*TOPAZ MARKETING, L.P., and DENNIS
LOWER, VILARR RANSOM, as
Trustee of the VILARR B.
RANSOM REVOCABLE
TRUST v.,* 41, 49–52
*TOPAZ MARKETING, L.P. and MR.
AND MRS. DENNIS LOWER,
FARR WEST INVESTMENTS v.,*
41, 49–52
Topaz Mktg., Ransom v., 49
Tort law, introduction to, 1–16
Tort liability, immunity from. *See*
Immunity
Tort litigation, defined, 7
Tortfeasor
defined, 3
in intentional tort, 19
joint, 119–120
in malicious prosecution, 26
Tortious conduct, defined, 3
Tort(s)
business, 203–207
categories of, 6–7
contracts vs., 4
crimes vs., 3–4
defined, 1–3, 6
elements of, 5–6
intentional (*See* Intentional torts)
personal, 201–202
personal property, 202
real property, 202
survival, 201–202
toxic, 40
wrongful birth, 203
wrongful death, 202–203
Townsend v. Townsend, 229
Toxic tort, 40
Trammel v. United States, 217
Transferred intent, 19, 22
Transferred intent doctrine, 19, 24
Treasury Employees v. Von Raab, 66, 68
Trespass, 41, 156
Trespass in cyberspace, 42–43
Trespass to chattels, 41–43
consent and, 55
defense of property and, 58
self-defense and, 57
Trespass to land
consent and, 55
defense of property and, 58
defined, 39–41

Trespass to land—*Cont.*
  elements of, 39–40
  self-defense and, 57
Trespassers, 151–152, 170
Trespassing livestock, 171
Triad, Inc., Crespo v., 99
Trier of fact, 23, 89

U

U.C.C. *See* Uniform Commercial Code
  (U.C.C.)
UNDER THE HILL CORPORATION,
  James M. BIGLANE and Nancy K.
  Biglane v., 164–166
Unfair competition, defined, 206
Uniform Commercial Code (U.C.C.), 184,
  185, 186, 187
Union Pac. R. Co., Alesko v., 50–51
Unit rule, comparative negligence and,
  104, 105
United Paramount Network, Whiteside v., 37
United Services Automobile Association v.
  Warner, 128
U.S., Berkovitz v., 223
United States, Elkins v., 66
United States, Trammel v., 217
United States Constitution, 232–247
United States v. Biswell, 67
United States v. Dotterweich, 147
United States v. Martinez-Fuerte, 66
Unreasonable conduct
  negligence and, 70, 75
  proximate cause and, 91
  tort law and, 2, 3
Unreasonable mistake, legal malpractice
  and, 200
Unreasonableness
  duty and, 78–79
  nuisance and, 157
Usage, 79

V

Vendees, defined, 154–155
Vendors, defined, 154–155
VERNONIA SCHOOL DIST. 47J v.
  ACTON, ___U.S.___ (1995), 65–69

Vicarious liability, 7, 130–148
  automobile consent statutes and, 140
  defined, 130–131
  employer-employee relationship and,
    131–134
  ethics for, 139
  family purpose doctrine and, 140–141
  independent contractor and, 136–139
  intentional torts and, 139–140
  joint enterprise and, 140
  negligent instruction and, 135
  negligent selection and, 135
  negligent supervision and, 135–136
  theories behind, 131–132
  websites for, 141
VILARR RANSOM, as Trustee of the
  VILARR B. RANSOM
  REVOCABLE TRUST v. TOPAZ
  MARKETING, L.P., and DENNIS
  LOWER, 41, 49–52
VILLANUEVA ex rel. U.S. v.
  COMMERCIAL SANITATION
  SYSTEMS, INC, 126–129
Volunteers, immunity and, 219, 220
Von Raab, Treasury Employees v., 66, 68

W

Warner, United Services Automobile
  Association v., 128
Warning defects, 182
Warrants, 24
Warranty
  defined, 184
  express, 185
  implied, 185–187
  product liability and, 184–189
  strict liability and, 184–189
Website(s)
  for Cornell Law School Legal
    Information Institute, 8
  for immunity, 223
  for National Personal Injury
    Attorneys, 80
  for negligence defenses, 107
  for product liability, 190
  for Reference for Business, 80
  for vicarious liability, 141

West Nile virus, public nuisance
  and, 158
Wheeler v. Yocum, 38
Whistle-blower, defined, 207
White v. Samsung Electronics America,
  Inc, 30
Whiteside v. Thomas Williams et al.,
  Norman v., 29, 38–39
Whiteside v. United Paramount
  Network, 37
Wholesaler, product liability and, 188
Wiggins, Williams v., 166
Wild animal, 168–169, 170
Williams v. Gannett Satellite Information
  Network, Inc., 37
Williams v. Wiggins, 166
Winfrey, Oprah, 204
Winnebago County Dept. of Social Servs.,
  DeShaney v., 67
Winzeler Excavating Co.,
  Borchers v., 112
Wisconsin, Griffin v., 66
Women, interspousal immunity
  and, 215
Words
  assault and, 22
  false imprisonment and, 23
Workmen's Auto Insurance Company,
  Myers v., 51
World-at-large test, 75
Wright, Ingraham v., 67
Wrongful birth tort, 203
Wrongful death tort, 202–203
Wrongful deaths, defined, 3

Y

Yocum, Wheeler v., 38

Z

Zoila GODOY v. ABAMASTER OF
  MIAMI, INC., Mike's Restaurant
  Equipment Corporation, Carfel,
  Inc., 195–196
Zone-of-danger test, 74, 75
Zoning ordinances, nuisance and, 157